UNCOMMON THREADS
Threads that Wove the Fabric of Baltimore Jewish Life

FIRST EDITION

Philip Kahn, Jr.

PECAN Publications
Baltimore, Maryland

Copyright 1996
Philip Kahn, Jr.
All rights reserved

Printed in the United States

Library of Congress
Catalogue Card Number
96-95005

ISBN 0-9655057-0-7: $19.95

UNCOMMON THREADS

For their interest and support and BETSEY's and my love for them, *UNCOMMON THREADS* is dedicated to our children BETH KAHN LEAMAN, PETER CHARLES AND LINA LEE KAHN LIEBHOLD, and for the joy she has put in our lives, our granddaughter AMELIA. Just because we want it this way, our sister LEONORE K. NEWMAN shares in the dedication.

Feb, 1997
To Harriet,
Many thanks
Phil

UNCOMMON THREADS

CONTENTS

ACKNOWLEDGMENTS		vii
INTRODUCTION		ix
PROLOGUE		xv

PART I — *BALTIMORE GERMAN JEWS*

1	Early Maryland Jews * The Jew Bill	1
2	Rhinelanders * Vocations * Napoleonic Wars * Migration from Hesse and Bavaria	3
3	Tobacco * Travel to German Ports * Voyage on the *LOUISE* * B. & O. R. R. and the North German Lloyd Steamship Co. at Locust Point	7
4	German Jews and German Christians * Tailors * Peddlers	13
5	Lloyd Street Synagogue * Pre Civil War congregations * Early Reform * Sephardic and Polish Jews * Cemeteries	17
6	Reform * Orthodox opposition	27
7	Hebrew Benevolent Society	29
8	German, Hebrew and secular schools * Jewish and Christian German publications	31
9	Civil War German Jewish merchants * Slavery and the rabbis * Know Nothings * Baltimore prosperity * German Jewish military * Post Civil War Peddler's letter home	35
10	Post Civil War Harmony Circle * Hebrew Hospital & Asylum * 1868 Masked Purim Ball Hebrew Orphan Asylum * Mercantile gains * Wave of anti-Semitism * Jews join German societies * Concordia Club * Chizuk Amuno	41
11	Public markets * Jewish retailing * Old Town	47
12	Christian German schools late 1800s * German-English Jewish schools * Catholic high schools for German Jewish girls	51
13	First Northwest Passage * Druid Hill Park * Eutaw Place * Hebrew Friendship watches German Synagogues move uptown * Early Polish and Russian Jews in German Baltimore * Board of Jewish Congregations * Comparison study, Oheb Shalom and Chizuk Amuno	55
14	Late 1800s politics * German Jews and Baltimore economy * Banks, insurance companies and Jews * Reality of Russian Jewish migration * Christian fears * Park School	63
15	Victorian Christian influence * German Jewish protocol * German Jewish Registry * German domestics * Rearing children * Summer camps, residences and vacations * Baltimore horses	67
16	Clover and Mercantile Club #1 * The Phoenix Club * The Harmony Circle * The Suburban Club * Money, art gifts in-kind * German Jews and Zionism * German Jews and education * 1904 Baltimore Fire * World War I	73

UNCOMMON THREADS

PART II   *BALTIMORE EASTERN EUROPEAN JEWS*

1	Pale of Settlement * Well to-do Russian Jews * Thinking and writing * Life in the Shtetls * Poland-Galicia-Bessarabia * Alexander II & III * Pogroms and 1882 May Laws * Marxizm and The Bund * Kishinev Riots and pogroms * Plea from Odessa * Migration II * Romania	81
2	Travel to North Sea ports * Baron de Hirsch Fund * Alliance Israelite Universelle * At sea	91
3	German Jewish reception * A Christian teacher's view * Entry travails * Locust Point * Post World War I immigration * Immigration Act 1921 * Johnson Act 1924	97
4	Emigrant Aid Society * HIAS * What to do? * Farm communities * Help and care programs * The United and Federated charities	107
5	Eastern European congregations * Cemeteries and federations * Kosher checks * Rabbinical Tribunal * Spiritual leaders	113
6	East Baltimore * Sweatshops * Public health and baths * Jewish Court of Arbitration * Street smarts * To become American * Parental attitudes and concerns * Americanized children	119
7	Non-heavenly marriages * Orthodoxy and the Sabbath	127
8	Urban peddlers - Garment Workmen's Circle * European tailors * Labor organizations * Family businesses	131
9	Cultural breeches * Summer camps * Holding the line	137
10	Maskilim * Russian Jewish night school * Hebrew schools * Schools for females * Public schools * Jewish Board of Education * Talmudical Academy * Baltimore Hebrew College * The Yiddish Press	141
11	Zionist political zealots * Zionism traced to Russia * Zionist organizations * Labor Zionists American Jewish Committee * American Jewish Congress * Balfour Declaration * The Jewish Legion	149
12	Jewish Educational Alliance * B'Nai Brith * Yiddish Theater	153
13	World War I and the Pale * Bolsheviks * Social conscience * Anti Semitism * Socialism * Hoolinganism * Jews in politics	159
14	Northwest Passage * Great neighborhoods * Easterwood Boys * Synagogues follow * Changing life styles * Regressive Reform * Family Circles * Yiddishkeit * East Lombard Street	165

PART III *COMMON CLOTH*

1	Mount Pleasant * United and Federated form The Associated * *The Passing Years* * Levindale	175
2	1920s Anti-Semitism	181
3	2nd Mercantile Club * Woodholme Club * Demise of men's clothing manufacturing * Brooks Lane * John Eager Howard School No. 61 * Robert E. Lee School No. 49	183
4	1929 Stock Market crash * Rise of Chancellor Hitler * A New Deal	189
5	Roland Park * Educational quotas * Barriers and fraternities * Johns Hopkins University * The University of Maryland * Atlantic City * The Catskills	193
6	Pre-WW II Germany * Kristalnacht * The Roosevelt administration before and after Kristalnacht * United Jewish Appeal * 2nd German migration * World War II	203
7	Post-WW II * United Nations * Meetings and conferences * Zionists * The British and Palestine * The Jewish Agency * German-Eastern European refugees * The Poles still at it * *President Warfield/Exodus 1947*	211
8	Roosevelt and Truman * Jewish underground * World Zionist Organization * State of Israel, May 14, 1948 * Displaced Persons Act * Joint Distribution Committee	217
9	Economic emergence of Baltimore's Russian Jews * Suburban synagogues * Orthodox to Reform to Conservative * Conservative * Liberty Road Judaism * Jewish foods * Suburban "Bars and Bats"	221
10	Talmudical Academy * Ner Israel * Bais Yakov * Baltimore Hebrew University * Hasidic Lubavitchers * Independent congregations	233
11	Demise of Eutaw Place and the Phoenix Club * Country and swim clubs * Vacationing singles * Marriages and interfaith marriages * Violence in Jewish marriages	237
12	Associated Agencies move Uptown * Park Heights * Pikesville-Stevenson * Jewish voting	247
13	The Jewish Historical Society of Md. * The Jewish Heritage Center * Lombard Street Revisited * Jewish Population * Holocaust remembered in bronze, concrete, and stone	251
14	2nd Russian Migration * Charedi * N.W.C.P. * The 16 mile Eruv * 1.5 million dollar Mikvah * Kosher vs Government * Jews in the news, June 1993 * Avalon * Genetics * Today's et cetera * Har Sinai	257

CONCLUSION 269
APPENDIX 275
GLOSSARY 277
BIBLIOGRAPHY 279
INDEX 295

ACKNOWLEDGMENTS

To research for the writing of *Uncommon Threads*, I extensively used the JEWISH HISTORICAL SOCIETY OF MARYLAND, my Judaica library, published books, newspapers, magazines, pamphlets, periodicals, encyclopedias, and oral histories. I attended lectures, read letters and papers, and interviewed a few persons. Ms. Virginia North, archivist and librarian of the Historical Society, was a big help to me. Virginia is a pleasure to work with, and the JHSM is fortunate to have such a gem. In a limited way, I used the libraries of the MARYLAND HISTORICAL SOCIETY and the ENOCH PRATT FREE LIBRARY. For their help, thanks to Francis P. O'Neill of the MHS and Jeff Korman and Eva Slezak of the PRATT.

Dr. Joseph L. Arnold, Professor of History at the University of Maryland Baltimore County, read the manuscript. His suggestions helped to transform *Uncommon Threads* into its present form. Liliane Hanke, former instructor of literary criticism at the Johns Hopkins University read and commented very favorably on an early draft *of Uncommon Threads*. Bruce Rosenberg, college English teacher in Hungary and former foreign service officer for the United States Department of State, read the manuscript, and he too commented favorably. Dr. Carol Schreter, a literateur, read the final text, did some copy editing, and offered relevant suggestions that became part of *Uncommon Threads*. Many thanks to these four.

Rabbi Louis Hoffman of the NER ISRAEL RABBINICAL COLLEGE, painstakingly answered dozens of religious questions for me. After reading the Introduction and Prologue, Rabbi Ira Schiffer of BETH AM (Unaffiliated) Congregation and the late Rabbi Abraham Shusterman of the HAR SINAI (Reform) Congregation advised that they felt it was historically important for *Uncommon Threads* to be written. Thanks to Sandra Lee Levin for allowing me to use some descriptive matter from her book *Vision*.

Several academicians read the Introduction and Prologue to *Uncommon Threads*: Dr. Aleine Austin, Sociologist and author; Dr. D. Randall Beirne, sociologist University of Baltimore; Dr. Robert Brugger, historian and Acquisitions Editor of the Johns Hopkins Press; Dr. George W. Calcott, Professor of History, University of Maryland College Park; Dr. Louis Galambos, Professor of Business History at Johns Hopkins University and editor of the Dwight D. Eisenhower papers, and Dr. John Higham, John Martin Vincent Professor of History at Johns Hopkins University and author of *Send These to Me* and *Strangers in the Land*, well known books about Jewish immigrants. I heeded their words of advice.

Suggestions were received from friends who read the Introduction and Prologue. Thank you Mark I. Baker, Harriet Bank, James H. and Mary Bready, William E. and the late Catherine Brown, Dr. Barry Buchman, Charles M. Cahn, Jr., Mary Caldwell, Estelle Cohen, Jerry B. Cohen, Moses J. Cohen, Martin Dannenberg, Jerome G. Denaburg, the late Henry J. Fensterwald, Samuel (Sandy) Frank, Allan T. Hirsh, Jr., Raf and Mary Hirtz, Harry and Lorraine L. Lobe, Miriam Lowenberg, Benedict Rosenberg, Esther Saltzman, A. Harvey and Phyllis Schreter, Helen Sollins, Alfred Strauss, Hildegard and the late Wilfred Wagner, and Lawrence Ziffer for your responses and remarks.

Thanks and thanks again to my wife Elizabeth (Betsey) Rosenfeld Kahn who, for the time it took to write *Uncommon Threads,* was my sounding board and advisor. She read and corrected draft after draft and because it's her natural way, she did what she did in a most cheerful and encouraging manner. For me, writing a book is very stressful, and Betsey patiently listened to my many threats to toss the computer out, followed by the manuscript. Betsey was the copy editor of *Uncommon Threads*. To our daughter, Beth Kahn Leaman, thanks for your computer technical support.

Philip Kahn, Jr.

UNCOMMON THREADS

ILLUSTRATION ACKNOWLEDGMENTS, courtesy of:

ALLIANCE ISRAELITE UNIVERSELLE, Pg. 179 HIAS desk. **AMERICAN JEWISH ARCHIVES,** Cover & Pg. 180 Morning prayers, Pg. 70Cohen's Lottery. **AMERICAN JEWISH HISTORICAL SOCIETY,** Pg. 177 Kishinev, Pg. 184 clothing factory. **A PICTORIAL HISTORY OF MD. JEWRY,1955),** Pg. 70 Etting Cemetery (1799), Pg. 78 Chizuk Amuno (1876), Pg. 83 Har Sinai (1894), Pg. 83 Sheareth Israel (1903), Pg. 83 Balto. Hebrew (1891), Pg. 83 Chizuk Amuno (1895), Pg. 83 Oheb Shalom (1893), Pg. 186 Balto. Talmud Torah (1916), Pg. 186 Jewish Educational Alliance (1952), Pg. 188 Beth Tfiloh (1927), Pg. 188 Shaari Israel (1921), Pg. 189 Second Zionist Congress (1898), Pg. 189 Theodore Herzel, Pg. 189 Certificate Central Committee (1916), Pg. 189 Poster Rev. Dr. Schepsel Schaffer, Pg 283 Sinai Hospital (1926), Pg. 288 Bais Yaakov School & classroom, Pg. 288 Planning Jewish Medical Center (1950s). **ARCHIVES, HISTORY OF THE JEWISH PEOPLE, JERUSALEM,** Pg. 177 Destruction in Ukraine (1881). **BALTIMORE AMERICAN SOUVENIR EDITION (1778-1894)** Pg. 81 Phoenix Club 1892, Pg. 180 S.S. Baltimore at Locust Point (circa 1880). **BALTIMORE COUNTY PUBLIC LIBRARY,** Pg. 84 Suburban Club (1921). **BALTIMORE JEWISH TIMES,** Pg. 184 Yaazor Farm (1903), Pg. 291United Hebrew Cemetery, Pg. 292 Map of Eruv. **BALTIMORE MUNICIPAL JOURNAL (1729-1929)** Pg. 70 Lottery Office, Pg. 73 Jones Falls (1832), Pg. 73 First Post Office, Pg. 284 First National Bank, Pg. 284 Savings Bank of Balto. **BALTIMORE SUN,** Pg. 183 Ice wagon, Pg. 184 map Yaazor Community, Pg. 292 map Northwester Citizen's Patrol, Pg. 283 Sherman's news stand.(1921). **BILDARCHIV DER OSTERR NATIONALBIBLIOTHEK, VIENNA,** Pg. 176 Advertising Yiddish Theater (1908), Pg. 287 Tietz Department Store. **A. AUBREY BODINE,** Pg. 82 Lexington Market (circa 1900, Pg. 187Lombard St. Chicken man. **CENTRAL ZIONIST ARCHIVES,** Pg. 178 Red flag. **CONGRESS MONTHLY** Pg. 176 Klezmer Band. **ELLIS ISLAND MUSEUM,** Statement of Russian Pogroms, wall exhibit. **ENOCH PRATT FREE LIBRARY,** Pg. 284 Ford's Theater play bill "Pins & Needles" (1938), Pg. 285 Garrison & Liberty Hgts. Ave. **ENCYCLOPEDIA OF TRAINS & LOCOMOTIVES,** Pg. 179 Russian Train (circa 1909). **GERMAN IMMIGRATION TO AMERICA IN THE 19th CENTURY,** Pg. 71 North German Lloyd sailings (1887), Pg. 72mid 19th century passenger quarters. **TIM GIDAL** Baalagoleh. **J. HAMMAN, HAMBURG,** Pg. 179 Emigrants registering in German Hall (circa1909). **ILAN RAT COLLECTION,** Herzziya, Pg. 176 Carpentry shop, Romania (1922). **NANHAN GOLDMAN MUSEUM OF JEWISH DIASPORA,** Pg. 178 Jewish worker (1904). **THE GRAIN DEALERS NATIONAL ASSOC. 1916,** Pg. 81 Eutaw Place (1916). **HARPER'S WEEKLY,** Pg. 75 German Singing Society. **ISRAEL OFFICE OF INFORMATION,** Pg. 289 Dancing the Horrah. **ILLUSTRATE ZEITUNG MUSEUM FLIER HAMURGGISCHE, GERSCHICHTE,** Pg. 71 German port (1866). **JEWS OF BALTIMORE (1910)** Pg. 74 Hebrew Friendship Eden St. Shul (1848). **JEWISH FAMILY ALBUM,** Pg. 173 Peasants in the Ukraine, Pg. 174 Synagogue in Gwozdziecz. **JEWISH HISTORICAL SOCIETY OF MD.,** Pg. 74 Interior Lloyd St. Shul (1845), Pg. 74 Hebrew Benevolent Society inscription (1866), Pg. 74 First Hebrew School (1842), Pg. 76 German English newspapers, Pg. 185 Yiddish Newspapers, Pg. 77 Purim Assoc. Bal Masque (1875), Pg. 78 Hebrew Hospital & Asylum (1868), Pg. 78 Hebrew Orphan Asylum (1872), Pg. 79 Interior Oheb Shalom (1858), Pg. 80 German/English School (circa 1890), Pg. 84 Jewish Social Register (1905), Pg. 84 Society Visiting List (1899), Pg. 84 Debutantes (1907-1908), Cover & Pg. 85 horses & carriage (1920), Pg. 179 Russian Travel Certificate, Pg. 186 Adult class JEA (1919), Pg. 186 American Citizenship paper (1912), Pg. 187 Lombard Street, Pg. 187 ritual killing, Pg. 188 Yiddish Theater broadside (1892), Pg. 190 Jewish Legion (1917), Pg. 282 United Hebrew Charities (1917), Pg. 291 Chevra Ahavas Chesed. **JEWISH MUSEUM, N.Y.,** Yehuda Penn (1914), Klezmer band. **JEWISH NATIONAL UNIVERSITY LIBRARY,** Pg. 177 Returning home. **THE JEWISH PEOPLE IN AMERICA,** Pg. 173 map of Pale of Settlement. **P. & E.R. KAHN,** Pg.71 Aschaffenburg, Pg. 75 Wiesenfeld factory (1853), Pg. 80 Lina Kraus card (1872), Pg. 81 Eutaw Place mansions, Pg. 82 Kahn's Store (circa 1880), Pg. 85 Eutaw Place family (1918), Pg. 178, 182 Ellis Island Museum, Pg. 180 Hansa Haus, Pg. 283 Brooks Lane (1917), Pg. 283 Atlantic City (1925), Pg. 286 Nazi photos (1929), Pg. 291 50th Anniversary of Kristalnacht memorial, Pg. 293 Mikvah, Pg. 293 Balto. Shmurah Matzo Co. **E.R. (BETSEY) KAHN,** Pg. 290 Snoeball stand (1979), Pg. 290 Chicken man closing door (1979), Pg. 290 Sign of the 1930s. **ROSS KELBAUGH,** Pg. 74 Lloyd St. Synagogue exterior (1945). **JACQUES KELLY,** Pg. 80 Academy of Visitation (1837), Pg. 82 Gay Street (circa 1890), Pg. 82 Harrison Street (circa 1900), Pg. 181 Arrival Locust Point (circa 1904) Pg. 183 Public bath, Pg. 187 Lombard Street woman sitting. Pg. 187 caged chickens, Pg 283 Upper Eutaw Place (1923), Pg. 285 Nos. 5 and 33 street car lines, Pg. 290 S. High St. (1934). **LEGACY OF A LIBERAL,** Pg. 76 Har Sinai (1849) Pg. 76 Rabbi Einhorn's writings, Pg. 83 Har Sinai interior (1894). **LEWY,** Pg. 282 The Passing Years (1922) **LIBRARY OF CONGRESS** (LC-USZ62-13459), Pg. 184 girls sewing, Pg. 73 Peddler. **MARYLAND HISTORICAL SOCIETY,** Pg. 75 Concordia Club (1847), Pg. 77 Masquerade Ball of the Harmony Circle (1866), Pg. 73, 183 East Baltimore row houses, Pg. 188 Early movie house, Pg. 188 Holliday St. Theater, Pg. 188 Gayety Burlesque **MUSEUM OF THE CITY OF N.Y.,** Pg. 185 English class, garment shop. **NER ISRAEL RABBINICAL COLLEGE,** Pg. 288 Study hall, Pg. 293 Sofar scribing a torah. **NORTH GERMAN LLOYD,** Pg. 287 Bremen. **ODENHEIMER FAMILY, JERUSALEM,** Pg. 287 1937 German passport- **OSTERR TAATSARCHIV/KRIESGARCHIV, VIENNA,** Pg. 173 Jewish Quarte Zborow. Pg. 174 Poverty in Eastern Europe, Pg. 175 Passover in Galicia (1915). **TEMPLE OHEB SHALOM,** Pg. 79 Synagogue exterior (1858), Pg. 79 Psalm 1 (1884), Pg. 79 Rabbi Szold's prayer book (1864). **THE PARK SCHOOL OF BALTIMORE,** Pg. 85 Entrance Hall (1912). **PICTURE HISTORY OF AMERICAN SHIPS,** Pg. 72 sailing vessel. **PEALE MUSEUM,** Pg. 181 Holding Pen Locust Point, Pg. 181Currency exchange (circa 1904). **SAIL STEAMER & SPLENDOR,** Pg. 180 Atlantic crossing (1890). **GLADYS SAUBER,** Pg. 291 Baltimore Hebrew Cemetery Holocaust memorial. **PROF. SCOPEC, PRAGUE,** Pg. 175 coffee vendor. **STAATSARCHIV, BERLIN,** Pg. 72 Deutsche Auswinder Zeitung (1852). **STATE MUSEUM OF ART OF THE REPUBLIC OF BYELARUSSIA, MINSK,** Pg. 175 Yehuda Penn 1914. **THE STORY OF THE JEW,** Pg. 179 Baalagoleh, **UNION OF AMERICAN HEBREW CONGREGATIONS,** Pg. 292 Russian Jews mid 20th century. **UNITED STATES BUREAU OF CENSUS, HISTORICAL STATISTICS OF THE U.S.,** Pg. 182 Jewish population charts. **PROF. ROMAN VISHNIAC,** Pg. 174 Market day in Poland. **GEORGE VEITH** Pg. 285 No. 32 street car line. **WOODHOLME CLUB,** Pg. 284 Woodholme Club. **ZIONIST ARCHIVES & LIBRARY,** Pg. 190 Balfour Declaration (1917), Pg. 289 Exodus 1947, Pg. 289 Palestine Post, Pg. 185 Editorial office.

REASONABLE EFFORT HAS BEEN MADE TO IDENTIFY AND CREDIT THE SOURCE OF EACH PHOTOGRAPHS AND ILLUSTRATION IN THIS BOOK. MANY PHOTOGRAPHS ARE IN THE PUBLIC DOMAIN, ESPECIALLY OLDER ONES CREDITED TO A FOREIGN MUSEUM. ALL CORRECTIONS OR SUPPLEMENTAL DATA IN THE IDENTIFICATION WILL BE APPRECIATED AND ACKNOWLEDGED IN SUBSEQUENT EDITIONS.

INTRODUCTION

The threads of the lives of German Jews who came to Baltimore from Germany in the early to mid 1800s were uncommon with those of Jews who migrated to Baltimore a half century later from Russia, Poland, Lithuania, Galicia, Romania, and Hungary, however, a few generations back, the fiber of their threads was identical.

One hundred seventy-five years after the beginning of the German Jewish and slightly over one hundred fifteen years after the start of the Russian Jewish migration, *Uncommon Threads* tells how a semblance of Baltimore Jews of the past, German and Eastern European, lived within their minds and in places apart. The subject matter is of primary sociological interest with emphasis on change and must be read within the context of its historic past. *Uncommon Threads* records that which in the opinion of Baltimore historians and sociologists with whom the author has consulted, of interest and significance about Baltimore Jewish life that should not be lost.

American Jews, including those in Baltimore, have come a long way and with certainty are not one of the ten Lost Tribes of Israel. We have retained a rigorous sense of community, and through a shared group identity, a deep concern for Israel's future, the painful memories of the Holocaust, and the ever present need to be aware of and to guard against discrimination. More than any other ethnic group, Jews had been influenced by separate currents of both secular and Jewish religious activities between 1880 and 1920. Eastern European Jews found a home in Baltimore and while enriching their own lives, I believe they have enriched the city's character more so than have the German Jews. Though Jews are no longer Dr. John Higham's *Strangers in The Land*, and although we don't know for sure, we appear to be getting close to defining our role and finding where the Jewish people fit in the jig-saw puzzle that is America.

Part of the text of *Uncommon Threads* is devoted to the stresses of Jewish life in Germany and Eastern Europe and to being immigrants who lived the adventure of steerage travel across the Atlantic Ocean. These experiences had a profound effect on the formation of the personality of American Jews. Hopefully, this brief look into the lives of our progenitors causes us to better understand ourselves. Our present images do not reflect us as refugees, but "lest we forget," we came from lands other than America and are the children and the children of the children of immigrants. It's good to back off at times and look at ourselves and, in doing so realize that Jews are like everyone else, but because of our innate intensity, a bit more so.

Research has established historical truths, and I feel at ease with this. My personal perceptions and observations have not been ignored though I feel less comfortable with them. I was fascinated, and I learned much while researching books, pamphlets, and periodicals. I have read magazines, newspaper articles, and letters about Baltimore Jews; listened to oral histories; attended exhibits and lectures; and received comments from academic historians and friends. From this wealth of material, I have gleaned those items and thoughts that I think are the most interesting and have included them in *Uncommon Threads*. As I researched, I renewed an awareness that many Baltimore Jews of the present younger generations are either not or only partially familiar with the subjects about which I have written.

While I am well aware that some writings in *Uncommon Threads* may be controversial or sensitive to some, I remind readers that this book is a social history and should be read as such. Hopefully accurate, I assure readers there is no malicious intent to arouse semi-buried or fragile feelings; nevertheless, the fact is that in the years of our fathers and grandfathers most Eastern European Jews could not stand those haughty arrogant Germans and the feeling was quite mutual. Unfortunately, these dislikes fed upon one another. Since to my knowledge *Uncommon Threads* is the first book of its kind in Baltimore, I am fully aware of my responsibilities.

Heritage and tradition, so important to all Jews, portrayals of Jewish religious and secular verve, foibles, and strengths have been a special social interest to many people and continue to be so with the uncommon threads that have become quite common. Woven throughout the book are a few customs and rituals of Judaism that are interesting and based on solid Talmudical interpretation and reasoning.

Mentioning names in *Uncommon Threads* presented a problem for me because the city has been fortunate to have had in the past and present a multitude of outstanding Jewish spiritual and lay leaders. Their contributions, financial and otherwise, are etched in our memories and have been well documented in the local, regional, and national press. Names that are mentioned are co-incidental to the narration. Thus *Uncommon Threads,* pursuing an interest of its own as a social history, is a departure from previous publications about Baltimore Jewry.

Uncommon Threads is written in three parts. PART I begins with a few words about Jews in Colonial Maryland and then describes conditions in early 19th century Germany and the perilous voyages of German immigrants to America. It discusses nineteenth and early twentieth century Baltimore German Jews in America, their religious life, education, businesses, intra-city migrations, and their social being.

PART II portrays how Jews lived in late 19th century Eastern Europe, immigrant voyages to Baltimore, and their struggles to become Americans. It covers religious and peripheral institutions and the Eastern European Jewish verve for education, a basic ingredient in their lives. *Uncommon Threads* tells of the early colorful life of Russian Jews in East Baltimore and its effect on later generations. It refers to Zionism, ignored by most German Jews but embraced by almost all Eastern European Jews.

PART III describes how German and Eastern European Jews became united, beginning with the founding of the Associated Jewish Charities and how through its influence, the Jewish community became friendlier and more closely knit. Differences faded rapidly after World War II with the financial and social successes and the intellectual accomplishments of thousands of the city's Eastern European Jews. These and lesser factors played important roles in the homogenizing of Baltimore Jewish life. PART III depicts the lives of Baltimore Jews through milestone events of the twentieth century: two world wars, a major depression, Zionism, *Exodus 1947,* the founding of the State of Israel in 1948, and country clubs, the latter of so much importance to some. Part

III explains the ways of the Charedi, the Torah observant Jews. Though relatively few, they are of much interest because their life style and religious verve tend to stand apart from the rest of the Baltimore's Jewish community. Nevertheless, ultra Orthodox beliefs and ways of life are paramount because some say Jews who practice strict conformance are by definition the Defenders of the Faith.

The Prologue and some of the corpus of *Uncommon Threads* explains the Jewish experience in Europe during the 19th and 20th centuries and earlier. From these experiences, combined with religious beliefs, evolved the Jewish heritage and customs that influenced Baltimore Jewish life and made it so colorful. How else can the reader begin to understand Jewish sociology?

Except perhaps for New York City, the writings in *Uncommon Threads* are fairly representative of the past and present of every American city that from 1820 had large German Jewish populations. Within the metropolitan area of Baltimore, Jews no longer fearing persecution, have, in some areas and not in others, socially assimilated within the community. Assimilation and acceptance can be measured only by degree, and the degree of acceptance by some non-Jews is not always apparent. By choice or otherwise, Baltimore Jews remain a separate and distinct community and within this community are thousands of German and Eastern European Jews. Partly as a residual of restrictive covenants of a few years past, most Baltimore Jews perpetuate their living in a defined geographical northwest pattern of the city; in Randallstown, Pikesville, and in the valleys of Owings Mills, Reisterstown, and beyond. For sure, they are no longer Emma Lazarus' "huddled masses," but Baltimore's almost 100,000 Jews find a degree of mutual comfort and understanding within the bounds of where they live. The exception is a recent and growing number of Jews who have moved into the high rise apartments of the North Charles Street corridor.

Uncommon Threads recognizes Baltimore Jews for their substantial dedication to charitable institutions that care for their own as well as others. Individual Jews and family foundations have assumed a visible lead as major benefactors of the city's musical, educational, medical, and art institutions; so much so, that Baltimore, a city of limited wealth for its size, could not exist on its present high cultural plane without its Jewish philanthropists.

Beginning a few years before the Civil War and continuing thereafter, *Uncommon Threads* relates how Baltimore German Jews with an ethic for hard work attained financial success in entrepreneurial endeavors. They also spent much time defining and refining their culture; those with great wealth lived elegantly. In contrast, in the late nineteenth and early twentieth centuries, many of Baltimore's immigrant Russian Jews lived in poverty, frustration, and turmoil. They were busy though, seeking opportunities for better material living and outlets for the fervor of their intellect. Very few could have foreseen that so many of their sons and daughters would be able to rise from peddling, small store keeping, and tailoring to become major players in a large number of more exotic and intellectual endeavors.

UNCOMMON THREADS

By the time Russian Jews arrived in Baltimore, the city's German Jewish community had become a major entity in the urban economy. Nationally significant, Baltimore German Jewish- owned needle trades are legendary. From 1860 to 1920, men's clothing manufacturing, almost 100% German Jewish owned during those years, was by far the city's largest and most important industry. German Jewish owned straw hat and umbrella factories became the nation's largest, and their shirt, underwear, and pajama factories were enormous. In retailing, with a single exception, no Russian Jewish owned businesses matched the size or community importance of Baltimore's great German Jewish-owned department stores; however, not so for wholesaling. The volume of a single firm founded by a Lithuanian Jew in the late 1800s probably overmatched the combined sales of all the other city's Jewish dry goods wholesalers.

That Baltimore German Jews of the mid and late 1800s generated much art, music, or literature, there is little evidence. For the early German Jews and later the Russian Jews, the possession of material wealth, earned or inherited, became a mark of social distinction. This was more pronounced than for other ethnic groups, probably due to centuries of deprivation. Though it is a difficult and somewhat tenuous comparison to make, and certainly an observation only, until the end of World War 11 there appeared to be differences in values between Anglo-Saxon Christians and Jews. During the great depression years of the 1930s, many Anglo-Saxons considered their social status based on their English culture and genealogy to be a more significant measure of the solace of life than the possession of wealth. If need be, and there was a need in those years, they felt the comfort of their family heritage rather than the wealth many no longer possessed.

Uncommon Threads tells how the passing of years and the coming of age of children evoked similar responses from both German and Russian Jews. Some encouraged their sons, and in a few instances their daughters, to continue family businesses while others wanted to spare their children the vicissitudes of such a demanding life. Restricted as tradesmen and money lenders as far back as recorded history, the range of Jewish activity in Baltimore has been wonderfully expanded into other ventures. Beginning in the late nineteenth century for the German Jews, and later for the Russian Jews, many first, second, and third generations have embraced advanced learning. Partly because the Russian Jews outnumber the Germans, and particularly since World War II, their talents have engendered an inordinate number of outstanding scientists, attorneys, educators, physicians, musicians, artists, authors, and pure intellectuals.

The social manners of many mid-nineteenth century German Jews are said to have been brash; this should probably be attributed to their Germanic heritage rather than to their German Jewishness. No shrinking violets they, Russian Jews have equaled the Germans in this respect; again this can be attributed to their national heritage. Both groups have been politically outspoken, liberal free thinkers, with the Russian Jews more so. A less tangible difference was the propensity for nineteenth century German Jews to adopt Protestant-like attitudes and genteel manners. Though discounted by some historians, this was evident by the introduction of organs and choirs into the services of the Reform temples and by the adopted social mores of the period. Russian Jews, because of their more recent arrival in America, have held more tenaciously to their Eastern European heritage, and perhaps this has made their American story the more colorful

For ethnic and ritual reasons, German and Russian Jews favored separate funeral establishments in past years. Until shortly after World War II, a period of much change, a single mortician served the needs of Baltimore's German Jewish community members who would not be caught dead in the three Russian Jewish undertaker's parlors. This ratio of funeral parlors correlated closely to the numbers of each group living and dying in Baltimore.

German Ashkenazi Jews tended to have fewer children than the more prolific Russian Ashkenazi Jews of a passing generation. Because of this and marriages between the two, German Jews as an identifiable group have dramatically diminished. It is apparent now that in the not too distant future, there will no longer be a distinctive sub-culture of Baltimore Judaism.

Philip Kahn, Jr.
October, 1996/5757

PROLOGUE

*F*ollowing the destruction of the Second Temple in Jerusalem and the conquest of the province of Judea by Titus' Roman Legions in 70 C.E., the Jewish people ceased to exist as a nation. Thus began the Diaspora, a life in exile for the Jews. Jewish people dispersed; some resettled in various parts of the Roman Empire including many areas along the Rhine River. Actually, elements of Jews settled in the Rhineland as early as the 4th century. Their adherence to tradition and faith kept them united while they suffered persecution during the Crusades (1096-1270). The Crusaders on their journey to Jerusalem destroyed synagogues and massacred unaccountable numbers of Jews. Following these persecutions, during the years of 1348-1350 the Black Death plague annihilated thousands of Europeans; the Jews were accused of poisoning the wells of the Christians. To escape this harassment, many fled east and settled in an area that is now Poland. Little is recorded about the Jews in that area before the First Crusade at the end of the eleventh century though there is every reason to believe Jews lived there before that time.

After the Diaspora, two distinct groups of Jews became identified and named for Biblical locations. Large numbers of Aramaic speaking Jews sought refuge in Spain and Portugal. Known as Sephardim, they adopted the Spanish language and in time formed their own dialect known as Ladino. Those Ashkenazim located in Germany in the middle ages spoke Yiddish, a mixture of Hebrew and German probably older than the English we speak. Both groups shared the same beliefs but they differed in customs, prayer and pronunciation of Hebrew. Spoken in a variety of dialects, the Yiddish language did not build a literature of its own until the mid-nineteenth century. As life evolved in their respective habitats, the Ashkenazim became primarily peddlers, peasants, poverty stricken proletarians bound to orthodoxy, superstition and Messianic dreams. A large number of Sephardim, at least those inculcated with the glory of Spain, became cosmopolitans, sophisticates, merchants, physicians, scientists, philosophers and advisors to bishops and kings. Few Sephardim ever resided in Baltimore so they are almost a non-entity in the city's Jewish history.

Aside from this, there are records of Jews living in Kiev in the twelfth and thirteenth centuries and in Little Russia and White Russia during the long periods when these provinces formed part of the Lithuanian and Polish dominions. Jews also lived in other areas that one by one fell into Russian hands during the course of that nation's expansion. Included as Eastern European Jews are Romanians, an amalgamation of Russian Ashkenazim and Turkish Sephardim, as at the end of the fifteenth century, some Spanish and Portuguese Sephardim fled to the Ottoman Empire.

Over a span of approximately five-hundred years, the language, customs, prayers, and synagogue chants of Jews who remained in Germany and those who fled developed distinctively differently. In Eastern Europe because they were Jews, they were forced to keep to themselves though they could not avoid absorbing some of the culture of the countries in which they lived for generations. Eastern European Jews preferred to speak

Yiddish, a polyglot basically German language but written in Hebrew characters, and long for their natural tongue, rather than adopt the language of the areas in which they lived. Jews who remained in a not quite so geographically restrictive Germany eventually discarded Yiddish and spoke only German.

Both groups brought their differences to America; they clashed when the German and Russian cultures faced each other, so much so that they coexisted here almost as unrelated peoples. For years, they lived each with their own synagogues and institutions. A few decades passed before the uncommon threads of their lives would combine to weave the fabric of a united and vital Baltimore Jewish community. *Uncommon Threads* **examines these differences.**

In the 1770s, long before Jews thought about coming to America, Moses Mendelssohn, the great German writer and philosopher, planted the seeds for their eventual migration. He believed that language and education were the important paths for freedom from the social and vocational restrictions for German Jews and for those confined to the Russian Jewish ghettos.

Beginning in colonial times, Sephardic Jews in America established themselves as the social hierarchy of American Jews. German Jews who arrived in the early to mid-1800s resented this snobbery; subsequently, Eastern European Jews who arrived in the late nineteenth and early twentieth centuries resented the snobbery of the Germans. Clearly it was not only the date of arrival in America that mattered, but it was also the geography, the countries from whence Jews came.

With neither intent to rob Volhynians or Bessarabians and other sub-nationalists of their heritage nor to explain their individuality, Russia at one time or the other controlled all of the Eastern Europeans except those living in the Austro-Hungarian and Ottoman Empires. At times Poles were Poles; however, at other times they were Russians as their territories and identities intermingled and changed. The general designation of Eastern European as Russians is used by many historians so at times I have done the same.

The trickle of Jews from Eastern Europe to Baltimore began in the 1870s and before then in a much smaller way. After the outbreak of pogroms in Russia in 1881 and the Polish and Russian May Laws of 1882, Jews left Eastern Europe by the multi-thousands and headed to America. Persecution was not the only reason for Eastern European Jews to emigrate to America; the lack of human rights and poverty were reasons enough to leave. In White Russia, the western province of Byelorussia, anti-Semitism was as rife, as was the poverty. This was cause to leave though the pogroms of the 1880s and 1890s did not spread to this province. Bessarabians left Russia because of a combination of poverty and pogroms, as did the Romanians, while the Galitzianers left primarily because of poverty.

Russian Jewish immigrants of the early years came from the shtetls where they were the poorest of the poor with no hope of their ever being without need. Many of this early group were peddlers and tailors though the latter had no concept of a garment factory such as those that existed in Baltimore at the time. The first Russian Jewish immigrants to arrive were extremely aggressive, and many became a success story after about twenty years in America. The middle class of Russian Jews continued to live in Europe at this time as they found a way to cope with life there.

Russian Jews heading for Baltimore and other United States cities passed through Germany in trains on their way to German and Dutch port cities. Some stopped for brief periods in areas east of Berlin before continuing their migration, and their pause was long enough to learn the German language and to assume German names. German Jews in America who considered themselves to be authentic Germans, unkindly referred to these Russian Jews as "Hinter Berliners" (Backdoor Berliners). Some of this group who continued their migration to America at a later date spoke an impure Yiddish known as Judeo-German. Others camouflaged their origins by stopping briefly in England and Holland where well-established Jews had lived since the days of the Spanish inquisition. Some of each of these groups denied their Eastern European heritage, claiming to be either German, English, or Dutch.

A re-birth of pogroms began on Easter morning of 1903 in Kishinev, the capital city of Bessarabia, a wayward section of Romania. This initiated a second wave of Russian immigrants culturally, intellectually, and economically more advanced than the 1880s' Jews from the Pale of Settlement. In Baltimore in the 1880s and for a decade or so thereafter, the origin of Eastern Jewish immigrants was a matter of significant social importance Jewish immigrants was a matter of significant social importance

Unlike the movement of other national ethnics such as the Greeks, Finns, non-Jewish Russians and, beginning in the 1890s, the Italians, the Eastern European Jews were the only ones to migrate as a people of a single village or region at the same time. Through the early years of the twentieth century, second to New York City, Baltimore was the largest port of entry for all Europeans, Jews and non-Jews and the largest port of entry for Germans of all faiths. In the three decades before the Civil War, close to 200,000 German immigrants landed in Fells Point.

*   *   *   *   *

*J*ews are considerably more than a religious group. Though Israel is a Jewish state, Jews are not a nation and anthropologists and others reject the notion of a Jewish race. They probably fit the description of a "socio-religious" designation that as a family have shared their history and can trace their genealogy back to Abraham in 2,000 B.C.E. Jews have been driven from one land to another; the wandering Jew is an eternal image who has retained Judaism as his functional theology.

Because the Jewish religion so dominates the theme of *Uncommon Threads*, it will be helpful for the reader to acquire some easy step-by-step knowledge of the expressions of worship and traditions and the complex religious laws which govern the Jews. Though *Uncommon Threads* is no lesson in theology, readers must understand first and foremost that monotheism is the Jews' belief; one God over all people, all beings, and all lands for all time. A basic declaration of faith, the watchword of the Jewish people, is expressed in the *Shema* prayer that begins with an affirmation of God as the

Unity of the Universe. "Hear O Israel, the Lord is our God, the Lord is One." Deuteronomy 6:4.

If indeed the Jews are God's chosen people, it is not because of any mark of superiority; Jews are well aware of this. Through centuries of persecution and wandering, Jews have questioned what they have been chosen for; many believe God's choice was because of the righteousness of their ancient forefathers. Others believe it is because of Tikkum Olam, the healing of the world.

The *Torah*, the sacred scrolls of Judaism, contains the Five Books of Moses (The Pentateuch), and the Ten Commandments. Its 54,976 Hebrew words and 304,805 Hebrew letters have been recorded for generations by scribes on scrolls of animal skin parchment or velum. Said to have been given to Moses by God on Mount Sinai, the *Torah*, a great human cultural document of 613 commandments, is the core of Jewish teaching. It is the Law, the Mosaic Code that defines the doctrines, ethics, philosophy, customs, and ceremonies of the Jews. The Mosaic Laws remain apart from secular laws and are extremely intricate. The Old Testament, the sacred Bible, is written in three sections: the Five Books of Moses, Prophets and Sacred writings.

Since their beginning, discussions of Jewish laws were transmitted by word of mouth from generation to generation. Interpretations grew so that it was no longer possible for scholars to memorize them. The destruction of the Second Temple in 70 C.E. triggered the writing of a document, the *Mishna*. Between the years of the destruction and 200 C.E., scholarly rabbis of the period compiled and codified interpretations of the oral laws. The *Mishna* written in Hebrew is the first of two components of the *Talmud* and the earliest written assemblage of Jewish laws. The *Mishna* is divided into six sections or orders that cover human behavior and life. They are:

"Seeds" deals with the fruit of the fields;
"Festivals" relates to the laws of various holidays;
"Women" deals with the laws of marriage and divorce;
"Damages" deals with civil and criminal law;
"Holy Things" relates to the laws of sacrifice;
"Purities" pertains to that which is ritually impure.

Sixty-three sub divisions or tractates of the six orders and five hundred twenty-three chapters cover all of the activities of the Jewish people.

Two *Gemaras*, commentaries and rabbinical discussions of the *Mishna*, were written separately by numerous Jewish scholars; one, in Jerusalem by the end of the 5th century C.E.; one, in Babylonia by the end of the 6th century C.E. The *Gemara* compiled in Babylonia is larger, more significant and the one scholars consider to be the most important. While the *Mishna* is a Hebrew text, the spoken language of the day during the development of the *Gemaras* was an Aramaic dialect. The *Mishna* and the *Gemara* combined are the components of the *Talmud*, the final writings of which ended about 700 C.E. The *Gemara* goes further than do the laws set down by the *Mishna*, but it is not simply a list of laws and rules. It consists of interpretations, additions, judgments, decisions, and modifications made on the laws of the *Mishna* by the ancient rabbis and scholars who interpreted, added, judged, decided, and modified that body of law.

Each day for approximately thirteen hundred years, thousands of scholars and rabbis all over the world study and interpret the *Talmud*. An Orthodox Jew is careful not to build his life around the literal meanings of the *Torah*. The question must always be asked, "How is this understood in application to Jewish life?" Unless the questions address minor everyday life, the inquirer must refer to the *Mishna,* and if the answer is not found there, then to the *Gemara*. After the commentaries in the *Gemaras* were written, the Jewish people had much information but didn't know exactly how to apply it. The *Shulcan Aruch,* the standard code of Halacha (Jewish Law) and its commentaries compiled by rabbis during the mid-sixteenth century, takes into account both Sephardic and Ashkenazi thinking, making it easier for Jews to know which laws to follow. Next to the *Talmud,* the *Shulcan Aruch* has become the most important guide to Jewish life and worship, tying the Jewish people together.

Baltimore Jews worship as either Orthodox, Conservative or Reform and in lesser numbers as Reconstructionists, Hasidic or unaffiliated.

To simplify the tenets, moderate Orthodox Jews are the classicists of the religionists and somewhat strict in their daily behavior. They literally believe that the *TORAH* was given by God to Moses on Mt. Sinai and that the Jewish scriptures foretold the coming of a Messiah. Observance of the Sabbath and the dietary laws are the most visible manifestation of their beliefs.

To the right of moderate Orthodoxy are the purist of the purists, the "black hatters," the fervently Orthodox *Torah* observant "Charedi" (those who tremble as with the fear of God); this includes the Hasidim who live in strict accordance with the *Shulcan Aruch*. Modern Hasidism stems from Baal Shem (Israel ben Eliezer), an historical figure who lived in early to mid- eighteenth century Poland and upheld a pantheistic doctrine and communion with God through joyous worship. Thousands of Jews flocked to the mystic sects seeking a spiritual escape that allowed them to combine their cultist ethical religious life and beliefs with a joy of life. Hasidim believe that unnecessarily denying the pleasures of the body and wallowing in sorrow are insulting to God. Food, drink, and love are gifts from God so they dance and sing of their joy in the Lord. The Reform movement that quickly gained popularity in northern Germany began with services in a small synagogue in Seesen, Westphalia, in 1810. While continuing the doctrines of Judaism, the Reform movement successfully moderated traditional worship, thereby allowing Jews to move more easily within commercial and social circles. In the spirit of the time, some rabbis declared that the essence of Judaism was a belief in God and immortality and that the ceremonies of religion were of lesser importance. Reform considered the influence of intellectual reasoning that grew out of the theology of the Protestant Reformation and the Jewish enlightenment of the 2nd half of the 19th century. The forward thinking of Reform followers eliminated the theory of the coming of the Messiah and the rebuilding of Zion from its liturgical references. Reform Jews considered their beliefs to be a valid contribution to the ongoing development of Judaism, as opposed to the Orthodox who have resisted change.

The Conservative movement founded near the end of the 19th century began as a reaction against Reform; it was not congregational but centered on the establishment of the Jewish Theological Seminary in New York City in 1886. The fact that it was founded as a school determined what the movement would become. Opposed to some Reform platforms, Conservatives could not identify with Eastern European Orthodoxy, then in its infancy in America. Conservatism struggled and had little influence until given support and guidance from a group of understanding and wealthy German Jews who were anxious for it to succeed as an amalgam of Reform and Orthodoxy. Conservatism links a loyalty to the old Orthodox traditions with a freer observance of religion in the modern world. For former Orthodox Jews, it relieves a spiritual and theological dilemma by moving slightly to the left towards liberal Reform but not quite so distant from the religious observances they practiced since birth. After World War II, many former Orthodox Jews of Eastern European heritage joined Conservative congregations. While the three principal sectarian divisions of Jewish religious practice appear to have well-defined differences, this is not the case. They actually overlap rather than divide.

Reconstructionism, somewhat akin to Conservatism, began in New York City during the first half of the century. Followers interpret Judaism as a way of life with the Jewish religion as its communal core. They emphasize the necessity of a Jewish community organized across lines of theological differences that encourage a more active participation in Jewish life. Reconstructionists believe Judaism is an evolving religion that must undergo constant change and development in their history, literature, art, music and traditions, in accordance with the religious needs of a changing civilization.

Philip Kahn, Jr.
October, 1996/5757

PART I-1   *BALTIMORE GERMAN JEWS*

Early Maryland Jews * The Jew Bill

A single Lithuanian Jew, Moses Mordecai came to Baltimore in the 1760s, and is said to be the first Jew from that region of Europe to arrive in North America. From Telz, the seat of Talmudical learning in Lithuania, Mordecai was considered to be an authority on Jewish law. It is significant that for the first time Orthodox Jewish needs could be respected in Maryland. The right which Jews value the most, that of economic freedom, seems to have been upheld without question in Maryland courts.

    A small Jewish group emerged in Baltimore in the 1780s shortly after Baltimore began to flourish as a market place during the Revolutionary War. They could hardly be termed a community when twenty years after the adoption of the State Constitution of 1776, the Baltimore City Directory of 1796 listed a mere 18 Jewish names. During the Revolution, Maryland's population numbered about 250,000 with only a handful of Jews counted; fifty years later a maximum of 150 Jews lived in several areas throughout the State. It does not appear reasonable that Jews could have been either a communal problem or a serious political issue of the time.

    After years of effort and frustrating defeats in the General Assembly, Maryland's Jews became full citizens of the state after being granted the same legal rights as Christians by a vote of 45 to 32. Less than five years after the Maryland General Assembly passed the Jew Bill in 1825 and confirmed it in January 1826, a trickle began that preceded the large migration of German Jews to Baltimore. These rights were given to the Jews, but it is important to understand that they were "toleration rights" only. The acceptance of Jews into the community was a social issue that had to be dealt with and is still being dealt with separately.

UNCOMMON THREADS

PART I-2

Rhinelanders * Vocations * Napoleonic Wars * Migration from Hesse and Bavaria

After a large number of Jews fled the areas around the Rhine River in the fourteenth century, those who remained survived five hundred years of suffering even into the nineteenth century. The majority of the German Jewish people continued to center in the south though others scattered throughout the Prussian states. Denigration attributed to their religion and economic conditions continued, and the Jewish ability to make a living was seriously curtailed. Since the Middle Ages, they had been denied ownership of land, work in agricultural endeavors, and membership in the guild-controlled crafts. Allowable vocations were pawnbroking, cattle dealing, raising flax for textiles, and buying grapes for wine makers. They traded in second hand goods and clothes and in grain for millers. Some Jews acted as agents between horse breeders and the government to obtain horses for the cavalry. House-to-house peddling made sure they remained poor and led simple lives although the "Hausierer" (peddler) played an important role in the rural economy of the German provinces. Some Jewish women performed domestic services; some men worked as laborers.

Nevertheless, Jews were welcomed, in fact encouraged, to come to the weekly fairs always held in Bavarian villages on Sundays. They rode into town in their wagons with the children perched on top of the goods being brought for sale. Traditionally, women and children were put in charge of the stall at the fair while the men moved about buying or peddling or both. The reasons for encouraging Jews to attend the fair were not paternalistic but because Jews sensitive to competition tended to force the prices down. In order to protect themselves from physical violence and discriminatory Jew taxes, the Jews frequently formed themselves into cooperative groups, boycotting those fairs where they were too abused. In many areas and in commodities such as furs, feathers, textiles, and tobacco, Jews were essential to the trade. Where Jews controlled these much wanted commodities, the nobility suppressed persecutions against them. The little pleasure they could derive from persecuting the Jews was not worth the cost.

After the Napoleonic Wars (1800-1814) and following Napoleon's victory over and occupation of Prussia in 1806, the Emancipation Edict of 1812 bestowed citizenship with full rights and duties on the Jews. Jews, happy to consider Prussia their homeland, felt so secure that many of them volunteered and fought in the German army against Napoleon. To become full partners in this joy, Jews adopted family names and kept their accounts and wrote their contracts in German. With the defeat of Napoleon during the Wars of Liberation 1813-1815, Jewish illusion was shattered. The Congress of Vienna in 1815 that followed those wars repudiated all of the liberal reforms, and Jews reverted to living with their age old restrictions. Some Germans in high office felt that it would be desirable not to have any Jews in Germany at all; however, since they were there, they would do what they could to make them powerless as a group. Thus, the government eased the way for Jews to be baptized; at first several were, but as this idea diminished, almost no Jews were baptized.

After the Napoleonic Wars, the states of Hesse and Bavaria figured prominently in the 39 separate political entities that formed the loose federation known as Germany. The largest concentration of German Jews lived in these states, and many of them constituted the mid-nineteenth century migration to America.

In Bavaria, and to a lesser degree in Hesse, Jews lacked almost every civil right and endured constant hostile governmental attitudes and harassment. The only property they were allowed to own was the small plot on which their houses stood; at times the government went so far as to confiscate those. To control propagation, German states listed the names of men who could marry, and they had to do so in turn as their name worked its way to the top of the town hall roster. In some of the smaller villages, Jews managed to ignore this restriction by having Jewish marriages that were religious in nature and not recorded in the village civil records. After the Congress of Vienna in 1815, the German army no longer welcomed Jews, and for this dubious privilege, they paid a special tax that excused them from conscription. Opportunities for education were limited to learning to read Jewish prayers written in Hebrew.

But for a handful, the early migration to Baltimore of German Jews, most of whom came from Hesse, began with small numbers in the decade of the 1830s. The numbers stepped-up and then dramatically increased in the late 1840s, when almost all German Jewish immigrants came from Bavaria. German Jews of this period called "forty-eighters" were small town rural cattle dealers, horse traders and store keepers.

In 1848, a revolution that began Bismarck's climb to power revolved largely around Berlin and the north. Though Jews achieved some political gains at this time, demands for civil rights independent of religious beliefs failed, resulting in a setback for Jewish emancipation. In the early 1850s, immigration mostly from Bavaria continued at a heavy pace, tapering off towards the end of the decade, and for most statistical purposes,[1] all but ended before the American Civil War. Rural German Jewish immigrants of this period formed a solid basis for the growth of the Reform Jewish movement in Baltimore. Small numbers migrated to Baltimore in the late 1860s. Bavaria, the most conservative and reactionary of the German states, a century later became the area in which Nazism gained a foothold and gathered its strength.

1   *City population statistics of Jews in 1820 are interesting and are of special note for Richmond and Charleston. Both cities with populations smaller than Baltimore, had more Jews because of the earlier large influx of Sephardic Jews and the beginning at this time of German Jewish migration to these cities as well as to New York, Philadelphia, Baltimore and Savannah. Jews became attracted to Charleston, especially because of its reputation as a tolerant city where they could live with all the freedoms America could offer.*

	Jewish Population	*Total Population*
Charleston	*700*	*37,000*
New York City	*550*	*123,000*
Philadelphia	*450*	*112,000*
Richmond	*200*	*12,000*
Baltimore	*150*	*62,000*
Savannah	*100*	*7,000*

Scattered in other parts of the U.S.: 500 - 600
Total in U.S.: 2,650 - 2,750 of which over 1,000 lived throughout South Carolina

PART I-3

Tobacco * Travel to German ports * Voyage on the *LOUISE* * B. & O. R. R. and The North German Lloyd Steamship Co. at Locust Point

Along with the other nations of Western Europe, the Germans' infatuation with tobacco created an unusual and favorable commercial exchange when the product became a catalyst that facilitated the departure of oppressed Jews from Germany to begin life anew in America. German ships sailing from Bremen carried German immigrants to the port of Baltimore, the largest American port through which Maryland and Virginia tobacco was exported to Europe. After discharging passengers in Baltimore, the ships loaded tightly packed hogsheads containing leaves of dried tobacco plants and returned to Germany. German shippers capitalized on the mass migration of thousands of Jews and Christians who chose to leave Germany in the 1830s through the mid 1850s because this arrangement sustained large and profitable exchanges for their shipping companies and the Maryland and Virginia tobacco interests. Ninety percent of all immigrants who landed in Baltimore during the decades of the 1840s and 1850s were German and by the beginning of the Civil War one fourth of Baltimore's population was of German descent.

Venturesome Jews who decided to leave Germany traveled overland from Hesse and Bavaria to convenient points on the Weser and Elbe Rivers where they boarded river boats and continued their voyage to the Atlantic port cities of Bremen and Hamburg. With the founding of the North German Lloyd Company in 1858, most of the vessels sailing from Bremen to Baltimore were ships of that line. Those who embarked from Hamburg usually sailed on Hamburg-American Line ships that connected that city with east coast ports other than Baltimore. As competition increased, offices of the shipping lines established contact points on several landings along rivers in the interior of Germany. From these stations, North German Lloyd representatives who wore dual hats, those of tobacco commissioners and travel agents, met Jews bound for Baltimore. They sold them passage for America at discounted prices; at least this is what they told the Germans emigrants planning to leave the country. Those who preferred not to purchase passage from advance agents bought tickets at the docks from other agents whose prices for passage were about the same as those sold along the rivers.

To sail across the Atlantic Ocean in the mid-nineteenth century on barque rigged sailing ships of only several hundred tons was a major adventure. The day and time of departure of these ships depended on the weather, on the tides, and on the ability of shippers to recruit crews to man the ships. Immigrants spent numerous days in port cities before embarking, sometimes waiting as long as a month to sail. In the German port cities, they were besieged by and became prey for tavern keepers, ship brokers, and land agents. The unscrupulous gouged them; some transportation agents misdirected or overcharged them for advance tickets purchased to destinations to inland American cities. Mid-nineteenth century German sailing ships provided no food so passengers supplied themselves. From "Emigrant Provision Stores" located on or close to the wharves, emigrants purchased rodent proof provision boxes, provisions, and cooking and eating utensils. For those who sailed from England on British ships, life was better in that they were promised three meals a day, tea with sugar and milk, and oatmeal for breakfast, beef for dinner and gruel for supper.

Some of those who left Germany carrying family heirlooms intending to take them to America were disheartened at the embarkation point when they discovered that the risk of breakage or loss was very high and the cost of shipping far too expensive. Those who chose to sell their family heirlooms to embarkation port sharks did so, but they received very little money for their precious possessions.

No matter how much the German agents charged the immigrants for passage, the agents paid the shipping company a fixed price, usually about M30 (30 marks) * for each passenger. Neither the agents nor the shipping companies displayed much concern over the fact that the ships usually sailed overloaded. The height of the steerage accommodations below the decks of mid-nineteenth century sailing vessels varied from four to six feet, and hard rough wooden berths were installed in double tiers. Living quarters filled the spaces on the steerage decks, and below that deck, areas were used for cargo. Passenger baggage was relegated to the lower hold. Passengers entered the steerage decks through hatches which when open were the only source of ventilation for those below. During rough seas, this source of light and air was cut off when the crew secured the hatches to prevent high seas from pouring into the lower decks.

Motivated partially because there was no separation of the sexes nor privacy during the voyages, brawls occurred frequently on the early to mid-nineteenth century crossings. Rudimentary sanitation facilities and the contamination of food and water during several weeks of the voyage resulted in cholera, small pox, and dysentery for many; death shortened the trip for others. Conditions were so bad, in fact, that fines were imposed on ships' captains for every corpse aboard ship when they docked, and there were lots of them. Supposedly, as many as one-third of the immigrants to America died as a consequence of their voyage. Ships' officers and crews were usually unrefined, rude and tyrannical, and as if that weren't enough, the fear of shipwreck always lurked. Then too, there was the ever present concern about the scourge of sea travel, fire. Needless to say, many German immigrants arrived in Baltimore ausgespielt (played out). For some, travel did not end here as the city was merely a stop-over on their way to other destinations,

For the very few who sailed to America in the early 1830s, conditions were far worse than mid nineteenth century; a partial and true relating of the voyage made by a German Jewish family of seven tells a story. Jonas Friedenwald, his elderly father Chayim,[1] his wife Merle and four children arrived in Baltimore January 14, 1832, after four months at sea aboard the brig LOUISE. They had sailed from Bremen, Germany, in September knowing full well how dangerous it would be to cross the Atlantic Ocean in winter, which turned out to be an exceptionally hard one. Added to the severe and dangerous storms that generated frightening black waves that caused the LOUISE to shudder and be tossed around, they dealt with the usual difficulties of life on board ship.

Sailing the high seas has always carried its share of superstition so some of the crew believed that because they had been lax in prayer, they were being punished. Passengers and others of the crew blamed the captain of the ship for the storms. The captain was a religious man who respected the German Jewish family, and he allowed them to use his private quarters for their daily devotions. The crew and other passengers could not help but hear the strange incantations going on behind the closed cabin door so, if it weren't the captain's fault, it was the Jews who brought thunder, lightening and torrential rains upon their innocent God fearing heads.

Had they heeded their doubts, the Friedenwald family may never have made the trip. Aboard ship, they were crowded together in a small cabin, and during the long voyage, the father of the children questioned himself as to the wisdom of their flight from Germany. They prepared their meals in a special small kitchen on the ship from their provisions of water, flour, biscuits, oatmeal, rice, and molasses. At times when the crew had the energy, they fished for themselves and the passengers. Despite the scorn of other passengers, they faithfully recited their daily prayers. The two men wrapped themselves in their tallit (prayer shawls) and attached one phylactery to their forehead and wound the leather thong of the other small leather box around their left arm seven times.

When the LOUISE arrived in Baltimore, the Patapsco River around the Fells Point wharves was frozen solid. It was before the Sabbath so Jonas left the ship and walked across the ice to find housing and fortunately located two rooms in the house of a fellow Jew. When the LOUISE was able to dock, the seven person family moved directly into their new temporary home. In Baltimore, the Friedenwalds and their descendants prospered and became outstanding business men and physicians.[2] Not the usual pattern for German Jews, members of this family continued their Orthodox Jewish religious practices well past the mid-twentieth century.

To determine with certainty the port of departure for all Germans, Jewish and Christian, or the towns or areas from where they had left is impossible. Ethnic Germans were widespread throughout Europe by the nineteenth century. They lived in Germany and Russian occupied Poland, in Austria-Hungary, Romania, France, Switzerland, and even in Russia near the Volga River. Between 1855 and 1910 many of those emigrating from Hamburg used a less expensive route on ships that stopped at intermediary ports such as Hull on the east coast of England. From there they traveled directly west by land to Liverpool where they boarded transatlantic ships. For those sailing from Bremen[3] to Baltimore on ships, sailing was direct. Some sailed from little known small German ports other than those thought of as the usual points of emigration.

Toward the end of the 1850s, some ships began to make Atlantic crossings under steam. The German government heavily subsidized their early steamships; they carried first class passengers at fares much too costly for immigrants. It was not until 1868, a date well past the pre-Civil War migration, that immigrants no longer crossed the Atlantic Ocean in sailing ships that tied up at the outdated moorings of Fells Point where facilities for processing immigrants was almost non-existent. Usually medical checks were performed by doctors aboard ships in the harbor, and in some instances on ships headed to Baltimore on the Chesapeake Bay.

In that year, the Baltimore and Ohio Railroad and the North German Lloyd companies signed a contract for two first-class iron twin screw steamships to be put on the route between Bremen and Baltimore; to be maintained for five years. Each of the companies had a half interest in the project. The United States Immigration Service built a reception center and processing facility at North Locust Point; adjacent to it, the Baltimore and Ohio Railroad Company erected piers Number 8 and 9, each 650 feet in length. These piers were capable of simultaneously handling the loading and off loading of six ocean-going vessels. Rails were laid onto the piers so that immigrants who disembarked and were ticketed for American destinations other than Baltimore could board Baltimore & Ohio Railroad cars waiting a few steps from the gang plank; destined for St. Louis, Cincinnati or Chicago. The shed-like reception center was a long open room with benches that held several hundred immigrants. Low wooden fences guided the new arrivals through the entry processing procedure. In later years, the Immigration Service built a quarantine facility at Fort Armistead. The North German Lloyd Company's Bremen and Baltimore Steamship Line was well-positioned anxious and ready to schedule regular steamship service between Baltimore and the German ports of Bremen, Hamburg and Luebeck. The arrangement was the answer to Baltimore's longtime desire to have a facility on equal footing with other east coast ports engaged in the Atlantic trade. In March of 1868, the magnificent first class German built S.S. Baltimore sailed from Bremen, the first steamship of the Baltimore and Bremen Line to arrive in Baltimore. This ship and its new sister ship the S.S. Bremen weighed only 2,250 tons, minuscule compared to the 25,000 to 100,000 ton behemoths of later years. The S.S. Baltimore arrived on March 26th flying the flag of the North German Confederation with no visible American emblem or ensign. The ship sailed at the time of the year when few people traveled the North Atlantic Ocean so on her maiden voyage, she carried an unusually moderate number of passengers. On the night of her arrival, the officers of the ship at attended a lavish banquet that featured almost unending speeches by Baltimore business leaders, most saying just about the same thing. All praised the Baltimore investors involved in the establishment of the new steamship service, especially the Baltimore and Ohio Railroad.

Subsequent sailings carried a full complement of steerage passengers. Baltimore shipping authorities expected steamships would bring a better class of immigrants to the city; It is not known if this proved to be the case or what criteria could be used to establish the class of immigrants. In addition to steam propulsion, the S.S. Baltimore was rigged as a sailing barque as were all the steamships of the day. Though steam engines of the period operated quite reliably, there were the rare instances of engine failures at sea whereby ships continued their voyages under sail.

Thus began monthly sailings from Baltimore and from Bremen. In 1881, at the start of the Eastern European migration, a North German Lloyd steamship sailed fortnightly, every alternate Wednesday from Baltimore and every alternate Thursday from Bremen. When additional ships became available later on, the line began weekly service. By the turn of the century, larger and faster ships of the Baltimore and Bremen line had a capacity of about 800 steerage passengers. The few Germans who came to America at this time generally traveled the better class, but in the steerage of these ships were hundreds of Russian Jewish immigrant on their way to freedom. When World War I began, the tobacco for people exchange ended after a period of over one hundred profitable years.

In 1914, the erection of a new complex was begun to handle immigration more efficiently through the port of Baltimore, but unfortunately for the city, World War I cut off immigration to the United States. Before the facility was opened, the War Department took over the buildings for use as a military hospital. For many years, Baltimore was second only to New York in the number of immigrants passing through the port. In other years, Baltimore was always among the top five ports along with Philadelphia, Boston and New Orleans.

* The author was unable to determine the value of the German mark in the early 1800s.

---

1   *Amelia Liebhold, the granddaughter of the author and his wife Elizabeth (Betsey) Kahn, is eighth generation American; a lineal descendent of Chayim Friedenwald.*

2   *Not the usual pattern for German Jews, members of this family continued their orthodox practices well past the mid-twentieth century.*

3   *Original passenger lists from Bremen between the years 1852 and 1875 were destroyed, but the DEUTSCHE AUSWANDERER-ZEITUNG published in Bremen preserved at least the number of passengers on each ship sailing from that city. As noted below, up until the Civil War, German emigration to America, Jewish and Christian immigration grew, and was by far the heaviest during the decade of the 1850s.*

1820-1829	*50,000*
1830-1839	*210,000*
1840-1849	*580,000*
1850-1859	*1,160,000*

UNCOMMON THREADS

PART I-4

German Jews and German Christians * Tailors * Peddlers

*I*nitially, German Jewish immigrants who arrived in Baltimore on the same boat, figuratively, stayed in the same boat socially and financially. Young unmarried men socialized together by spending their spare time learning the English language, trying to accumulate a little capital, and at the same time, helping peddler friends stock their back packs. After inauspicious beginnings for all, some unmarried men and families bettered themselves while others remained poor and through their lifetime depended on community services during the winter's hard times when the port shut down or when illness made it impossible to work. A very special kinship existed with those from the same German state. In Baltimore, they felt comfortable living in the same section of the city as their co-religionists and fellow countrymen. These feelings also related in a somewhat vague sense to their integration with Christians from the same German state, an association without assimilation. Neither German Jews nor German Christians felt imbued with intense German nationalism. They considered themselves to be Germanic though Germany was not a united country in the early 1800s; so they were Bavarians or Hessians or from whatever German state they had come. Christian Germans who had a need to learn about business welcomed the Jewish Germans who had a good basic understanding of the subject.

English presented only a partial communication barrier for the immigrants as Baltimore's heavy immigrant population and first generation Germans conversed in either English or German. In no mid-Atlantic state, except for Pennsylvania, did Germans play a more important part than in Maryland. Thousands of Germans came to America in the first part of the nineteenth century but their numbers were small compared to the latter half when the primary source of immigration to the United States was Germany.

There is little justification to assume that all early to mid-century German immigrant Jews sewed garments for his or her livelihood, but for certain, a very large number of them did. From the Middle Ages to the Renaissance and into the nineteenth century, Jews acquired little agrarian know-how due to being denied ownership of land, even though they played a leading role in the craft of tailoring, and for centuries were tradesmen. When the German Jews began their migration to Baltimore in the 1830s, Elias Howe had not yet invented the sewing machine so the industrial revolution in America at that time did not include machine sewing. In close family interaction, Jews, accustomed to sewing by hand in their homes back in Germany, continued to do so in America. The multitude of social restrictions in the small German communities allowed Jews to be only non-guild craftsmen, artisans and merchants so these few skills tended to pervade their American lives.

Many German Jewish immigrants, particularly those who arrived in the 1850s, earned a living by peddling in the city streets or in the countryside. They, too, along with those who sewed, laid the foundations of the German Jewish business enterprises of the future. Some peddlers and their families left the city and moved into rural areas where they continued peddling while others maintained a residence for their families in Baltimore. This allowed family members an opportunity to earn a wage or conduct a small business while the titular head of the house roamed the countryside.

Historians recognize the importance the peddler played in the development of America, particularly those who traveled through the rural areas. They were the link that connected the countryside and the urban centers, part of the commercial infrastructure of the day. Our concept, and this a concept only, has been that bone-weary peddlers all looked as though they had just walked out of the Old Testament. With backs bent, they were unkempt, bearded, and shaggy-haired as drawn renditions and early photographs show them to be. What we do know is that those who traveled on foot trudged the dusty back roads shouldering huge back packs weighing between 80 and 100 pounds; some accounts say as much as 150 pounds. About two thirds of the total weight strapped to the peddler's back was balanced by about one third of the weight carried in the front.

Rural peddlers differed in the wares they carried. Some sold tin and copper wear (pots, pans and utensils), others shoe laces, stockings, dry goods (textiles and clothing), notions (threads, ribbons, pins and needles), and some peddled picture frames and jewelry or a variety of items not otherwise available in small rural communities. He was the original "catalogue house" because customers could place orders for items that peddlers ordinarily did not carry in their packs, and these would be brought to the customers on his next trip into the area. Rural folks preferred to buy from a country peddler because he had a business like character and sold goods for less than the country store. Peddlers preferred to receive cash for a sale; however this was not always feasible, so many accepted rags, furs and feathers in barter.

For peddlers walking on foot for scores of miles, some days were probably not too unpleasant. On other days, they wilted in the searing heat and humidity of summer and winced when they faced the snow and icy winds of winter. Those on foot saved their money for the day that they could purchase a horse and wagon, the traditional middle step between pack peddling and opening a small store. A horse and wagon enabled a peddler to carry a larger and more profitable stock of goods and to service a wider territory. This increased the peddler's chance of finding a favorable location where the possibilities of opening a small store seemed good.

The lack of being able to adhere strictly to kosher diets tested the peddler's religious beliefs so they dealt with their conscience as best they could. They seldom returned home for the Sabbath; usually it was not possible for peddlers to participate in Sabbath services though they tried to avoid working on that day of rest. Because of the time spent away from their homes, relations with their wives and children were close to being non-existent. Peddlers who worked city routes allowed time for them to have a closer family relationship and a conscience free feeling concerning their religion.

By the time of the Russian Jewish immigration of the 1880s, most German Jewish peddlers abolished traveling in the countryside. Rural roads had been improved, and farmers and others living in outlying areas began to come to the cities and towns more often. Many peddlers saved a little money, and that allowed them to open retail and wholesale businesses, usually in conjunction with or in a partnership with a son or sons or a brother. For decades, peddling remained a viable occupation on the urban streets of the cities where those who dealt in scrap iron, old pots and assorted discarded metal items did well financially, more so than those who had worked the rural areas of an expanding country.

Many 19th century German Jewish women bore the painful brunt of economic distress. Greatly due to the fact that they married men a number of years older than themselves and because peddlers and small store keepers worked so hard they were short lived. A disproportionate number of German Jewish widows continued to operate their husbands retail stores but certainly not their peddling routes. Those not having self support factors opened boarding houses or lived through the generosity of their families and charity.

UNCOMMON THREADS

PART I-5

Lloyd Street Synagogue * Pre Civil War congregations * Early Reform * Sephardic and Polish Jews * Cemeteries

*E*stimated at 300 persons in 1835, Baltimore's German Jewish community in five years grew to just under 1,000. About one fourth of the almost 15,000 Jews in America lived in New York, Philadelphia and Baltimore. Those who came to Baltimore between 1820 and 1830 were largely Dutch born and came to the city primarily from New York and secondarily, from Philadelphia. Curiously, almost one half of the heads of Jewish families in Baltimore in 1820 were American born, but partly due to the Dutch influx at the end of that decade, the 1830 figure changed to about one quarter. Despite the fact that Baltimore had a population in excess of 100 Jews in 1820, it was the largest city in the country without a synagogue. Because of this, some Jews who came to Baltimore from Philadelphia retained memberships in the latter city's Mikvah Israel and Rodeph Shalom congregations. There is no telling of how they managed to attend services in those synagogues or if they actually did after moving to Baltimore. We can safely assume that Baltimore Jews, except perhaps for the high holidays, did not mount a horse or engage a carriage for such a lengthy trip to observe the Sabbath.

Being poor, and with few material possessions, did not stand in the way of the German Jewish immigrants' need to worship. It is recorded that the initial service in 1829 of the city's first organized congregation, Baltimore Hebrew, consisted of a minyan of thirteen German, Dutch and English Jewish immigrants who gathered together for this purpose. The founders of the congregation, in accordance with the Jewish tradition, alluded to their heritage in the naming of their congregation. The Hebrew name chosen Nidche Yisrael (The Scattered of Israel) aptly described this group whose ancestors identified with the Diaspora and who had so recently left Germany. The petition for their charter to the General Assembly was granted in 1830 in the name of the Baltimore Hebrew Congregation in the City of Baltimore and their Hebrew name Nidche Yisrael did not appear in that document.

In the beginning, the founders, their families, and others worshipped in a grocery store at Bond and Fleet Streets, and in homes and public halls on Exeter Street, at #2 Harrison Street near Etna Lane, and in 1835, on High Street. At this last address, the fifty-five members demonstrated their need to become an incorporated Jewish congregation. They had no rabbi so lay members with the knowledge to be readers conducted services.

Fifteen years after its founding, the Baltimore Hebrew Congregation completed the erection of a synagogue on Lloyd Street. There are anomalies surrounding the use of the congregation's English name and the synagogue's erection. From its earliest founding, why did this German-speaking-reading-writing Orthodox Jewish Congregation consistently use their English name rather than their Hebrew name? Although some members had advanced economically, how could this congregation, most of whom as far as we know still in modest circumstances, justify the engagement of Baltimore's best known and highest priced architect, Robert Carey Long, Jr.?

In the early 1800s, classicism was fashionable in Baltimore so Long, famous as the architect of the Peale Museum and of several Gothic churches, presented plans to the synagogue board. For the synagogue building, his plan replicated an age old classic Greek Revival style known for its beauty, simplicity, and quiet grandeur. Ancient Greeks built temples of this general design for the storage of offerings and their treasures. Was this design Long's idea or had this style been suggested to him? It is reasonable to assume that some members of the board would have done so as they were certainly aware that the nationally known Beth Elohim Congregation in Charleston, S. C. had completed a Greek Revival style synagogue in 1840.

There is no trace of Jewish identity on the front of the synagogue nor along it side facades. In accord with Long's ecclesiastical orientation, the stained brown church-like pews enclosed by low doors are similar to those usually found in Protestant churches. The extent of the free reign given to Long, or if he had any in designing the interior of the synagogue is not clear, but for sure he complied with the necessary inclusion of a beautiful ark and a bimah. Supported by cast iron posts, lattice work screened balconies concealed the faces of the women from the possibility of a few lustful gazes of some of the men seated or standing in the pews below. At the time the congregation adopted Reform worship in 1870, the screening was removed and replaced by high balustrades that partially shielded the women worshippers. Shortly before he left the pulpit, Baltimore Hebrew's first rabbi, Abraham Rice, complained "had the synagogue not been a convenient place for them to show off the newest and latest fashions in hats and dresses, the ladies' gallery would be empty most of the time."

High in the wall facing east are three round stained glass windows, the center one of great value and merit. Designed by architect Long, this window with a white star of David on a cobalt blue ground encircled in red was originally installed above the ark in 1845. As the major change during an 1860 expansion, workers extended the east wall a distance of thirty feet, and the reinstalled windows were placed above a newly constructed Ark. Jewish Historical Society scholars believe the circular Shield of David window to have been the first of its type to be installed on the exterior of an American synagogue and the earliest piece of this type of glass installed in Baltimore. Shortly before the purchase of the synagogue for restoration, vandals broke the Shield of David window. Fortunately, the restorers were able to gather enough shards and pieces of lead molding to enable them to exactly replicate the original window. The matzoh baking oven and the present mikvahs in the basement were installed by an Orthodox Ukrainian congregation that owned and occupied the synagogue at a later time. The present brass and glass chandeliers are uniquely ecumenical. Some years after the erection of the Lloyd Street Shul, the Second Presbyterian congregation started the construction of a church on the corner of Lloyd and Baltimore Streets, one they couldn't finish due to lack of funds. The Baltimore Hebrew Congregation loaned the Presbyterians money to complete the church, a loan that became a gift when, at a later date, the Jewish congregation canceled the debt.

In the late 1920s, the church was razed and the magnificent chandeliers were discovered buried in the debris. The finder had them restored and gave them to Rabbi Avrum Nachman Schwartz of the Orthodox Shomrei Mishmeres Hakodesh Congregation, then the occupants of the Lloyd Street Shul. They were to be hung in the sanctuary, but the congregation quarreled over the question of accepting objects to be installed in a synagogue that had previously been an adornment of a Christian church. The Rabbi took full responsibility for the questions that could be answered only by Talmudic guidance. Scholars decided that no synagogue or any sacramental content should ever become a part of a house of worship of another faith, but the opposite is perfectly permissible. It is acceptable to convert a church or parts of a church into a synagogue.

The Lloyd Street Shul is listed on the United States National Register of Historic Places as it is the third oldest extant American synagogue building. However, in 1959-1961 it was vulnerable to being demolished or simply collapsing from decay, Dr. Wilbur Hunter, Director of Baltimore's Peale Museum and a preservationist and professional historian felt very strongly that the synagogue could and must be saved. He brought his concerns to the attention of interested Baltimore Jewish leaders who heeded his fears. They founded the Jewish Historical Society of Maryland in 1960 for the sole purpose of saving the Shul, and through that organization, the synagogue building was not only saved but restored. Today, the Lloyd Street Shul is one of two (the other is B'Nai Israel, also restored) synagogues standing with dignity each on a side of Baltimore's Jewish Heritage Center of the Jewish Historical Society of Maryland. Nowhere in America, paired in a single location, are two such historic, architecturally beautiful, and spiritually important nineteenth century restored synagogues.

By the time the Baltimore Hebrew Congregation completed the Lloyd Street Synagogue, known as the First Shul, two other Baltimore German Jewish congregations had been founded and were active, and a third one formed that did not survive. At this time, a custom of numbering the Baltimore shuls began, in order to signify their order of establishment. The custom fell out of use by 1885. Fell's Point Hebrew Friendship, its Hebrew name Oheb Israel (Lovers of Israel), was founded in 1832 and the Har Sinai Verein in 1842. Hebrew Friendship was the first of several congregations founded by former members of Baltimore Hebrew. A minyan called the Irische (Irish) Chevra regarded the new congregation to be a continuation of their minyan.

The Irische Chevra was the third German Jewish congregation mentioned and the one that withered away. Exact details of the history of the Irische Chevra are vague though it is known that the minyan held their first service in 1832 in the same combined grocery store and inn previously used by the Baltimore Hebrew Congregation at Bond and Fleet Street. The use of the word Irische is unclear and likely not the minyan's formal name. One explanation is that an Irish woman frequently sat at the door of the place of worship. A more plausible explanation is that the minyan's actual name was Iris Chevra.

UNCOMMON THREADS

In addition to holding religious services, members of the Irische Chevra who had risen to leadership in Baltimore's German Jewish community founded the United Hebrew Benevolent Society in 1833. The society, a mutual benefit society for the relief and burial of each member and their respective families, also aided less fortunate Jewish families during days of illness, death, or other stressful times. The early date of the society's founding indicates that there could have been only a fine line of financial difference between the recipients of the help and of the givers. Leaning and fallen stones in a small cemetery on the south side of Pulaski Highway near N. East Street are a sign of neglect of the burial grounds known as Die Irische Hebra Cemetery.

Historically for American Jewish congregations, former members of a mother congregation began new ones for a multitude of reasons. The formation of the Hebrew Friendship Congregation was due to the fact that many Baltimore Hebrew members had moved to homes in a location slightly east of the Jones Falls and west of Central Avenue. Because the Jewish religion does not permit riding on the Sabbath, orthodox Jewish Baltimore Hebrew members who continued to live in Fells Point found Lloyd Street too distant. The area of rapid growth of the German Jewish community was in the neighborhood of the Lloyd Street Synagogue so by 1860, Lombard Street between Lloyd Street and the bridge over Jones Falls became the center of Baltimore's German Jewish activity.

The Lloyd Street Synagogue became known colloquially as the Stadt Shul (City Shul) to distinguish itself from Oheb Israel (Hebrew Friendship), the Second Shul, known as the P'int Shul (Point Shul) that was located on Canton Avenue in the dock area near the foot of Broadway. In 1848, Hebrew Friendship erected a synagogue on Eden Street between Baltimore and Lombard Streets. Known by this early congregation of German Jews as the Eden Street Shul, at a later date the name lingered with confusion. After the Hebrew Friendship Congregation membership fell apart, those who remained sold the synagogue to the Aitz Chaim Congregation, the Prushnitz Shul, and this orthodox Russian congregation became the second one to use the name Eden Street Shul. A few years after Aitz Chaim moved from Eden Street, parts of the walls of the old synagogue crumbled and the structure was completely razed in 1976.

For some German Jews, the practice of orthodoxy hampered commercial intercourse with Christians. The observation of religious tenets forbade working or exchanging monies on the Sabbath which presented a barrier to the determination of many German Jews to become successful in the mercantile markets. A small group rejected these restrictions, these demands for worship that interfered with their latitude for trade and assimilation. In 1840, Rabbi Abraham Rice, the first ordained rabbi to come to the United States, became the spiritual leader of the Baltimore Hebrew Congregation. He was born in Wurzburg, Bavaria and graduated from the Talmudical Seminary in that city. Rice, who limped, was not considered to be eloquent in the pulpit. As reported in the Christian press, he came to Baltimore to become the "Chief Rabbi," whatever that meant in an American German Jewish community. It took about two years for Rice's strict orthodox leanings to alienate a number of younger members who were influenced by the Reform worship that would allow them to better compete in the mercantile world.

Many German Jews had strong Masonic loyalties as this secret ritual organization admitted adherents of all religions. Seven masons took part in the founding of the Third Shul, Har Sinai Verein (Har Sinai Association). They met at the home of Moses Hutzler at Exeter Street and Eastern Avenue in 1842. Masons objected to Rabbi Rice's opposition to the performance of lodge rituals at Jewish burials. Har Sinai offered an opportunity to adapt a way of worship in the Reform Jewish religious manner that did not frown on Masonic and other secular rituals.[1]

The name Har Sinai is derived from the belief that God gave his law, the Torah, to the people of Israel through Moses on Mt. Sinai. From the beginning, members of Baltimore Hebrew and Hebrew Friendship congregations harbored unfriendly feelings existed towards Har Sinai. Though requested to do so, both congregations refused to loan the new congregation a Sefer Torah, almost an essential for Jewish services. After worshipping in a number of locations, Har Sinai completed the erection of a two story Norman design synagogue in September 1849, fronting 36' on High Street near Lexington. It was completed in September at a cost of $ 5,000. To disavow orthodoxy, Har Sinai congregants installed a melodeon (a small reed organ on which they played symphony music) opposite the ark and played it during their English, German and Hebrew services. Although one might think organ music to be taboo in an orthodox synagogue, this was not so. In Germany, orthodoxy was not of the same degree as orthodoxy practiced in Eastern Europe, and it was not unusual for synagogues in Germany to have an organ and a choir as well. In its beginning, Har Sinai had no rabbi so members of the congregation gave the sermons. A measure of guilt, though, prevented the congregation from completely shedding their heritage so most members continued to cover their heads in the synagogue and in their homes. Har Sinai male members sat apart from their women and observed the dietary laws. It was not until 1869 that men removed their hats when entering Har Sinai. The congregants perceived themselves to be liberals, innovators, and reformers, and for that day, indeed they were. As early as the late 1840s, a few extremely liberal and apparently misguided members suggested moving the weekly Sabbath service to Sunday, an innovation that would put Har Sinai in conformity with Christian America. This was actually being done at this time in New York's liberal Reform Temple, Emanu-El.

In the 1930s, Har Sinai's Rabbi Edward Israel, probably the most liberal in its history, conducted Sunday morning lectures in the synagogue. They were limited in length to make sure he would not be late for his appearance on the golf course. He wore neither yarmulke nor tallit while delivering his Sunday morning lectures in the sanctuary; some say he wore golf knickers under his robe. The Reform Rabbi Morris S. Lazaron of Baltimore Hebrew of this period uncovered his head only while delivering the Sabbath sermon. Although some congregants considered this quite daring, rabbis probably wanted to be more comfortable and appear less formal during that part of the service. Uncovering the head could be seen as a symbolic step from the role of rabbi to a more secular posture in keeping with the subject of his sermon. The rabbis of Oheb Shalom would have none of this.

Bavarian born and overtly liberal, Rabbi David Einhorn came to Har Sinai in 1855. The next year he wrote a prayer book for his congregation and began to publish *Sinai*, a German language magazine. Expressing his opposition to slavery through *Sinai* and from his pulpit, in April 1861, Einhorn was forced to flee from Baltimore. His Hebrew and German prayer book *Olath Tamid* was adopted as the model for the *Union Prayer Book* used by every Reform congregation in America. Re-chartered in 1873, the congregation removed the Germanic word Verein from its name when they moved into a remodeled church building at Lexington and Pine Streets. Six years later, their rabbi conducted his first service in Hebrew and English; no German spoken here. Through the years Har Sinai, the oldest continuously Reform congregation in America, has remained the beacon for Baltimore Reform liberal Judaism.[2]

Oheb Shalom Congregation (Lover of Peace) was founded in 1853 by a group of young men who were influenced by German Reform and who felt Baltimore Hebrew was too orthodox and Har Sinai was too liberal. Oheb Shalom, the Fourth Shul, has remained traditionally, even now, the most conservative of the Baltimore Reform Jewish congregations. Founding members of Oheb Shalom worshipped on the third floor of a Gay Street building until numbers of its congregants moved to homes west of the center of the city, after which, Oheb Shalom purchased an abandoned church on Hanover Street between Pratt and Lombard. They added a gallery, built an ark and built a bimah; thus converting the church to a synagogue that could accommodate nine hundred worshippers. Their first rabbi, German speaking Benjamin Szold, was born in Nemiskert, a small village east of Bratislava, Hungary. Until the 19th century, Bratislava, high on the left bank of the Danube River near the meeting of the present frontiers of Slovakia, Austria, and Hungary, was a base for many German traders. After completing his education at nearby Vienna, Szold came to Baltimore. An organ and a choir were introduced into the service; the congregation used Rabbi Isaac Wise's prayer book *Minhag Amerika* until 1861 when Rabbi Szold published the first edition of his own prayer book *Avodot Israel*. Wise was the prime organizer of Reform Judaism in America.

By the year 1855, four well-established congregations tended to the spiritual needs of most of Baltimore's 4,000 German Jews, a number that increased to between 5,000 and 7,000 by the beginning of the Civil War. Though the synagogues acted as the central institutions of Judaism, and the religion itself sacrosanct, in 1860, only about half of Baltimore's Jewish families affiliated with synagogues. By 1865, German Jews numbered about 10,000, and by the 1870 census, 26,700 Jews of all backgrounds lived in Baltimore. By the outbreak of the Civil War, Oheb Israel, the Hebrew Friendship Congregation, was Baltimore's largest. Though the monetary worth of many of its members had grown substantially as had the fortunes of members of the other synagogues, congregants were less than anxious to increase the cost of spiritual leadership and guidance. They denied continuous requests for raises for their rabbis who remained extremely low paid; as for the cantors, their pay remained at near poverty level.

Numerically unimportant, but not to be overlooked, the small numbers of Sephardic and Polish Jews who arrived early and lived in Baltimore, worshipped each with their own minyan. A few Sephardim followers, descendants of Baltimore's early notable and most recorded German Jewish Cohens and Ettings, rejected associations with synagogues practicing the Ashkenazi ritual; they prayed in the Sephardic minhag (custom) in their homes. The parents and grandparents of both families had come to America at a time when no Ashkenazic Jewish congregations existed in the city so they joined a small Baltimore Sephardic minyan of mostly Portuguese for spiritual worship and companionship.

In 1856, the Cohens and Ettings and the city's few Spanish and Portuguese including Solomon Nunes Carvalho, Baltimore's great painter, explorer, photographer, inventor, and writer founded the Beth Israel (House of Israel) Congregation. For the first time in Baltimore's history, Jews recited Sephardic prayers in congregational worship, and Carvalho acted as chasin (cantor) at their services held in the hall of the Hebrew Young Men's Literary Association on Gay and Fayette Streets.

Plans advanced for more permanent housing, and in 1857 the Beth Israel Sephardic Synagogue was dedicated in the Red Men's Hall at 24 N. Paca Street. As set down by the founding fathers, Rabbi Jacob Lesser preached the sermon in English to congregants who were largely American born. Members erected a succah in the yard of the synagogue; it was the first public succah ever erected in Baltimore.

In the same year Carvalho's wife Sarah opened a Hebrew-English Sunday school modeled after the Sephardic school in Philadelphia where she had previously taught. The congregation's children who attended daily secular schools studied Hebrew and Jewish subjects taught in English. She urged parents to "educate your children in the English language and have the divine principles of their religion taught and explained to them in the vernacular of the country." This was quite upsetting to Har Sinai's Rabbi David Einhorn who verbally attacked the idea of a woman teaching Jewish subjects, and of all things, teaching them in English. The Germans were certainly dogmatic about their beliefs and rituals and, in their typical Germanic mind set of what was right and what was wrong, there was no argument.

Though Beth Israel members were individually quite wealthy, they numbered too few for the congregation to survive. In a last attempt to do so, Beth Israel appealed to out-of-town Sephardic congregations for financial help which was denied. The Carvalhos left Baltimore in 1859 to take up residence in New York City. Their loss was a fatal blow to Beth Israel so the doors of the shul were closed that year, never to re-open. At no other time has Baltimore had a Sephardic population large enough to support a congregation.

Two small groups withdrew from the Baltimore Hebrew Congregation.[3] The first was in 1851 when Rabbi Rice formed the Shearith Israel Congregation, the Fifth Shul, located at the southwest corner of Howard and Lexington Streets. The second group became the Shevet Achim Congregation in 1862, and they worshipped on the second floor of a well-known Baltimore landmark building on the southeast corner of Eutaw and Fayette Streets. This building, listed on the National Register of Historic Places, was erected in 1857 by the Eutaw Savings Bank and is now occupied by the Baltimore Equitable Society. In 1879, the two congregations joined and became the Shearith Israel (Remnant of Israel) Congregation. They moved into the deserted First Constitutional Presbyterian Church erected in 1855 at the intersection of German (Redwood) and Greene Streets.

Known at the time by some as Rabbi Schepsel Schaffer's Shul and by others as the Strauss Shul, Shearith Israel was without doubt the most orthodox of the German Jewish Congregations; to this day Shearith Israel has not strayed from its direction as the oldest continuously orthodox congregation in Baltimore. In 1903, Shearith Israel built a synagogue on McCulloh and Bloom Streets, and the congregation is active today in a newer and smaller synagogue they erected on the corner of Park Heights and Glen Avenues. Through the years, Shearith Israel has not reached the prosperity and importance of other German Jewish congregations in Baltimore. Almost all of its German Jewish families left the shul some years ago, and its present members are a handful of older German Jews and neighborhood Jews of various backgrounds.

The Sixth Shul, founded in 1852 was the Beth Hamedrosh Hagodol Claus Congregation. This congregation lost many of its members in 1870 and 1871 when they joined those who seceded from Baltimore Hebrew to form Chizuk Amuno. In 1886, Beth Hamedrosh Hagodol Claus, called the "mother synagogue" of all orthodox Jewish synagogues in existence at that time, occupied a building on Harrison Street and Etna Lane formerly occupied by the Baltimore Hebrew Congregation in 1845 while they waited for the completion of the Lloyd Street Synagogue

Although in the eighteenth and nineteenth centuries it was customary for wealthy families, Christians or Jews, who lived on large estates to bury their dead on their own properties, the German Jewish Sephardic worshipping Cohens and Ettings maintained personal burial plots apart from their homes. The earliest recorded Jewish burial in Baltimore, that of an infant daughter of the Ettings, was an interment in 1786 on land owned by Charles Carroll of Carrollton. Later, in 1801, Carroll conveyed this plot to Solomon Etting and his uncle Levi Solomon. This could be confusing because the term conveyed meant the passing of ownership. At that time Jews in Maryland by law could not own land or form a corporate body; however, for burial purposes, land could legally be conveyed to a Jewish owner. The plot on Jew Alley, a blind narrow passage way in Ensor Town, ran north from Monument Street between Ensor Street and Harford Avenue. One hundred feet north of Monument Street, a lane called Abraham Street connected Jew Alley with Harford Road. After the passage in 1826 of the Jew Bill that allowed Jews to own land, Ettings purchased a plot for a family cemetery on what is now North Avenue east of Pennsylvania Avenue. The infant Etting was re-interred and rests in this family cemetery.

In 1830, Jacob I. Cohen, Jr. acquired a very small parcel of land past the city line west of Baltimore. Much too small for farming, he apparently had in mind that the plot was to be used as the Cohen family cemetery. Over a period of 120 years since the first burial in 1832, a total of forty-five family members had been buried in this west Saratoga

Street cemetery, the last burial being in 1952. In later years, the Cohen Family cemetery became a legal muddle because the land had been conveyed in trust by a deed in 1837 to trustees who died in 1870 and 1879 and who had named no successors to hold legal title to the land. Monies to care for the cemetery were derived from three separate Cohen trusts, one of which was paid directly to the Baltimore Hebrew Congregation. However, as time went on, there was no longer enough income from the trusts to adequately maintain the plots, the tomb stones, and the deteriorating brick wall. So in 1960, the synagogue suggested to the trust company that the bodies be moved to the safer and continuously supervised Belair Road cemetery of the Baltimore Hebrew Congregation. After long and complicated legal maneuvers, plans to move the bodies were made in 1974, and they were finally moved in 1975 to a low granite post and chained area in the Belair Road Cemetery. In 1976, sixteen years after its beginning, the saga ended with the sale of the land of the original Cohen family cemetery.

In 1832, two years after its incorporation, the Baltimore Hebrew Congregation purchased land on Belair Road, adjacent to Clifton Park, for the purpose of establishing a cemetery. The far sighted board of the congregation wanted a land parcel large enough to satisfy the needs of the fast growing German Jewish population, but they apparently misjudged the future. They added 50 acres in 1866 and 9 more acres in 1884 which made this cemetery at the time the largest Jewish burial ground south of New York. Har Sinai preferred to continue an arrangement for the burial of their members in the private cemetery of a Sephardic family until they purchased land on Brehm's Lane near Loney Lane (Erdman Avenue and Edison Highway).[4]

In the 1850s, Baltimore Hebrew approached the Har Sinai and Hebrew Friendship Congregations with a proposal that the three groups share the cost of burial for indigent Jews. They agreed and continued to do this until the establishment in 1867 of the Hebrew Free Burial Society (now, The Hebrew Burial and Social Services Society of Md.). Shortly after its founding, the Society refused an offer from Johns Hopkins of an acre of land on Harford Road that could be used as a pauper's field. The Society saw no merit to the burying all of the poor together as in a Potter's Field. For Baltimore German Jews, this refusal perpetuated the Jewish doctrine of dignity for all Jews even in death. It was agreed by the four German Jewish congregations in existence at that time of the founding of the Hebrew Free Burial Society, that burials would take place in each of their respective cemeteries in turn.

Jewish funeral traditions and practices were and are still meticulously precise. A code of Jewish law, the *Schulchan Aruch,* prescribes the rituals followed by the Hassidic, orthodox and some conservative Jews. At the time of death the Chevra Kadisha, The Sacred Society the Jewish funeral society, makes all of the funeral arrangements. In the 1800s, and well into the 1900s, all funerals were held from the home of the deceased until funeral homes, (undertakers), came into being in the early twentieth century. Undertakers coordinate the funeral and prepare the body, but members of the Chevra Kadisha to this day perform the orthodox ritual washing, purification and dressing of the deceased in the white kittel (burial shroud).

UNCOMMON THREADS

Since the founding of the State of Israel in 1948, soil from that land is placed in the casket of Jews being buried everywhere in the world to symbolize that every Jew is a son or daughter of Israel.

---

1   *German Jews were welcome in Freemasonry lodges.*

2   *Einhorn insisted that German would be the language in which Reform Jews would be able to understand religious innovations. He argued with his congregants and others about almost everything and it seemed that his continuous anger was for anger's sake. He objected to female teachers in religious schools, maintaining that they were ignorant about Judaism and how were they going to be able to teach about such a delicate matter as circumcision.*

3   *Since the beginning of Jewish congregational worship, members have always left synagogues for one reason or another. Baltimore Hebrew's services were too orthodox for some, but not enough for others, and the board became quite picky about petty issues of decorum. They set up a system of fines that had a negative effect on mature congregants. Members were subjected to a fine of between twenty-five and fifty cents for talking or chewing during services, for gathering on the sidewalk in front of the synagogue, and for leaving services without the permission of an officer of the congregation.*

4   *The Hebrew Friendship's Philadelphia Road cemetery has an unusual configuration; originally a stone wall with no entrance to the enclosed area. Pall bearers passed caskets over the wall after which, for interment, mourners transversed the wall by the use of ladders.*

PART I-6

Reform * Orthodox opposition

*T*he Jewish Reform movement began in a small synagogue in 1810 in Seesen, Westphalia; in 1818, Reform services were held in Hamburg, Germany by young men who wanted the practice of their religion to be more attractive and understandable. In Maryland, greatly due to enfranchisement, Jewish men felt a loyalty to the temples in Berlin superseded any loyalties they may have had to temples in Jerusalem. Incongruously, they referred to their synagogues as temples, a contradiction of a sort because the word temple was usually associated with houses of Jewish worship in ancient Jerusalem. As previously mentioned, music was introduced into Reform services; again a contradiction, because music was heard during services in the ancient temples of Jerusalem. The rejection of a sense of attachment to the Holy Land was an apparent reason for most Reform Jews to be anti-Zionists.

German Reform services tended to be more decorous and dignified than those of the orthodox. New Reform prayer books omitted prayers for the coming of the Messiah, and stressed the enlightenment of Judaism. In time, German American Reform rabbis became educated in the secular system as well as in the advanced Jewish schools; for sermon purposes, they learned the nuances of the English language of their modern generation. Hebrew was removed from some parts of the service because young educated Germans were not prone to learn the language. In some sense, Reform movement's attempt to water down traditional Judaism brought the religion closer to that practiced in 19th and 20th in Germany. Certainly the Jews in Germany provided many, and maybe all, of the different modes of worship and traditions of Judaism, the diversity of which has enriched our world. The concepts of all forms of Judaism as we know them today have always been a part of German Jewish culture. Contrary to this, Reform Judaism did not happen in Eastern Europe probably because it could never have gained a foothold with the poor, simpler, and closer community minded Jews of Poland and Russia.

In Baltimore, the practice of Reform split the community more than it did individual families, although not in all cases. The movement attracted many young German immigrants who answered only to their own conscience and not to parents who remained in Germany. When two generations lived in America and the younger generation adopted Reform, some did so with deceit for fear of the wrath of parents.[1] Brothers who seldom opposed each other frequently did on the issue of Reform though it was not a cause for deep family differences. The fact was that the concept of Reform had become so widespread that it became a non-issue for most families who understood the economic considerations that prompted religious changes. Those favoring Reform wanted to be released from the bonds of tradition, the extensive use of the Hebrew language and the drawn out synagogue and home services of orthodoxy. Reform Jews perceived the orthodox services as being too disorderly, lacking dignity and decorum while organ music in the Reform deepened the spirituality of services. Orthodoxy did not recognize the equality of women in their synagogues; in Reform services a man and his wife could be seated together and could worship together, without the discomfort of head coverings. Reform granted merchants and their employees the freedom to work on the Sabbath, the best day of the week for retail business and an important factor for Jewish merchants facing the competition from Christians. Usually appropriate for those in the retail business, some, both Reform and a few Orthodox, eased their conscience by attending Saturday morning services after which they left the synagogue and went to their place of business.

Traditionalists remained rigid in their belief that any change would endanger the entire structure of Judaism. Today, so many Jews have practiced Reform for so many years, it is difficult to realize how threatening Reform was in the 1840s. To have a single law, ritual, or tradition changed without fear of changing their fundamental beliefs was unthinkable for many Orthodox Jews. Bitterness on either side was understandable. Those favoring Reform were convinced that Orthodox reactionaries held back progress and enlightenment; in turn, the Orthodox thought to be radicals and heretics.

Those who remained orthodox presented reasons to oppose the new Reform, and they considered the entire concept of religious freedom for individuals a threat to Judaism.[2] In Germany, the government, through its oppressive ways, forced Jews to practice an inner discipline of unity that built up a self defense mechanism. Through this spartanism, Jews could, at times, avert or at least endure hardships. A split in the practice of their ideology in America was construed by the Orthodox to be a threat to the unity of Judaism, that would upset the harmony of their American life. Orthodox Jews expressed concerns that the differences in religious observance could draw public attention to the Jews that might arouse prejudices of Christians. The underlying German Jewish insecurity, fueled by so many years of oppression, was always present when the community tried to deal with its religious and social issues.

In time, neither the Orthodox nor those who favored Reform were correct, as Judaism remained a precious heritage for both. Through all of the fears and comments, Reform Judaism endured and flourished in Baltimore and so did orthodoxy. Each group embraced the Torah, and its doctrines strengthened the "Threads of Life" of the Reform and the Orthodox alike.

---

1   *The son and daughter-in-law of a prominent Baltimore German Jewish family pitted their conscience against their love of fried oysters. At dinner, Mother arrived unannounced and the platter of oysters was hastily put on the floor under the dining room table where the family dog usually waited for table scraps; thus, this tale ends.*

2   *Freedom to practice as one pleases sought by Christian German groups such as the Mennonites and Dunkards who allowed no freedom within their own sect, was a reason for them to come to America.*

PART I-7

Hebrew Benevolent Society

*P*robably unaware of what was happening in their community, German Jews were in the process of building a strong Baltimore Jewish presence. Most lived in the same neighborhoods east of the Jones Falls and were part of the establishment of foundations for their religious and educational needs. Organizations for social services to care for the less fortunate were close to being founded, and ways to raise funds were being considered. Centers for recreational and cultural activities, lodges and clubs for mutual help and protection were in the not too distant future. Jewish people have managed to survive, because in every land in every age, they were able to live in well structured communities, enabling Jewish teachings to be transmitted from generation to generation. Baltimore German Jewish immigrants did not seek, nor did they expect help from the outside. Freedom permitted them to help themselves and to help each other. The necessity to be fed, sheltered and clothed superseded all other needs. Sewing jobs in Fells Point, where immigrants landed, enabled them to meet their needs, and little did they know that the garments they made that day were the modest beginning of Baltimore's great needle trades industry. The monetary return from the tedium of sewing allowed the immigrants to retain only small surplus funds above those needed for essential basics. Some men who migrated to America without their families were very frugal, enabling them to put aside a little money whenever they could; in time, they accumulated enough to pay for the passage of family or prospective brides left behind in Germany. A few who prospered, went back to Germany, married there and returned to Baltimore with their brides.

German Jewish immigrants, many of whom were in their early adulthood when they landed at Fells Point were cognizant of their needs. This is evident considering the early dates of the founding of a Jewish charitable institution that met individual and communal obligations. In 1846, a few individuals founded the United Hebrew Assistance Society that was reorganized in 1856 to become the Hebrew Benevolent Society.[1] The Society's scope extended to such a degree that during the Civil War they examined the feasibility of establishing a Jewish hospital. The Hebrew Benevolent Society evolved into an assortment of social agencies and services that in later years became agencies of the Associated Jewish Charities. In 1893, a member of the Board of Management of the Society, Jonas Friedenwald, left $5,000 in his will to provide matzo for poor Jews at Pesach (Passover). Cards were issued to be presented at matzoh bakeries for fifteen pounds of matzoh. Because needs were usually immediate, the direct approach to relief seldom included attempts to understand or eliminate the reasons for the needs, thus perpetuating the poverty of recipients. As the stages of life lengthened and needs changed, benefits overlapped and fund raising was duplicated. Frequently widowhood produced a condition of dependency but little evidence of demoralization. The avidity and eagerness with which beneficiaries became wage earners and self supporting was a bright chapter in Baltimore's German Jewish history of charity. As soon as children became of age to get jobs, they did, and their wages became part of the family income.

---

1 *Miss Myra Kraus, a cousin of the author's mother, was a pioneer case worker of the Hebrew Benevolent Society. She became the second wife of Dr. William Rosenau, rabbi of the Oheb Shalom Congregation.*

PART I-8

German, Hebrew and secular schools * Jewish and Christian German publications

*I*n 1817, several years before the arrival of the large influx of German Jews to Baltimore, the Society of Friends built the McKim School on the corner of Aisquith and Baltimore Streets. The school building that replicates in miniature the Temple of Theseus in Athens stands to this day in the center of the Jewish neighborhood of the past and still under the proprietorship of the Society. As customary for the Society of Friends, the school located in the heart of the German Jewish neighborhood was open and free to all who would come. In fact, it is only a half block up the street and around the corner from the Lloyd Street Shul. Even then, the McKim School attracted no German Jewish children because the parents, so imbued with German roots and German language, did not enroll their children in English speaking schools. Furthermore, the German Jews neither knew what nor who "Friends were for" nor who Quakers were. German Jews knew that Friends were different than they, but whether they attempted to surmount these differences and become good neighbors will probably never be known.

The Hebrew and English Benevolent Academical Association of Baltimore located on Bond Street between Pratt and Gough Street in 1842 organized the city's first Hebrew-English school. Cognizant of a need in 1848 both the Baltimore Hebrew and the Hebrew Friendship congregations began programs that were at best inadequate attempts to educate the children of the city's Jewish community which had grown quite large. In addition to the young of prosperous families, orphans and children of the poor needed to be taught. The Society for the Education of the Poor and Orphan Hebrew, the forerunner of the Baltimore Jewish educational system was founded in 1852 by Cantor Alois Kaiser of the Oheb Shalom Congregation; he was its first president. Since 1850, all of the congregations conducted schools on Sunday where students who attended non-secular weekday schools learned religion and Hebrew. Customarily, rabbis of both the Reform and the Orthodox synagogues personally taught the children. Rabbis of this era, stern and egotistical who demanded attention and respect, enforced these demands by inflicting corporal punishment. Until the time many years later when Chizuk Amuno changed its basic religious school curriculum to English, all children in their school were taught in German and in Hebrew, even though almost all first and second generation German Jews continued to speak German in their homes.

A few young German Jews who considered themselves intellectuals in 1854 founded the first Jewish community center in the country, the Young Men's Hebrew (Literary) Association. Active for only a few years, this Y.M.H.A. had an entirely different agenda than the Christian Y.M.C.A. and had no connection with a later Y.M.H.A. organization. Within ten years, three important literary associations followed: the Cliosophic, the Mendelssohn and the Hebrew Independent. The later Y.M.H.A., founded in 1920 and housed at first on Madison Avenue, stressed physical fitness. In mid nineteenth century Baltimore, the German Jewish community had a real need to offer advanced education beyond the high school level. Collectively, in 1864, the Cliosophic, the Mendelssohn and the Hebrew Independent organizations, societies that specified fines for using profane language, urged community educators and leaders to establish a Hebrew National College in Baltimore. In great haste; they established a college within one month; it no longer exists.

Education was not well structured for adults whose businesses and jobs consumed many hours of their time. Their avenue for learning and keeping abreast of world and local affairs was through the reading of German language, Jewish and Christian German newspapers. *Der Deutsche Correspondent* (1841-1918) and *Der Wecker*[1] (1851-1878) both carried accounts of German Jewish events, and because of this many Jewish businesses advertised in them. Started as a weekly, *Der Deutsche Correspondent* which became a bi-weekly and then a tri-weekly before becoming a daily in 1848, was a strong supporter of the conservative leanings of the Democratic Party, and before the Civil War, it became the state's most widely read German newspaper. Although written in German, *Der Deutsche Correspondent* had the distinctive make up of an American paper. On page one, a news column presented concise accounts of the news. This was not a controversial paper and when it was faced with the necessity of taking a stand, it did so with a degree of tact and reserve. Der Deutsche Correspondent lasted longer than any German language newspaper published in Maryland.

The Baltimore *Der Wecker*, a voice of liberals ran for decades as the constant opposition and competitor of the *Correspondent*, and it was the only Republican Party newspaper published in Baltimore a few years before and during the Civil War. *Der Wecker*, the only Baltimore paper that expressed opinions against slavery, a courageous thing to have done in "Mobtown Baltimore," was popular with those German Jews who wanted to read German language newspapers. *Der Wecker* was a bit off base when it compared the position of the Germans in America with that of the Jews in Germany. It claimed that the American German Jews legally had the same rights as others though prejudice against them remained. Liberal German Jews read Rabbi Einhorn's *Sinai* (Ein Organ fur Erkentniss und Veredlung des Judenthums), first published in 1855. An ultra liberal paper, Sinai attempted to enlighten and persuade Jewish thought against "forces of darkness" and took a strong stand opposing slavery. The publication of *Sinai* ended abruptly in 1861 when pro-slavery mobs destroyed that paper's presses along with those of *Der Wecker*.

1 Other popular newspapers of the time were the OCCIDENT, the ISRAELITE (published in Cincinnati), the JEWISH MESSENGER and the JEWISH RECORD (both published in New York). THE JEWISH MESSENGER began to publish as an organ of Orthodoxy, in strong refutation of the Reform movement. It was not until 1875 that the widely read German periodical, THE JEWISH CHRONICLE, appeared in print for 1 cent per copy. THE HEBREW AMERICAN, a weekly published in New York, became deeply concerned in 1881 about the persecution of Jews in Tsarist Russia. They took a leading part in the establishment of the Hebrew Immigrant Aid Society (HIAS). In the early to mid-nineteenth century in Baltimore, there was no dearth of publications. In fact, between 1820 and 1869, twenty-five German language newspapers alone rolled off Baltimore presses.

PART I-9

Civil War German Jewish merchants * Slavery and the Rabbis * Know Nothings * Baltimore prosperity * German Jewish military * Peddler's letter to his Mother

*F*ollowing the American Revolution, the next most significant event in American history was the Civil War. For the German Jewish immigrants there can be little argument as, in the few years before, during and after the war, the consequences for them were without doubt. Far reaching effects emanating from those emotional years reshaped the lives of Baltimore German Jews. Within the two decades of pre-Civil War German Jewish immigration, Baltimore Jews enjoyed almost complete freedom and social acceptance, primarily from Christian Germans. Those who could be termed merchants made a lot of money, umbaschrien (thankful and lucky) and began to enjoy staple niches in the city's mercantile circles. They were a thrifty lot, enterprising and materialistic; they welcomed the competitive circles of business. Unfortunately, their stampede to make money out paced their cultural advances because many Jews of the time were still immigrants, and their most singular interest was their personal economic and social adjustments and gains to be made in America.

Based on their recently acquired wealth, some German Jews were extremely conscious of their "neulich" (recent) high social standing, one they assumed themselves. They attempted to force themselves into the company of the so-called higher Baltimore Christian society by clamoring for admission to prestigious circles. In a few instances, some Jews associated and others assimilated with Anglo-Americans to the extent that a very few were accepted into Christian clubs and dancing assemblies. Not often but nevertheless statistically measurable, some German Jewish men married out of their faith, raised their children as non-Jews and sent them to Christian schools. So in Baltimore today, there are quite a few Christians with at least a single Jewish forefather. This is partially borne out by names that appear to be Anglican on the grave markers in the Cohen family section of the Baltimore Hebrew Congregation's cemetery on Belair Road.

Before and during the Civil War, most Baltimore German Jews were ambivalent on the question of slavery though a few took strong sides on the issue. In some instances, business partners parted over their differences as did some families. The popular newspapers read by most German Jews differed in their views on all Civil War issues, and this tended to drive a wedge into Jewish thought. *Der Deutsche Correspondent* opposed the abolitionist view of *Der Wecker* and *Sinai*.

Rabbis, who up to that time had been totally enmeshed in religious fundamentalism, injected additional confusion and doubts. Slavery per se became a big issue with them. No one knew what they honestly thought; were their opinions their own or did they reflect those of their congregants? Rabbi Bernard Illoway of the Baltimore Hebrew Congregation preached that slavery was sanctioned by the Bible and the South had every right to secede from the union. Rabbi Einhorn of Har Sinai was an abolitionist who felt the issue was a moral rather than a political one. Rabbi Szold took no part nor side and it seemed almost pre-ordained that he would remain neutral. After all, he was at the time rabbi of the Oheb Shalom, Lovers of Peace Congregation, and this appellation had a literal meaning for him. His thoughts paralleled much of the thought of his congregation, mentioned previously in this text as the most conservative of the Reform congregations. Szold felt that Jews should stay completely out of the controversy though he was not a pacifist. He had fought in Vienna for the revolution of 1848; subsequently he migrated to the United States. After the Civil War, Szold advocated the education of freed Negroes, and for this he was dubbed as the Rabbi of Timbuktu by his opponents. The rabbis bickered over their opposing positions on slavery when slavery at that time was not, and had not been, the major issue, at least for Baltimore long before the war began.[1]

For some, the intense feeling of the rabbis was not easily understood, but certainly there was a correlation between the slavery issue of mid-nineteenth century America and the Jews of biblical days who were delivered out of Egyptian slavery. Because only a few years had passed since the Jews left Germany, they well remembered the rigidity of government controls over their lives in Bavaria and Hesse. Social issues of the day appeared to have been a bit muddled for American German Jews; the issues of slavery and the rights of humans, the economic consequences, Reform or Orthodox, would not go away. Restrictions on Jews in America were fresh in their minds as it had been only thirty-plus years since the General Assembly of the State of Maryland recognized equality and political freedom for them.

On the other major mid-century pre Civil War issue, Jewish thought concurred. The Know Nothing Party (Native American Party, a misnomer) was a threat to all who were foreign born. Though the Know Nothing's scope was national, Baltimore became a major active target for the faction's intense wrath. The party concerned about its members losing jobs to immigrants attempted to have the doors of immigration shut and to impose limits on the rights of the newly arrived. To accomplish this, they implemented violence against them. Though primarily focused on Irish Catholics, the party also considered Jews and other minorities a threat to their well being. Nevertheless, Know Nothings did not zero in heavily on the Jews because by this time many Jews were self employed, while most of the Irish Catholics worked as employees for others. The Know Nothings disturbed meetings, picnics and other gatherings of immigrants and harassed those who had become American citizens. Members were sworn to secrecy, and if asked their social or political opinions, members replied "I know nothing." At the polls, they threatened voters with clubs, knives and pistols. After several elections in which Know Nothings were victorious, their star waned; the German Jewish vote an important factor in the demise of their demagoguery.

At its beginning, the Civil War placed the prosperity of Baltimore in limbo as city merchants had lost their southern market, but as the war gained momentum, Union money began to pour into the city. At the war's end, Reconstruction benefited Jewish merchants in a munificent manner. Manufacturers who had been engaged in tailoring of uniforms during the war turned to the clothing needs of the South and the mid-West. During the post war years, several Jewish owned men's clothing manufacturers and dry goods wholesalers seized the opportunity to expand into mainstream mercantile America.

Events of the Civil War changed attitudes of Christians towards Jews and inspired a mild flurry of ideological anti-Semitism which brought suspicions and accusations of disloyalty upon some German Jews.[2] Factually, some Jews crossed military lines and made business jaunts into the South. This included a few peddlers who lived in Baltimore and for several years prior to the war, traveled the rural areas of Virginia. As the supply of Union currency dwindled in that state and with the risk involved, crossing the military lines became increasingly less compelling for Baltimore peddlers and other business men.

Baltimore's location as the nation's largest and most commercially oriented border metropolis placed it squarely in the middle of the war's non-military movement, and German Jewish merchants became an important economic factor. Mercantile learnings and experiences of generations for German Jews were compressed into the four years of the war. Though they had uncertainties as the war progressed, German Jews became emotionally drawn into the conflict as they could no longer escape being caught up in the excitement of a war so physically near them. They became a part of the drama of military victories and defeats and became politically involved in issues that affected their well being. Too small of a group to contribute significantly to the military, they also had no overwhelming desire to do so. Many of the German Jews who arrived in the 1850s had lived in America only a few years, and they lacked the verve to fight for issues that they really never fully understood. A number of German Jews of military age took advantage of the legally allowable custom of the day; upon being drafted into the army, for a payment of a set sum, they found substitutes to serve for them. The American Hebrew stated that "There were not more than thirty Union men among the Baltimore Jews in the early days of the war." By the war's end, seven Congressional Medals of Honor were awarded to Union Army Jews, none of whom were from Baltimore.

Those who served in the military hastened their assimilation as Americans, whereas in previous years as immigrants, they tended to adopt Americanism with a cautious approach. The son of a Prussian born Baltimore German Jewish clothing manufacturer and a congregant of Har Sinai, Leopold Blumenberg chose not to buy his way out of the Union Army. He was commissioned a major in 1861, was instrumental in forming the Fifth Regiment Infantry of the Maryland volunteers, and spent much of his own money to do so. In 1862, Blumenberg led his troops against Lee's army in the battle of Antietam where he was seriously wounded. After convalescing for a year, President Lincoln commissioned him a Brevet Brigadier General in the Union Army and appointed him provost-marshal of the Third Maryland District. When the war terminated, Blumenberg was appointed Postmaster of Baltimore; he later served with the Internal Revenue Service.

In an act of no particular bravery, and unconfirmed, is the report that a few German Jews joined the gang action of stoning the Sixth Massachusetts Regiment on

Pratt Street. The regiment, summoned by President Lincoln to protect Washington, arrived from the north at the President Street Station. At the time of the stoning, the Sixth Massachusetts was en rout on foot, headed for the Camden Street Station where they planned to entrain for the Capitol.[3]

Those clinging to extreme Orthodox Judaism appeared to be less concerned about the war and actually continued to be somewhat withdrawn from the city's wartime problems. Several groups never became part of mainstream Baltimore and probably had little desire to do so. Among them were the author's paternal grandfather who continued to eke out a living as a poor peddler on Maryland's Eastern Shore, far from the areas of conflict.[4]

---

[1] *Due to Maryland's climate, except for the Eastern Shore and the southern Western Shore, the ownership of slaves was no longer economically feasible. The cost of feeding, clothing, and sheltering slaves on a plantation situation for twelve months of the year was too expensive when they could productively work the fields for only seven months. Some owners of large estates used slave labor as household servants and continued to do so long after abolition in 1863-1865. They then had to pay them for their services.*

[2] *During the Civil War, Moses Wiesenfeld, a prominent German Jewish clothing manufacturer and a great grandfather of the author's wife, Betsey, suffered a humiliating defamation of his fine character when, under orders from the military governor of Washington, he was arrested, his business shut down, and his goods and accounts confiscated. Wiesenfeld was accused on four charges of selling goods to be taken into the States in Rebellion. He was convicted on two of the charges as well as a charge of bribing a federal witness. He was fined $ 25,000, and sentenced to three years in the Federal Penitentiary in Albany, NY. Events during and after the war strongly indicated that this merchant as well as others had been falsely accused and convicted through contrived evidence. Along with Moses Wiesenfeld, principals of other businesses were arrested including the German Jewish firm of Simon Frank & Sons.. However, it does not appear that Jewish business owners were singled out because five principals of Christian owned firms were arrested at the same time as Wiesenfeld.*

[3] *In 1884, German Jewish Meyer Katzenberg, an alleged stone thrower at the Sixth Massachusetts in his youth, named his eldest son Alexander Stephans Katzenberg to honor the Vice President of the Confederacy Alexander Hamilton Stephans. The son in turn perpetuated this honor by naming his middle son Alexander Stephans. Paradoxically, two other Katzenberg sons living in Baltimore today are staunch Republicans.*

[4] *The author's grandfather Bernhard Kahn was typical of the German Jewish immigrant of his day; the following eloquent letter of 1865 tells an interesting social story, and except for the personal color he added to the calling of peddling, there is no record of his contributing anything whatsoever to the community. He arrived in Baltimore in 1853 from Bavaria, landing as did hundreds in Fells Point. Though he lived in the city with his family on week-ends, during the week he peddled on the Eastern Shore of Maryland, traveling his territory with a horse and wagon. A letter to his family in Germany is pitiful; a plaintive cry although it appears that he philosophically shielded himself from the war. He made no inference to whether his financial reverses were or were not caused by war so apparently to him; the conflict was a mere current event with no particular impact on his life. He expresses no great expectations for his life in America; no fulfillment of an American dream whatever that may have been for a German*

Jewish immigrant in 1865. Probably typical was the pathos of his never being able to see his mother again though she remained alive in Germany. Letters from immigrants to their families in Germany were few and far between. They were expensive to send and slow to be received. Because of their rarity, letters like these were saved and passed down through the years. Another letter written twenty-four years later to Bernhard Kahn's sister and brother-in-law who remained in Germany indicated a definite upgrading of his fortune. Its pertinent portions are covered in Part II.

TRANSLATED FROM THE GERMAN

Trappe, the 25th of July, 1865

Beloved Parents, Sisters and Brothers,
    A long time has passed to show you my hand again. All of us thank G-d are healthy and well; the same I hope, of you. It was a relief when receiving your letter and i could determine that you are doing well. I want to advise you that again i have a little son. He was born in February, is now five months old, his name is Moses; he was sick, he had a cough, is now well again. I want to let you know that i no longer live in the house where i had earlier lived. My home is now number 74 Harrison Street. We had sold our house for 500 dollars and we have bought for this amount a city Bond which brings 7.3 percent. Where i now live i am renting; i pay 18 dollars per month in rent. I had started a clothing store, but i had bad luck with the store. I could not make a living, so i have now begun my old business again, namely pelts, or to go out into the country. I had bought someone's stock for 1,000 dollars, and it was not worth 500. I also lost 300 dollars on wool, and i lost 300 dollars on cowhides and feathers..so my money is gone.
    I am writing this letter from the country, about 100 miles from Baltimore, where everything looks very pretty and everything is growing well. The war, thank G-d is over. The North beat the South. The army all went through Baltimore on its return way, which numbered at least 10 to 18,000; also, the southern prisoners came through here. Abraham Lincoln was shot through treacherous murder, but last Friday two weeks ago four of the conspirators were hanged. Also I want to report that my sister Bertha and her two children are well. They bought a nice house and paid for it. It cost 900. She also had 900 dollars at the Savings Bank where she gets 50 dollars interest yearly. Things are going well for her, and she has a small store in the house. Last week Nathan Friedman visited me. I had not met him before in America. He lives in Philadelphia, has a spice factory, and his father Abraham Friedman lives with him in the house. Also his brother is married. That is all i can write, dear parents. Dear, dear mother, you can imagine how i weep when i think of you and can no longer see you. I hope that you may all live in joy, and may never any harm come to you.
Farewell, i greet you all heartily, and remain your son.
    Bernhard Kahn
Write me soon.

While Bernhard did not follow the lead of hundreds of peddlers who at this time made a transition to store owner or manufacturer, his sons became retail and manufacturing merchants.

PART I-10

Post Civil War Harmony Circle * Hebrew Hospital and Asylum * 1868 Masked Purim Ball * Hebrew Orphan Asylum * Mercantile gains * Wave of anti-Semitism * Jews join German societies * Concordia Club * Chizuk Amuna

Baltimore suffered no physical damage during the Civil War. Its location, ideal below the Mason-Dixon line, astride and adjacent to the agricultural regions of the nation, enabled it to become a trade center for a sizable section of the nation. German Jews, traditional traders and now becoming important in Baltimore's mercantile circles, learned through their wartime business experiences that they had to break away from their own small community. Manufacturers became aware of the necessity to become associated with national as well as local organizations through which they could expand into greater markets.

During the fifteen years following the Civil War, the Jewish community grew slowly. Immigration from Germany had become a mere trickle and the great wave of immigration from Eastern Europe had not yet begun. Data gathered for an 1868 police census[1] in Baltimore included name, age, sex, race, country of birth, naturalized or registered as a voter, and religion.

The immigrant generation of Baltimore German Jews was part of the city's German-American society, with very few indications of anti-Semitism among the German-Americans of the 1840s and 1850s. Apparently as long as the German Jew spoke German and allied himself with the German-American group, he was welcomed into their community. Following generations of German Jews became more closely identified as being either Jewish or American. If they were Orthodox, the Jewish element outweighed their German background; if they were liberal, the process of Americanization overcame the German-American isolation.

Along with the changes and development in religious patterns, there were those who considered their social consciousness to be exclusive. These were a well-to-do group of German Jews who perceived themselves as having attained a social position that was a level above the others. They had charitable concerns that they supported liberally, and except for this, they wrapped themselves in a cocoon of social elitism. Started as a small organization prior to the Civil War in 1855, this group of successful German Jewish merchants founded the Harmony Circle. The Circle's rooms provided reading and billiard areas for the men and a parlor for the ladies. Ostensibly a social order, the Circle was oriented towards raising funds for the Hebrew Benevolent Society. The Harmony Circle fell upon hard times during the Civil War; curtailed their activities and successfully revived them in 1866.

Baltimore's German Jewish population increased three-fold in the decade before the Civil War and because the sheer numbers inflated community needs, leaders planned new institutions while the war was in progress. They recognized that better care for sick Jews to be a critical need when it was brought to the attention of Jewish community that a Jewish man had recently died unattended in a local Christian hospital. With assistance from the Hebrew Benevolent Society, in 1863, the Hebrew Hospital[2] and Asylum Association founded the Baltimore Asylum for Israelites to care for aged Jews. The cornerstone for the new hospital was laid in 1866 on Ann Street (now Rutland Avenue), and the ten room hospital building was completed the following year. In its first year of operation, the staff treated forty-eight patients. In 1868, the hospital was incorporated and renamed the Hebrew Hospital and Asylum; by 1886, a new wing was built. A nursing school was added in 1906; in 1926, fifty-eight years after its incorporation, the name of the large hospital building on Monument Street east of Broadway was changed to Sinai Hospital of Baltimore, Incorporated.

German Jews of this era were extremely philanthropic, and through their generosity, the hospital was able to offer medical care with no fees charged to those unable to pay. Though the hospital furnished excellent care, it was several years before Jews able to pay became patients there because of the stigma of its being a charitable hospital. A stay there was considered beneath their dignity. Conscious of a moral commitment to the people of Baltimore and its environs, when space permitted, non-Jews were cared for in the Sinai Hospital. Time has changed this policy; now admission is completely secular.

In 1866, the Baltimore Purim Association[3] was founded. Officers of the association contacted the Harmony Circle directors to join with them in sponsoring a masked ball for the benefit of charity. Initially, the Circle declined; however a meeting was held in November 1868, in the vestry rooms of Oheb Shalom's Hanover Street Synagogue where arrangements were made for the jointly sponsored ball. The proceeds of the their first annual masked balls benefited the Hebrew Hospital; at subsequent balls, the Hebrew Orphan Asylum for Sheltering the Orphans was included. There were almost no Jewish physicians in these years, so the hospital's staff was mostly Christian and the elite of Baltimore's Christian community joined Jews at the ball. All danced the waltz, schottishch, quadrillo, polka, waltz and hop, and the gallop.

The Hebrew Orphan Society founded in 1872, was located at Rayner Avenue and Dukeland Street in the Calverton section, 3 blocks north of the 3000 block of Edmondson Avenue; at the time just outside the city line. Given to the Jewish community by German Jewish William S. Rayner, it was a large residence structure, formerly the Baltimore City Almshouse. At the dedication of the newly constructed building, sixty-five voices of the combined choirs of the city's Reform synagogues sang.

Jews recognized a need for courage, discipline and strength to combat a new pattern of discrimination in the 1870s that threatened to negate business and social advances attained during the Civil War. In the years before the war, some Christians experienced difficulties differentiating between Christian Germans and Jewish Germans. Now along with the increase of German Jewish shopkeepers, wholesalers, and manufacturers they knew for certain to be Jewish, traditional dislikes were reborn into the Christian community. Caricatures of peddlers appeared in publications, songs, and stories and tended to display Jews as dishonest. Possibly envious of the Jewish economic situation that grew and prospered, Christians related being Jewish to greed, deceit, vulgarity, and ostentation. Through it all, German Jews expanded their community interests, and participation in non-work activities became attractive to them. To satisfy needs for physical and recreational activity, particularly those who were artisans, many joined the non-denominational though unmistakably German, Sozialdemocratische Turnverein (the turners), and after the Civil War, the Turnverein Vorwarts. The Turners primarily attracted liberal, free- thinking young working class men. In their meetings, they engaged in arts and science debates, lectures, and readings. Their primary outlet, however, was physical, and in the form of quasi-military gymnastics. German Jews who loved to sing became members of the German Zion Church sponsored Liederkranz, the Arion, and the German Mannerchor singing societies. Others joined fraternal associations such as the Masons, the Elks and the 100% German Odd fellows.

Noting the Germanic orientation of several of the organizations German Jews joined, it is indicative of the difficulty they had in shedding their German characteristics; maybe they didn't want to. German Jews remained Germanic to the degree that they habitually deposited their monies in commercial and savings banks founded after the Civil War by non-Jewish Germans,[4] some of whom were also political refugees.

In 1847, cultured Germans founded the not particularly elitist Concordia Society, a social organization on an intellectual level. The programs designed to educate its members covered a multitude of musical, scientific, literary, dramatic, agricultural, and charitable interests. Members dabbled in politics, and there was a large secessionist group in the society. At its founding, the Society rented rooms for their meetings and continued to do so through the Civil War years. In 1865, the Concordia Club built a large combination hall and opera house fronting on Eutaw Street on the southeast corner of German (now Redwood) Street. The Society chose a location that after a few years was surrounded by the red brick loft type buildings of the 1870s, constructed to house Baltimore's expanding garment industry.

The literary and musical programs of the Concordia appealed to the upper middle class, and over the course of years developed into an entertainment organization for Germans; the music and drama programs became the most important functions. The opening of the Concordia Hall and Opera House marked the beginning of a period of excellent sponsored German performances. The Concordia Club held tightly to its German orientation by renting the hall to other German organizations for an assortment of functions. Charles Dickens lectured there in 1868, and the Grand German Opera Company performed in 1872 in the magnificent ballroom of the club's opera house. Concordia presented weekly concerts, and both American and English theatrical troupes performed regularly.

After the Civil War, hundreds of German Jews moved west from East Baltimore to Baltimore, German (Redwood), Lexington, Lombard and Fayette Streets between Hanover and Carey Streets. In a short while, many joined the Concordia, and as more and more joined, more and more Christians resigned. There were two reasons for this change in membership; one, factual; one, conjecture. The fact: Improved intra-city street transportation became a catalyst for thousands of Christians to move out to Edmondson Avenue, Frederick Road and other west Baltimore thoroughfares so the location of Concordia was no longer convenient for them. The conjecture: Jewish members began to outnumber the Christians, and that didn't work well. It seemed that Christians were less likely to be comfortable with this weighted degree of social association. Probably a finishing touch for the Christian members was when the Yiddish Theater played an engagement at the Concordia. During the years of the development of the "Loft Area," primarily the home for Baltimore's garment industry, large numbers of German Jews moved away from east Baltimore and settled within walking distance of the Concordia. A disastrous fire in 1891 destroyed the Concordia and all of its records, ending the most important social organization of its day, or any day, for Baltimore's German Jews.

New associations and degrees of assimilation and feelings of being American fueled the expansion of Reform Judaism. The sacrifice of some Jewish traditions through the movement resulted in some aloofness directed to those who had retained their Orthodoxy. Reform Jews considered the adoption of Jewish traditions to the American climate was the way to worship in America. In a matter of months after the Civil War ended, the Baltimore Hebrew Congregation lost many members because of their Orthodox regime.[5] To the consternation of many of those that remained, in 1868, the congregational leaders voted to change their orientation to Reform. They introduced an organ into the services; women sat with their men folk; and the wearing of tallit became optional. In protest, a group of twenty members in 1870 sued Baltimore Hebrew for its infractions of ancient Jewish rituals. They settled out of court and in 1871 founded the Chizuk Amuno (Strengthening the Faith) Congregation. Those who worshipped with the new Orthodox Chizuk Amuno congregation actually strengthened and defended the faith. While temporarily housed in a small Exeter Street hall, led by the author's wife's family, Chizuk Amuno, also known as the Friedenwald Shul, raised funds for a synagogue. In 1876, they completed the erection of a Moorish style synagogue, a popular design for European shuls. Located on Lloyd Street near the corner of Lombard Street, Chizuk Amuno is less than a half block down the street from the synagogue they left, Baltimore Hebrew's "Stadt Shul."

1   The 1868 census showed that:
        57 percent of Baltimore Jews were native born.
        51 percent were under the age of 20.
        Females slightly outnumbered males.
    Of employed males:
        62 percent were managers
        19 percent were clerks or salesmen
        11 percent were skilled artisans
        3 percent were semi-skilled
        2 percent were unskilled
        2 percent were professionals
    Of 54 Jewish women between ages 30 and 49:
        10 were in households with no children
        13 were in households with one to four children
        16 were in households with five or six children
        15 were in households with seven or more children

2   Moses Wiesenfeld, (a great grandfather of the author's wife) was the first president of the Hebrew Hospital in addition to being president of the Baltimore Hebrew Congregation.

3   The Association's first president was the author's wife's grandfather Goody Rosenfeld.

4   One of the popular four banks with expressive German names was the Deutsche Bank von Baltimore, founded in 1868 as a savings bank. It was converted in 1874 to a commercial bank and the name changed to the German Bank of Baltimore. The other three were the Deutsche-Amerikanische Bank organized in 1871 and the name later anglicized to the German-American Bank; the Deutsche Central Bank founded in 1874 became the German Central Bank; and the Deutsche Sparbank von Baltimore founded in 1876 became the German Savings Bank.

5   The AMERICAN HEBREW of October 1885, reported that since the founding of Chizuk Amuno, "Baltimore Hebrew has been losing ground and were it not for the large revenues received from its cemetery, it would be in a sore plight." In the same issue of the publication, it noted that "We now have in Baltimore eight synagogues besides a great number of little congregational halls."

PART I-1I

Public markets * Jewish retailing * Old Town

*T*he development of Baltimore's early retail business areas and market places trace back to the colonial era, and along paths Indians once trod. Farm wagons traveled rudimentary roads from rural areas to bring produce into the city, and they gathered in the areas with the largest concentrations of population. These same roads became the turnpikes used by stage coaches to transport people to and from central Baltimore; today they remain major traffic arteries.

A correlation between the location of public markets and Baltimore German Jewish owned retail businesses took place largely during the post Civil War years, establishing a pattern of German Jews living in small enclaves near the markets. Baltimoreans of all manner of being made weekly trips to the markets to buy food which resulted in a concentration of buyers in the area of the markets. Although almost all of the city's markets predated their arrival in Baltimore, German Jewish retailers joined others in taking advantage of the large buying power of people who, in addition to buying food in the markets, purchased other needs on the same day in nearby stores. This sound reasoning continues to exist in modern retailing where a large food market is frequently the anchor store and main attraction of a strip shopping center. For Christian working people, Saturday was market day. Although it is the Sabbath, German Jewish owned stores opened and sold clothing, hats, shoes, furniture, notions, jewelry, and pawnbroker's items. Many of the German Jewish merchants offered credit, enhancing the growth of their businesses.

Centre Market, known colloquially as Marsh Market and by some as Mash Market, was located south of Gay and Baltimore Streets where it intersected with Harrison Street, almost immediately across the Jones Falls from the large concentration of German Jews living in East Baltimore.

Baltimore's nationally known Lexington Market attracted both large and small German Jewish businesses and a concentration of German Jews lived nearby. Centrally located, the market, designated as such over 200 years ago by John Eager Howard, became the attraction for the development of Baltimore's principal downtown retail shopping center. The market became operational in 1803, and a permanent structure was erected just before the War of 1812. Near the market in the late 1800s, German Jewish retailers built large department stores.[1]

Though the owners of the these stores became wealthy, their fortunes never approached the size of those made by the city's Christians who were involved in banking, shipping, railroading, and heavy industrial manufacturing. Because they were store keepers, their names were well known to the public; so their importance in the community was magnified, and they met this challenge by being generous to the city's needs. Although they were grateful for their good fortune in America, their pedestals were not all that high. While most were paternalistic, they never paid their employees one cent higher than they had to; they were not saints because for the most part, saints do not operate in the highly competitive retail markets of the world.

North on Howard Street, the Richmond Market surrounded by only a few Jewish storekeepers and homes, catered to the city's elite, both Christian and Jewish, the so called carriage trade. In East Baltimore, the Fells Point Market, also known as the Broadway Market, existed many years before German Jews landed in Fells Point. This market continued to have a strong hold for German Jewish businesses long after the store owners moved from their homes on the Point. Several blocks east of Broadway smaller enclaves of German Jews resided where the Northeast Market attracted a large group of German Jewish owned retail stores on Monument Street, an artery leading to Philadelphia. In West Baltimore, Hollins Market, just north of the Baltimore and Ohio Railroad's Mt. Claire Station, and the Lafayette Market on Pennsylvania Avenue, the old Reisterstown Turnpike, there were fewer Jewish residences; nevertheless they were important market areas for Jewish owned businesses. Along the corridor leading from Anne Arundel County, German Jews moved into two story houses and established retail businesses in South Baltimore adjacent to the Hanover Street, the Camden Street and the Cross Street markets. German Jews continued to live in these areas until some time after World War I when they gradually moved their residences northwest. By the 1930s, most Jews had left these areas.

The Belair Market on Gay and Forest Streets was a latecomer to the city's market system, not being built until the 1850s. Gay Street, the main artery from Harford County, fed directly into the area known as Old Town, one of the most popular of the city's retail areas. Anchored in the middle by the Belair market, a string of German Jewish owned retail stores, housed in structures built before the Civil War stretched along Gay Street from the Fallsway to Aisquith Street. Several merchants who previously lived above their stores on Harrison Street moved to Gay Street after the Civil War where they continued the custom of maintaining living quarters above their stores. During store hours and well into the turn of the twentieth century, merchants hung wares on racks on the stores' exteriors under awnings on wooden frames. At closing time, these awnings were rolled up and shutters secured the store fronts.

Gay Street was a working man's neighborhood and its merchants evolved into a sub-culture of Baltimore German Jews. The atmosphere of Gay Street was more Old World than uptown, and families who owned the stores had a limited interest in almost any activity other than their businesses. They placed great stock on family succession so that their businesses would continue rather than placing emphasis on education and refinement. Financially, they did well, but socially they did not enjoy the communal acceptance of wealthier German Jews who owned the large uptown department stores, wholesale dry goods firms, and clothing factories. Their need to keep their stores open for business day and night precluded serious social associations. Gay Street retailers were a clan of their own, not matched by German Jewish retailers in other parts of Baltimore. Either owners or employees took turns standing on the sidewalk with their backs to the street, facing their store's entrance to bark and catch, a quaint old world method of retailing frowned upon by the more sophisticated larger downtown stores. Barkers and catchers enticed passers-by to enter their stores, hopefully to buy. Once inside, the prospective buyers were subjected to the art, and it was an art of intriguing leverage where the pressure to buy reached a new high or new low, depending upon how the customer perceived being caught in such a trap.

Gay Street's best years were after 1880, perhaps up to World War I, as at that home ownership in the area began to decline and most German Jewish store owners moved into uptown residences. Though Jews still own most of the Gay Street stores, blacks have replaced the once all white Christian German, Polish and Italian customers.

---

1   *Among the large Jewish owned department stores in the vicinity of the Lexington Market were Posners, Hutzler Brothers, Hochschild-Kohn & Co., Bernheimers, the Leader, Joel Gutman, Julius Gutman, Bragers and Eisenbergs.*

PART I-12

Christian German schools late 1800s * German English Jewish schools * Catholic high schools for German Jewish girls

Although all of the German Jewish synagogues conducted schools, by the end of the Civil War many families could afford to have their sons educated in the private Deutsche und Englische Schules of Frederich Knapp and of the libertarian Heinrich Scheib.[1] Both Lutheran educators, German to the nth degree, opened their schools to children of all faiths. Several other smaller German-English schools did not seek non-Christian pupils.

Knapp's school opened in 1853 with 60 pupils. He advertised in the Jewish periodical *Sinai*, and for the most part, his students came from well-to-do families. In 1859, it was incorporated as F. Knapp's German and English Institute, and after changing locations several times, Knapp found a permanent home on Holiday Street opposite City Hall. Pupils came to the school from several states of the Union, and in the year prior to the Civil War, 700 pupils were enrolled. In later years, Jewish students rubbed elbows with the Knapp Institute's legendary alumnus, H. L. Mencken, who in his writings had few kind words to say about his Jewish classmates. At the beginning of the 1870s, the school gradually declined, and in 1874 it was taken over by the city and continued then as a public English-German school. The growth of the public school system in the late 1870s spelled the eventual demise of all but one of the private German-English schools.

Scheib, pastor of Baltimore's Zion Lutheran Church located on the northeast corner of Lexington and Holiday Streets, established that church's secular school in 1836 with 71 pupils, and it was not disbanded until 1896. The number of pupils whose parents did not belong to Zion Lutheran Church out-numbered those that did. An early believer in free thought, Scheib encouraged the thinking that secular education should take precedence over religious teachings and that young boys of German heritage, Christian or Jewish, should be well prepared to make their way as Americans. Thus, religious instructions were not allowed in Scheib's school; the curriculum remained entirely free of church dogma. All of the classes were conducted in English or German. Just before the Civil War, the school had an enrollment of 418 pupils in seven grades. Corporal punishment was strictly prohibited. For one year, between 1839 and 1840, Scheib published a paper for the teachers, the parents of pupils, and anyone who was interested in educational matters. The audience to whom the paper was directed constituted a kind of early parent teachers association.

Strangely, even at the height of the German-American era, no one ever succeeded in establishing a German kindergarten in Baltimore in spite of the fact that the idea of the kindergarten originated in Germany and brought to America by Germans. In 1876, a local German educator attempted to start this type of kindergarten in the city but failed miserably. He found support only from German Jews, who alone were responsible for the fact that he did not go completely bankrupt when, he closed his school after a year in existence.

Other Jewish boys attended week-day German-English, though Jewish oriented schools, those of Professors M. Seligman, Joseph Sachs and Jonas Goldschmidt. M. Seligman's school, located at 310 S. Broadway, served as a combination day and boarding school. The curriculum was designed to "educate the better class youth of German immigrants who were anxious to preserve their superior culture in the new world." M. Seligman taught courses in German, French and English, the languages the boys spoke in his school. He offered Hebrew courses as well as an extensive curriculum in geography, history (modern and ancient), mathematics, writing, composition, bookkeeping, music, and drawing. All of these studies could be had for $ 5.00 each semester; the schoolmaster allowed a reduced fee for indigent students of "good character and from good families."

Starting in 1848, Sachs taught classes at the city's first Hebrew School housed in the Baltimore Hebrew Congregation's new synagogue. Later in his own school at 30 N. Calvert Street, Sachs taught Hebrew, English, French and German, much the same subjects as Seligman though he also included philosophy. In 1859 at age 16, Leher (teacher) Goldschmidt began teaching in the Hebrew Friendship Congregation's Eden Street Shul and in 1864 replaced Samuel Gump in a school conducted in the basement of the Oheb Shalom Synagogue on Hanover Street. Goldschmidt's school, one of the leading schools in the country, enrolled students from other cities. In the evenings, Goldschmidt taught French to a class of selected students; the school was disbanded in 1867. Jacob Levy wore dual head-coverings of two professions. A schochetim, Levy traveled from Philadelphia to Baltimore on Mondays and Thursdays to perform the ritual killing of cattle and chickens. While in Baltimore, he fulfilled his primary interest early in the day; in the afternoon, he taught Hebrew and German and any other language desired by his co-religionists. He specialized in preparing young boys for their Bar Mitzvah, all of this for the bargain price of 25 cents per lesson.

Those who could not afford private schools or desired their sons to associate with Christians enrolled their children in public schools. In 1879, the Baltimore City School Board introduced courses in the German language but only in those schools located in the German neighborhoods. Public Primary School #2 on High Street near Fayette and Secondary School #3 on Baltimore and Aisquith Streets, with a nearby annex, enrolled almost 100% German Jewish students. These effective German-English schools infringed on the popularity of the private German schools so much so that they hastened their demise.

The German-English schools, for many years the foundation of German Jewish education until the 1870s, experienced a modest revival in the 1920s. Most often German synagogue schools were poorly funded and depended largely on untrained volunteer teachers. During these years, mainly for the Orthodox children who did not attend Sunday Schools, daily afternoon religious schools operated under the auspices of the Orthodox shuls.

For young ladies, education was indeed a problem and not overly popular. Choices were few as there were no private Jewish-run secular schools for females. There were always women teachers, mostly untrained unmarrieds or widows who in order to make a living conducted small classes for younger girls in the their homes. For the most part, these classes stressed domestic arts. Many females of high school age attended the Western Female High School,[2] Baltimore's first public all girls' high school. By the standards of its day, it was an excellent school at a time when co-education was unthinkable. Those German Jewish parents desiring a more suitable finishing school style of education, and not too expensive, enrolled their daughters in either of two local Catholic institutions, the Institute of Notre Dame or the Academy of Visitation. In addition to their studies, students at the Catholic high schools learned how to do needle work, especially tapestries depicting biblical subjects worked on large canvasses.[3]

---

1   *Families of marginal finances interested in the upward mobility of their sons could at times afford to send only one son to the Knapp or Scheib schools. Parents expected that this son would impart his acquired knowledge to his younger brothers.*

2   *Henrietta Szold, daughter of Rabbi Benjamin Szold of the Oheb Shalom Congregation was one of the best known Western High School graduates*

3   *A 4' x 3-1/2' tapestry titled Jacob Blessing the Sons of Joseph hangs in the author's home. His maternal grandmother Lina Kraus worked this piece in 1874 while she was a 16 year old student at the Academy of Visitation founded in 1837. In Lina's years, it was located on the north side of Center Street between Howard Street and Park Avenue. The author's wife's paternal grandmother Rosa Wiesenfeld while a student at Baltimore's Institute of Notre Dame on Aisquith Street in 1875 worked a slightly larger size tapestry titled Rebecca at the Well. It has been given to the Chizuk Amuno Congregation.*

PART I-13

First Northwest Passage * Druid Hill Park * Eutaw Place * Hebrew Friendship watches German Synagogues move uptown * Early Polish and Russian Jews in German Baltimore * Board of Jewish Congregations * Comparison study, Oheb Shalom and Chizuk Amuno

*I*n the late 1880s, many German Jews abandoned their east, west, and south Baltimore homes and synagogues and began an exodus that continued through the 1890s. During this Northwest Passage, German Jews moved into large houses in uptown areas that had the amenities of electricity, indoor plumbing and telephone lines. In the past in all cities, those who could afford to sought residences on the heights; those without the money to do so lived in the lower lying areas near to the industries in which they were employed. It has never been desirable to live downwind from meat packers or chemical plants; so in Baltimore with prevailing northwest winds, northwest was the choice of the German Jews.

Less well-to-do German Jews moved into lesser uptown houses that were much improved over where they had previously lived in East Baltimore. For the most part, these were situated along Eutaw Place, Bolton Street, Linden Avenue, Madison Avenue, McCulloh Street, and Druid Hill Avenue corridors. Socially conscious German Jews considered the better addresses to be helpful in establishing their community standing. Except for North Avenue, there were almost no homes on the east and west streets. The houses facing the north and south streets were quite large with alleyways separating the back yards of the homes. The newly established electric street railway lines on Madison and Linden Avenues that fed into the center of the city added to the desirability of northwest residences. By 1900, virtually the entire Baltimore German Jewish Community had moved uptown; an exception being a group of Gay Street merchants who continued to live in quarters above their stores.

Houses built above North Avenue adjacent to the estates of Chauncey Brooks and Dr. Thomas E. Bond and not too far from Druid Hill Park, the former estate of Lloyd Nicholas Rogers, were in demand. Heading south, the value of residential properties gradually lessened. At no time in the late 1800s did these neighborhoods become all Jewish; they remained perhaps 60% to 70% Christian. Although both the Christians and Jews in the neighborhoods maintained cordial relationships, there were marked cultural differences. Christians verbalized about how nice their Jewish neighbors seemed to be and how happy they were to have them living alongside, but these remarks did not include social acceptance. When neighborhood boys played games, the lines were usually drawn; a team of Christian boys played against a team of Jews.

Several wealthy German Jews seeking pretentious homes on Eutaw Place bought large and gracious mansions vacated by prominent Christian families who were perhaps wealthier at the time than the Jewish buyers. The 1899 Society Visiting List names well over 150 German Jewish families living on Eutaw Place in the ten blocks between Dolphin Street and North Avenue. Many of the family names such as Ambach, Bendann,

Erlanger, Frank, Friedenwald, Greif, Gutman, Hamburger, Hecht, Hess, Hochschild, Hutzler, Rayner, Rosenfeld, Schloss, Sonneborn, Stein, Strauss, Strouse and Wiesenfeld were household names by the turn of the nineteenth century and well into the twentieth century.

Paved with Belgian blocks in 1856 as an extension of Eutaw Street on land partly a gift to the city, Eutaw Place stretched from Dolphin Street as far as North Avenue by 1876. Considered by some to be a better address than Mount Vernon Place, it was perhaps Baltimore's most distinctive and elegant residential neighborhood. Until 1888, North Avenue, formerly named Boundary Avenue, was the northern boundary of Baltimore City.

'Tis said that Eutaw Place was modeled after Paris' Champs-Elysees or after Unter den Linden in Berlin, but most likely after neither; it was not quite that grand. Either way, its green lawns and irregular concrete walkways interspersed with huge cast iron urns and fountains complemented great planted beds of tulips, annuals and cannas, depending on the season. For years past, city gardeners meticulously cared for the plots, and householders' assessments supplemented city funds to do this. Weather permitting, strollers rested on green wooden benches from where they watched the play of water in the ornate fountains. North of McMechen Street, a female figure stood atop a three tiered cast iron fountain in the center of a 30 foot pool while seraphs spouted water. The fountain was built for and displayed at the Philadelphia Exposition of 1876. It was scrapped sixty-six years later during World War II to make tools of destruction. Topping off the grandeur of Eutaw Place, in 1911, a Christian wholesale tobacco merchant, Charles L. Marburg, presented a white marble monument to the city in honor of Francis Scott Key, author of our national anthem, the Star Spangled Banner. Situated within a circular drive at the top of one of Baltimore's highest land points at the intersection of Lanvale Street where Oheb Shalom built their Eutaw Place Temple, Key is depicted standing in a small row boat looking up at his poem held by a female figure atop a four column pavilion.

In 1895, the completion of twelve houses opposite the Gill estate pioneered the building of dwellings on Eutaw Place above North Avenue. It was not until well after the turn of the century that monied and socially minded German Jews moved into exclusive and expensive high rise apartments erected on the property of the former estate of Chauncey Brooks. The Esplanade, built in 1912, and the Emersonian, in 1915, fronted and faced each other on Eutaw Place, five city blocks north of North Avenue at the entrance to and overlooking Druid Hill Park. Residents of the upper floors of those buildings and in the later built Temple Gardens, erected in 1926 could see for miles. The Riviera and the Lake Drive Apartments high rises on the edge of the park enjoyed spectacular panoramas of Druid Hill Park and Baltimore City. Eutaw Place remained a desired residential address for many years. During the 1920s, 1930s, and early 1940s[1] an inordinately large number of both German and Russian Jewish physicians maintained their homes and offices on Eutaw Place.

Except for the Hebrew Friendship Eden Street Orthodox Congregation, all of the German Jewish synagogues accompanied the northwest move of their members. The leadership of Hebrew Friendship, Baltimore's second oldest German Jewish congregation, would not acknowledge to themselves that their old East Baltimore community was disappearing. It happened gradually as one family after another vacated the area and moved uptown. With half their congregation gone, Hebrew Friendship made an overture to Baltimore Hebrew to unite the city's two oldest congregations and proposed to join them in the erection of the new Madison Avenue Synagogue; however, a group of Hebrew Friendship members who continued to live downtown succeeded in having the proposal withdrawn. Hebrew Friendship membership continued to dwindle and the congregation survived until 1899, far too late to make the decision to relocate. Two years later, with most of their former members worshipping at the uptown Madison Avenue and Oheb Shalom synagogues, Hebrew Friendship sold their Eden Street shul, including its one hundred cut glass chandeliers, to the newly formed Russian congregation, Aitz Chaim (Tree of Life). When a shul dissolves, the future of its cemetery presents a problem, particularly so for a large congregation such as Hebrew Friendship whose many members pre-purchased burial lots. To perpetuate the cemetery, it incorporated and burials are still being made there.

In 1891, Baltimore Hebrew transferred ownership of their Lloyd Street synagogue to a Lithuanian Roman Catholic congregation that converted the building into the Church of St. John the Baptist. In 1905, Shomrei Mishmeres Hakodesh (Guardian of the Holy Commandments) congregants, all Ukrainians from the province of Volhynis, purchased the Lloyd Street church, thus returning it to Jewish ownership. Shomrei Mishmeres Hakodesh at the time was considered to have been Baltimore's leading Orthodox synagogue.

The Baltimore Hebrew congregants dedicated their new synagogue on the northeast corner of Madison Avenue and Robert Street in 1891. Architects said at the time that the building was America's single example of pure Byzantine architecture. The Baltimore Hebrew torah ark was removed from Lloyd Street and re-installed in the Madison Avenue Synagogue, so Shomre Mishmeres installed their own and at the same time built a matzoh oven in the basement of the Lloyd Street shul. Sadly, in a subsequent move of the Baltimore Hebrew Congregation to Park Heights Avenue, the original Lloyd Street torah ark was thoughtlessly abandoned. When it was needed later for the restoration of the Lloyd Street Synagogue, it had mysteriously disappeared. In its new environs, Baltimore Hebrew's prolonged conversion to Reform was completed, and they now referred to their synagogue as the Madison Avenue temple.[2] The use of street nomenclature became common usage for Baltimore synagogue congregants because it differentiated the present synagogue building from the one the congregation had abandoned. After only twenty years of occupancy in their Lexington and Pine Street synagogue, the building committee of Har Sinai chose a site for a new temple on the southeast corner of Bolton and Wilson Streets. The congregation, with fewer members than Baltimore Hebrew or Oheb Shalom, built a less pretentious structure than the others.

Dedicated in 1894, the architectural design of the stone exterior of Har Sinai, though no less attractive, had simpler lines than those of the other Reform temples. The absence of interior supporting pillars enhanced the beauty of the sanctuary and unobstructed views of the two massive candelabras that adorned the bimah.

Through a combination of pledges from well-to-do members[3] and a grand fair, the Oheb Shalom Congregation raised enough money to move from Hanover Street. The members were very anxious to occupy their new synagogue. It was not only that most of their members had moved uptown but, also when they converted the church to a synagogue almost thirty years before, they were not aware that they had chosen a location that later become a noisy commercial area of Baltimore. In 1892, members of Oheb Shalom laid the cornerstone of a magnificent house of worship on the crest of the hill on the northeast corner of Eutaw Place and Lanvale Street. Designed by Joseph Evans Sperry, Oheb Shalom, huge and domed, was the only Baltimore Reform congregation to build in accordance with ancient tradition of a domed temple on the heights. (See Appendix)

In 1882, Oheb Shalom joined the Reform Union of American Hebrew Congregations and in 1890, the Conservative Jewish Theological Seminary Association. Nevertheless, it was not until 1902 in their new temple on the mount that the men of Oheb Shalom doffed their hats, eliminated the German language from their services, adopted the Union Prayer book and heard female voices in their choirs.[4] Oheb Shalom, the most traditional of the three Reform congregations and its members among the wealthiest of Baltimore's German Jews, even then in the eyes of many of its members, was not fully mainstream Reform. An observation by their rabbi in 1928 was that Oheb Shalom was never either Orthodox or Radical in its interpretation of Judaism and in its ceremonial practices.

In their new homes and synagogues, except for attending an occasional Friday night service, Reform German Jews began to limit their synagogue attendance to the two holiest religious holidays, Rosh Hashonah and Yom Kippur. At Sabbath services, atmosphere in the Reform temples was almost indistinguishable from that of Christian churches. Children attended Sunday Schools where teachers made feeble attempts to teach them Hebrew, Jewish history, the Bible and ceremonial rituals. Most boys continued to be Bar Mitzvah, but certainly not all. After Bar Mitzvah, although the temples offered two more years of Jewish education in the Confirmation classes of the Sunday School, few boys continued their religious education. The enrollees in confirmation classes that ended the additional years of study were predominantly female. Consecration services, held at the end of confirmation study, renewed the pledge of the class to their forefathers to observe the teachings of the Torah. Bat Mitzvah for girls was unheard of at the time in a Reform synagogue, and in most homes of the Reform, the ushering in of the Sabbath became a ceremony of the past.

The David Sondheim & Sons Funeral Home buried almost every Reform German Jew who lived and died in the Baltimore area. Strategically located on Eutaw Place and Robert Street, Sondheims was in the neighborhood when and where they were needed. In

1962, Sondheim closed their body shop because they could no longer maintain it in the fading Eutaw Place corridor. Two Baltimore orthodox funeral establishments, Jack Lewis and Sol Levinson & Bros. operated homes in East Baltimore and near Sondheims. All three promoted the advantages of holding funeral services in funeral homes rather than in the residences of the deceased.

In the 1850s, about thirty years before the mass migration of Eastern European Jews, a handful of Polish Jews migrated to Baltimore apparently from Poznan, parts of which were the cradle of the Polish State. In 1865, this handful of indigent Yiddish speaking Polish-German Jews formed the Bikur Cholim (Visiting the Sick) Congregation. They moved into a building on Gay near Lexington Street that had been vacated ten years before by Oheb Shalom; later they worshipped in two other buildings on Exeter Street near Fayette. Bikur Cholim endured united for eight years until a split in 1873 when some of its former members founded the B'Nai Israel Congregation. Space was set aside in the Hebrew Friendship Cemetery for the burial of members of Bikur Cholim, and in that cemetery several stones erected in the 1870s, 1880s, and 1890s mark their graves.

While the mass migration of Jews from Eastern Europe did not begin until 1881, in 1875, there were enough Russians from Bialystok (Byelo-Russia) living in Baltimore to establish a second Eastern European congregation, Ohel Yaakov Bialystoker. Colloquially known as the Frantzoisishe Shul (French Shul), its origins stemmed from the fifteenth century. At that time, French Jews wandered as far east as Bialystok, and presumably the founders of Ohel Yaakov were of French descent. Officers of Ohel Yaakov Bialystoker wore formal wear and top hats to shul on the Sabbath and Jewish holidays.

An early group of Lithuanians in 1877 founded the Pokroyer Shul. Lithuanians, who are referred to by some as Litvaks, endured probably the worst economic conditions in all of Russia. Their land was poor and these peasants of the Russian province had sunk into the lowest depths of poverty and ignorance even though they were known to be intellectually superior to the Russians. Lithuanians numbered by far the largest Russian group living outside the Pale of Settlement.

In 1895, Chizuk Amuno sold their Lloyd Street synagogue to an Orthodox Russian Jewish congregation, B'Nai Israel (Sons of Israel). In 1896, Chizuk Amuno dedicated their newly constructed synagogue in a changing neighborhood at McCulloh and Mosher Streets. This was a location mistake, so in 1922, after only twenty-six years on McCulloh Street, Chizuk Amuno moved again, this time to a grand new synagogue building on the northeast corner of Eutaw Place and Chauncey Avenue. Because B'Nai Israel was the second largest Eastern European Jewish synagogue in Baltimore, it came to be known as the "Russische Shul." Until five or six years ago, B'Nai Israel, the only active Jewish congregation in the inner city, could barely support a minyan. The synagogue has been recently listed on the National Register of Historic Places and has been designated a Baltimore Historic Landmark. B'Nai Israel has been restored and rededicated and is one of the two anchor synagogues of the Jewish Historical Society of

Maryland's Jewish Heritage Center. Now during the high holidays, it's seating capacity for 200 men and a like number for women is filled by worshippers, mostly former residents of East Baltimore, who return for the comfort and meaningful uniqueness of being able to worship again in this historic synagogue. Oheb Shalom kept its minutes in German until 1880; Chizuk Amuno kept theirs in English from the date of their 1871 founding. Supplementing this, the Chizuk Amuno religious school with some secular orientation abandoned the German language and replaced it with English before this date. Oheb Shalom's great German oriented, though Hungarian born, Rabbi Szold, who officiated from 1859 to 1892, stressed German. Although his English was not fluent, in 1882, Rabbi Szold condescended under pressure to deliver his sermon in English every other week for the benefit of the younger American born members. Chizuk Amuno's rabbis of the same period were American born and favored Hebrew and English in their services. Rabbi Henry W. Schneeberger, the first American born ordained rabbi, became Chizuk Amuno's rabbi in 1876, and he favored Hebrew and English in their services.

By the 1890s, Oheb Shalom's members were the richest Jews in Baltimore, and many of the men resisted further religious changes, keeping Oheb Shalom the most traditional of the three Reform congregations. On the other hand, the German Jews who founded Chizuk Amuno were just as affluent and Americanized and only slightly less wealthy. They certainly enjoyed the same level of prosperity as did members of the Baltimore Hebrew Congregation from which they had withdrawn. They attained similar patterns of upward social mobility and their occupational distributions were quite the same except that Chizuk Amuno had a significantly higher percentage of "wunderkinds" who became doctors and lawyers. By 1920, a large percentage of Chizuk Amuno members pursued careers as employees, but this was offset by a higher percentage of American educated professionals.

The curriculum in Chizuk Amuno's religious school was derived from the synagogue's firm commitment to Orthodoxy and not from the yearnings for small-town German roots. Thus, unlike Oheb Shalom's religious school, they did not teach German. The English language was used in the translations and conversations with the pupils. Though the curriculum did not replicate traditional cheder learning, it did emphasize Jewish learnings in Hebrew and related Jewish subjects. The original 1871 founder members of Chizuk Amuno differed from the members of Oheb Shalom in where they lived. Thirty percent lived in quadrant I, forty percent in quadrant II and ten percent in quadrant III. (See Appendix)

Differences in member's wealth between Oheb Shalom and Chizuk Amuno showed in their financial structures and where they lived after moving uptown. Two years after Chizuk Amuno's founding, their rabbi received $1,200 per year; Oheb's $4,500; Oheb Shalom rented its pews from "$25.00 to $50.00" and single seats from "$6.00 to $13.00." Chizuk Amuno rented seats for the high holidays from "$3.00 to $6.00." About one third of Oheb Shalom's congregants lived on Eutaw Place; the rich of Chizuk Amuno lived in far less pretentious houses on McCulloh Street. Baltimore

Hebrew and Har Sinai congregants tended to live on Druid Hill and Madison Avenues, streets virtually shunned by Oheb Shalom members.[5]

It is interesting to note that many of the well-to-do Orthodox German Jewish families, after joining Reform synagogues, continued their memberships as well in Orthodox shuls such as Shearith Israel. They joined the Reform synagogues not because of their financial wealth but because of personal preference. They also wanted to worship in a synagogue that could better their business contacts or to worship with a relative who had joined a Reform congregation.

Consistent with change, in 1898, the German Jewish synagogues formed the Board of the Jewish Congregations in Baltimore. Its purpose: to encourage the firm pricing of seats, to outline conditions for officiating at non-synagogue Jewish services, and to encourage the attendance of children at the synagogues' religious schools. To add strength to the intent of the board to advance synagogue membership, they introduced a penalty for not being a member of a synagogue; the denial of rabbinical officiating at family functions. The barring of non-synagogue members from Jewish privileges was only partially effective.

---

1   *In the 1940s during World War II, Eutaw Place literally became trashed. At first the change was below North Avenue and later above to accommodate the need for housing an influx of Appalachian people who moved into Baltimore to work in wartime industries. Owners of the beautiful mansions sold them to unscrupulous landlords who converted the large single family homes into small apartments. The area south of Lake Drive, west of Mt. Royal Avenue, north of North Avenue and east of Madison Avenue, unofficially renamed Reservoir Hill, is one of the city's poorest neighborhoods and presently fighting blight and large-scale abandonment.*

       At the time of this writing, all of the high rise apartment buildings on Lake Drive, their interiors run down, their views unchanged are no longer occupied by well-to-do Jews. Several years ago, the city renamed the Esplanade, Emersonian and Temple Gardens complex Renaissance Plaza, a rather amusing name for the condition of the buildings but one that sent a message of promise. In December 1993, the Baltimore City Board of Estimates approved a loan to a developer who, along with state, federal, and the developer's equity, plans to "restore," a poor term for cheap renovating and modernizing, the three buildings for low income occupancy.

2   *A small squib appeared in the Baltimore SUN of September 15, 1891, which stated that "The sale of pews at the new temple of the Baltimore Hebrew Congregation on the corner of Madison Avenue and Robert Street, began last night. The building was filled with people and the bidding at times very active."*

3   *The Strouse, Sonneborn, Schloss, Schoeneman and Greif families who owned the five largest men's clothing manufacturing firms in Baltimore all worshipped at Oheb Shalom. The reason is conjecture, but it must be assumed that it had something to do with the Oheb Shalom location on South Hanover Street, literally in the back yard of the clothing factories and within walking distances from the west Baltimore homes of its members. When Oheb Shalom moved to Eutaw Place and Lanvale Street, it became a neighbor of the Eutaw Place mansions of many of its congregants.*

4   *Throughout the years, the female voices of the Reform synagogues' choirs have been outstanding. For the most part they have been, and still are, the voices of Christians. The organs have been played by Christian men and some say, although this is questionable, the reason is that Christians sang and played better than Jews.*

5   *In 1985, seeking material for a study, Dr. Marsha Rosenblit, an associate professor of history at the University of Maryland, sifted through the records of the Oheb Shalom and Chizuk Amuno Congregations. Pre-studies indicated that through the years these two congregations had been the city's most stable German Jewish congregations and two of the most intrinsic interest. They possessed, albeit incomplete, membership records and minute books, but there was enough to reveal some outstanding facts. In the 1870s, a large number of Baltimore's upwardly mobile Americanized German Jews rejected Reform and chose to continue worshipping in the traditional Orthodox manner. As previously mentioned, the founding of Chizuk Amuno by prosperous German Jews resulted from a split within the congregation at the time that Baltimore Hebrew members adopted Reform.*

The study found no basis for the belief that as German Jews became prosperous they became affiliated with the Reform movement as a symbol of their success and higher degree of Americanism. Contrary to this popular assumption, there is little correlation between wealth and Reform Judaism, though by 1890 most well to-do German Jews, owners of clothing factories, the large retail stores, and wholesale firms, worshipped in Reform synagogues. Congregational members were not rich at the time the Baltimore Reform synagogues were founded. The fact is that the listed members of the Reform groups between 1853 and 1862 indicate they were far from well to-do. Fewer than 20% were merchants, and none were professionals. The same research revealed that the Americanized German Jews who rejected Reform and retained their orthodoxy were economically better off in the final decade of the last century.

PART I-14

Late 1800s politics * German Jews and Baltimore economy * Banks, insurance companies and Jews * Reality of Russian Jewish migration * Christian fears * Park School

Socially and financially, during the last quarter of the nineteenth century, things went well for Baltimore German Jews. The 1880s were years of enormous economic growth and business owning German Jews gained a measure of wealth. Too early to become actively involved in politics after the Civil War, many German Jews became supporters of the new Republican Party of Lincoln and their descendants remain affiliated with that party today. Not until the end of the nineteenth century did they become politically active; serving on civic boards and commissions. In 1895, Louis Putzel was elected to the Maryland House of Delegates and in 1897 he became a state senator. Previously, a well-regarded Putzel had been a member of a commission that framed Baltimore City's new charter. Jacob Moses was elected to the House of Delegates in 1902 and to the State Senate in 1904. In that year, Martin Lehmyer was appointed to the Baltimore Supreme Bench, the first Baltimore Jew ever to served in such high legal circles. Isaac Lobe Strauss served as Attorney General for the State of Maryland between 1907 and 1911. Isador Rayner served three terms in the Maryland House of Delegates before he was elected to the United States Senate in 1904. Although a lifetime member of the Har Sinai Congregation and sympathetic to Jewish problems, he kept a distance from becoming involved in Jewish affairs. Rayner married a Christian woman, raised their only son as a Christian and was buried in a Christian cemetery but he never converted to Christianity. Nevertheless, most German Jews had little appetite or enthusiasm to engage in politics as did the Eastern European Jewish Democrats of later decades.

Though anti-Semitism remained apparent, many well respected German Jews appeared to have been accepted by the Christian business community, albeit in a condescending sort of way. Distinctively in the distilling business, a few German Jews formed partnerships with members of old Maryland Christian families. Jacob Ulman, a German Jew, and in a partnership with the Christian Goldsborough family, married a Christian woman of high social standing. On the strength of her being a collateral descendent of Thomas Jefferson, he was accepted as a member of the Maryland Club. Ulman subscribed to the Bachelor's Cotillion and also joined the Elkridge and Gibson Island Clubs, living to be the last survivor of the five steeplechase enthusiasts who founded the Maryland Hunt Cup in 1894.

The German Jewish owned department stores flourished as did the large clothing manufacturers and the general merchandise and dry goods wholesalers; all played an undeniably important role in the Baltimore economy.[1] In fact, if there were a way to measure or equate their intrinsic importance, their communal roles probably exceeded their financial worth to the city. The physical locations of German Jewish businesses helped to determine the upward economic climate of the city because the areas in which they chose to build large mercantile establishments increased the real estate values of those areas. For the banks, the Jewish owned enterprises were often their largest depositors and borrowers; their employees, their steadiest bank customers. A few banks elected a token number of prominent Jewish merchants to serve on their boards, and they made sure they selected only important Jewish officers of firms that were large customers of the bank. There were never enough Jews selected; their numbers were disproportionate to their communal importance. But then, this was better than in later years, when Jews, German and Russian alike, were excluded almost entirely from the city's largely Christian controlled financial institution's boards.[2] It was difficult for German Jewish white collar workers to be employed in Christian owned banks or insurance companies or any type of financial institution. Most public organizations seemed to have felt comfortable accepting the money of Jews, but somehow they were uncomfortable working with or being in a position of having to associate with them.

Beginning in 1882, the reality of the Eastern European Jewish immigration sent shivers down the backs of the German Jews arousing their deep seated feelings of insecurity. Continuing for several years, the migration became a momentous issue causing unrest within the German Jewish community. They conjured fears of economic reversals and fears of Russian immigration motivating social repercussions in associations German Jews and Christians had formed. It is difficult to know if these fears were founded or if the arrival of Russian Jews had anything to do with a noticeable underlying resurgence of anti-Semitism directed mostly, but not exclusively, towards German Jews. In 1892, idle threats that bombs would be placed in Russian Jewish neighborhoods were contained in messages received by city officials. In the nation, anti-Jewish demonstrations were directed towards Jewish landlords and businesses but in Baltimore only a few felt personal taunts.

In 1905, President Cleveland's determination to retain the gold standard spawned a political situation and a phony reason for Christians to dislike and mistrust the Jews. Obviously not justified, in 1905, some Christian Americans conjured up a bizarre idea that Jews could and would acquire the nation's gold reserves and ship all of the gold out of the country. Emanated from rumors and mixed fears surrounding Jewish traditions with gold, a somewhat nebulous connection arose to the literary stereotype of Shylock. Because of an increased Jewish business presence in the nation's communities, some Christians expressed the fear of a Jewish take over of American businesses. Some claimed there was a Jewish conspiracy to rule the world, though there was never any factual evidence to support any of these confusing but not so amusing fabrications.

Of a sobering nature, almost all of Baltimore's female private elementary and secondary schools discriminated against the enrollment of Jewish girls, and private schools on the same level set up quotas for boys. An exception, the Quaker's Friends School, always liberal, remained open to all and enrolled several Jewish students. This blocking of enrollment and the quota system presented an impenetrable educational barrier for Jewish children that lasted for several decades.

The political turmoil in the public schools after the turn of the century reduced public school education to a low ebb, so the Jewish community took steps to do something about the education of well-to-do Jewish boys and girls.[3] The Park University School opened on September 30, 1912, with 104 students in a converted residence on Auchentoroly Terrace, and in the spring, some classes were held under the trees in Druid Hill Park. This was a special school from its beginnings which were relatively small; the first class to graduate in June 1914, numbered four students. The founders were not aware of it at the time, but the establishment of this school was a major event for Baltimore and American education. The school began with bold concepts and standards of education on the elementary and secondary levels, an entirely new approach to the existing methods of educating children.[4] In the 1920s, a modern school building was erected on Liberty Heights Avenue; now it is on a thirty-six acre campus on the south side of Old Court Road near Falls Road. Today, secure in their Brooklandville campus, the Park School welcomes and embraces a diversity of students from all ethnic and socio-economic backgrounds. Enrollment today is about fifty percent Jewish and eight percent Afro-American. On the subject of Hebrew schools, the 1995 Seventy-fifth Anniversary issue of the Baltimore Jewish Times stated "and several sizable Hebrew schools including Park School." The reader should not be misled as there was not a single word of Hebrew uttered in the early days of the Park School, not then, not now.

---

1   *The Henry Sonneborn Company, Baltimore's largest men's clothing manufacturer, in 1904 erected what was at the time the world's largest single clothing factory at the northwest corner of Pratt & Paca Streets.*

2   *See illustrations in PART III for The Savings Bank of Baltimore and the First National Bank of Baltimore in 1929. Note the name of Jewish Leonard Greif. In the 1990s, the line-up has scarcely changed.*

3   *Baltimore Public School Superintendent James H. Van Sickle made a ten year effort to remove public education from the spoils system by refusing to allow teachers' appointments to be controlled by the political patronage system. For this, Mayor Preston dismissed him and three of his proponents, Eli Frank, Dr. J.M.T. Finney and Dr. J.M.H. Rowland. In protest, Goucher professor Hans Froelicher, Sr. and General Lawrason Riggs resigned from the board. Within a few months, Froelicher and Riggs combined with Eli Oppenheim, Louis H. Levin, and Siegmund B. Sonneborn, Jonas Hamburger, Dr. Louis P. Hamburger, Dr. Guy S. Hunner, Sigmund Kann, George C. Morrison, Francis E. Pegram, Karl Singewald, Isaac A. Oppenheim and Eli Strouse to join with Eli Frank to found the Park University School.*

4   *The progressive Park School promoted freedom of pupil expression and emphasis was put on educating children for productive citizenship in a democracy where respect for the rights of the individual citizen including the respect for the right to religious choice.*

PART I-15

Victorian Christian influences * German Jewish protocol * German Social Registry * German domestics * Rearing children * Summer camps, residences and vacations * Baltimore horses

Circa 1900 ended the Victorian and began the Edwardian Era, and accounts of the social life of the German Jews focused on the well to-do. Only a few years removed from hearing their parents and grandparents tell of their lot in Germany, turn-of-the-century German Jews through social activities reinforced their awareness that they were Americans. The reality was that they were not able to discard their Jewish insecurity, although these feelings could be partially ameliorated by a blending of their lives with and hope for a better acceptance from the Christian community.

There was a question though: Which Christian community did they want to be a part of; the Protestant Anglo-Saxon Episcopalian, the German Lutherans or Irish Catholics?[1] It was difficult for German Jews to be accepted by mainstream Baltimore Episcopalians, as well as the German Lutherans and Irish Catholics. Beginning in the 1800s and continuing to the mid-1900s, marriages between Anglo-Saxon Episcopalians and Christian Germans, Jewish or non-Jewish, were frowned upon. Prejudice against Germans, Irish, and after 1890, the Italians, played an important role in Baltimore's social and ethnic structure for generations. Episcopalians and Presbyterians controlled the power structure of the city, as they do to this day but less effectively. Earlier when most German Jews adopted the Reform movement and introduced choirs and organs into their services, they paralleled the Protestant church service decorum. Reform Jews not only experienced a similarity in their worship, but also some actually joined with Christians in celebrating their holidays. On one of the two holiest days of Christianity, Christmas, some German Jewish families celebrated with an interchange of gifts lovingly placed at the foot of their decorated pine trees. At Easter, they dyed eggs and filled Easter baskets for their young children so that they could participate in traditional Christian egg hunts.

The propensity to refine German Jewish culture became an obsession, and many adopted as their role model the manners and the social graces of the Anglo-Saxons. As they pursued the eloquent etiquette of the day, the right German Jewish families made certain that their homes would not be without a publication prescribing the detailed commandments of Christian society's social dos and don'ts; there were no maybes. Maids in the homes were properly dressed in the European manner, black dress and white apron. Several families employed butlers, and this being Baltimore, their Jeves was more likely an Afro-American than English. Most wore a white coat jacket for daytime duties and the informal supper service. For a formal dinner, there were those who served wearing a dinner jacket and a black tie. Butlers wearing a white tie and tails in a German Jewish home at a formal dinner was not the Baltimore German Jewish style. With Our Crowd in New York City, this dress was de rigueur.

German Jewish women joined literary societies and sewing circles and took turns hosting lecture groups in their homes. In the evenings, men frequently gathered to enjoy a lively pinochle game. For the upper echelon of cultured German Jews who had cultivated a deep feeling and understanding of the arts, Friday night after dinner musicales were held in their homes. A musical friend or two, a professional musician or two joined the family in the drawing room where a family violinist, pianist, harpist or vocalist accompanied them.

The intellectual level of the German Jew in Baltimore during these days was certainly equal to the desired social level. The national characteristics of the Germans, Jewish or not, were self-confidence that bordered on arrogance, competitiveness and not so subtle feelings of superiority, a stereotype that had some basis in fact. They loved music, education and the theater, and most important, they thought in broad concepts and theories. They came from a country that had produced, for good and bad, a Heine, a Mendelssohn, a Wagner, and later a Marx and Hitler.

While the customary tradition was to attend Saturday morning services, have lunch and be free for afternoon family visits, social interchange took a far more serious turn. Visiting became refined and re-defined and developed into a social art. The grand mansions of Eutaw Place and the lesser ones of Linden Avenue, Park Avenue, and Bolton Street became the picture perfect settings for social activities of first and second generation German Jews. Usually on Wednesdays, and if the rules[2] were faithfully followed, between 11 AM and 3 PM, unannounced callers paid brief visits. Obviously, the homes to which visits were made were mostly within the select area south of North Avenue. Visiting became a social strategy whom you could and would visit and whom you would have visit you. Even so, without the benefit of calling cards, German Jewish families continued their age old custom of interchanging visits on Rosh Hashonah with family and close friends.

To clarify the turf on which socializing became acceptable, in 1899, the elite Hebrew Directory or Visiting Register was published. In 1905 and 1908, and possibly in later years, the Register Publishing Company of Baltimore listed several hundred names in The Jewish Social Register. To be listed meant it was OK to maintain a social relationship with others on the list and that extended to the acceptance of invitations to teas, dinners, and balls given by fellow German Jewish listees. These were not games that people played; they were serious maneuvers of a society with definite inferences of social strata.

Owners of Baltimore German Jewish mercantile firms, on business trips, established solid relations with German Jewish retailers in the South. They formed friendships and social associations with those customers whom they considered to be acceptable and who lived within a reasonable visiting range. The Jewish Social Register of 1908 listed separately the names of those socially acceptable in Baltimore, Washington, Richmond and Norfolk. This register was of particular interest to those families with children of an eligible age for marriage. Almost every German Jewish family who lived in these four communities and who had some wealth and finely honed social instincts automatically became part of a network that either knew, knew of, or were perhaps related by blood or marriage to other German Jewish families within this geographic boundary. The larger German Jewish communities of New York and Philadelphia, not a part of this tightly knit Maryland, Virginia, and Washington German Jewish circle, maintained their own social separatism.

It was proper to employ the services of a non-Jewish German governess and young domestics to live in with the families. Shortly after the immigrants arrival at Locust Point on North German Lloyd steamships, German American Christian fraus made it a business, to deliver an endless supply of frauleins directly to the German Jewish homes where they were to be employed. Hundreds found jobs in this manner; many never married and through the years established special relationships with their adopted families, living with them for the rest of their lives. Other young German girls, after working a few years as a governess, domestic or cook in a German Jewish home matured, met a German men, married him, and left their jobs to raise a family of their own. Considered to be disciplinarians, German governesses influenced the children through a constant relationship that taught them proper manners and a sense of responsibility and orderliness. German governesses satisfied a hope of the family, and it was a hope only, that the German language would be perpetuated within the household.

Some families engaged tutors to teach French to their children. When spoken in the best circles, French, the language of culture and of romance, appealed to German Jews. Tutors attended family dinners at least once a week, and at this time, the children and the tutor conversed in French at the table. Most of the time, pappa and momma, or if the parents demanded a more refined address, father and mother, who most likely did not speak French, sat silently through their meal listening and wondering of what they had done.

To acquaint their children with life's better things, important family dinner tables were set with rosepoint lace tablecloths, expensive German bone china, heavy silver, and the best crystal. More than likely the dinner itself fulfilled the German Jews appetite for their traditional foods. A favorite main course was gansebraten, (roast goose). The goose's skin was partially removed and rendered into crisp, crackling grieben; the legs and wings, good only for stew, were cooked separately; and the large roasted carcass was served with apple sauce and kartoffel kloese (Potato dumplings with croutons in the center).

Talented or not, German Jews enrolled their children in Saturday classes at the Maryland Institute of Art or the Peabody Conservatory of Music; some children attended both. Children of both sexes attended ballroom dance classes[3] at Professor and Mrs. Tuttle's on North Avenue where the boys' trouser pockets were sewn to prevent the socially taboo habit of standing with their hands shoved in them. Girls went to classical dancing schools that held frequent recitals for the pure admiration but not necessarily the enjoyment of parents. A few were enrolled in elocution and poetry reading classes. Hidden in the thoughts of many Jewish parents was the hope that one of their offspring harbored the soul and talent of an artistic genius who would not have to work in the family business for the rest of his or her life.

For a recreational day in the park, parents or governesses took their charges to the wide lawns of Druid Hill Park to play and romp on the green. On the hillside in front of the Mansion House, if the timing was right, they experienced an introduction to natural studies while witnessing the grazing of the park's flock of sheep in residency.

During the summer months when well to-do German Jews traveled abroad, they crossed the Atlantic on huge ocean liners and spent time in the European capitol cities or in expensive spas and resorts. The children were shuffled off to summer camps for eight week sessions. The camps all had authentic sounding Indian names and those located in Maine and New Hampshire were considered to be the best; certainly the most expensive and exclusive. None of these camps offered two week stays as did summer camps in other New England states, in New York State and in Pennsylvania. These camps were quite nice and a bit cheaper, but were not quite the same as camps in the State of Maine.

To escape the summer's heat, less affluent Jews rode unglamorously in the evenings, on the Madison Avenue open-sided trolleys of the United Railways and Electric Company's No. 16 line. They rode to Riverview Park and back to the Madison Avenue car barn. Seeking comfort for the entire summer, families who could afford to rented or bought houses in outlying areas. Typically wooden, these structures with spacious center halls, tall first floor windows and wrap around porches on shaded lots encouraged a free movement of cooler air. After dark the family gathered on the porches to enjoy the wooden swing that hung from eye bolts affixed through the porch ceiling, to rock on the rockers, to just talk, and maybe to have a little ice cream before the mosquitoes got too bad. The most desirable houses were located near street car or train transportation so that the commute to father's office or place of business was not too difficult. If his business or profession allowed, father spent only a part of the entire summer day at his office.

Houses in and around West Arlington, Windsor Hills, and Mount Washington were popular as were those in Glyndon in Baltimore County, northwest of the city. Houses in the Greenspring Valley near the Chattolanee Hotel and Springs were in demand and very expensive. In this location, pappa was able to take the hotel bus directly to the station for the train trip to Baltimore. Sudbrook Park,[4] designed by Frederick Law Olmstead, Sr. in 1891 on 204 acres, was a suburban summer resort. The Western Maryland Railroad made Sudbrook Park ideal for summer use as it provided nine daily trains to and from Baltimore. Sudbrook Park is listed on the National Register of Historic Places.

During the summer, families vacationed in Pen Mar, Braddock Heights, and other resorts high in the Blue Ridge Mountains, and a few went to tidewater spots along the Chesapeake Bay. Some German Jewish families who kept kosher traveled far to spend their summers in mountain resorts such as Tannersville in the Catskills[5] of New York State. Other families vacationed in the big white clapboard-sided hotels in New Hampshire or Maine while the very rich ventured to coastal resorts in the Jewish Newport of Deal, (now the summer refuge of America's Syrian Jewish Community) of

Elberon, Long Branch or Sea Bright in northern New Jersey.[6] Less affluent Jews more than likely vacationed in the cheaper off-boardwalk hotels of Atlantic City.

Several well-to-do German Jewish bankers and owners of department stores in the large eastern cities tended to summer vacation in the same places. Baltimore families were among those that built camps on the Rangely Lakes in northwestern Maine. They sent their boys and girls to the expensive camps, where there was little danger of their meeting too many Russian and Polish Jews. There was always a pattern of a few German Jewish families that discouraged meaningful associations with Russian children and a few Russian Jewish parents were guilty of the reverse of this social indiscretion. Some mid-western and Baltimore families built homes in Charlevoix on the northern shores of Lake Michigan. To this date, a few of these family summer vacation camps in Maine and homes in Michigan are still used by their Baltimore German Jewish owners. These vacation spots translated into plans and assumptions, premeditated or not, that the children of fine German Jewish families would meet the children of other fine German Jewish families. At Charlevoix, Rangely and elsewhere, friendships were formed that lasted through college years and in many instances in marriages, because most German Jewish families wanted their own to marry their own and they did.

Families well off enough to own and stable a single or a pair of thoroughbred horses, and if they were very rich, a pair of matched stallions, hitched the animals to the family phaeton for a spirited afternoon, evening, or Sunday ride through the arteries of Druid Hill Park and around its reservoir. A few families retained their horses and carriages long after the advent of the automobile, primarily for the joy of drives through the park. Some of the mansions had attached or detached stables and carriage houses. Others boarded their horses and housed their rigs at nearby livery stables. On Sunday, it was popular to hire and saddle a horse for a canter through Druid Hill Park's extensive bridle paths.

Before World War I, several German Jews engaged in horse, mule and live stock trading and exporting to Europe. The German Jewish Fox Family, the largest live stock dealers in the city, in 1933 converted their horse dealership into an automobile agency. Between World Wars I and II, a number of well-to-do young German Jews, as a hobby, appeared on the horse racing scene as owners of thoroughbreds. Some had financial interests in breeding and training farms, and to German Jew Harry L. Straus, horses and a major horse breeding farm were more than just a hobby. Straus, a Baltimore engineer/entrepreneur/inventor/sportsman was a member of the class of 1917, the first person to complete the engineering curriculum at the Johns Hopkins University.

Because horse breeding and racing was his business, and pari-mutuels so much a part of the king of sports, he got to thinking what a great idea it would be to have a system that would instantaneously register a bet into an electronic device that would immediately provide a printed bet ticket with up to the moment odds on the horse. Straus and a fellow engineer proceeded to invent the Totalisator that can arguably be considered to have been the world's first computer. In 1930, the first installation of the Totalisator

UNCOMMON THREADS

was at Baltimore's Pimlico Race Track and now, in a more sophisticated form, at race tracks all over the world.

---

1   *A study by Elinore Bruchey of the Baltimore business elite in 1890 revealed startling facts. Episcopalians and Presbyterians combined represented only 5.3 % of the city's population, yet were 56 % of the city's leadership. 18 % of Baltimore's residents were Catholic, and they represented only 8.5 % of the leadership. For the German Jews it was much better. They were 8% of the city's population and 6 % of its leadership.*

2   *A proper Victorian lady carried an aide memoir (memory aid) in her purse. This was a book cover that held her calling cards and a few sheets of note paper. Loops in which a silver mechanical pencil was inserted held the front and back covers together. In most socially active German Jewish homes, a small silver salver was kept on a table in the entrance foyer; in some homes, in the vestibule. A servant answered a ring of the door bell, received and placed the visitor's calling card on the salver, and took it to the lady of the house. During the "calling hours," it was most likely that this lady was sitting in the drawing room awaiting visitors. Providing the caller was socially acceptable, he or she was escorted into the drawing room and properly received for a brief visit; an exchange of pleasantries and a bit of gossip. If not on the acceptable social listing, or for other reasons, the servants advised the caller that the recipient of the visit was either not at home or was indisposed. The calling card itself established communication with the use of a simple code. Turning down the upper right corner of the card denoted a personal visit. Turning down the upper left corner indicated a congratulatory visit and turning down the lower right corner meant that "adieus" were to be given. Turning down the lower left corner implied that the visit would be a condolence call. If the entire left side of the card was creased, it indicated that the call was being made on the entire family.*

3   *In April 1993, the author attended a small sixtieth reunion of his ballroom dancing class.*

4   *Though not restricted by covenants, residents of Sudbrook Park were overtly unfriendly to Jews so only a handful of acceptable German Jewish families spent their summers there. A probable "gentlemen's agreement" allowed property owners to pick and choose their neighbors. During "the season" the Sudbrook Hotel accommodated city visitors until it burned in 1926.*

5   *Jewish vacationing in the Catskills began in the early 1900s, at a time when some of the more exclusive resorts in other areas were off limit to them. Jewish vacationers boarded at farms owned by Jewish immigrants who were trying their hand in agriculture. When the farmers found summer boarding provided a more lucrative income than planting and harvesting, large popular Jewish Catskill resorts grew from these modest farms.*

6   *The wealthy Baltimore German Jewish Henry Sonneborn employed eleven household servants and they took all of them along for summers spent in Long Branch, New Jersey. The family and their entourage traveled from Baltimore in a private railway car accompanied by their coachman, stableman, carriages, and horses in a separate car.*

PART I-16

Clover and Mercantile Club # 1 * The Phoenix Club * The Harmony Circle * The Suburban Club * Money, art gifts in-kind * German Jews and Zionism * German Jews and education * 1904 Baltimore Fire * World War I

*I*n 1892, former members of the Concordia Club founded the Mercantile Club, which occupied a building on the southwest corner of Fayette and Paca Streets, formerly the home of the defunct Crescent Club. In 1895, the club moved to 1412 Eutaw Place into the former residence of Isador Rayner a German Jewish community leader and U.S. Senator. The Mercantile Club faded from the Baltimore picture and another club by the same name was founded at a later date. The story of the second Mercantile Club is covered in Part III of Uncommon Threads. After failed attempts to reorganize and rebuild the Concordia Club, in 1896 former members founded the Clover Club. For all purposes, the Clover Club was to be a continuation of the Concordia Club. Members of the Clover Club met first at 810 Madison Avenue and later at 1511 Madison Avenue. In 1910, they moved to 1914-1916 Madison Avenue in the middle of a block of large four story row houses. The Clover Club and the Mercantile Club's membership reflected slightly different levels of German Jewish social strata.

A childless German Jewish couple, Aaron and Lillie Strauss, major benefactors of the Baltimore Hebrew Synagogue, bought the Clover Club property in 1922 and deeded it as a gift to the Congregation. After their death, the Aaron and Lillie Strauss foundation continues to endow the Baltimore Hebrew Congregation. Named Synagogue House, its principal use was to house the Congregation's Sunday School. In 1922, the couple added to the original gift when they purchased the property at 1912 Madison Avenue. As the initial step in the Congregation's plans to build a new synagogue in upper Parks Heights, Baltimore Hebrew purchased land on the Southeast corner of Park Heights and Slade Avenues. At this time, the donors of the Synagogue House property at 1912-1914-1916 Madison Avenue bought it back from the congregation, and in 1943 they made a gift of the land and building to a Y. M. C. A. satellite of the main Franklin Street Baltimore Y. M. C. A.

In 1885, before Concordia burned, a group of men listed in the 1899 Society Visiting List, resigned from Concordia and founded the socially elite Phoenix Club for male members only. Concordia, never elite, could no longer, if it ever could, offer the higher plane of social brotherhood wanted by the new well-to-do garment manufacturer members of the Phoenix Club. The club moved from their Park Avenue quarters in 1892 to a magnificent red sandstone three and a half story clubhouse they built at 1505 Eutaw Place. Perfectly user located and architecturally blended with the Eutaw Place mansions, the building's graceful center entrance stairs were flanked by bow windows. Three broad, rounded-top windows spanned the second floor; on the third floor, an inset portico with double large windows on each side was offset by balustrades. This elegant mecca for Baltimore's elite German Jews served the best food in Baltimore, offered the best services, very important to Jewish society, and hosted many of the special social events of the Harmony Circle. In the basement of the Phoenix Club, members bowled or played billiards; were shaved, and had their hair cut in the club's barber shop. A large dining room occupied part of the first floor, and the ladies' parlor, a men's sitting and reading room, and the spacious entrance hall occupied the remainder of the first floor. The sitting room and its oversized deep chairs and modest illumination followed the traditional signature appearance of British men's clubs. Absolute quiet allowed the men to concentrate on their reading, so no mortal would dare to start a conversation and disturb the tranquillity of this room. Ballrooms occupied the second floor and men played pinochle in third floor card rooms.

The regular Saturday night Phoenix Club dances were indeed civilized; men wore dinner jackets and women dressed in evening gowns. For special events, such as New Year's Eve, men usually dressed in white tie and tails. Customarily at Phoenix Club dances, in an overt act of refinement and foppishness, a few men who considered themselves gallant, drank only wine or champagne as they considered it vulgar to drink hard liquor in front of their ladies.

Thoughts such as expressed by some members of the Phoenix Club towards the end of the nineteenth century, though probably not deemed to be shallow at the time, would probably not be uttered today at a meeting of any Jewish group. Two hundred members attended the club's annual banquet in November 1882. In replying to a toast "Our Ambition," the Christian guest speaker, Joseph S. Goldsborough, began by saying that "the most prominent among the ambitions of the members of the Phoenix Club was the promotion of good fellowship among its members and that the climax of that purpose each year was the annual banquet." He urged upon the members the importance of allowing nothing to interfere with the continuance of this custom. The lavish decorations and the atmosphere of the event seemed to indicate that the well-to-do German Jewish club members of 1882 were carried away with themselves and their prosperity.

A selected few Jewish families who established a high degree of stature in the commercial community saw a need to express their social standing in their sectarian community. Considered "persona non grata" in the Christian First Monday German's Bachelor's Cotillion and Junior Assembly, they formed the Harmony Circle. Three Harmony Circle balls were held during the winter months in various public rooms. Those attending balls shortly after the Civil War danced in the New Assembly Rooms at Lombard and Hanover Street. However, on the night of November 22, 1893, the Harmony Circle Ball where debutantes were introduced to German Jewish society was the initial event in the ballroom of the new Phoenix Club. After the New Assembly Rooms were razed in 1901, the festivities moved to the new and elegant Belvedere Hotel, completed in 1903. Harmony Circle balls continued to be held there and at the Lyric Theater until a few years before World War II when the Circle again used the facilities of the Phoenix Club.

How were the debutantes selected? Who were the fine German Jewish families, and how was their status determined? German Jews had not been in America long enough to establish an impeccable blood line so this premise did not exist. Without doubt, the most important measurement of social acceptability was wealth. Unofficially, exceptions were made for a few especially physically attractive and personable girls, but invitations were usually extended only to those young ladies whose parents, or close relatives, had enough money and social standing to be members of the Harmony Circle and the Phoenix Club as well. Young escorts, having taken a social step-up from membership in the Junior Cotillion, net-working through a tightly knitted German Jewish Society, had much to say about who would be invited to the ball. They did not extend invitations to Cinderellas.

Popular girls were asked months in advance by several escorts for all three Harmony Circle events, the most important being the Debutante Ball. By invitation only, daughters of prominent German Jewish families were introduced to Baltimore's German Jewish society when they made their bows on Thanksgiving eve. In 1909, a typical year, thirteen girls of German heritage and one of Lithuanian decent were asked. These were edgy times for young German Jewish girls who, with emotions of uncertainty, anxiously awaited an invitation to make their Harmony Circle debut. Those invited joined in a full social season of pre-coming out dinner dances and other lesser events. For those who traveled socially within the same set and were not extended invitations, it was cruel and crushing. Usually several escorts accompanied a single debutante, and those with the most escorts were usually the gayest and most sought after girls of the year's crop.

For the Debutante Ball, proud parents dressed their daughters in elegant, expensive, and, as required, full length white gowns. They purchased couturier creations from exclusive Charles Street shops for these young girls who, so recently, were mere children. On the night of the ball, usually each debutante received several corsages and bouquets from her friends and family. Escorts to the Harmony Ball and other attending male club members, in order to fully participate in the Circle's festivities, wore full dress: tails with white ties, vests and gloves. Those men who chose to wear a dinner jacket could attend, but that dress was considered too informal for the balls; therefore, they were not allowed on the dance floor. In a formal procession, debutantes and their escorts walked from the ballroom to the supper room to be seated at assigned tables beautifully decorated with lighted candles and flower arrangements. Making their bow was that simple. The Board of Governors engaged the finest orchestras, ones that played almost exclusively for socially elite functions of east coast Christians and Jews. At some of the balls, famous singers such as Lucretia Borja and Beniamino Gigli, considered to be the greatest Italian tenor of his day, performed. The Harmony Balls of the twentieth century were a far cry from the nineteenth century; especially the seventh Purim Ball held in 1875. Then, operatic selections were played during the mask, and no hats, caps, or overcoats were allowed in the ballroom except for mask. The unmasking was at 11 PM.

A slightly younger set of equally high social status prepped for their debuts the following year by being invited to the Junior Cotillion. This organization held a series of three annual dances in a less formal vein and with much more gaiety than those of the Harmony Circle. The last dance of the season, always in costume dress, was held at the

Belvedere. No one could appear on the dance floor unless he or she were dressed in costume, most of which were extremely elaborate. Many of those attending had their outfits made to order by the costumier services of Brooks Brothers of New York. The leading orchestras such as Paul Whiteman and Benny Goodman played at the balls. In one year, the walls of the twelfth floor ballrooms of the Belvedere were decorated as Chinese walls, and although it was February, the decorators used fresh wisteria. In another year, when the costume ball was held at the Lyric Theater, the theme was Mount Vernon, and all who attended dressed as either George or Martha Washington. When functions of this sort were held at the Lyric, the seats on the main floor were removed, and the stage converted into an elaborate supper room. Purim Balls benefited the Hebrew Benevolent Society until 1910. By that time, charity balls per se were no longer the vehicle to raise money for charities because more money could be raised through a sophisticated well-organized network of direct solicitation.

In 1901, the Suburban Club of Baltimore County, the second and last of the larger exclusive German Jewish social clubs, was founded. Located on beautiful rolling land, just North of Slade Avenue the wooden structured club house topped an elevation that rose from the club's entrance driveway leading from Park Heights Avenue. In the summer at the Suburban Club, ausgelassen (carefree) German Jews played tennis and golf during the day and dined and danced under the stars on Saturday evenings. By 1910, the club had five hundred members, most of whom were also members of the Phoenix Club. Because the Suburban Club functioned as a country club and the playing of golf and tennis were neither popular nor feasible during the winter months, the original club house was not constructed to be heated comfortably for winter social use. The two clubs worked together to a large degree, so the Phoenix Club, located near the members' in-town houses, held Saturday night dances and other social functions during the winter months. Most of the staff of waiters and kitchen personnel served both facilities, and when the Suburban Club reopened at the end of April, they borrowed dinner and silver-ware from the Phoenix Club, whose dining room was quiet during the hot summer months. In 1959, the Suburban Club buildings were razed and an all weather clubhouse was completed so starting the following summer, the Suburban Club operated the year around.

Suburban and Phoenix club members, many of whom volunteered their time as charity workers, also contributed large amounts of money to the Federated Jewish Charities and to Baltimore cultural institutions. As years passed, it became a membership requirement to give a required minimum sum to the Associated Jewish Charities. In the early years, while it was thought that the Phoenix and Suburban clubs restricted membership exclusively to German Jews, this was only ninety-nine percent true. Exceptions were made for one or two very successful and prominent Eastern European Jews. It was expensive to belong to either the Suburban or Phoenix Club so club people encompassed only a small segment of Baltimore's German Jews. To this day, as if it were the only Baltimore Jewish country club of social substance, the Suburban Club is affectionately and smugly referred to by its members simply as "The Club"; but this is not too different from any other club.

In many instances, friendships that had endured through the years fell apart as those who could neither afford to nor had a desire to belong to social clubs became relegated to a different social life. It is safe to presume that, in some instances, the feelings of non-joiners became embittered toward some former friends who now acted ueber geschnappt (too good for them). Nevertheless, German Jews had come a long way socially. They had become genteel, but a few were distressed because they were not born Gentile, from whose social interaction and clubs they remained persona non grata.

Though the issue of Zionism was present for years all over Europe, it was brought to the attention of American Jews in the late 1800s. Not particularly tuned in to the social or religious picture of Reform German Jews, Zionism was of little interest to them; in fact, most of them disdained the movement. Baltimore Reform German Jewish life was far removed from the distant mid-eastern lands of the Turks, the Jews, and the likes of those Christians and Muslim Arabs. Russian Jews established early settlements in Palestine and as far as the German Jews were concerned, the Russians could continue to establish settlements if that is what they wanted. A few prominent German Jewish families, foremost among them included the Friedenwalds and some of the Strausses who remained Orthodox, embraced the Zionist movement and were brothers of the Russian Jewish Zionists. A line was drawn in the Baltimore Jewish community simplifying the perception that Zionists were Russians and Orthodox and the Germans were Reform and American.

Before the days when German Jewish wealth could be termed "old money," many newly well to-do became involved in a wide variety of interests and activities not related to their businesses. A few became connoisseurs of art and acquired representative collections.[1] Some German Jews, ignoring the social clubs and castes in any form, joined the Society of Truth Seekers dedicated to scientific, literary and esthetic interests. They considered social shenanigans merely a facade; they felt they needed more eloquent meaning to their lives. Many German Jewish scholars stemmed from these intellectuals and several became scientists and professors on the faculty of the Johns Hopkins University. Some rose to become international leaders in fields that helped establish the academic credence of the Hopkins. By the end of the 1800s, the make-up of the professorial faculty of the school was about 80% German, and quite a few of these were German Jews who had been schooled in Germany.

Baltimore's German Jewish community contributed on a large scale to national scholarly and culturally oriented institutions, such as the Hebrew Union College and the American Jewish Archives in Cincinnati and to Dropsie College in Philadelphia. For very special educational advantages, some German Jews sent their sons, and occasionally their daughters, to study and travel in the great cultural centers of France, Austria and Germany.

In the late nineteenth and early twentieth centuries, well-to-do Baltimore German Jews, no longer associated with the German-American cultural structure, traveled to and from Europe for both business and pleasure. Due to their business and social experiences, these men were quite cosmopolitan, though some of their short, stout, heavy-bosomed, thin legged, firm-jawed women retained traces of old world charm. Because their lesser degree of Americanization, a few women could not be fully at ease when communicating with the strangers they encountered during their travels. When in Berlin, a world centrum and leader in education, fashion, finance, and night life, American German Jews saw no resemblance to the rural countryside and mountains of Hesse and Bavaria that their parents or grandparents had left perhaps only fifty years before.

On the quiet but cold and blustery Sunday morning of February 7, 1904, the households of the German Jewish community, as well as those of the entire city, were aroused and traumatized. By word of mouth they heard and from the city's higher grounds they saw the burning buildings of Baltimore's downtown commercial area. While the fire raged, many business people hired horses and wagons in attempts to rescue valuable records from burning buildings and from those in the fire's path and likely to burn. Due to the prevailing winds, damage was not quite as devastating to the German Jewish owned garment sewing factories, most of which were adjacent to and west of the burning dry goods area. Before the fire was extinguished, virtually the entire wholesale dry goods area had been demolished. Though most of the destroyed structures were owned by Christians, the losses of inventory and business interruption of the German Jewish businesses that rented these buildings were quite high. Through bank loans and help from friends, practically none of the German Jewish businesses failed to re-open, and the commerce of the area recovered and prospered.

Baltimore's Great Fire did not interrupt immigration for long. On Monday, February 8th, the North German Lloyd S.S. Willehad with four-hundred seventy passengers arrived in the Baltimore harbor and the immigration authorities would not allow her to dock at Locust Point. Passenger's, mostly immigrants, first view of America was the sight of an American city smoldering from the conflagration of the previous day. Some of the immigrants considered remaining on the Willehad and return to their old world European homes; however, they were allowed to disembark the following day.

In 1914, a conflict began in Europe that erupted into the raging World War I. Two and one half years after its beginning, the United States became a participant. German Jewish clothing manufacturers made thousands of uniforms and bound hundreds of thousands of blankets. From 1914 to 1920, German Jewish dry goods firms, clothing manufacturers, and retailers thrived financially while their sons served in the military. In World War I, there was no buying-out of the service and a Baltimore German Jewish Brigadier General Charles Henry Laucheimer served with the United States Marine Corps.

1   *Added to the liberal giving of funds to the city's cultural institutions, from Baltimore Jews, their gifts-in-kind are the foundation of the Baltimore Museum of Art. The works of old master painters and sculptures of the Post Renaissance and 19th century collections of Jacob Epstein and Abraham Eisenberg; the twentieth century and medieval art from Sadie May are important to the scope of the museum. Most of the important pieces in the Oriental room were given by Julius Levy. Much of the Baltimore Museum of Art's nationally outstanding print and paper collection are gifts from the Benesch Memorial collection and from Blanche Adler. Gertrude Rosenthal willed an important book collection and recently, George H. Dalsheimer has given the museum his enormous photography collection.*

One cannot put a label on individual collections in order to measure their importance but certainly the Allan and Janet Wurtzburger gifts of pre-Columbian and indoor and outdoor sculptures by the best of modern internationally acclaimed artists is of great importance. The sculpture garden donated by Robert H. and Ryda Levi, contains several of their enormous modern pieces and hopefully more from this collection will be given to the museum in future years. Visitors from all over the world come to the Baltimore Museum of Art to see the enormous French impressionist collection of the Cone sisters, Dr. Clarabel and Etta, that features a large number of Henri Matisse.

Germane to UNCOMMON THREADS, two German Jewish families arrived in Baltimore several years before the migration of other German Jews. The Etting family came to the United States in 1758, settled in York, Pennsylvania and the widow of the family moved to Baltimore in 1780. Her son Solomon became extremely wealthy and important in the community. Samuel, a son of Solomon, one of the five Baltimore Jews who served in the defense of Ft. McHenry in in September 1814, was wounded in action.

The Cohen family settled in Richmond, Virginia, about 1784. The widow of the family moved to Baltimore about 1803. The family, heavily involved in finance engaged in the lottery business, a method of raising public funds. In 1831 they turned to banking; later Jacob Cohen, Jr. became a director of the B. & O. R. R. and the president of two large financial institutions.

After confirmation of the Jew Bill in 1826, both Solomon Etting and Jacob Cohen became members of the Baltimore City Council.

It must be noted that neither the Ettings nor the Cohens had social contacts with or assumed their threads as being common with the German Jewish immigrants of the early 1800s; their social contacts were with German Christians. Nevertheless, both families were seat holders in the Mikveh Israel Congregation in Philadelphia.

The Etting Cemetery on North Avenue near Pennsylvania Avenue is still there.

**Lottery advertisement
The Cone Bank**

**Lottery office
Baltimore & High Sts.**

IN THE EARLY 1820s, JEWS BEGAN TO MIGRATE FROM THE GERMAN STATES OF HESSE & BAVARIA TO THE UNITED STATES

In the early 1850s, the author's paternal grandmother Amelia Lowenthal left this provincial town of ASCHAFFENBURG BEI KLEIN OSTHEIM, BAVARIA to come to Baltimore

Sailing date postings from Bremen, North German Lloyd Co. - 1887

Near sailing time at a German port - 1866

Deutsche Auswanderer-Zeitung

№ 83.   Bremen, 15. October   1852.

Between 1852 and 1875, DEUTSCHE-AUSWANDER-ZEITUNG, published in Bremen, kept passenger lists of emigrants who sailed from that port.

Typical mid-19th century ocean going sailing vessel

Smaller ocean going sailing vessel in port at Fells Point

Passenger quarters in a mid-nineteenth century Atlantic crossing.

When Jonas Friedenwald arrived in Fells Point in 1832, this is the nearby Jones Falls he saw.

Baltimore's first post poffice at Front near Exeter Street was in the area in which the early German Jews lived.

Early 19th C. East Baltimore German Jewish immigrant housing.

Many German Jews of the 19th century made their living peddling in the countryside on foot until they acquired horses and wagons.

Baltimore Hebrew Congrgation - Lloyd Street - 1845

Hebrew Friendship Congregation's
Eden Street Synagogue - 1848

BALTIMORE, MARCH 28, 1842.

SIR,

You are respectfully invited to attend the CONSECRATION of the **New School-house,** erected by the *Hebrew and English Benevolent Academical Association of Baltimore,* in BOND STREET, between Pratt and Gough Streets, on Wednesday morning, the 30th inst., at 9 o'clock.

R. Goldsmith, Secretary.

Baltimore's first Hebrew School - 1842

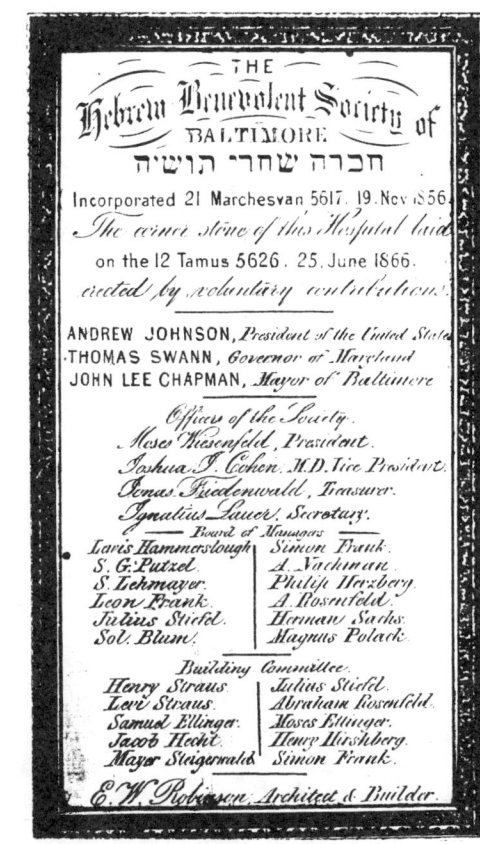

Inscription on cornerstone
Hebrew Hosp[ital and
Asylum - 1866

Moses Wiesenfeld's men's clothing factory Baltimore opposite Hanover Street - 1853

Performance of German Singing Society Maryland Institute - 1869

German "Die Kunsthalle der Concordia" - Concordia Club founded 1847

Har Sinai Synagogue, High St. (1849-1873)

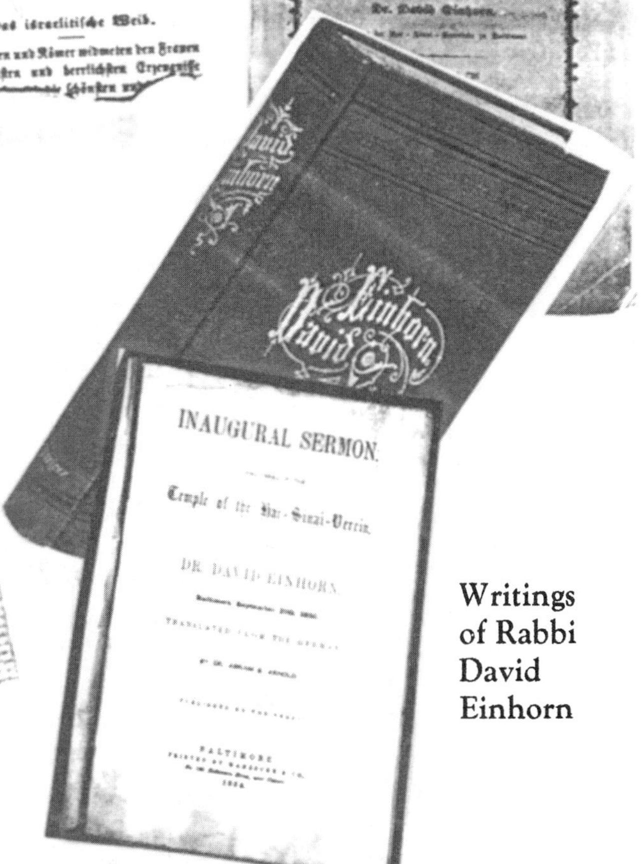

German/English newspapers

Writings of Rabbi David Einhorn

MASQUERADE BALL OF HARMONY CIRCLE
NEW ASSEMBLY ROOMS, MARCH 1ST 1866.

Selected German Jewish girls made their debut at the Harmony Circle Balls

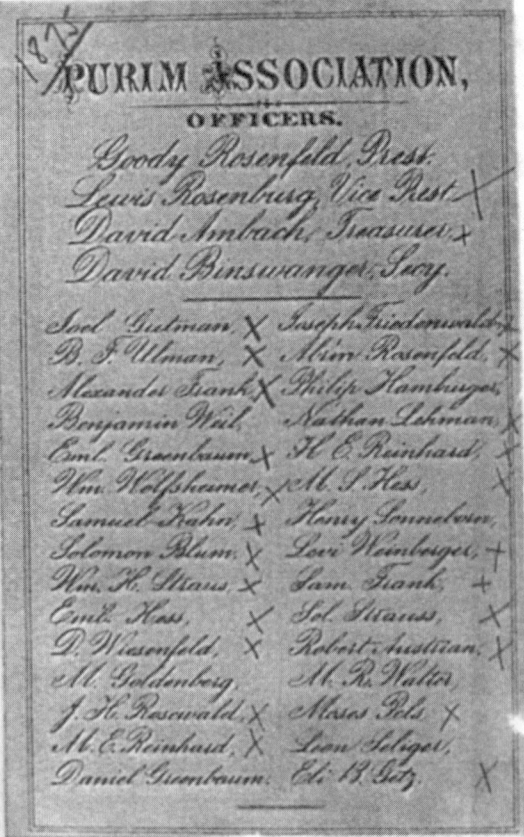

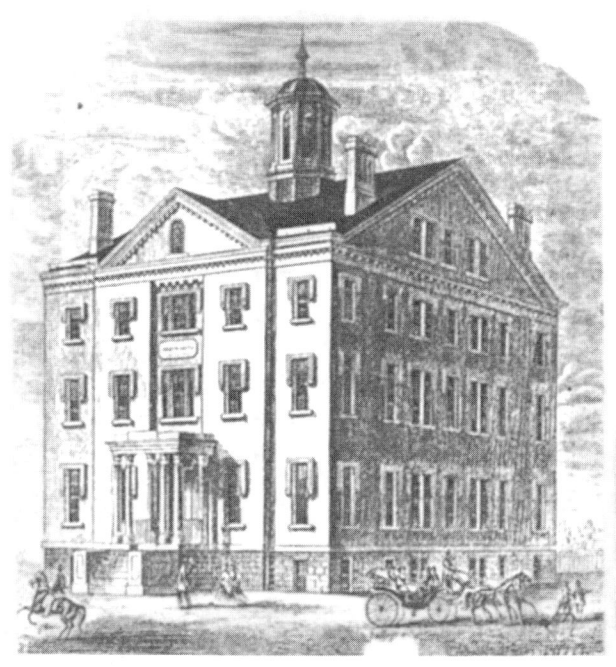

Hebrew Hospital and Asylum
Ann Street (Rutland Ave)
(1868)

Hebrew Orphan Asylum
Rayner Ave. & Dukeland St.
(1872)

Chizuk Amuno Congregation's Lloyd Street Synagogue (1876-1895)

Oheb Shalom Synagogue -Hanover between Lombard and Pratt Sts. (1858-1892)

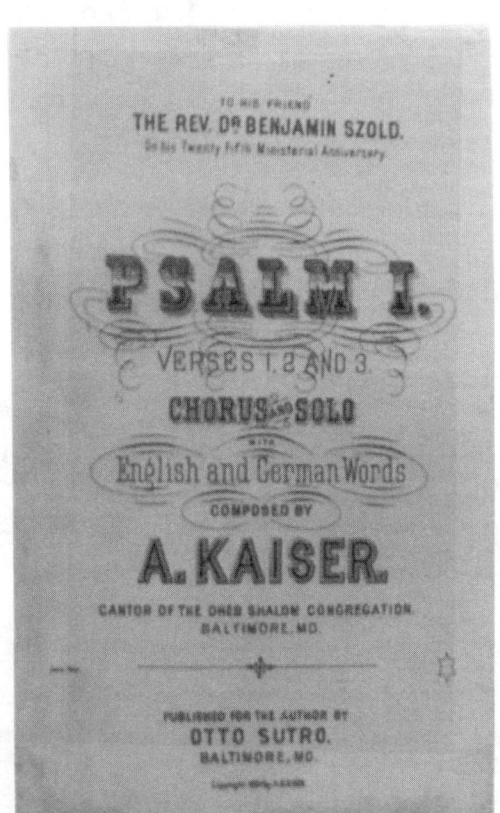

Composition honoring 25 years of of the rabbinate of Rabbi Benjamin Szold - Oheb Shalom Congregation 1884

Title page - Rabbi Benjamin Szold's 1864 prayer book Avodat Israel - 1873 edition

Card awarded to the author's maternal grandmother Lina Kraus, while a student at the Academy of Visitation

Physics class - Academy of Visitation - Park Ave. and Center Street founded 1837

The German/English School - circa 1890

Eutaw Place

and it's mansions

The David & Ella G. Hutzler mansion - 1801 Eutaw Place

Phoenix Club
(1892 - 1960)
Note the members
list, most were
in the men's
clothing business

Gay Street - circa 1890

Lexington Market - circa 1900

German Jewish Merchants
Harrison Street - circa 1900

Author's paternal grandmother
Amelia Kahn's second hand
men's clothing store
Harrison Street - circa 1880

Five German Jewish Congregations moved to mid-town near 1900

Har Sinai Temple
Bolton & Wilson Sts.
(1894 - 1959)

Baltimore Hebrew Temple
Madison Ave. & Robert St.
(1891 - 1951)

Har Sinai Temple

Chizuk Amuno Synagogue
McCulloh & Mosher Sts.
(1895 - 1921)

Shearith Israel Synagogue
McCulloh & Bloom Sts.
(1903 - 1925)

Oheb Shalom Temple
Eutaw Pl. & Lanvale St.
(1893 - 1960)

SOCIETY VISITING LIST.
1899.

Jewish Social Register - 1905
Debutante List - 1907 - 1908
Society Visiting List - 1899

A

Aaronsohn, Dr. A.,	1601 Linden Ave.
Aaronsohn, Miss Estelle	1608 Eutaw Place.
Adelsdorf, Mr. and Mrs. Joseph	2224 Eutaw Place.
Adler, Mr. and Mrs. S. J.	1944 Linden Ave.
Adler, Mr. Sam	1944 Linden Ave.
Adler, Mr. S. C.	1313 Eutaw Place.
Adler, Miss Blanche	1313 Eutaw Place.
Adler, Mr. and Mrs. Charles	1313 Eutaw Place.
Adler, Dr. and Mrs. Harry	1215 Madison Ave.
	1601 Linden Ave.
	1601 Linden Ave.
	1601 Linden Ave.
	Herald Office.
	1619 Madison Ave.
	1619 Madison Ave.
	2038 McCulloh St.
	2038 McCulloh St.
	2044 Linden Ave.
	2044 Linden Ave.
	1809 Madison Ave.
	706 W. North Ave.
	1412 Linden Ave.
	1932 Madison Ave.
	1031 N. Gilmor St.
	2007 Madison Ave.
	2007 Madison Ave.

JEWISH SOCIAL REGISTER

BALTIMORE

1905

A Directory of Names and Residences of Members of Jewish Society, Clubs, Synagogues, Hospitals, Cemeteries and Organizations

PRICE, — — — TWO DOLLARS

BALTIMORE:
REGISTER PUBLISHING CO.
301 FIDELITY BUILDING

DEBUTANTES
1907-1908

Miss Eileen Adler. 809 Newington Ave.
  Daughter of Mr. and Mrs. H. S. Adler.
Miss Ethel Epstein. 1729 Park Ave.
  Daughter of Mr. and Mrs. Jacob Epstein.
Miss Alice Frank, 1506 Eutaw Place.
Miss Carlyn Friedmann. 2210 Eutaw Place.
  Daughter of Mr. and Mrs. Henry Friedmann.
Miss Sylvia Greenwald. 1512 Madison Ave.
  Daughter of Mrs. F. Greenwald.
Miss Elizabeth Gutman, 1321 Eutaw Place.
  Daughter of Mr. and Mrs. Louis K. Gutman.
Miss Mary Kraus. 1817 Madison Ave.
  Daughter of Mr. and Mrs. Henry Kraus.
Miss Mosella Lauer. 1807 Linden Ave.
  Daughter of Mr. and Mrs. S. Lauer, Jr.
Miss Evelyn Morris. 2229 Eutaw Place.
  Daughter of Mr. and Mrs. Edward Morris.
Miss Regina Ottenheimer. 1634 Linden Ave.
  Daughter of Mr. and Mrs. Reuben Ottenheimer.
Miss Hilda Rosenheim. 2032 Eutaw Place.
  Daughter of Mr. and Mrs. Benjamin Rosenheim.
Miss Aimee Stein. 1323 Eutaw Place.
  Daughter of Mrs. Emma Stein.
Miss Rita Strauss. 2206 Callow Ave.
  Daughter of Mrs. A. Strauss.
Miss Harriet Wolf. 2012 Bolton Ave.
  Daughter of Mrs. Katie Wolf.

The Suburban Club of Baltimore County - founded 1921

Fiftieth Wedding Anniversary on Eutaw Place - Family of the author's wife 1918

A well-to-do German Jew driving his carriage and matched pair around the Druid Park Lake - 1920

Entrance Hall - The Park School 3440 Auchentoroly Terrace (1912-1917)

UNCOMMON THREADS

PART II-1 *BALTIMORE EASTERN EUROPEAN JEWS*

Pale of Settlement * Well-to-do Russian Jews * Thinking and writing * Life in the Shtetls * Poland-Galecia-Bessarabia * Alexander II & III * Pogroms and 1882 May Laws * Marxism and the Bund * Kishinev riots and pogroms * Plea from Odessa * Migration II * Romania

*E*normous numbers of Eastern European Jews lived in virtually medieval conditions under six Russian Tzars, suffering greatly under each one. Russia, outrageously anti-Jewish throughout its history, inherited the largest population of Jews in the world. Beginning in 1772, and fully achieved in 1795 under the reign of Catherine the Great, Russia, Prussia, and Austria partitioned the old Polish Republic which ceased to exist as a political entity. Although Russia was anxious to partition Polish land, they were not anxious to acquire the Polish Jews who would become Russian Jews overnight.

In 1791, Catherine created the Pale of Settlement, a legal territorial expanse of 386,000 square miles within which an enormous concentration of over 5,000,000 Russian and formerly Polish Jews lived. The Pale was bounded on the north by just a touch of the Baltic Sea in Lithuania and from there extended over 800 miles south. It skirted west of Poland along the eastern boundary of Austria, into the Ukraine at the northern edge of Romania and the northern shores of the Black Sea. This land prison of Russia included twenty-four provinces as it extended on the east, north from the eastern edge of the Sea of Azov. The important cities of Vilna, Warsaw, Minsk, Pinsk, Kishinev, Bereditchev, Volhynia, Kiev, Kharkov, Donetsk, Dnepropetrovsk, and Odessa lay within the boundaries of the Pale.

In the early days of the Pale, Jews were restricted from living in some designated areas occupied by non-Jewish Russians. Jews were barred from the vast Russian expanses not included in the Pale of Settlement except for a few who in the later nineteenth century managed to become wealthy. They and some students were permitted to pay a special fee that allowed them to move into Moscow or St. Petersburg. Two of the largest banks in Moscow, located a distance from the Pale, were Jewish owned. Within the Pale, two banks in Odessa and two banks in Warsaw also belonged to Jews. Three families of Jewish railroad tycoons[1] lived inside the Pale of Settlement; they were builders of seventy-five percent of the railroad that ran across Russia and Siberia. This handful of wealthy Jewish Russians lived much like the court Jews years before in Germany in a totally different environment than the Jewish masses in the Pale. About 40% of the heads of the Jewish families within the Pale were petty merchants of one sort or another. 40% were artisans and providers of personal services, mostly to the gentiles of the shtetls (small towns) in which they lived and the remaining 20% made a living any way they could or were recipients of the charity of their neighbors.

Life in the shtetl was simple. Each family had a wooden house of its own, usually part of a cluster surrounded by or very close to the market place. Other than on the Sabbath, market places were busy with peddlers, customers, and hangers on. Here and there a woman had a basket of eggs or a bundle of old clothes for sale. Livelihoods were

81

drawn from the market place and there was considerable back and forth discussion on prices. At the very center of the Jew's daily existence in a shtetl was the synagogue in which each family had an assigned pew. If the shtetl happened to be located on a river as were many, it was there that generations of Jewish boys learned to swim and fish.

Study and scholarship were by far the most important consideration in the shtetls. While the man with financial security carried much weight as he would in any community, the greatest influence was wielded by the learned man. Study was the path to greatness and the only lasting riches one could acquire. A rich man seeking a good match for a daughter sought not the son of another rich man; he preferred to look for a good student. The best wedding present he could give was not a house but a promise to support the new family for a stated number of years during which the new son-in-law could spend his day in study. Families of rabbis tended to marry into families of rabbis and this preference carried over in America.[2]

For the poor, many families were supported by the meager earnings of the wife who either peddled or had a stall in the market place while her husband spent his days in the Beth haMidrash (house of learning). Life revolved around births, marriages, and deaths; about fast days and feast days; about rain and sun. Brought up under the stern discipline of the cheder and the synagogue, they rebelled inwardly and expressed their feelings by playing truant and mumbling prayers at home or in the synagogue. Given time, they came to understand and accept what their fathers had accepted years, the necessity of continuous Torah study.

Shut out of the modern world with their age old patterns of customs and their life as it was, whispers of grand new thoughts found their way into the shtetls. The Russian Jews began to think and to write. Haskala (cultivation of the mind), the movement of Enlightenment, begun in Germany in the second half of the eighteenth century, found its way to the Jews in the Pale of Settlement. In the Berlin of Frederick II The Great, King of Prussia, families of wealthy privileged Jews brought young Polish Jewish intellectuals to Berlin where they came under the influence of Moses Mendelssohn. There they met Italian-Dutch Jews and from these contacts, they developed a moderate tendency toward westernization and an orthodoxy that included an essential element, the veneration of Hebrew and of medieval western Jewish literature. Following Mendelssohn's lead, scholarly Jews in the Pale began to write in Hebrew; however, Haskalah never reached the consciousness of the traditionalists, the masses who fought back claiming it was sacrilege to use the Loshen Kodesh (Holy Tongue) for non-religious communication. Paralleling the development of Hebrew, was the growth of Yiddish as a literary language. Young Jewish scholars throughout the Pale secretly read books, frequently hiding them in the open covers of a volume of the Talmud. After the pogroms of the 1880s, Haskalah, which was basically assimilationist, did an about face when it became particularistic and Jewish nationalistic, a backer of the Zionist movement.

Interesting but not germane to Russian Jewish life during the reign of Tzar Nicholas I, the most brutal autocrat of all the Tzars, was a treaty between the United States and Russia signed in 1832. This agreement guaranteed the freedom of travel in the territories of either country. Beginning under the regime of Tzar Alexander II in 1855 and ending abruptly in 1865, Jews were given educational opportunities, and some actually graduated from Russian colleges. Regardless, it was quite evident that the great majority of Jews in Russia during these few enlightened years continued to be ingrained with their studies of the Talmud, so much so that they paid little attention to the secular education being offered. During these wondrous and precious almost eleven years of Alexander II's reign, the government also allowed Jews to settle in Russia proper, away from the Pale of Settlement. For those who took advantage of Russian education, civil service positions and professional vocations became available. Striking out the orders of previous tzars, Alexander abolished conscription into the military for boys twelve years of age or under. The historic Edict of Emancipation of 1861 instituted reform in the military, the judiciary, and in local governments, and systems of representation were established that came close, but not quite close enough, to creating an all Russian parliament.[3]

At the end of the eighteenth century, Austria partitioned Galicia, a former land section of Poland, north of the Carpathian Mountains. After World War I and the disintegration of the Austro-Hungarian Empire, the western part of the country including the city of Krakow was ceded to Poland; the eastern half was absorbed by the Soviet Ukraine after World War II. In 1881 in Galicia, about six hundred thousand Jews, the largest minority, lived with about five and one-half million non-Jews. Most of the Jews were Russian settlers from the Pale of Settlement who had recently come to Galicia where all people were allowed to own land. Of the little over six million population, about 80% were peasants, half of whom were Poles who occupied the western part of the state. West Ukrainians, known as Ruthenians, lived in the eastern section. The new province enjoyed relatively free and equal rights of citizenship for all of its people, as this was guaranteed by the Austro-Hungarian Constitution of 1867. Unfortunately, the enjoyment of such privileges was tempered considerably by extreme poverty, so much so that poor Galitzianers became one of the largest single European groups to emigrated to America. They did so because of a yearning for a better way of life in America, for freedom from their economic squalor in Galicia, and more freedom for their religious practices.

Later in 1881, at the time of the beginning of the mass migration of Jews from Russia, thousands of Ukrainian Jews fled to the ancient city of Brody in Galicia. The number of newcomers exceeded the permanent population of the city, and there they encountered other Jews who spoke a strange dialect of Yiddish and who combined coarse manners with Germanic airs of cultural superiority. Many of its Jews were recognized leading adherents of the Maskilm, supporters of the Haskalah. These people were not friendly towards the fleeing Ukrainians though they felt a responsibility for them because they were their Jewish brethren. They set up information stations that helped the travelers find food and lodging and to buy railroad tickets to German port cities. The Russian Jewish flight to this area swelled the Jewish population of Galicia to almost a million people. The city of Brody, once a center of commerce and culture, was impoverished, squalid, and run down because Galicia failed to industrialize. As was to be expected, the migrants ended their flight in hunger because there was little food to be had even though persistent and tumultuous gatherings of Russian Jews in Brody demanded bread.

Ukrainian Jewish families without accommodations roamed the streets and slept outdoors or camped out at the railroad station, in abandoned factories and in stables. In October of 1881, the Secretary of Vienna's Israelitische Allianz on a mission to Brody was struck by the presence of poverty everywhere. He described the scene as "a young mother, squatting with her scantily clothed children by her side, pressing a suckling infant against her breast and handing a crust of bread to the other little ones. There, a father limps along, held up by his children, a large tattered bundle dragging behind him, in which the pathetic remnants of the family's clothing is visible. And over there, an old woman, panting from exhaustion, helped along by two grandchildren who have themselves, lost their source of sustenance. Here a woman with despairing eyes, pushes through the crowd in search of her children who have strayed. There, a whole family whispers, racked with hunger and cold -- everywhere misery, confusion and want. Relief for these people began when agencies such as the Baron de Hirsch Fund and the Alliance Israelite Universelle took charge.

In the same year, Russian Jews began a mass migration to the United States. In 1880, approximately 250,000 Jews lived in the United States. Slightly more than 200,000 were German Jews and several thousand were Sephardim. The others were Poles, Russians, Romanians, Galicianers, Silesians, Bohemians and Slovakians who had migrated earlier to America. Because Baltimore was the leading port of entry for German Jews, the percentage of German Jews in the city was considerably higher than the national figures. To realize the magnitude and understand the phenomena of this migration, bear in mind that 80% of the world's Jews (approximately six million) lived in Central and Eastern Europe, and 90% of the Russian Jews lived in the Pale. The Russian dominated Polish and Lithuanian Jews suffered alternating periods of brutality and religious and social intolerance for well over one hundred years. At times the government made attempts to "civilize" the Jews by establishing elementary type schools. Except for brief intervals, Jews were denied higher education. While many rights of citizenship were withheld, the Russian government had no hesitancy about conscripting them into the army.

Alexander II of Russia was assassinated by terrorists and revolutionists in March of 1881, and Alexander III succeeded him. This change of tzars signaled the start of pogroms in Elisabethgrad directed against the Jews. Before the Christmas night blood bath of 1881, it became the official Russian policy to rid the country of Jews in one of three ways: Jews could convert to Christianity; they could emigrate; or they could be slain. Beginning in the Ukraine, Cossack attacks took place within a month after the assassination, and in one year's time, spread to over one hundred fifty Jewish communities. Encouraged by government authorities and the police, hundreds of Jews were massacred, their homes plundered and burned. The destruction of small businesses numbered in the thousands. Russian Jews mistakenly thought that the organized persecutions and murders had climaxed in 1881 with the Christmas night blood bath, only to suffer from additional dreaded laws the following year.

The restrictive Russian and Polish May Laws of May 1882 followed the harassment, rapes and murders of the previous year. These laws, that literally made Jews who lived in the western provinces prisoners in their own country, initiated tremendous urbanization of Eastern Europe, causing tens of thousands of Jews to be driven from villages and towns into the overcrowded but larger urban ghettos of the Pale of Settlement. The laws promulgated the confiscation of Jewish shops and set limitations on property ownership. They controlled the right to travel and stated how a person could make their living; could a person be a watchmaker or a baker? The laws controlled the licensing of Jewish doctors and lawyers and set drastically low quotas for university entrances.

From the shtetls of the Pale in the 1880s through the 1890s, Jews left Russia and Poland in a mass migration to the United States. Russian Jewish intellectual leaders and almost all of their figures of moral authority chose not to leave for America. Unwillingly, the Russian Jews left a large segment of their culture and religion in mother Russia. Not all Eastern European Jews emigrated to America to escape persecution and pogroms. In White Russia, the part of western Russia known as Byelorussia, the situation for Jews was somewhat different from the rest of the country. Though anti-Semitism was rife in Byelorussia, the notorious pogroms of the 1880s and the 1890s did not spread to this province, easily the most socially and economically backward in the land. Most of the White Russian Jews and many Christian neighbors as well emigrated in the years before the Russian Revolution simply to escape their poverty.

During the reign of Alexander III, middle class Russian Jews educated their children and that encouraged the emergence of a Jewish proletariat. The peasant orientation of Russia started to change, hastened by rapid industrial progress. No longer immune to Western European socialism, Marxist thinking penetrated Russia and began to take a strong hold on its working class population and revolutionary thinking intelligentsia. A renegade German Jew Karl Heinrich Marx, founded Marxism that had an understandable appeal to Jewish intellectuals.

Along with Marxism, Jews in the provinces of Lithuania and Poland, almost spontaneously formed organizations of their working classes. In 1897, the year of the first Zionist Congress in Basel, Switzerland, Jewish workers gathered in Vilna, Lithuania to give birth to the socialistic Jewish Workers Federation, Der Algemeiner Juddisher Arbeiter Bund. This organization and its activities eventually became known to Jews on both sides of the Atlantic as the Jewish Socialist Bund. Fired by a group of young rabbinical students, workers began to preach Marx instead of Moses. Through the underground Marxist party in the following year, events began that eventually changed the world; the founding of the Russian Social Democratic Party of Lenin, Trotsky, and Stalin. Unions were formed and the great strikes of 1895 and 1896 were successfully organized. The Bund was anti-Zionist because it believed Zionism gave the Jews the dream of a future state in a far off country, and this weakened the fight for justice in their present land. The Bund opposed Orthodoxy because it tended to wait for the Lord to wipe out the social injustices rather than fighting for rights themselves. The Bund was strongly Jewish in a nationalistic and cultural sense, so much so that it split off from the Russian Socialists who would not recognize the Bund's nationalist demands.

When the Russian Revolution destroyed the power of the Tzar and his Cossacks in March, 1917, the Bundists hailed the event as the birth of freedom in Russia. When the Bolsheviks took power six months later, the hopes of the Bundists were betrayed. They had not fought for a government that would shoot and kill Russians without the benefit of a trial. In Poland the Bund remained strong but in Russia the Bolsheviks wiped it out because it was too democratic.

Throughout the history of Eastern Europe, by 1903 there had been no major anti-Jewish incidents to equal those that followed. Almost twenty years of Russian Jewish life passed without any significant riots; there were always minor ones. Alexander III died in 1894, and Nicholas II succeeded his father. Nicholas held a personal hostility toward Jews much more profound than that of his predecessors. It took a little time, but events that followed in Kishinev and other cities showed Nicholas' true colors as the pogroms made the riots of the 1880s seem to belong to an age of civility. It is important to understand and try to share the feeling of the Jews living in the city of Kishinev. This was the beautiful and prosperous capital of Bessarabia, and Jews living there had attained a large degree of assimilation with the Russian populace. The prosperity of Kishinev had to be attributed to the Jews who built up the city's commerce, established banks and promoted and engaged in cultural activities.

Not necessarily unusual for the Eastern European press, a Russian language newspaper in Kishinev published stories that Jews had infected their country, whatever that meant. In addition, the paper carried the age old false accusations that Jews were the slayers of Christian children. Everyone has heard this ridiculous and sickening falsehood of how Jews used the blood of Christian children to bake their matzoh. Rumors of slayings fed upon rumors. A second newspaper, always thought to be liberal in the past, turned into an anti-Jewish giant when its headlines and articles agitated and inflamed the Christian population. Both newspapers erroneously blamed Jews for the so called ritual murders of two specific young Christian children. On April 19, 1903, Easter and the last day of Passover coincided. On that day, the Chief of Police, his officers, and a small band of strangers incited the non-Jewish population to stone and curse Jews on the streets of Kishinev. The confrontation exploded as members of several half-drunken mobs released pent up hatreds towards Jews, hatreds the Russians had harbored for centuries. The assailants, mainly Moldavians, included Greeks, Serbs, and Albanians who lived in the city, smashed windows and cracked doors of Jewish dwellings. They turned to looting and demolishing Jewish owned businesses, and they beat Jews they encountered on the streets.

Toward the end of the first day, the looting and destruction gave way to murder and rape. A strange calm followed in the evening; it seemed the worst was over, though it proved to be only a prelude to the likes of horrors not seen since the Middle Ages.

When word of the atrocities in Kishinev reached Baltimore, the local Committee of the Alliance Israelite Universelle sent four thousand dollars to Paris for Kishinev sufferers. The pogroms, though heavily concentrated in the Ukraine, continued throughout Russia for three years[4].

On October 17, 1905, Tzar Nicholas II issued a manifesto promising constitutional reforms, and Jews and Christians alike were exuberant. Jews literally danced in the streets and soon red flags of freedom of the Russian Social Democratic Party became evident during the celebrations. It is said that Jews pulled down the Tzar's emblems in the villages and cities and cried, "Down with the Emperor." This proved not to have been the best thing Jews could have done because melees ensued between Jews and Ukrainian cossacks along with hooligans protected by the police. The killings and rapes, heaviest in the large Ukrainian port city of Odessa, spread to other localities throughout Russia. The pogroms triggered a new wave of emigration from every part of Russia, the largest since the years 1891 an 1892.

During the years of the pogroms[5] that peaked in 1906,[6] large numbers of Russian intellectuals who managed to escape their horrors started for America. They harbored a disdainful and snobbish attitude towards the poorly educated Jews who had come to America fifteen to twenty years before. A definite line of separatism between the two generations was drawn, though the line could never be as sharp as the one drawn in the 1880s between Eastern European and Germans Jews. Feelings between separate Eastern European groups existed far back in history. Russians and Poles always disliked each other and collectively they disliked Lithuanians. The haughty and condescending Hungarians had a long standing dislike of Galitzianers. Though the Russian Jewish migration to America between 1890 and 1910 was tremendous, it accounted for less than 15% of the total immigration from all countries for those years

In Romania, the large area that lies south of Russia, Jews were partly Russo-Polish and partly Turkish. This amalgamation of Ashkenazic and Sephardic cultures existed in no other country on the European continent. Here Jews lived under the comparatively benevolent rule of the Sultan of Turkey. First proposed as an independent state at the end of the Crimean War in 1856, and actually created in 1859, the nation of Romania was finalized by international agreement in 1862. Romania's land, formerly part of the Ottoman Empire, became a haven for Sephardic Jews who fled Portugal and Spain at the end of the fifteenth century. Sephardim in this area considered themselves to be native Jews. Beginning in the sixteenth and culminating in the seventeenth century, Yiddish speaking Russian foreign Jews, refugees from Russian massacres, infiltrated Romanian areas along the Russo-Turkish trade routes. Juxtapositioning of Eastern European Jews in Romania created a country that was home to Sephardim who spoke Yiddish and Romanian and Ashkenazi, who spoke Ladino and Romanian.

Largely due to non-Jewish Russian influence and church codes, anti-Semitism was inherent to Romania's existence. Jews there suffered the same general Eastern European indignities, the denial of full rights of citizenship although these indignities were directed primarily towards the foreign Jews. In 1870, the United States concern for Romanian

UNCOMMON THREADS

Jews resulted in severe anti-Jewish riots and vicious pogroms; nevertheless, the greater Romanian exodus to the United States did not occur until the turn of the century, almost twenty years after the beginning of the Polish and Russian migrations. Even then, some of the Romanians who fled were young artisans who organized committees to obtain horses, buggies and tents, handed out newspapers and sang and performed to raise much needed funds for their journey. There were others who fled as fusgeyer (walkers), tramping hundreds of miles across the countryside. These Romanian Jews depended on being fed by Jewish communities along the way.

---

1   *The building of the Russian railroads had a strong Baltimore though non-Jewish connection. Before the Civil War, Baltimorean Thomas Winans played a large role in developing the imperial Russian railroad system.*

2   *In Baltimore in August, 1994, Rebitzen Judith Neuberger, wife of the late head of Ner Israel Rabbinical College, died. She was not only a rabbi's wife, a great honor in itself, but the daughter of a rabbi and a rebitzen, a sister of a Rabbi and the mother of five rabbis.*

3   *Concurrently with the ending of partial Jewish civil latitudes in 1865, the Russian government reneged on the Treaty of 1832 when they denied some Jewish citizens of the United States their rights to travel under the treaty. Inequities dragged on for years and years; it was not until 1912 that the Treaty of 1832 between Russia and the United States was officially terminated.*

4   *Eastern European Jews have little regard for their mother countries, but they have great regard for their fellow villagers. Landsmanshafts, organized by Eastern European immigrants to preserve their traditions, lasted only so long, disappearing in a generation or so. Not so for the Bessarabian Society of Baltimore, formed in 1945 to honor and keep the refinement, great intellect and traditions of their country alive in America. The founders had survived the Kishinev riots of 1903 but they could not survive the toll of passing years. By 1982, when there was no one left to remember Kishinev, the Bessarabian Society disbanded. For the thirty-seven years of the Society's existence, one man, Leon Moss, held the office of President.*

5   *On a wall in New York's restored Ellis Island is a Statement of Pogroms in Russia, and it covers four days of absolute horror from October 31st to November 3, 1905. The statement accounts for 640 separate pogroms in 13 named communities and 13 isolated places. 37,775 families totaling 159,001 individuals were affected in this brief period. Of these individuals, 937 were killed and 1,190 wounded. 351 women became widowed; 179 children were orphaned 1,278 lost one parent.*

6   *In the files of the American Jewish Historical Society in Waltham, Massachusetts is a dramatic letter of desperation that follows:*

   Odessa Oct. 27th. 1905.
   My dearly beloved sister,
   Know, my dear sister that I do not write this letter with ink, but with bloody tears and trembling hands. I suppose you have already heard of our terrible calamity. So awful a catastrophe has occurred that it's like has not been seen since the world began. Thousands of people have been slaughtered, and not only have the stores been robbed, but each private dwelling. House to House.

UNCOMMON THREADS

We ran first to the cemetery to see the extent of our misfortune. What shall I say to you my dear sister? We have been left utterly destitute. Until to day we have all been lying hidden in a cellar, and we have come out like corpses. We have no Home. God only knows where we get the strength to come back, after seeing and realizing the great misfortune and great sorrow that has befallen us Jews. It is not in human power to describe this. My eyes are strained with bloody tears and my head is dizzy from the terrible shricks.

It is now three days that the dead are being buried and there is no end as yet. The graves take up one half of the field, and 85 bodies are buried in one grave. Bodies are scattered all over the grave yard, so battered and disfigured that they are unrecognizable. Limbs and heads of the children are strewn about. They lay as thick as steep, covered with tarpaulin. The morgues are full. Woe to our years that we should live to see this sorrow. Happy are they who dies before our misfortune overtook us, and cannot see how our blood flows through the streets. Of God; who sees and does not help us. Our troubles and sorrows are not to be endured and what is yet to come, who can say?

Many, many of our people have been killed. A. (list of those killed) Woe is me that I can say in a breath that this is a thousand times worse than in Kisheneff. It was in reality a war. God in heaven, how have we survived the noise of the shooting. And now, the ambulances and Red Cross carry the wounded as though from a war. Happy indeed are they who died in time to be saved from witnessing all this.

What I write you here is but a small part of what I could tell you if I had the strength. I would write more, but cannot, as I am broken; from fasting and worry. The streets are knee deep with blood. It is impossible, my dear sister to describe our circumstances. We find ourselves in a stable. Do not ask about food. The only thing that could help us, would be to taking out of this accursed land. Do not for a moment think we want you to send us money, but merely to take us all out, as we could not tear ourselves away from each other. We have nothing wherewith to live. I do not know, how we will exist until your letter reaches me a month to live in a stable, myself, my husband and our four children. You must send me tickets and some money, and how we will live till then I do not see. Do not think I am asking just for the few dollars No. If I do not receive an answer, enabling us to go forth away from this land, the only thing left for us to do, is to throw ourselves into the sea. Save us from our terrible misfortune, or else we and our children are lost. When you send the tickets, see that we will have no trouble with them. My hands are trembling as I write this letter. How, how can we exist in a stable, waiting a month for your letter? Yankel is 13 years old, Ellie 11, Esther 10, and Rachel 3. We will go forth upon receipt of the steamer tickets. We have nothing to sell. Everything is broken or sold. And if we do not receive any tickets from you, then we will throw ourselves into the sea. That is all we can do.

Your sister,
Sherva Sandelman

PART II-2

Travel to North Sea ports * Baron de Hirsch Fund * Alliance Israelite Universelle * At sea

*T*o understand the mental and physical hardships endured by migrating Eastern European Jews is to respect and to be aware of a tenacity born of despair. It is not possible to relate to or to compare the travail of Russian Jewish flight experiences with others who have in the past and are in the present fleeing their native lands. It is safe to say, though, that the flight of the Russian Jew to America was born of psychological challenges for a new life resulting from the abuse they suffered for hundreds of years.

It was unusual for Russians who lived in the Pale to have ever seen a train. To begin their trip from Russia, they, and what luggage they had, left their shtetl homes in horse carts and boarded dilapidated rail cars at the nearest railhead. From there, they traveled to the Russian terminus at the east German border where the cars were emptied and passengers required to show a passport indicating their destination. The authorities made sure that each document bore a police stamp, the essential form of Russian authorization required to leave the country. Permission to enter Germany was predicated on the possession of tickets for passage on German shipping lines although lobbying by United States labor groups in 1885 forced a change in the rules for obtaining those tickets. Previously, friends in the United States could purchase tickets and send them to their Russian friends, however, after the change, only relatives could buy and send tickets to their migrating relatives. If they could afford them, emigrants themselves could buy tickets directly from German or American contacts, but the whole emigration issue presented a problem of some delicacy for Germany.

It was possible to sail to America from Odessa but it was much more expensive than traveling overland to German ports. The logistical problems of moving thousands of emigrating Jews from Eastern Europe were best served by the geographic and transportation advantages of traveling through Germany. Historically, Germany, then and now, reacted to and then rejected the thought of foreigners being on their land for whatever reason. Though they disliked the idea of interlopers, at the same time Germans succumbed to a higher calling; that of recognizing the possibilities of turning a quick mark. German shipping lines had great economic clout, so they encouraged the government to keep the emigration going. As written in Part I of this book, at the time the German Jews emigrated to America in the mid-nineteenth century, German shipping interests acted as agents to facilitate their voyage on German ships.

In principle but not always in practice, the moment Russian Jews set foot on German soil, German Jewish charitable organizations took them under their wing. Once in charge, the Baron de Hirsch Fund and the Alliance Israelite Universelle operated under the auspices of a Central Committee established in Berlin in 1882. Baron Maurice de Hirsch of Paris, son of the German Moritz von Hirsch who amassed a fortune in railroading by building the Oriental Railway (The Orient Express) linking Europe and Constantinople, continued his involvement in Russian Jewish emigration from the time of his first donation of one million francs in 1881. Hirsch's grandfather was the first Jewish land owner in Bavaria. The Baron de Hirsch Fund extended its help to the United States, where it aided the reception of Russian Jewish immigrants, conducted classes to teach them the English language, and helped in the development of their mechanical skills. The Baron's first philanthropic interest was the Alliance Israelite Universelle, founded in 1860 in Paris. The Alliance was a form of secular philanthropy that was the first international Jewish agency formed to give relief to distressed Jews anywhere in the world. The Alliance subsidized the emigration of destitute Russian and Polish Jews to the United States by paying the cost of travel from the frontiers of Russia to the European ports. It is significant that the organization was founded and headquartered in France, a country not known to have been overly friendly to Jews. A Baltimore branch of the Alliance was founded in 1888 to educate Jewish boys and girls in intellectually starved lands that denied them schooling. The children were taught trades and were prepared for farm life.

The two agencies required that the heads of families register with German authorities and that they fully describe the family with whom they were traveling. Only then were they allowed to board German trains headed west to the North Sea German ports of Bremen and Hamburg. A lesser number traveled further to Antwerp, Belgium, or to Rotterdam and Amsterdam, Holland where they boarded ships. During the 1880s and 1890s, most of the ships went only so far as the east coast ports of England, and from there immigrants entrained to Liverpool. Before embarking on the trans-Atlantic steamships, immigrants underwent cursory physical examinations. Although this examination was made to screen from the masses those who were not likely to pass the physicals at the American ports; it was an emotional sewer for some families. They had come this far as a family and wanted to remain a family. They knew they would never lay eyes again on whoever was left behind. Now about to board ship for a new life in an unknown country, a family member was not allowed to continue because of a health problem, often a minor one. It is difficult to imagine how this tore an immigrant family apart; the decision to continue their voyage to a new land without a family member or to return to Russia with the family intact. Not all, however, intended to continue their voyage to America. Some remained in the eastern section of Germany and others stayed in England, ventured to London, and became part of an Eastern European community that exists to this day in Whitechapel.

Primarily in the early years of migration, some Russians Jews, for one reason or another, could not obtain the proper police clearance that would allow them to leave Russia. There were those that left regardless, and they traveled on foot with few belongings, enduring not only the physical difficulties but also the fear of being caught during their flight by either Russian or German authorities. They walked miles by night; they hid and slept during the day until they reached Bremen or Hamburg where they were able to purchase passage to America. For Ukrainians forced to travel on foot, the distance to the German and Dutch ports was greater. The most direct route was to cross the Austro-Hungarian borders illegally, and this they did. On their way to the ports, whether from the Ukraine or from Poland, smugglers and con artists found Russian Jews to be easy prey. Usually, families and groups from a single village traveled together, and they proudly bore a flag and a Torah they had removed from the synagogue of their village. Though they had provided themselves with loaves of bread and flasks of drinking water for the overland trip, those who traveled on foot arrived in the port cities faint from near starvation and reduced to a state of helplessness. For the few who managed to fortify themselves by carrying cheese and brandy, travel was more tolerable.

The presence of so many preparing to board ships for America or England presented a logistical tribulation that strained the facilities of Hamburg, Bremen, Rotterdam, and Antwerp. No port city could provide proper lodging and food for so many at one time, as most of the emigrants arrived days before their day of sailing. Though the Jewish charitable agencies housed many in barracks type quarters and fed them in soup kitchens, there was usually an overflow that needed care. Frequently, those traveling without friends or family slept in the streets.

The momentum and mass of the migration challenged the transatlantic facilities of the steamship lines that provided passage for the additional thousands of immigrants. Russian Jews in the 1880s and the 1890s traveled on steamships that had largely replaced the smaller sailing vessels used by German Jews who crossed the Atlantic Ocean fifty years before. The voyage for the Russian Jews was of considerably less duration, from twelve to twenty days up until World War I. Conditions aboard ships were far less primitive than those of the mid-nineteenth century, when in an effort to handle the heaviest demand for space, steamship lines converted some cattle carrying vessels to passenger use.

On the morning of the day a ship was scheduled to sail, horse drawn wagons went from one lodging place to another and gathered up those due to leave. The emigrant men, women and children and their baggage were deposited on the dock to which their ship was moored. There, the shipping authorities introduced them to the mashgiach (poor 19th century counterpart of the modern day Cruise Director) who would accompany them on the ship and would make arrangements for Kosher food to be served aboard ship. He was to make sure that the passengers had no hesitation about eating the food served. Poverty dictated that most Russian Jewish emigrants book passage in the cheapest facility on the ship: steerage. Passage fare in the late 1880s for this class of accommodation usually ran about 35 German marks ($ *). To travel steerage meant to be a part of hundreds of passengers quartered below in suffocating spaces near the bow where the rolling and pitching of the ship could be felt the most or aft of the ship over the screw where vibrations were endless when under way. The shipping lines provided shallow wooden boxes mounted on iron frames in tiers for the emigrants to use as beds.

Some of the women traveling steerage boarded ships juggling large bundles or packs on their heads, and they used these for bedding. They hand carried the family's two silver candlesticks, needed for Sabbath kiddish prayers, and a few other precious possessions because there was no way they could send for articles they left in Russia. Though the shipping companies provided receptacles for those who became seasick, there were never enough. Most of the men had little luggage, their possessions so few they could fit them into a package carried under their arm. They made sure though that these belongings included a tallit, phylacteries and a small prayer book. No one carried a tooth brush or tooth paste because personal hygiene as such was almost unknown to immigrants of the 1880s. Each passenger hung on their person a small bag containing their personal tin eating utensils. These jingled like spurs as the men ran up the gang planks, jostling and shoving, to reach the narrow and slippery steps that led below in order to find the most comfortable space for his family.

On some of the smaller ships, crews herded men, women and their children together in the discomfort of a single space in the hold of the ship. By the turn of the century, condition on ships improved greatly, at least on newer German ships that offered modified state rooms with eight berths and better sanitary facilities for a slightly higher fare. For this, men were assigned to one stateroom and women and children to another. They too slept in tiers on wooden bunks but the extra fare for these deluxe accommodations included a stack of straw for bedding and a dipper for rationed drinking water. While waiting to sail, some few emigrants purchased pillows and thin mattresses from dock venders, and they carried these aboard ship to replace the straw. Sanitary facilities usually included two water closets per deck, each used by both sexes. The wash room consisted of a long trough and a line of faucets that spouted salt water used for body washing, laundry and dishes.

In the morning at sea, a slovenly crew member ladled a non-definable black soup into bowls. In the late afternoon, immigrants were confronted with an exquisite cuisine of bread, almost raw herring, potatoes in the skin, and moldy cake laid out on a ship's table in ample quantities. There was enough to eat, though passengers had to accept the fact that in the 1800s, creamery butter was not an item of ship's fare. Instead, the so called butter furnished in steerage was a barely edible fatty oil that remained solid at ordinary temperatures and closely resembled moldy wax. Before sailing, agents for the steamship lines and the mashgiach assured the passengers that the food served would be kosher, and it may have been. However, being sea sick for the most part, the passengers ate very little At times when meat was served, passengers who were able to eat also became ill. As could be expected, the mashgiach who had made unfulfilled promises seemed to have disappeared from the ship. There was no one to complain to so they grumbled to each other and being seasick for the most part, ate very little. By the early 1900s, conditions improved to the extent that some ships provided better cooks and stewards in steerage and general passenger comfort continued to improve. The length of the journey shortened with the use of newer ships; a few of which made the crossing in six days. Immigration for a growing America was good business for steamship lines as the number of immigrants grew each year, enabling the ship owners to keep their large liners in service.

On ships that sailed during daylight in good weather, passengers crowded the decks and watched the sights on shore. As darkness fell, and the ship reached the open sea, passengers became panic stricken so the emigrants huddled together. Even in good weather, Atlantic Ocean waves buffeted the small ships of the late 1800s, that caused them to roll and rock. The sound of eating utensils banging against the sides of the ship's hull vied with the wails and groans of those who were seasick, which included almost everyone at some time during the voyage. For sure, living in the interior of Russia, emigrants had never seen the sea and had little beforehand concept of what an ocean voyage would be like. The much used word hardship no doubt derived from the hard life aboard ship. Fear of a fire breaking out aboard or having a collision added to the passengers' psychological discomfort. German crews, completely unsympathetic to the plight of the poor emigrants on their ships, added to the passengers' discomfort by referring to them as "Russian Pigs." During storms and high seas, the crews warned passengers of the danger of seeking a breath of fresh air on the open decks. Those who did became frightened by the sight of huge angry black waves, created by the churning dark waters of the Atlantic Ocean. Below, the distance between decks was usually too limited for most of the passengers to stand upright so they sat or lay down on their bunks. As the ship rolled and pitched, they watched trunks and benches slide from side to side across the hold.

Weather permitting, passengers welcomed the air on the crowded open decks. On the days the sun shone, it uplifted their spirits, and they enjoyed the tranquillity of gazing out at the sea. As it waned and the colors of sunset appeared, immigrants became nostalgic, and they longed for home. Many gathered in groups to dance and to sing the songs of their Russian shtetls that they would never see again; nevertheless, and not to be forgotten, life aboard ship was a lot better than their existence had been in Russia. They felt the touch of freedom, and this sensation filled their days with hope and a kind of joy. Immigrants kept their hopes alive not only by the prospects of life in America and the freedom it offered, but also by what they would do after they landed. Discussions centered on whether they would or would not build a synagogue for their group from the same shtetl and what Yiddish language books they would need to start a library. Their dreams of starting a synagogue came true, because in 1910 in East Baltimore, there were 20 to 25 congregations of Eastern European Jews, each founded by Eastern European Jews who had lived in the same shtetl.

Meanwhile, they tried to erase from their minds thoughts of not being allowed to enter the United States, because they knew there was always that possibility. At some point near the end of their voyage, the steerage passengers became somewhat used to the ship and its crew so the discomfort of their trans-Atlantic travel lessened. On the Sabbath, the mashgiach fellow suddenly appeared for services and tried to verbalize some sort of indoctrination for going ashore in America. At this juncture in their long voyage from eastern Europe to America, emigrants technically became immigrants. Before the ship docked, the captain made sure that all of the passengers, whether they could write or not, sign a paper stating that they had received only the best possible treatment aboard ship. Some passengers could not sign; they had passed away during the voyage.

PART II-3

German Jewish reception * A Christian teacher's view * Entry travails * Locust Point * Post World War I immigration * Immigration Act 1921 * Johnson Act 1924

*I*n 1881, immigration was a trickle; only seven Russian Jewish families made their way to Baltimore; in early 1882, approximately 375 Eastern European Jews lived in the city; however by the end of the year, the composition of the city's population began to dramatically change. Baltimore German Jews realized that those Russian Jews who had landed were merely a vanguard of thousands to follow, and a sobering thought this was. Their arrival was in some ways similar to that of the German Jews who had arrived in Baltimore fifty years before, but what followed would be on a much larger scale. Though both the Germans and Russians practiced Judaism, culturally they were a century apart. In 1830, a handful of Portuguese Sephardic and German Jews lived in Baltimore, and worshipped together as Sephardim and they felt the same about their cultural differences with the German Jews as the German Jews felt about the Russian Jews. Now in 1881, there were too few Sephardim in the city to be concerned about threats to their well being. In 1882, well-established Baltimore German Jews considered themselves to be American Jews of German descent and cultural refinement. In fact, they were already almost indistinguishable from their American Christian German neighbors. For their everyday social and business exchanges, most had completely changed their German tongue to English.

Baltimore German Jews were joined by small groups of Jews from Germany who arrived between the end of the Civil War and the beginning of the Russian migration. Though not rich, they seldom arrived penniless. They were literate, having been secularly educated, and their transition to being Americans was easily accomplished with the help of Baltimore friends and relatives. Few of the German Jewish immigrants of this period resembled the strangers who arrived at Locust Point after 1881.

Initially, German Jews reacted with shock over the arrival of shiploads of illiterate Russian Jewish immigrants, the waves of which rocked German Jewish boats. They feared that their reputation would suffer because of the tendency of Christians to judge all Jews to be alike. A small group of highly cultured and well-to-do Baltimore German Jews responded more receptively to their arrival. Although small in numbers, at the beginning of the Russian Jewish migration, this was the only sector the Russian Jews could turn to for empathy and help.

The author's wife Betsey is named after her great grandmother Betsey Friedenwald Wiesenfeld. Because Wiesenfeld lived in the 1800s and she was part of the small group of German Jews who were so helpful to the new immigrants, the author has included a first hand observation of her. The following vignette by Baltimore's well-known author, poet and Western High School teacher, Lizette Woodworth Reese was written in 1929 in her book *A Victorian Village*. Before coming to Western High, Miss Reese taught in a German-English elementary school in East Baltimore.

UNCOMMON THREADS

"It was the spring of 1876 when I entered Number Three School. A few years later a new, much larger building was provided for us, on East Baltimore Street near Aisquith Street, and thither accordingly we were removed. It was a modern structure, for its time, well-lighted, well-heated, a welcome contrast to the stove-warmed, steep-staired, narrow, inconvenient building on Trinity Street. The change was most necessary, as the number of pupils had increased at a most astonishing rate."

"And was it only the teaching of the German language which increased the number of pupils in this school, and others of like character throughout the city, and kept there those who had entered several years before? Yes. But as time went on. I found, by examining my records, that often, when a child, on account of change of residence or some other sufficient reason, was transferred to another public school, as likely as not it was to a purely English one. Germans are the most thrifty of people and eventually the mere sentimental attachment to their mother tongue was not strong enough to militate against a system so much more efficient and financially firmer than the ancient parochial one. The children became Americanized; the parents, also; little by little the foreign language was dropped from the curriculum; the English-German schools became as purely English as the other public schools of the city."

"A few years after my establishment at the Baltimore Street building, the first of the Russian Jewish refugees commenced to pour into the city; the streets in the neighborhood, especially Lombard and Pratt, rapidly filled up with poorly nourished men, women, and children, the latter entering the large, newly built, important Number Three."

"A widow lady by the name of Wiesenfeld, who lived in one of the fine houses across the street, constituted herself a veritable Mother in Israel to those forlorn people.[1] She fed them with hot soup, standing all day long on her kitchen stove. She saw that they were adequately clothed and warmed. Any hour of the daylight, you could see her walking briskly, her gray skirts billowing around her stout knees, the dark purple ribbons on her black lace cap flying straightly about her, upon her errands of mercy. She was not a young woman, she was not a handsome woman, but the kindliness in her eye, her inherent and responsive friendliness, gave her the real affection of those of her own creed and race who knew her the best, and the undoubted respect of every Gentile. It was a heavy hour to the community when she died. As the time for the funeral drew close, a throng of people, most of them her grateful, old pensioners, arranged themselves on each side of the doorway. When the short, plain, bare coffin -- for strict Jewish custom would not allow a single flower -- was carried to the hearse, they stood and watched it in silence. There were tears in their eyes."

By the end of 1882, a large number of Russian Jews had arrived in Baltimore, and they, the Russian Jews, appeared to the discomfited Germans to be an uncouth and unmannerly lot that neither read, spoke, nor wrote English. Baltimore's German Jews were appalled at the outlandish appearance of the new comers. They looked as though they could be Italians or Slovak immigrants, and to the Russians, the Germans Jews looked like Christians. Their percentage of illiteracy was high, and their material wealth well below that of immigrants who arrived at this time from other European countries. Some were actually without funds, without job skills, and without the names or addresses of friends or relatives in America. The Russian Jews observed dietary laws and smelled of garlic, a horror in itself; no self respecting German Jewish frau used this bulbous herb in her cooking. Visually, most Russian Jews seemed to adhere to their religious orthodoxy, now an unusual and almost strange image that Reform Jews abolished years ago.

The Russian Jewish men, their appearance unkempt, traveled in rumpled suits, some made of canvas, and they wore common fabric white shirts that they buttoned to the neck. They wore no ties; not a negative to their appearance as the four-in-hand tie was unknown before the late nineteenth century. In Baltimore today, it is common to see extremely Orthodox Jews wearing a white shirt buttoned to the neck with no tie. The immigrant men wore either a soft Russian peasant type visor cap or a modified derby. Women in long dresses covered their shoulders with shawls and their heads with a large triangular kerchief, the babushka. A few men in long caftan type garments sported black undisciplined beards and payes (earlocks). This image of dress, was one that German Jews had never seen before, and it did not encourage social overtures. Within a few weeks after landing in America, it seemed propitious for many Orthodox Russian Jews to shave their beards and cut off their earlocks.

Quite a few Russian Jews, formerly tailors in their homeland, emerged from steerage compartments with a sewing machine strapped to their back, looking as if it were an extension of their body. Russians called these sewing machines their katerinka, figuratively translated from Yiddish the word means music box. They depended on these machines, the use of which enabled them to make a living. Most immigrants had not reached step one in their understanding of anything mechanical so the internal workings of a katerinka were a mystery to them; so when katerinka malfunctioned and needed repair, the tailor malfunctioned.

Russian Jews, wounded and suffering emotionally from their experiences in Eastern Europe, arrived in America somewhat bewildered and confused. The long train trips and the voyage across the Atlantic Ocean tended to tire them, and their sensitivities became dulled by the authorities frequently herding them from one place or another in the immigration station. Some were turned away and sent back to Europe by immigration inspectors and doctors who had the authority to deny admission to the United States for an assortment of reasons. Red eye, a frequent physical condition, caused the doctors to be suspicious of trachoma, a severe form of conjunctivitis that is contagious and can lead to blindness. This disease, somewhat widespread among immigrants, was curable though the United States immigration authorities considered it a cause for rejecting individual immigrants. Actually the large numbers of immigrants who appeared to have red eye indeed had red eyes; usually caused by salt water they washed in, since aboard ships, this was all that was available.

Effective in August 1882, under the terms of a new law passed by Congress, statutes permitted the screening of immigrants for past criminal convictions in Russia, for mental incompetence, and an assortment of other new medical deficiencies. The new law required that arriving immigrants not become public charges. The minimal amount of money required by each immigrant upon entry was set at $20.00. Word spread through the towns and villages of Europe that this amount of money was sufficient to get into the United States so rarely did arrivals declare more than that amount. For each person on a ship's passenger list an entry form inquired if in possession of money, was it more than $30.00, and how much more, and if less than that amount, how much. Often, immigrants resorted to carrying their life savings sewn in the linings of their coats and in the hems of their skirts, and they had no intention of revealing their treasure to any uniformed official.

Prior to 1891, as immigrants were admitted, one by one, they experienced the terrifying travail of clerks at desks who registered their given name, age, country of origin, the name of the vessel they came on, and their destination. The answers to a total of twenty-nine questions needed to be recorded. In the event an immigrant did not know or could not make his or her name clear to the immigration agent, the agent simply assigned that person a new name. What a dehumanizing experience to be given a new name by a sometimes insensitive stranger -- a name that replaced the name they had been given at birth, and one they would legally use for the rest of their life. Immigration records became the provenance of the Russian Jew in America. Because of records lost or non-existent in Russia, some immigrants did not know the date of their birth. It was logical, therefore, to use their date of landing in America as their birth date, an easy date to remember; it represented the birth of a new life. By the time the authorities finished their processing, some immigrants became so terrified that they sat and cried and wished they could return to the bosom of Mother Russia.

After 1891, United States immigration affairs became separated from custom matters, and the United States sent standard forms to ports of embarkation around the world to be filled in by ships' pursers before landing. Additional columns to the document were added in 1903 and again in 1906 which allowed the government to keep in depth statistical profiles of immigrants. Though pursers transcribed each passenger's name from a passport or travel papers and other identification as best they could, they were not familiar with the Cyrillic or Hebrew alphabets. They resorted to asking the passengers their names and listing them as they sounded. The immigrant passengers, for the most part with no knowledge of the Latin alphabet, were unable to correct the purser's transliterated listing. The government was not entirely insensitive to the immigrants' feelings, so officials who questioned them during processing made corrections where they could. Purser errors which resulted especially from this practice, were no more accurate than those of immigration officials before 1891.

After the immigrants completed their entry processing and formalities, the Hebrew Immigrant Aid Society (HIAS) arranged for room and board in Baltimore for those who were not scheduled to entrain to other destinations that day. They were furnished food and given comfortable places to sleep and until less transitory living arrangements could be made.

The United States government required that a bond be posted for each immigrant to appease the concern that immigrants would become wards of the state. The demand from the authorities that these bonds be posted was discretionary and frequently waived. Fortunately for Russian Jews, German Jews posted the bonds when needed; had they not done so, who else in the city could or would have? There was no way that the German community could afford a bond for each of the thousands of immigrants who landed at Locust Point. In one instance, two ship loads of Russian Jews arrived in the Baltimore harbor from the port of Hamburg, and they were about to be deported because the United States immigration authorities demanded a $1,000 bond for each passenger. This was impossible to obtain from Baltimore German Jews, particularly on such short notice. Unauthorized to do so, community leaders offered to pledge the buildings of the Hebrew Hospital and Orphan Asylum as collateral for the immigrants' entry. United States Treasury Department officials responsible for immigration services rejected the offer which presented the immigrants with the alternative of being returned to Russia and again being subjected to the terrorism from which they had fled. A prominent German Jewish physician Dr. Harry Friedenwald persuaded another influential Baltimorean to go with him to Washington and present the immigrants' dilemma to government officials. They successfully used the old method shtadlanuth (pleading with someone they knew), and the Russian Jews were allowed to disembark from their ships.

The Sephardic, the German and the Russian Jews shared a religion, but they differed in culture and in the languages they spoke. When the German Jews came to Baltimore, it was a city inhabited by many Christian Germans of a similar aestheticism and a minimum of language dialect differences. The Russian Jews arrived in a city much different from the shtetls they had left. Even if there had been Christian Russians living in Baltimore, few Russian Jewish immigrants could have communicated because they did not speak the language of their native Russia. Their language was Yiddish, the mama loshen (the mother tongue). Russian Jews called the uptown Germans Yahudim, a mocking variant on Yehudim, the Hebrew word for Jews, and some Germans in derision referred to downtown Russian Jews as Yiden.

As a sequel to the scenario of pre-Civil War German Jewish immigrants, Russian Jews were poor in their homelands, perhaps poorer than the Germans had been in theirs. For centuries, the Russian Jewish culture accepted the fact that it was a distinctively high honor to be poor, as the Talmud taught that the poor man was more blessed than the rich man. Rabbis preached "to be a Jew, one had to be poor and suffer." As with the German Jews, many of the early arrivals were single men who found jobs and saved their money until they accumulated enough to send funds to Russia to enable others in their families to join them in America. After two or three brothers and sisters settled here, they naturally wanted their parents to join them. It was not too difficult to encourage younger brothers facing four years of conscription in the Russian army to leave, but for older parents, it was another matter. To sever their Russian connections and the life they were used to and to establish themselves in a new country required a great deal of courage. If they traveled to America they faced the fact that they would never see their European families and friends again. It was not only that leaving seemed difficult but also the sea voyage that added to the long overland journey seemed insurmountable; nevertheless, for thousands, love for their children overcame their questions and fears, and so they came.

Between 1882 and 1890, approximately 25,000 Russian Jews landed in Locust Point, Baltimore. In the following decade, 18,000 additional arrivals came to Baltimore aboard ships of the Baltimore-Bremen Line of the North German Lloyd Company. All entered through the immigration facility adjacent to the Baltimore and Ohio Railroad piers. Many stayed in Baltimore, while others faced the challenge of opportunities in other communities where they had relatives. The synchronized arrangement used for years worked well for immigrants. Those who made pre-ticketed arrangements in Europe to destinations other than Baltimore, with no planned Baltimore layover after processing, boarded Baltimore and Ohio trains on the pier.[2]

On those trains, immigrants formed an immediate liking for America. Though large trunks were not allowed in their passenger cars, handbags and suit cases were conveniently hoisted onto overhead racks. The comfort of the trains provided a sense of order to the passengers, and they became less inclined to have noisy conversations and annoying nervous laughter. On some trains an entire car was reserved for smokers. By this time most immigrants had learned to say "all right" and "OK," and they were on their way to settling in, in America. As the train passed through cities and towns, they noted that the streets of America, as they had heard in Russia, were not paved with gold, as the use of that precious commodity was mostly for jewelry and filling teeth. They also learned that good strong Vodka would not be available to them in America.

While the subject of this book concerns Baltimore Jews, there is a compelling reason to mention the specter and experiences of Russian Jewish immigrants who entered America through the facilities of the port of New York. Entering through the port of Baltimore was considerably different and much easier for the immigrants. The grand scale of New York City, the electricity of sheer numbers of immigrants being processed, though frightening to the Russian Jews, was a spiritual experience that could never have been matched in Baltimore.[3] Russian Jews who arrived in the early 1890s brought accounts of the continuing and increasing atrocities against them. They told of the Russian soldiers and their use of guns and bayonets to enforce the government edicts. They hesitantly told of the rapes of women, too sensitive a subject for them to talk about easily. On arrival, Russian Jews held meetings to vent their feelings and to protest the evil treatment of their countrymen who remained in Russia, but no one from the Russian government was around to hear their protests.

Labor organizations, fearful of their members' jobs, opposed the seemingly endless migration, and they had reasons to be fearful. Searching for cheap labor, agents of several Baltimore men's clothing manufacturers offered immigrants employment as they stepped on to the pier from the ships' gangway. In 1885, and again in 1891, stronger immigration laws passed by Congress took aim on protecting American workers from the influx of those who would, and no doubt did, work for less wages.

Roadblocks of all sorts added to the difficulties of would-be immigrants. In 1897, a bill, introduced and passed by Congress, required the rejection of immigrants who could not read the written language of their native country. Because of the high percentage of illiterate Russian immigrants, this bill, obviously designed to effectively lessen the large Eastern European migration to America, met with protest. Because of the heavy lobbying by a group of German Jewish Baltimoreans, Congress modified the bill to require the reading of any language. Even in its watered down version, President McKinley vetoed it.

In 1914, the plight of the Jews remaining in Russia and Romania worsened when these countries adopted policies forcing Jews from their lands. Hundreds of thousands of Jews in Poland, Galicia, and the Baltic countries fled westward into Germany and Austria where they became caught up in the ensuing World War I.

During the post war period, Europe was ravished by famine and uprisings, and pent up millions wanted to migrate to America. Although immigration resumed to some extent, the numbers allowed to enter were seriously curtailed. Never again would the count reach that of the great mass migration that occurred between 1881 and 1914. America reversed itself, and no longer opened its arms and its heart to immigrants. With the passage of an immigration act in 1921, the United States temporarily established quotas; the gates to freedom for the millions of oppressed who lived in foreign lands began to close. The 1921 act resulted from a well-prepared propaganda scare that had officials believing the impossible. A rumor spread through the country that there were 8,000,000 Polish Jews and 1,000,000 Italians poised and ready to come to the United States. There is little doubt that numerous Poles wanted to come to America at this time but 8,000,000? How they could be transported and how long it would take to do so was not a consideration of the issue facing a frightened nation. At Congressional hearings, twisted testimony convinced that august body to believe that the United States faced a grave situation; therefore the 1921 act was passed as an emergency bill that temporarily stopped immigration to allow Congress time to lay the groundwork for another bill three years hence.

The Johnson Act, passed by Congress in 1924 and signed into law by a benign President Calvin Coolidge, established the first permanent immigrant quotas based on the national origin of the population of the United States in 1920. In addition, the Johnson Act established the visa requirement, the processing of a permit from a United States consular office abroad as a condition for entering the Unites States. Under the restrictive 1921 laws, 50,000 Jews entered our country that year and under the Johnson Act of 1924, only 10,300 Jews entered that year. This law, certainly anti-Semitic, tilted immigration to favor those from northern and western Europe so much so that the annual British quota of 34,000 was raised to 73,000. The German quota then 51,000, was reduced to 23,000. In 1924, American Jewish leaders had no idea how desperate immigration conditions would become in just a few years. The Johnson Act had an immediate effect on the Associated Jewish Charities. The virtual hand-cuffing of immigration stopped the flow of needy Russian Jews who, except for World War I years, had been coming to Baltimore.

This began a change of direction for the Associated Jewish Charities. Indeed, unknowingly, the stage was set for the catastrophe of the 1930s and early 1940s when there was no place in America for large numbers of German Jews forced to flee the Nazis.

At this time thousands of Jews who had left Russia many years earlier and never proceeded to the ports to come to America lived in Berlin and an area east of Berlin. Because of conditions in Germany and immigration laws at this time that favored Germans over Russians, many of this group came to the United States. While they called themselves German Jews, the Baltimore German Jewish community referred to them as "Hinter Berliners."

America was becoming America for Americans though no one, no matter how they felt, advocated the removal of Emma Lazarus' words from the Statue of Liberty "Give me your tired, your poor, your huddled masses yearning to be free," but there arose a question that has probably been answered in recent years: Was America in the day of Emma Lazarus, the day of America past?

UNCOMMON THREADS

1   *In the late 1800s, many German Jews continued to live in East Baltimore. Wiesenfelds eventually moved to Eutaw Place.*

2   *In December 1993, a local real estate broker proposed "a journey back to the turn of the century" when Eastern European immigrants stepped off boats at Locust Point near a Baltimore & Ohio Railroad warehouse. His plans were to convert the old warehouse into a museum honoring immigrants, much like the Ellis Island museum that opened in New York in 1990. Though the nearby warehouse was never a part of the actual processing of immigrants, it was until a fire in January 1996, almost destroyed it, the only building of the Locust Point complex to remain standing.*

3   *Affixed to a wall in New York's restored Ellis Island, a photo-mural lists the number of immigrants entering the United States in twelve ports, both east and west coast for the seven years of 1897 to 1903. New York is by far the largest, followed distantly by Baltimore.*
   New York, N. Y.   706,11
   Baltimore, Md.   69,541
   Boston, Mass.   64,358
   Montreal, Quebec   33,048
   Philadelphia, Pa.   29,926
   The total for the remaining seven ports was 41,887.

PART II-4

Emigrant Aid Society * HIAS * What to do? * Farm communities * Help and care programs * The United and Federated Charities

The numbers of Baltimore German Jews who harbored a propensity for prejudicial attitudes towards the Russian Jews was large and not too different from the attitudes and dislikes the earlier Sephardim directed toward the German Jews. A well to-do minority of Baltimore's German Jews, mostly business men and community leaders, dealt more reasonably with the situation. Certainly, their philosophies about aid for the Russian Jews helped to defuse the possibilities of any overt demonstrations or public expressions by the German Jewish community. This group understood the plight of the Russian Jews so they offered help and comfort. German and Russian Jews took small steps, though not always jointly, to establish agencies that would ease the transition to life in a new country. Of great concern were the large numbers of Russian Jews who continued to land in Baltimore. How many years would their migration continue, and how many immigrants would eventually come to Baltimore?

German Jews founded the Hebrew Emigrant Aid Society in 1903, which acted as a central agency to help the Russian Jews with the technicalities of immigration. The Society found homes and jobs for the immigrants and helped them with their desire to eventually become naturalized American citizens. Without doubt, during the early years of Russian Jewish immigration, the Emigrant Aid Society was the dominant helping hand. In 1914, the Society joined with the Russian Jewish founded Hebrew Immigrant Protective Society, founded in 1881; the joint agency was renamed the Hebrew Immigrant Aid Society (HIAS). The Baltimore chapter along with others in America became the premier helping agency for Eastern European Jewish immigrants. By this year 1914 with World War I about to erupt, the flower of Russian Jewish immigration withered and died.

During the height of the eastern European migration, the Hebrew Emigrant Aid Society of Baltimore contacted its counterpart, the Hebrew Emigrant Society of New York, and requested that New York send no more immigrants who landed there to Baltimore. The Baltimore Germans were vehement, there were no jobs for Russian Jewish immigrants, and "genug ist genug"(enough is enough). As expected, the New York Society had problems of their own. The Hebrew Emigrant Aid Society also urged the British government, in whose land many Russian Jews awaited ships for America, to send neither families nor farmers. It was OK to continue to send single girls because they could be placed in jobs as domestics; single men, with tailoring experience, could be employed in clothing factories. Garment factory wages were too low to support an entire family, and economic conditions were such that it made it difficult to find work for other types of tradesmen. Farmers could not be placed because so many had arrived, and existing farms had absorbed as many as they could. Rumors spread to Russia that those who farmed in Russia would be given land to cultivate in America. Russian Jewish immigrants, who had neither planted a seed nor tilled the soil, claimed they farmed in Russia. Actually, at the turn of the century, only about 3% of the Jewish population farmed, partly due to their long history of displacement. These non-farmers made it difficult for genuine farmers from the Ukraine who came to America in 1881 and 1882. Farming was the ideal of intellectual Jews in this area, but as to the means of carrying out their aims they were divided into factions: One demanded that the emigration be to Palestine to settle the Land of Israel; the other insisted that the emigration should be to the United States.

Separate and distinct groups of German Jews and individuals were at odds with one another about the what to do with the Russian Jewish immigrants. Several impractical ideas were suggested, one of which was to deport them back to Russia. Others thought it was a good idea, with little concern for the details, to disperse Russian Jews at random throughout the country and to let localities deal with the problem as best they could. Efforts to educate Russian Jews in the mechanical trades, never popular with the Russian Jews, failed. There was some truth to the rumor of land being given to farmers. It seemed to be an excellent idea to send Russian Jewish immigrants from the cities and encourage them to pursue livelihoods in rural environments. Agricultural colonization for immigrants on farms, paid for by German Jews, became a very strong movement; the idea of its concept reached into the Ukraine where societies were formed for the purpose of facilitating the emigration of Russian farmers to America.

In January 1882, The Community Benevolent Society met to try to determine what could be done for several hundred Russian Jews recently arrived in New York City. The Baltimore Society raised $3,000 and bought a 700 acre farm outside of Washington in Charles County, Maryland. Named the Pisga Community, this venture in communal farming succeeded for a while and then failed. The Hebrew Colonial Society of Maryland established a colony in Baltimore County on the outskirts of Baltimore City in 1902. It occupied a 351 acre tract, 3 1/2 miles off Johnnycake Road, in Hollofield, about nine miles west of the Baltimore city boundary line. Named Yaazar (He will help), its 200 residents spoke no English, only a little Russian and much Yiddish. About 1910, the farmers themselves erected a small synagogue, and the community built a small one room schoolhouse. In addition to the three Rs, the boys learned to weave, and the girls learned to cook and can. The Society divided the acreage into about 25 narrow parallel lots, and each farmer bought his land through loans from the Baron De Hirsch Fund that contributed fifty million francs to bring Jews from Eastern Europe and to establish them as self supporting farmers.

The settlers were unable to raise enough money to purchase the necessary farm equipment, and their farms were not large enough to produce excess crops to sell. Twice a week, on an all day trip by horse and wagon, the settlers traveled to Baltimore to buy supplies and to sell the eggs and poultry they raised and the cheese they made. With no automobiles or public transportation, the bleak cold winters kept the farmers in isolation from the city's cultural life so the immigrants began to drift back to the city. Near the end of its existence, Yaazar farmers rented rooms during the summer to Jews seeking an escape from the heat for a couple weeks. By 1931, the noble experiment ended. Christians purchased some of the land and houses after the Jewish farmers returned to Baltimore. Other acreage was sold to the state for The Patapsco State Park. With little agricultural training for immigrants, and little leadership, Russian Jews never became suited for farm work.[2] With the exception of a highly successful Polish community in Vineland, New Jersey, no amount of money could successfully change Jewish small shop keepers and artisans from the shtetls of Russia into farmers.

Shortly after the arrival of Russian Jews, they themselves organized societies, fraternal organizations, and even labor unions. German Jews offered care for the sick in the Hebrew Hospital and started minimal community centers and educational facilities. Russian Jew's propensity to help themselves strengthened their already strong social ties, ties that go back through several generations when Jews could not depend on non-sectarian help. With the experiences of generations in which it was obligatory for Russian Jews to help themselves, they assumed that they must continue to do so in America. Then too, non-sectarian groups, as helpful and well meaning as they were, could in no way understand the unusual fundamental needs of Russian Jews. During that first year of their arrival in Baltimore, Russian Jews, with almost no resources, organized a committee to deal with the issues of immigrants. Though modest in scope, it is evident that the committee took action to form self help groups. Records do not indicate the depth to which they reached the community, but it is known that several were "Landsmanshafts," mutual aid associations for self help formed by immigrants from the same town or region. Landsmanshaft members contributed to a fund to be used for sickness and death benefits and for the payment to doctors who agreed to reduce their fees for group treatment.

In 1888, immigration of Lithuanians accelerated, prompting Lithuanians who preceded them in Baltimore to found the Hebrew Young Men's Sick Relief Association, a combined health and life insurance concept. For small weekly dues paid to a young physician on the Association's staff, medical costs were taken care of in the advent of serious and disabling illnesses. When there was a death in the family of a member, the Association paid a small sum towards burial the costs.

In the following year, the Russian Relief Association furnished direct relief for an assortment of needs, and in 1890 several other agencies were founded. German Jews established the Daughters in Israel that operated a home for immigrant wayward and single working girls. Hundreds of young girls experienced difficulties sustaining themselves on a $5.00 a week paycheck earned as a machine operator in garment factories. Russian Jews organized a distinctively different home, the Friendly Inn. This organization raised enough money to buy a house on Lombard near Lloyd Street. In a short while, they purchased a large building on Aisquith Street where for over sixty years they cared for transient and homeless elderly Jews. After the move to Aisquith Street, Aged Home was added to the name. Many of those who lived in the house contributed to their own support by selling matches and trinkets on downtown street corners. Later known as the Hebrew Home for incurables, it is now the Levindale Hebrew Geriatric

Center and Hospital. In 1894, German Jewish women founded the Baltimore chapter of the National Council of Women. Along with a variety of charitable activities in 1898, they started a Milk and Ice Fund that assisted the poor directly and so discreetly that the recipients' names never appeared on a charity list. In 1898, the Hebrew Free Loan Association (Gemilath Chasssodim) made funds available to help all Jews to start their own businesses.

German Jews founded the Children's Sheltering and Protective Association for the care of both German and Russian homeless and neglected children; in 1909, the Russian Jews founded the Hebrew Children's Sheltering Association that served the same purpose but for a more defined group. In the early twentieth century a substantial need existed to care for orphan children, as statistically, immigrant parents did not live long. Upon the death of a parent, or the desertion of the father from his family, it was likely that the remaining working parent could not properly care for their young children. Recorded is the tale of a few Jews who intervened when a policeman was seen leading a group of homeless children to one of the city's public institutions. As the story goes, they persuaded the policeman to turn his charges over to them, and they cared for and sheltered the children until they could be placed in the proper quarters of the Hebrew Children's Sheltering Home. For years, this home was well supported by door to door solicitation of funds. The German Jewish community founded the Hebrew Education Society in 1903 to educate the Russian Jewish children, and in 1908, they added a training school for the teachers. Also in 1903, a group of Polish immigrants began the Radomer Russian-Polish Verein, a labor Zionist group.

After twenty to twenty-five years of unremitting Eastern European migration, the Jewish community stabilized to the extent that existing agencies and societies provided effective care for just about all of their physical, emotional, and educational needs as well as their general well being. At the time of the founding of new institutions, missions frequently overlapped existing ones. Most likely due to the friction between German and Russian Jews, little note was taken of the existence of dual agencies serving identical purposes; nevertheless, in 1890, civic leaders made unsuccessful attempts to consolidate the administrations of the Hebrew Benevolent Society and the Hebrew Hospital and Asylum Association. Several years later in 1906, the German and Russian Jews consolidated their institutions apart from each other. Twelve German charities formed the uptown Federated Jewish Charities; one year later, seven of the Russian downtown charities joined to become the United Hebrew Charities. The Federated Jewish Charities served the needs of both German and Russian Jews. Their services indicate that not all late nineteenth and early twentieth century German Jewish families could care for themselves.

1   *By the beginning of World War II, the Vineland community became known as the Egg Basket of the East, and poultry farmers there built schools and a synagogue. They developed a cultural life that lasted until the ways of American living caught up with them. By 1966, half of the Jewish farmers had left the area.*

2   *The author's maternal grandparents Charles and Lina Kraus Baernstein farmed in Cass County, North Dakota, having taken residence there when it was Dakota Territory. A family narrative is that Henrietta Szold was instrumental in sending newly arrived Eastern European Jewish men to them for care, so that my grandparents would be able to help these immigrants establish themselves as farmers. Grandmother Lina Kraus, two years older than Szold, was born and raised on south Hanover Street, near the Szold residence and she was a close friend of Henrietta. It is a recorded fact that North Dakota was the only western state to which Eastern European Jewish immigrants were sent to farm, lending credence to our family narrative.*

PART II-5

Eastern European congregations * Cemeteries and federations * Kosher checks * Rabbinical Tribunal * Spiritual leaders

As did the German Jews fifty years before, Eastern European Jews prayed in homes, halls and rooms above grocery stores. Not every Russian Jew communed with God, but most of those who did prayed in the Orthodox manner. The Reform movement held little appeal for them; they actually had little or no knowledge of it. Many Russian Jews came from the same towns or districts, and they shared experiences during their migration that formed a camaraderie. It was natural for them to form a chevra or a minyan, a gathering of at least ten men required to conduct divine worship. Though chevras occupied no specific quarters of their own, members bonded and found a comfort in praying together. In 1880, there were only twenty Orthodox congregations in the entire country. By 1890 in Baltimore, at least fifteen Orthodox Eastern European chevras[1] with beautiful Hebrew names are known to have worshipped in buildings they converted for use as synagogues. Almost every one of the early shuls experienced splits and mergers, long a phenomena of structured Judaism. Some minyans ceased to exist when members dropped out, leaving them without enough men to conduct a Jewish prayer service. History records almost endless associations and disassociations of Russian Jewish Orthodox synagogues. Many of these individual groups either evolved or just joined with others to become larger and more prestigious congregations.

Differing from a secondary naming after families of early German Jewish congregations, many Eastern European Jews named their synagogues after the Russian towns or districts from whence they had come. The Hebrew word Anshe means The people of, and is frequently used in the names of Orthodox Russian Jewish shuls. Thus the names such as Anshe Emunah Tavriger (The people of Tavriger), Anshe Neisen Nusach Ari, (The people of Nesina), Beth Jacob Anshe Kurland (The people of Kurland), Beth Jacob Anshe Riga (The people of Riga) and Anshe Wolyn (The people of Wolyn) and so forth. Other Eastern European congregations did not include the town of origin as part of their formal name, but they did use the town or area of origin in Eastern Europe as part of an identification of landsmanschaften who started a minyan that evolved into a congregation. For example, Agudas Achim Anshe Chernigov Nusach Ari was the Chernigov Shul; Aitz Chaim, was known as the Prushnitz Shul; Mikro Kodesh, the Pokroyer Shul; Beth Jacob Anshe Vesher, the Visheyer Shul; Ohel Yakov the Byalistoker Shul; Shomrei Mishmeres Hakodesh, the Volhynia Shul, and Adath Yeshurin, the Shadover Shul.

Jews from a specific area of Romania and from all of Bulgaria,[2] lying south of Romania, frequently included the word Sphard (Spain) in naming their American congregations because of the Sephardic Jewish influence in those countries. Ashkenazi congregations that use Sphard as part of their name do so because Sephardic prayers recited by Jews in most Mediterranean countries are considered to be more authentic in their origins than those of the Ashkenazi. It is believed that Sephardic prayers can be traced directly back to Moses. These congregations usually with Ashkenazic European Hasidic roots north of the Black Sea have no relationship to the Sephardic heritage. They doven (pray) both in the Sephardic as well as the Ashkenazi Nusach (ritual).

At the turn of the century, a handful of Russian Jews dropped their associations with Orthodox shuls and joined the five existing German Jewish congregations, three of which worshipped as Reform. This early relationship between German and Russian Jews had only a modest effect on both groups; it only slightly strengthened the Reform movement and had little effect on Orthodoxy. Most, but not all, Russian Jewish immigrants went to shul at least several times during a year, but they especially went on Rosh Hashonah and Yom Kippur. Shuls were institutions taken for granted by some immigrant Russian Jews, and they were an integral part of Jewish life for those who were religious, and at times, for those who were not. They could not be considered houses of prayer only since they also functioned as mutual aid societies and the centers of the social and intellectual pursuits as well.

Bonded in life, Russian Jewish immigrants remained so in death. Almost without exception, they used the services of three Baltimore Orthodox Jewish funeral homes. A large cemetery at 6700 Bowley's Lane became the burial grounds for members of ten Orthodox congregations and societies. Occupying separate acreage on each side of the 6800 block of German Hill Road, east of Dundalk Avenue, a combined Hebrew cemetery provides plots for eleven Orthodox congregations and societies. Included is a section for the burial of persons after 1909 by the Chesed Schel Emes, the Hebrew Orthodox Free Burial Society founded in 1894. A children's plot is set apart from the others because children's graves require less space. At the height of World War I in 1918, a virulent influenza epidemic swept through the country and took the lives of thousands of young children; they were buried in children's plots in both the Reform and Orthodox Baltimore cemeteries. A huge cemetery in the 6300 block of Hamilton Avenue, the United Hebrew Cemetery, is the resting place for members of over thirty Orthodox congregations, societies and earlier burials of the Hebrew Orthodox Free Burial Society.

In 1902, Orthodox rabbis from eastern Europe banded together, although rather loosely, to form the national organization Agudath ha-Rabbanim (Association of Rabbis) in an effort to reach American born Jewish youths. They wanted to create in America a large scale old European type yeshivah. Six years later in 1908, the Baltimore Russian Jewish shuls united to found the Federation of Orthodox Jewish Congregations. Their purpose was to emphasize Jewish learning and to engage in activities that promoted Orthodox Judaism. Several of the Orthodox congregations forbade the reading of secular books in their synagogues, because they felt very strongly that the written word of man should not be allowed to compete with the word of God.

In practice, the observance of dietary laws inside and outside the home is a sacred precept of Judaism and Torah observant Jews adhere strictly to Halachah (Jewish rules of conduct). In the event of illness that required hospitalization, Orthodox Jews would be sent only to the Hebrew Hospital, the only health facility in the city where they could have a Kosher diet. The Federation organized a committee to oversee the city's kosher butcher shops; the issue of the integrity of the kosher butchers was of great concern to all Jews who kept kosher. The East Baltimore Jewish community grew so large that rabbis could no longer keep an eye on and control the dishonest practices of some butchers. For an issue so basic to Orthodoxy, the finagling with kosher food had to be monitored continuously, and the perpetrators of dishonest handling of food dealt with.

As written in the Talmud, strict Orthodox laws forbade a Jew from participating in the jailing of another. Where secular laws are affected, such as the kosher question, the Talmud encourages Jews to keep such disputes within their own community so that they are not aired in civil courts. Because of this, the Rabbinical Tribunal has the responsibility to form a beit din (House of Judgment) to settle disputes. The basic reasoning for not wanting disputed problems settled in public courts was that those courts were most likely administered by Christians. Orthodox Jews felt that Christians neither understood nor could fairly adjudicate a Jewish religious legal question. Talmudical laws based on religious theological persuasions had been prescribed only for Jews, so some Talmudical laws did, and some did not agree with secular civil law. Halacha prohibits suing in secular court before petitioning a beit din. In the summer of 1994, the Va'ad HaRabonim, the Rabbinical Council of Baltimore, organized a more formal community wide beit din with a paid three rabbi panel to judge cases by Halachah. Because of the increase in the presence of Orthodoxy in Baltimore, the old system of beit din could not handle the case load; and even now in 1996, there are over thirty cases being adjudicated in the city. Baltimore's new beit din is a ground breaker in the United State; there is one in Toronto. There are many battei din in New York City but none are community wide. The new Baltimore beit din is open to all Jews, not only Orthodox.

In America, well versed in Judaism and intellectually qualified, spiritual lay leaders frequently acted as rabbis, an arrangement almost the same as it had been in Russia. There, the rabbi usually had no connection with a specific shul but considered himself to be the spiritual leader of a town or district. Congregations depended on the wisdom of a core of Russian Jews who maintained a strong tie to their orthodoxy by spending their lives in the study of the Talmud. Except during the hours of prayer, and almost exclusive of anything else in life, a group of ultra Orthodox gathered in the bet ha-midrash, the house of study within the synagogue considered to be more holy than the sanctuary. There they studied and discussed the Talmud, an occupation that consumed about sixteen hours each day. This left them little time to devote to the welfare of their sizable families. Dutiful and believing wives of these men supported their families by peddling or owning small retail stores.

In the early years in America, Orthodox Russian rabbis worked for little pay, some for no pay. They survived on the donations given to them for performing services at life celebrations: births, Bar Mitzvahs, marriages and deaths. At a later date when business men in the congregations began to take an interest in their synagogues, rabbis became employees of the shuls. It was customary for the larger cities of Eastern Europe to appoint Chief Rabbis.³ Research does not reveal that Baltimore ever had an official Chief Rabbi although Rabbi Avrum Nachman Schwartz, a founder of the Talmudical Academy acted as an unofficial one.

The Hazan (the cantor) was of utmost importance for Eastern European shuls so the better financed congregations considered it a good investment to import the best voices from Europe. When they did, the Yiddish Press heralded the arrival of important cantors.⁴ The cantor, usually the recipient of adoration and respect bestowed upon him by the congregants, at times precipitated a confrontation when he undermined the authority of the rabbi. Russian Jewish shuls opened early in the morning so that worshippers could attend morning services and then go to their work place. They usually closed late at night although at some shuls, the doors were never locked. Afternoon and evening services seldom attracted women who, when they attended, sat in segregated spaces in the sanctuary, a requisite in Orthodox synagogues. The capacity of Orthodox Jewish worshippers to combine disorder, prayer, and fervor during their services baffled those who were not used to witnessing this sort of service. The Hebrew prayers recited in Orthodox shuls were and still are recited in a sing-song chant. A trace of these intonations can be detected at times in the English speech of Jews during ordinary conversations.

1	Technically, though not all, had incorporated; they became congregations. They were:

Adath Yeshurin (Congregation of Jeshuron Israel),(Shadover Shul), founded 1888
Ahavas Achim (Love of Brethren), founded 1889
Aitz Chayim (Tree of Life), founded 1887 Anshe Emunah (People of Faith) (Tavriger Shul), founded 1887
Anshe Neisen (People of Neisen, Chernigov) Nusach Ari(Form of worship), founded 1890
Anshe Sphard (People of Sphard), founded 1887
Beth Israel (House of Israel) (Little Eden Street Shul), founded 1890
Bikur Cholim (Visiting the Sick) (Prushnitz Shul), founded 1865
B'Nai Israel (Sons of Israel) (Russiche Synagogue), founded 1873
B'Nai Jacob (Sons of Jacob), founded 1883
Mikro Kodesh (Holy Convocation) (Pokroyer Shul), founded 1886
Moses Montefiore Emunath Israel (Faith of Israel), founded 1888
Oheb Hasholom (Lover of Peace) (Hill Street Synagogue), founded 1869
Ohel Yakov (Lover of Jacob) (Bialystoker Shul), founded 1875
Rodfe Tzedek (Pursuers of Justice) (Hill Street Synagogue), founded 1890

Ten years later, twenty-eight Eastern European Jewish Orthodox minyans were founded, and all were located downtown, primarily in East Baltimore. Listed are some of the additional congregations founded between 1891 and 1901:

Agudas Achim (Association of Brethren) (Chernigov Shul), founded 1896
Anshe Wolyn (People of Wolyn), founded 1894
Beth Hamedrosh Hagodol (Great House of Study), founded 1899
Beth Jacob Anshe Kurland (House of Jacob) (People of Kurland), founded 1895
Mogen Abraham (Shield of Abraham) (Galician Synagogue), founded 1891
Ohr Knesseth Israel (Light of the Assembly of Israel), founded 1894
Shomrei Hadath (Guardians of the Religion), founded 1890s
Shomrei Mishmeres Hagodesh (Guardians of the Holy Service) (Volhynia Shul), founded 1892
Zichron Yaakov (A Memorial to Jacob), founded 1896

2	The Great Synagogue of Sofia was the largest Sephardic synagogue in Europe when it was completed in 1909. It may also have been the largest synagogue in Europe to survive Nazi terror and destruction. Bulgaria was an ally of Germany during World War II and though the anti-Semitic Nuremberg laws were enacted there, it is said that no Bulgarian Jew went to Nazi death camps.

3	The appointment of a Chief Rabbi is indeed a delicate maneuver. A rabbi in New York City, shortly after his arrival from Moscow, hung a sign outside a prayer room, CHIEF RABBI OF AMERICA. When asked who gave him that title, he replied, "The sign painter."

4	Several years ago, the Agudas Achim Anshe Sphard Congregation at 4239 Park Heights Avenue offered a Yom tov (holiday) special. They stretched a sign across the front of their shul; it read, "Twin Cantors for the High Holidays."

PART II-6

East Baltimore * Sweat shops * Public health and baths * Jewish Court of Arbitration * Street smarts * To become American * Parental attitudes and concerns * Americanized children

*B*eginning in the early 1880s, the arrival of Russian Jews into the living spaces vacated by German Jews changed the neighborhood and gave birth to the legendary Russian Jewish East Baltimore. The dwellings, a mixture of small and semi-grand single family row houses along Baltimore, Lombard and intersecting streets were modified to accommodate a multiple number of expanded and expanding Russian Jewish families. They crowded into living quarters, and by doing so, hastened the deterioration of an already marginal and fading city district. Within a very few years, in order to accommodate all of the Russian Jews who wanted to live in this sector of East Baltimore, a moderate urban sprawl spread into contiguous neighborhoods. Roughly, the increased boundaries became Jones Falls on the west, Eastern Avenue on the south, Patterson Park Avenue on the east, and Orleans Street on the north.

Most of the late nineteenth century residents of East Baltimore lived in multi-family dwellings, ninety percent of which were without indoor plumbing.[1] Open flame gas pipes near the ceiling lighted each room. During the cold winter months, heat for their entire living areas emanated from a single coal or wood fired cooking stove in the kitchen, the immigrants living room. In the summer, the intense heat permeated and stayed in the pores of the walls, and immigrants endured almost unbearable discomforts especially in the unventilated inside rooms. Seeking some relief from the summer heat, although temporary at best, families boarded open-sided trolleys and rode to the eastern ends of the car lines and back at a cost of 5 cents for each adult, free for children. Up to the early twentieth century, people kept perishable fresh foods in well-insulated wooden ice boxes serviced by horse drawn ice wagons that plied regular routes through the neighborhoods. Five cents bought a large piece of ice, split from a hundred pound block. Children flocked around the ice wagons whose drivers shouted loudly, "Fill-up your ice box for five cents." They scrambled for cold chips of ice to suck on, ice that had splintered when the ice man hatcheted the large chunks.

Children were also attracted to roof repairmen who brought trailers with fiery heating devices into the neighborhood. In these, they melted pieces of tar chopped from huge round blocks and poured the black semi-liquid into the cracks of leaking roofs; children picked up tar chips that splintered from larger pieces cut to be melted. Chewing tar substituted for chewing gum, and the rationale for its use was good for strengthening the jaws and whitening the teeth. In reality, chewing tar came close to causing major maxillary dysfunction and no noticeable whitening of the teeth.

Kitchens served the multi-purpose of cooking, eating, studying and family gathering. Almost without exception, immigrant women prepared and served meals on oil cloth covered wooden kitchen tables while father seated on a wooden rocker read his Yiddish paper. Slouched on the straight back kitchen chairs pulled up to the table, children did their homework. At night at times, the father of the house sat alone in the dark, smoking and staring straight ahead, his thoughts to himself. Some conjured what their life would be in America without the burden of a family; there were other fathers who transferred their dreams to reality by deserting, leaving a wife to head the household. For some families, this was worse for the wife than being a widow without insurance. When a father who bought insurance died, his widow would at least have some slight financial benefit.

Judaism is a matriarchy which can be personified best by the mother in her kitchen, the emotional crutch to whose bosom all turned for comfort. The kitchen was the family control center, and Russian Jewish immigrant mothers were the guiding and forceful influence for the entire family. Sensitive to their family needs, she set the family pace, its morality and its values. The kitchen, this haven for others, trapped mama in a cocoon of toil and anxiety which left her worn with fatigue, probably sexually drained, prematurely aged and physically shapeless. This was her life and there was no escape. In the kitchen the ubiquitous family boarder, a blessing in disguise for most immigrant families, ate his meals. After the family went to bed, the kitchen became his bedroom. He, never a she, and frequently either a relative of the family or someone from the same Russian shtetl, was welcome because his board payment supplemented the family's meager income. Boarders in Russian Jewish immigrant homes became an institution because so many men migrated to America without their families.

Living in close quarters offered little privacy, much bickering, and a lot of intimacy, all of which made life difficult for children anxious to become Americanized. If youngsters had a relationship with another person, they felt embarrassed when that friend met their mother who hardly spoke English and their father, half nodding in his chair, wearing slippers and suspenders half dropped off his shoulders. This ungracious demeanor of many homes was ill fitted for the comfort of young Russian Jewish girls who wanted to have relationships with male friends. Most refrained from inviting any one in; it was so awkward to do so, but why? Families were facsimiles of each other. Nevertheless it was not easy to whisper innermost and confidential thoughts and feelings, hopes and plans while sitting in a room that doubled for a living room and a bed room. Sometimes a few feet away and within earshot, two or three younger brothers, and or sisters, were bedded down, presumably and hopefully asleep; probably they were not. Large families resulted in tight quarters for sleeping little ones. Older children slept in beds in conventional bedrooms with other family children or with their mother, and in some situations in another room with their father.

The problems of East Baltimore were not the same for all; specifically not for the families of clothing contractors, whose living conditions were more difficult. In 1900, over 5,800 East Baltimore Russian Jewish residences housed "sweatshops," the blights on society created by the ruthless system of sewing and pressing garments called "sweating." Families living within these quarters existed with the continuous discomfort of the noise of sewing machines and the heat of pressing irons. In these overcrowded rooms where the immigrants worked, gas lamp lighting was poor. Keeping the windows closed during the cold winter months allowed the kitchen wood or coal burning stove to offer little heat as they consumed much oxygen; thus, the air in the unventilated rooms became stifling and fetid. In these conditions, a clothing contractor, usually the family head, his family and employees in the sweatshops worked the Task, an incredulous system used at the time in the manufacture of clothing. The Task was a piece work system in which three to five persons worked as a team. Workers were paid a weekly wage conditioned upon completion of a predetermined number of garments for the work period. If the team failed to complete the weekly Task, wages were reduced. Overwork, sleepless nights, and exhaustion exacted a severe toll as poor health became the workers' constant companion. Immigrant workers slept on unswept floors and pushed unfinished garments on the tables aside to clear a space for them to eat their meager meals.

Customarily, men and women alike expectorated on the floor while they sewed, and this spread the tuberculosis bacilli. Russian Jews feared this disease because they were especially susceptible to it. The tragedy was not only the wage earner's contraction of tuberculosis but the removal of that individual from the home which frequently led to the break up of that family. After recovery from the illness and discharge from hospital care, there remained an inability of many Russian Jewish immigrants to alter their way of life. The cycle of illness and recovery recurred.

Dangers are recumbent living in overcrowded conditions because of the difficulties of maintaining a moralistic home life. The unit of society is the family and the stress of overcrowding that tended to spread illness was in some cases a root cause for crime and vice. Considering all of the factors of life as it was, for the most part, Russian Jewish families remained extremely close, though frequently they could not keep their problems from spilling out into the streets where some children turned for guidance.

Seemingly strange, in spite of the unhealthy living conditions of the Russian Jews, their infant mortality rate was for years the lowest of any defined Baltimore city group. This was possibly due to their diet and the fact that almost all Russian Jewish mothers nourished their infants at the breast for long periods. Old country mid-wives delivered and attended to the new born infants; an immigrant family could afford a doctor for birthing and more than likely they would not have wanted one. Doctors were for real medical needs. In the days after the arrival of a new baby the nextdoorster (neighbor), frequently from the same Russian shtetl, cared for the mother and infant. The close relationships of immigrant Russian Jews with their neighbors assured help for each when needed. This camaraderie, created by their shared way of life, also lessened the hardships of their working life. Russian Jewish immigrants spoke the same language, worshipped in the same manner, more often than not in the same shul, and had identical problems.

Each East Baltimore dwelling was a microcosm of the area. Russian Jewish immigrants of the 1880s appeared unkempt. Not too often, mothers bathed their children in galvanized wash tubs in water heated on the kitchen stove after which they sent them off to bed. The Maryland Public Health Association advised the people that regular bathing was the most efficient means of guarding against infectious diseases and the spread of epidemics.

When the need arose, the privileged member of the family, the father, frequented one of Baltimore's public baths for a "drei cente budd" (five cent bath). For easy access to East Baltimoreans, the city located a bath at 131-133 S. High Street near the Shot Tower, another at Jackson Place, and a third on Eastern Avenue and Bond Streets. The High Street Bath was a gift to the people of Baltimore from the philanthropic Baltimorean, Henry Walters. It opened in 1900 and closed in 1950s and was the first public bath in the city and the first of three given by Mr. Walters. Inside, the bath attendant peered through a small window, and after the fee was paid, issued a small towel and a minuscule bar of soap, that allowed the bather five minutes in the showers. Men stood in line, waiting for the attendant to call out, "Next." When the bather entered the shower stall, the time was chalked on a small piece of slate affixed to the exterior of the stall door. If the day was not too busy, the attendant extended an extra two minutes to the bather, and at the end of this largesse, he knocked on the shower door. The concrete floors of the baths were kept clean, and there was a distinct moist antiseptic odor about the baths, probably due to a liberal use of chlorine.

Due to their exalted position as titular head of the house, men who could afford to, indulged themselves; no public baths for them. Justifiably or not, they spent Sunday mornings at Maggid's Turkish Bath which was located on the northwest corner of Lombard and Central Avenue. Bathing at Maggid's lasted well over an hour as bathers, draped in a towel, passed through a series steam rooms of increasing temperatures. They sat on tiers of wooden benches, pausing long enough in each room for the steam to open their pores. Then, given a brisk rubdown, they took a cold shower. In accordance with Orthodox religious teachings, before attending either bath, men cut their finger nails since they had been taught through the years that evil spirits lurked under the dirt in the nails. In later years, men boarded a street car that took them uptown to the Biltmore Hotel and Turkish Baths on Paca and Fayette Streets, a hotel in the garment manufacturing area that catered to business men and commercial travelers. The women were not completely left out; after all, they had the mikvah to go to, probably not the most pleasant of ventures. One day a week, Turkish Baths confined their facilities to women and their young children. The Women's Turkish Bath Club met every Monday at the Biltmore.

Immigrant Russian Jews, not too venturesome in this new and strange country, stayed within the streets on which they lived. They accepted their plight which was not all that bad compared to life in Russia. Except for an assortment of juvenile offenders, immigrants generally abided by the laws and caused little civil disturbance. Though Orthodox Russian Jews used wines freely for ceremonial purposes, and almost any occasion called for a shot of shlivovitz; the evil of excessive drink never became their style; no drunks staggered through the neighborhoods of Orthodox Russian Jews. Their respect for the law was also tempered by over 700 different grounds for deportation including being found shicker (drunk) within five years after entering the United States

The community contained dance halls, pool rooms and run down hotels, along with three bawdy houses that scarcely raised a communal eyebrow on Lombard Street, East Street, and Watson Street. Even after the community aged, hard criminal activity was rare for Jews; they seldom murdered, they never kidnapped; and they were not incestuous. Jewish legal problems generally involved contracts, sales of merchandise, personal injury, and bankruptcy. Divorce, almost unheard of in Russian Jewish families in East Baltimore, was not considered an acceptable way to solve marital problems. Litigation, large or small, petty, business and domestic issues were usually arbitrated in the Jewish Court of Arbitration as prescribed by Talmudical Law. The court was founded in 1912 by German Jews for Russian Jews who spoke such poor English it was difficult for them to appear in the public courts. Litigants paid a fifty cent docket fee which allowed them to argue their case in Yiddish. In its first two and a half years, the court handled 351 hearings and only 35 litigants refused to abide by the court's decision. The adherence to both Talmudical and civil law kept many Jews from appearing in the city courts and in the public eye, so the forum settled differences quickly and for little expense. On occasions, greenhorns, newly arrived immigrants unfamiliar with the ways of America, ran afoul of little known city ordinances. With neither knowledge of nor any intent to break the laws, they were nevertheless arrested for non-obeyance and transported to the district police station. There, ward politicians helped to straighten out their indiscretions, and in doing so, befriended them and counted them as loyal voters for life.

Low wage, hard working immigrant parents did not know how to provide outlets for the energy of their children since there were few facilities available for them after school let out for the day. Six, seven, and eight year old children roamed the streets, and by the time they were ten, many sold newspapers on East Baltimore streets. Young Jewish girls had games of their own, and the separation of boys and girls in the public schools carried through to their street play. Girls played hop-scotch and jumped rope, and few had dolls to play with because they were much too expensive. They practiced for motherhood with the real thing; little brothers and sisters.

Children were aware that their lives were hard, but they didn't feel deprived for they hardly had a glimpse of how uptown Jewish children lived. Had there been other public parks and playgrounds available, except for those living near Patterson Park, East Baltimore Jewish boys may have participated in more quasi-organized sports. In later years, Jewish boys by the hundreds joined the city sponsored Public Athletic League (P.A.L.) and participated in sports programs at the Jewish Educational Alliance (J.E.A.). As in most all neighborhoods, children played in the streets, knocked balls through windows, and performed pranks while keeping an eye peeled for the local beat cops who were anxious to keep caps on petty street violations. Possibly a lack of understanding of the Russian Jewish immigrant culture prompted the Baltimore City Police Department to especially train officers to recognize juvenile antics that they thought would eventually lead to serious criminal activity.

UNCOMMON THREADS

Children of immigrants found a wonderful new world in the free public schools. For the first time in centuries, they were allowed to study in the schools of the nation in which they lived. Not only were they free to attend school, but also the law demanded that they do. Educational facilities were well used as hundreds of parents attended classes in these same public schools at night. After weekday school and on Sundays, immigrant children attended the traditional religious schools usually conducted in the synagogue in which they prayed. These schools were often dirty and the level of teaching frequently poor. Teachers had little patience for slow learners who more than likely received the crack of a ruler across their knuckles instead of an explanation of the subject. Talmud Torahs, supported by German Jewish philanthropy, had better quarters and better teaching. Immigrant children tried their best to play hooky from the religious schools after sitting so many hours in the secular schools. The religious schools kept them from releasing their pent-up energy in the freedom of the streets.

Within the congestion of cities such as Baltimore, street environment frequently outweighed home environment. Almost all children of Russian Jewish immigrants acquired "street smarts," and in turn, some became ill-mannered and spoke a vulgar and profane English. Unfortunately but understandably, some regarded their immigrant parents with disdain and refused to accept the environment that kept their parents' heads bent to the sewing machines and pressing irons. As the gulf widened between the generations, the young tended to reject everything their parents did and stood for. Many gave up everything Jewish except ethnic food, even Anglicizing their Jewish names. For these the family lost its authority, the traditional morality of Judaism was weakened, and the synagogue was no longer an influence. Immigrant children walked a fine line between two opposing cultures. On one side were their parents and centuries of ethnic tradition; on the other, America, new friends and ways and public school teachers, many of whom frowned on foreign ways.

While immigrant parents rejoiced to see their children studying in the great public school system, it was the secular education that was partially responsible for forming a barrier between the generations. The older people who had come to Baltimore as adults were the products of the ghettos, and to their children they remained Greenhorns. For the most part, parents looked different, spoke differently, and thought differently from the well-established German Jewish uptowners. Immigrants preferred to speak Yiddish in their homes and in the workplace, as English was hard for them, and they had difficulty making themselves understood. As an example, an immigrant whose spoken language was Yiddish would say in English that he was a "codder by men's clodding," meaning a cutter of men's clothing. Their children became their English interpreters to the outside world.

Frequently, the children became the family's principal breadwinner, and in order to earn good money, they found jobs that required them to have the appearance of an American. If they had not already done so previously, almost all young men shaved; they no longer wore earlocks that looked very much out of place in the Baltimore mercantile world. While most did not reject Judaism, at the same time, many sons of Jewish immigrants took further steps toward assimilation through dress and acquired mannerisms. Glad as they were to see the fine appearance of their sons, older Jews suppressed their true feelings when they saw their shaved faces when they sat at the kitchen table for breakfast. They had not affixed their phylacteries, said their morning prayers, washed their hands before eating, or recited the blessings after eating. On the Sabbath, parents had to deal with a mixture of emotions, when Orthodox Jews witnessed the departure of their children to their daily occupation.

Because of their importance to the existence of the family, many young boys assumed the role of linchpin or go-between that allowed the family to at least function within the community. Not through lack of respect for their parents, youngsters set the family rules because they spoke English and were able to adjust to living in America. Obviously, this tended to sap parental authority at the time when the parents should have been the strong familial force. Intensely attached to their parents, their children suffered deep feelings of guilt. Every day situations became constant battle grounds within themselves because of their need to become Americans and still remain Jewish. Few East Baltimore boys had role models outside of their neighborhoods so they defined their own lives; Jewish girls faced the problem of whether there could be any definition whatsoever of theirs. While their parents remained foreigners in their thinking, social advances became important to their children in their pursuit of Americanism.

Russian Jewish immigrant parents seldom expressed outward affection for each other, which probably stemmed from their arranged marriages. Immigrants had so many personal problems, they psychologically blocked out displays of affection towards their children as an expression of love for them. On another level of family relationship, young Russian Jewish immigrant children seldom sat with their parents to listen to tales of their former lives and experiences in Eastern Europe; in turn, parents found it difficult to convey their innermost thoughts and emotions to their children. The immigrant life in America was difficult for both parents and children, although the emotional stress for the parents seemed to be far greater. Words to a Jewish folk song say: "When a father helps his son, both smile; when a son must help his father, both cry."

At the end of World War I, America experienced the throes of change resulting from a culmination of fifty years of intense industrialization. Regardless of the mass arrival of immigrants of all faiths from many countries, the United States continued to refine its own culture, oriented towards the Christianity. In the 1920s, daily newspapers, magazines, movies that cost five cents, and radios in the homes taught the children of Jewish immigrants to walk, talk, and dress like Christian Americans. The young people, excited by the stories they read in books of the great American heroes, of the pioneers and of the opening of the West opted to be more American than the Americans and as different from their parents as possible. They sipped coffee from china cups rather than the Russian customary holding a cube of sugar under the upper lip or on the tongue to sweeten the steaming tea as they sipped it from a glass. Sophisticated advances included a multitude of mannerisms such as chewing gum, holding a cigarette between two fingers, and properly applying lipstick for the girls

Partly due to the fast life of America in the twenties, parts of their past were irretrievably lost to the children of Russian Jewish immigrants.

---

1   *Baltimore had no sanitary sewage system until 1908.*

PART II-7

Non-heavenly marriages * Orthodoxy and the Sabbath

*T*hough many Eastern European immigrant Jews chose not to affiliate with a Baltimore synagogue, they could not shed their ancient theological heritage passed down from the time of Moses. The influence and learnings of Judaism in one's life are not easily discarded because the strength of Jewish ritual in the family home combined with that of the services in the synagogue is a forceful domination of Jewish being.

Praying in the home is essential for Orthodox Jews beginning with daily prayers quite early in the morning. Except for the Sabbath and holidays, Jewish males over the age of thirteen lay tefillin. Tefillin, a reminder that the Torah must be studied every day, is a Greek word that applies to the use of phylacteries, two small square leather boxes containing scriptural passages traditionally placed on the left arm and forehead for the morning prayers.

To relate to the family life of Orthodox Russian Jewish immigrants, it is important to keep in mind that marriages made in the shtetls of Russia, and for some in late nineteenth century America, were not marriages made in Heaven. Rather, they were the products of the Schadchen, the match maker, the professional marriage broker, an important member of immigrant Russian Jewish society. It was common for a schadchen to enter preliminary negotiations with the parents of the boy and girl to establish the ground rules for a prospective union. The customary rate for matchmaking was 5% of the bride's dowry plus a modest flat fee. The rate was actually negotiable and was never enough to make the schadchen a rich man. Unless the clients were physically attractive, matchmakers did not use photos even though a girl of eighteen would have wanted to see what her man looked like. If the unmarried daughter reached the age of 25, she was concerned what a prospective husband did for a living; if she were 30, she wanted to know if there would be a prospective husband.

Non-affairs of the heart frequently created unhappy unions. If the relationship could be tolerated, husbands and wives remained together because it was simply so ordained; however, for extremely Orthodox Jews and otherwise, arranged or not, there are a myriad of religious customs and Talmudic restrictions and directions. Among them is the Ketubbah, the ancient Jewish marriage contract usually written on a single page and signed by the groom before the wedding. This document insures the traditional rights for the protection of the woman in marriage and the stated obligation of the husband.

Extremely Orthodox marriages parent many children since there is no provision in Talmudic Law for the practice of birth control.[1] Quite the contrary, and not a concept of romanticism, married men and women are expected to engage in sexual intercourse only for the purpose of fulfilling God's commandment, "to be fruitful and multiply." In Russian Jewish immigrant families, the boarder was frequently targeted as a prospective husband and in some cases, he had been deliberately picked to be a prospective son-in-law. Supposedly, the boarder never thought of the marriageable girl in the family in terms of sex; however, if he asked the girl to go out with him two or three times, it meant only one thing, marriage. In almost all arranged marriages, there is no engagement period in which the prospective bride and groom got to know each other. Fortunately in America for the most part, it is understandable that many Russian Jewish immigrant parents, especially the mother, found happiness in seeing their children educated and almost always married to the choice of their hearts.

Like no other religion, Orthodox Judaism differs in the attention given to the technicalities of living that would not be considered so important in other religions. There is the issue of Yikhes, of great concern in Eastern Europe and in some areas of America. In a marriage, yikhes is the pedigree of the family and more than that, it is an honor inherited through family lines but one that must be continuously earned. Yikhes has nothing to do with wealth or personal achievement in the secular world but has a lot to do with various levels of learning in the religious world. The highest degree of yikhes is the scholar of the Talmud, followed by other scholars, teachers, and rabbis. In arranging a match, the shadchen is careful to make mention of the family pedigree to both principals searching for a marriage partner. The longer the list of scholars, teachers, and rabbis in a family, the larger the yikhes, and that is important to even a poor Jewish family who would rather their eshes chayil (good wife material) daughter marry a rabbi than a rich man. For their son, to marry the daughter of a rabbi would be very special.

In a deeply religious Orthodox marriage, practitioners do everything they can to hide the married female from being too physically attractive. Rabbinic teachings are that it is a sin for a Jewish woman to be seen by any man other than her husband. On their wedding day, pious Jewish women shave their heads. For the rest of their lives they wear a sheitel (wig) so that they are not attractive to men, and as a sign of modesty. According to the Talmud, women are considered such a potent source of attraction that a man must avert his eyes in order to protect the sexes from each other. Some Orthodox men will not speak directly to a woman and some of the pious, aware of the possible and constant danger, enter a room walking sideways. Women and girls are not supposed to appear in public with their arms or legs exposed, reflecting a slightly less sentiment than the one that led Victorian ladies to put skirts around the legs of their furniture.

On Friday morning, Orthodox Jewish women begin to prepare for the Sabbath, the day of rest. After cleaning the sleeping spaces, scrubbing the kitchen floor, washing the clothes, making lokshen (noodles) and chopping carp and pike for gefilte fish and baking the "cholla," (the special egg bread for the Sabbath), women turn to their personal care. Before each festival and after each menstrual period, they frequent the mikvah, the public ceremonial bath. As the men do before bathing in the public baths or private steam baths, an Orthodox Jewish woman cuts her nails. She then brushes her teeth, combs her hair, removes her clothes and washes her body. Under the eyes of a matron, she descends the stone steps into a large cistern of running water and completely immerses herself. The Sabbath is particularly meaningful to Orthodox Jews as on that day, the humblest man becomes a king in his household, and his wife a queen. The best meal of the week is prepared, and it is eaten with the best utensils from the best plates placed on the family's best linens. No longer widely practiced by others than the Orthodox, as the hour to begin the Sabbath neared, in the spirit of tzedakah (righteousness), Orthodox Jews put money in the pushke (usually the blue tin charity box of the Jewish National Fund) to contribute to building a homeland for the Jews. So it was always visible and not forgotten, the pushke frequently hung on a kitchen door leading to the basement.

On Sunday, the day most Jewish people are home, meshullach (money collectors for accredited Orthodox Eastern European Jewish institutions) wearing the traditional long caftan type coats and wide brimmed black hats appeared at residential front doors in Jewish neighborhoods. They collected money from pushkes and for the Jewish orphan children of Jerusalem. On the same day, shnorers (a type of beggar), appeared to collect funds for other special charitable interests, usually local in nature. Schnorers were always careful to make sure that they solicited contributions from Jewish families; after their knock on the door was answered, they always asked, Do Jews live here? Since the ancient prophets Isaiah and Ezekiel, Jews have been taught that charity is an indispensable requirement for a life of faith. Even those who themselves depend on charity are obliged to give to help those less fortunate. In doing this, they observe Tzorchei Tzibur, (responding to the needs of the community). Acts of unselfish giving instilled within Orthodox Eastern European Jews a profound sense of their Jewish identity. Some former Orthodox Jews who had become Reform retained a guilt for doing so, so they tried to assuage some of their guilt by giving liberally to schnorers.

Jewish holidays and the Sabbath begin at sundown because the world began in darkness. The Bible in both Exodus and Deuteronomy refers to God's commandment to keep the Sabbath. As written in the Talmud, there are two acts required by Jewish women. One is baking the cholla and the other is bringing in the Sabbath, so eighteen minutes before sunset, the family gathers. Eighteen is a meaningful number for Jews; it means life. Showing respect for God, the housewife covers her head, usually with a shawl, and in conformity with Jewish law kindles at least two candles. Each candle honors the opposites of life; man and wife, light and dark, good and bad, full and empty. Once they are lit, Sabbath has begun and fires of any kind may no longer be kindled for the next twenty-four hours during which the family obeys religious restrictions as ordained by the Torah and refined in the Talmud.

After lighting the candles, the housewife places her hands over her eyes as a symbolic gesture, actually a pretense as though she has not actually lighted the candles; this allows her to continue with praising God for his Commandment of rest and peace and she asks His blessing upon the house. The father of the house, facing towards Jerusalem, raises a cup of wine and recites the traditional kiddush, the ancient prayer that sanctifies the Sabbath. He praises God for creating the fruit of the vine, sips the wine and passes it to the others. In the author's family the tradition is that the oldest person present sips the wine first, followed by the others of descending ages. The father praises God for bringing forth bread from the earth, then breaks off and passes a piece of the ceremonial cholla bread to each one present. Over bowed heads, he asks God's blessing for his children. The woman of the house speaks the blessing, and as she does, she moves her arms three times in a circular gathering motion over the candles which symbolizes bringing the holiness of the Sabbath unto herself and in turn spreading it to the family.

Rituals for bringing in the Sabbath and other Jewish ceremonies held within the home vary within families who inject their own personal customs into each service. Orthodox Jews conduct no business on the Sabbath. Family members occupy themselves in accordance with their own ideas; some rest, some read, and others engage in Shabbus shmues (small talk, opinions and such, not always accurate).[2] The Talmud outlines the dos and don'ts of the Sabbath and interestingly, there are many more dos than don'ts. It has been said, "It is not the Jew who has preserved the Sabbath, it is the Sabbath which has preserved the Jew." Orthodox Jews used the services of the Shabbus goy a non-Jew who of years past, raked the fire and shook the ashes from the grates of the kitchen stove or the house furnace. Shabbus goys turn on and extinguish lights in the homes in accordance with the Talmud.

---

1   *The Talmud has more to say about intercourse, actually going as far as dictating position. It is written that during intercourse the man must face down, looking at the earth from whence he came. The woman must face up to the place from which she was created, a man's rib.*

2   *Shmuos in Hebrew means things heard. Shmues in Yiddish means conversation. Somewhere between the old and the new World, Eastern European Jews adopted the unattractive sounding word shmooze that sounds like ooze that makes one think of an infected sore. Unfortunately, shmooze has been picked up and used widely by the press. German Jews continue to say shmuos.*

PART II-8

Urban peddlers * Garment Worker's Circle * European tailors * Labor organizations * Family businesses

*U*nlike the Germans Jews, few Russian Jewish immigrants ventured into the vocation of rural peddling. By the end of the nineteenth century peddling, probably one of the most humiliating and intensively difficult occupations, was no longer a viable way to earn a living. In the approximately fifty years between the beginning of the migrations of the German and the Russian Jews, the nation experienced a vast change in ways of distributing consumer goods. The 1870s was a decade of tremendous growth in the United States, and the Baltimore economy benefited from business expansion. The development of railroading made the trip to the cities easier for those living in rural areas so their dependency on the countryside peddler lessened and lessened. The Sears Roebuck catalogue, the beginning of Rural Free Delivery by the United States Post Office in 1903, and the parcel post system ten years later, contributed greatly to the demise of the rural peddler. This was not true for urban peddling that lingered in a small and quaint way up until the mid 1970s.[1]

Both the rural and the city peddler endured hardships. Unlike those who dealt with the weather and the arduous physical burdens of selling in the countryside, those in the city managed to conduct their businesses in spite of the almost continuous harassment from hoodlums on the streets. As the city peddler went from door to door, purchases were frequently made out of a feeling of pity. Possessing the character to stomach the insults, peddlers managed to survive. Some city peddlers followed a set route and sold large ticket items such as furniture and jewelry to be paid for on scheduled installments each time the peddler called. Transportation being what it was, buying from a peddler was convenient though expensive because there were considerable finance and built in charges. Peddlers maintained relationships with wholesalers and retailers who were their sources of merchandise supply. Though the city peddler gave birth to retail store installment selling, the purchaser paid fifty cents down and fifty cents a week; his role was never as essential in the distribution of merchandise as was that of the rural peddler of the nineteenth century. In later years, retail stores that sold on the installment plan employed collectors who sold selected promotional merchandise items at the time they stopped at a house to collect installment payments for previous purchases. If the customer had good credit, the concept was to keep that customer in debt by continuous buying and paying almost the same installment each week. The cost of an item was not unimportant; it only cost fifty cents or a dollar a week. Changes in the way Americans lived after World War II and the danger of being on the streets with large amounts of cash on one's person ended the era of the collector.

The last to cease peddling in the city were older women,[2] usually widows who spoke only Yiddish. They carried wicker baskets from door to door from which they offered various sundries for sale: needles, pins, threads, combs, matches, Chanukah candles and Yahrzeit candles in glass containers that could later be used as drinking glasses. Women peddlers carried a card for the prospective customer to read. It stated, "I'm from Russia, I didn't speak no English, please buy from me." It must be presumed that these women, forced to earn their keep in this manner, were poor, probably true for most of them.

From the day they landed in Baltimore, thousands of Russian Jewish immigrants became immersed in the needle trades, certainly more so than the German Jewish immigrants of the 1840s and 1850s. Russian Jews worked inordinately long hours in Baltimore garment factories, and many ate their meals while they worked in order to earn a few extra pennies. Legends of Russian Jewish immigrants in the needle trades moderately mirrored legends of immigrant workers in other trades.

Through the instigation of the Socialist self-help oriented New York Workmen's Circle, the Baltimore Workmen's Circle (Arbeiter Ring) branch No. 9 was formed. The majority of the Young Men's Progressive Club members joined the circle, and they consolidated the Club's large library with that of the Circle's. The joint library became the Baltimore Russian Jewish community's largest and best circulating library of Yiddish books and periodicals. By 1898, at least 900 labor reform-minded Russian Jews joined the Workmen's Circle Branch No. 9. Renamed the Progressive Labor Lyceum Association in 1931, the organization became the center for almost all Russian Jewish labor activities. The Association's East Baltimore Street building housed rooms for members' meetings, lectures, a synagogue chapel, and provided headquarters for striking labor unions. In addition they set up a soup kitchen for them during strikes. In the 1920s, the Circle conducted Baltimore's only Yiddish speaking secular school. Members of the Workmen's Circle were close knit in life and in death.[3]

In 1890, about one hundred Baltimore cloak makers carried membership cards in the United Garment Workers of America even though there was no Baltimore local in existence. In 1894, the International Ladies Garment Workers Union (ILGWU) was founded and Baltimore Local # 4 was organized within the year. At that time, United Garment Workers of America controlled union activities in the men's clothing manufacturing industry. The Baltimore market endured several notable strikes, most of which centered on the usual issues: wages, working conditions, hours, and the worker's rights. With the exception of one, discussion of these strikes is beyond the scope of this book.

A landmark issue and its related strike parted the Russian Jewish immigrant tailor from his katerinka, and so it became a vestige of the past and an antique of the future. Workers won the Machine Strike[4] of 1901. Prior to this, tailors working in a shop furnished their own sewing machine and accompanying stand. After the strike, the tailor no longer had to do this because manufacturers were required to own and maintain the sewing machines used in their factories. Until this time, the unions helped the workers in a small way, thus this important gain for workers in the garment industry sent a positive message to their members and the garment factory owners. For the first time, workers were convinced that there was a wide range of possible benefits to be made through unions organized under progressive labor leadership, which attracted strong new union endorsement.

The influence of the Russian Jewish members of the Amalgamated Clothing Workers of America, founded in 1914, also had a profound effect on men's clothing manufacturing. Mostly English, Irish and non-Jewish Germans controlled the leadership of the older unions that the Amalgamated replaced. These union leaders accepted the capitalist system of production as an inevitable evil in which workers were not destined to rise from the lowest rung of the economic ladder. Their mission went only as far as to improve the conditions in which members worked within the structure of the existing order. The new Amalgamated Clothing Workers of America union's leaders, mostly intellectuals born in Russia, included some who had been trained for leadership by the revolutionary organizations of Eastern Europe. Many immigrant workers embraced strong or pseudo-socialist tendencies born of their need to cling together in Russia, throughout their migration, and during their American experience. This dedication to a socialist philosophy ordained a refusal to accept the myth of the almost divine origin of Capitalism and rejected the existing property relations as a final decree of natural law. In plain words, They wanted a piece of the action.

Paradoxically, Russian Jewish women in labor organizations functioned with much less intensity. The women in labor unions believed that working all day and discussing labor problems in the evening limited their horizons. They broadened their interests and activities to include courses in reading literary works and holding picnics. The classic manifestation of the cultural interests of the ILGWU took place in 1938 when they produced the New York musical production *Pins and Needles.* The show played to sold out houses in Baltimore's Ford's Theater and in theaters throughout the nation. Members of the ILGWU wrote the script, the musical compositions, staged, costumed, directed, produced, and publicized the show. They performed all of the acting and singing roles.

Economic conditions in 1893 caused financial distress for most of Baltimore's German Jewish ladies' cloak manufacturers, and combined with labor problems, caused the liquidation of several factories. German Jews almost completely dominated this industry from its inception, and at this time chose not to take the risk of dissipating their hard earned wealth by reinvesting in their businesses. Prior to the turn of the century, rich women employed dressmakers to make their clothing, and some shopped in Europe. The German Jewish manufacturers had become merely merchants rather than innovators, lacking the motivation and imagination needed for the future of their businesses. Perhaps they had been making ladies' cloaks too long to recognize the changes wanted by the modern woman of the day. Working in their homes and in small shops, tailors of Galician origin introduced innovations that only their knowledge of tailoring could have produced. By the end of the 1800s, they were well positioned to enter ladies' wear manufacturing, and several of them did. The Russians were artisans who understood colors, textures, and fabrics. Having worked as tailors in Russia, they knew how a pleat should fall and how a skirt should hang. They knew where to place a gusset, a gore, or a

UNCOMMON THREADS

dart. From that time on, Russian Jews dominated the manufacturing of women's wear in Baltimore.[5]

Removing themselves from the proletariat, some Russian Jews joined others who began small tie, shirt, and men's clothing factories. Several Russian Jews were on their way to becoming well to-do. Literally hundreds of needle trades ventures started as partnerships; however, after a relatively short period, their principals very often changed. Many business associations formed by brothers, for example, dissolved due to family differences and pressure.[6] At times, the wife of an owner caused friction by letting it be known that, in her opinion, one partner (never her husband) did not contribute as much to the business as her husband yet was receiving compensation equal to her husband's. Some wives believed their husbands performed more important functions than their partner and should therefore be compensated accordingly. Pursuing these inequities to a logical solution led to dissolution of the partnership.

Becoming manufacturers was a very big step for Russian Jews. They were no longer completely isolated from the German Jews, and through mercantile lanes developed a closer relationship with each other. Recognition of the Russian Jews by Christian groups was not as easy as it had been for the German Jews fifty years before. What was important however, was that common threads were beginning to bring the German and Russian Jewish communities together.

---

1 *The author's grandfather, Bernhard Kahn wrote another letter which was addressed to his sister and brother-in-law who had remained in Germany. As mentioned in Part I - 9, he made his living as a peddler. The excerpts from this letter, written in October 1, 1889, 34 years after the one previously mentioned, are his socially revealing observations. Peddling out in the country had become a thing of the past for German Jews so we read first hand why Bernhard no longer peddled. Views on the Russian Jewish migration by a run-of-the-mill German Jew are valuable. A letter written over one hundred years ago is documentary evidence of the writer's feelings and a primary source for historians.*

"On August 15, I was 60 years old, am thick and fat, weigh 210 pounds, have not done much for three years. Before, I went out to the country with horse and wagon, but business got bad and rheumatism bothered me.
Jews were persecuted in Russia and then settle in America and spoil the land here; so that hardly one can make a living here, in Baltimore are 20,000.
The authorities make regulations for patents or licenses, peddling in a county costs $100; a horse and wagon costs $150.00. It is not a free country, the way you might think in Germany. Many who traveled to the wide West are coming back. Labour is paid badly and the land gets too full with human beings, the population is 69 million souls."

2 *One elderly woman continued to peddle a route that took her through the Madison Ave, Eutaw Place, Linden Avenue corridors. She was the mother of a prominent Jewish pediatrician, and well-taken care of by her son, but she could not stop peddling; this was her way of life until the 1940s.*

3	*Many of its members are buried in graves in the Jewish cemetery on German Hill Road on a plot of land adjacent to that used for the Hebrew Orthodox Free Burial Society.*

4	*Females, not always prone to strike, did at times remove their rings and other jewelry and offered them to the union leaders to sell or pawn to support a strike.*

5	*As America entered the 1920s, Baltimore German Jews owned the large and important Baltimore clothing factories. The national manufacturing of men's clothing during these years, became recognized as a major American industry that set standards for all manufactured products.*

6	*A recent study at Loyola University of Chicago focused on two hundred family businesses during a sixty-year period. It determined that while twenty-six survived as privately owned family businesses, only six continued to grow and prosper. The study indicated that the families that work together are destroyed, and that only thirty percent of family businesses survive their founders and continue into a second generation; others are sold, go bankrupt, or quietly close. Statistics grow dimmer with the passage of time as only half the companies that live through the transition to a second generations survive as family businesses. Ventures run by families faced challenges similar to those encountered by non-family owned businesses, though minor issues tended to become highly emotional in family firms because they involve two distinctly different but equally demanding organizations, the family and the business. There is, obviously, a profit motive in business, but that is not all. When power and prestige become involved, or when family members' personal ambitions come to the fore, tensions caused by familial differences all too often turned family businesses into battle grounds.*

A second and later study at Babson College in 1993 determined that family businesses account for half of the gross national product; half the nation's jobs are in family businesses. For the most part, family businesses are not designed to last and preserve a family's wealth as few owners have laid any ground-work for transferring their businesses to the next generation. Only three in ten family businesses survive into the next generation and only one in ten into the third generation. Though outside advisors can plan the continuance of a business, squabbles caused by family dynamics frequently derail the process.

PART II-9

Cultural breeches * Summer camps * Holding the line

*B*y the turn of the century, German Jews involved in helping immigrants hoped that the Russian Jews would ease up on their separatism and turn to the them for guidance. They felt sure that if they did, they would use German Jewish institutions to broaden their Jewish scholarship and adapt to a more enlightened concept of Jewish ideals and a more inclusive interest in Jewish world issues. This attempt on the part of German Jews was to entwine the threads of both groups so that there could be an Israel in America. Unfortunately, the Russian Jews at this time had not reached a degree of Americanization and assimilation that would allow them to accept such a concept. The breach between the two cultures continued and manifested itself most noticeably in the garment trades, an unlikely arena for agreement, as owner and union member workers functioned on different thought waves. The established uptown German Jews and the equally entrenched Russian Jews of East Baltimore stood their ground. Other than a lack of understanding of the cultural ways of each that prompted the dislikes, multitudes of other problems and differences existed well into the twentieth century.[1] Causes for mutual resentment were many, such as instances when the recipients of charity were employees of those who contributed to the charity.

Russian Jewish families, whether they adhered strictly to Orthodox religious precepts or not, were extremely prolific. Family needs for food, clothing and shelter increased in proportion to the size of the individual family, putting a strain on the resources of charitable organizations. However, the spirit and verve of Russian Jews themselves became an offsetting factor that lessened the charitable load. Large numbers of immigrants and first generation Americans left their charitable dependency behind when they moved into a higher economic society. An example aside from a single family situation occurred when a few Russian Jews intervened when a policeman was seen leading a group of homeless Jewish children to a public city institution. They persuaded the policeman to turn his charges over to them, and they temporarily sheltered them in private homes. Organized by Russian Jews in 1900, the Hebrew Children's Sheltering and Protective Association purchased a house for children, and for many years, funds raised by door to door solicitation supported the association.

Russian Jews founded the Baltimore Sheltering Home in 1909, and in 1914 the Hebrew Home for Incurables and the Jewish Children's Bureau. In 1910, a Polish group of Ostrolanker Landsleit (townsmen from Ostrow, Poland), founded the Baltimore Young Men's Relief Association. The Hebrew Immigrant Aid Society, organized in 1914 by the United Hebrew Charities, played a singular important role in a broad range of aid to Russian Jewish immigrants. Several Russian Jewish immigrant women's groups became active with the founding of the Independent Ladies' Farein of Baltimore in 1920, and in 1927 the Pioneer Women's Organization and the Hebrew Noble Ladies were founded. In 1931, the Lutzker Social Relief Society dealt with the issues of Russian Jews who wanted to start businesses or to get married. A women's group, aided by their husbands, founded the Jewish Convalescent Society and Home in 1936. German Jews continued tirelessly to help the Russian Jews, with a special emphasis on child care.

About 1920, the German Jewish Daughters in Israel established a recreational camp in the Catoctin Mountains, far from Baltimore. The camp offered a retreat and brief respite for the many young Russian Jewish females who worked in the city's garment shops, some of whom had lost their parents. Many supported themselves and lived alone in rented rooms; prisoners of the garment industry. They worked constantly under conditions that were too embarrassing to describe, and they were exhausted and vulnerable. They paid for the thread and needles they used. If the shop foreman forgot to charge them for several days, they knew what came next; a suggestion of how to repay the foreman's act of kindness. Unless fortunate enough to get married, they remained Baltimore's lost souls of the immigrant world. In 1922, Aaron and Lillie Straus, a wealthy and childless German Jewish couple acquired the camp and renamed it Camp Louise. Shortly thereafter, in 1924 at a nearby site, the couple established Camp Airy for boys.

Though the number of aid organizations appear to have been adequate, Baltimore lagged behind most American cities in the amount of money collected by charities for the Jewish poor. To supplement the charities, on Fridays and the days before the holidays, male and female couples begged from door to door. Identified by red and white handkerchiefs carried in their hands, they collected money for individual poor families.

In families where circumstances forced the mother to be the wage earner, long hours of work in a factory made it difficult for her to control her children. Situations of this sort exemplified the need for help, and because of the sheer numbers of Russian Jews, their needs were greater and more diversified than those of the earlier German Jews. Due to deprivations in Russia, far greater than in early to mid nineteenth century Germany, Russian Jews landed in Baltimore poorer than the German Jewish immigrants of thirty to fifty years before, and with health problems infinitely more serious. Paternalistic German Jewish organizations made sincere efforts to preserve the Russian Jewish family structure that, at times, tested the religious traditions and threatened the health and education of the Russian Jews. Many reacted adversely to German Jewish help because their offer worked against their anxiety to establish their own self esteem.

At a time when the Russian Jewish United Hebrew Charities continued to raise money by peddling tickets for lotteries and by conducting bazaars, the German Jewish Federated Charities developed sound practices through which they efficiently solicited, collected, and disbursed funds.

1 *Fortunately for the Baltimore community, though relationships produced tensions, no open hostility existed as it did between similar New York East siders, the distinctive mind set and picture for most Americans of the Russian Jewish immigrants.*

PART II-10

Maskilim * Russian Jewish night school * Hebrew schools * Public schools * Jewish Board of Education * Talmudical Academy * Baltimore Hebrew College * The Yiddish Press

*M*embers of the Russian Jewish Maskilim, proponents of the Haskalah, the scholarly and enlightened, founded the Hebrew Literary Society in Baltimore in the late 1880s. For several years in Russia, the small and non-influential Maskilim circle opposed extreme Orthodoxy and the intense exclusive study of the Talmud. At the Society's meetings, Hebrew intellectual discussions ran the gamut of Jewish philosophers and Jewish literature from medieval ages to modern times. The Maskilim advocated changes within the prevailing way of life. They looked down on the Yiddish language as an illegitimate slang, the language of radicals, and they preached that it be replaced with the classical Hebrew of the Bible. Some of the Maskilim went as far as suggesting that those Jews who continued to speak Yiddish in America should be returned to Russia; English was the language of America. Many enlightened Jews, because of these teachings and because of the Society's commitment to the Zionist movement, became Zionist activists.

Religion and education go hand-in-hand in significance to Jews, German and Russian alike. The presence of so many uneducated Jews, many of whom were unable to speak the language of their native Russia, presented a challenge for the 1880s. Though neither scholarly nor secularity educated, most Russian Jewish immigrants had an appreciation and respect for learning even though Russians of the early migration were meager achievers. It was not until the early 1900s that the first large numbers of Yiddish intellectuals arrived in America, and they kept coming until the surge of Russian Jewish immigration ended.

Russian Jews lived in a culture of deep religious passion. By the 1890s, scholars who succumbed to secular temptations still bore a heavy rabbinical and theological stamp. After the turn of the century, some Yiddish scholars devoted themselves to secular themes which met with hostility from rabbis. They suffered ridicule, not only from within the American Jewish world but often from other cultures. In contrast by the turn of the century, German Jews had worked out a conciliation between their Judaism and styles of American thought. Neither group was sure that a Jewish scholar, with a beard and earlocks, and son of a tailor, could have anything of value to say about the great philosophers of history. Many male immigrants in Baltimore were well-versed in the teachings of the Talmud and in Yiddish literature, and these learnings acquired in their shtetls, helped to sustain them in America.

Henrietta Szold, raised as a non-Zionist daughter of the Oheb Shalom Reform Congregation's Rabbi Benjamin Szold, became a most respected world renown Zionist and educator a founder of Hadassah in 1912. In November 1889, the Russian Jewish Hebrew Literary Society joined Henrietta in establishing the Russian Jewish Night School for immigrants in a single room on N. Gay Street where Miss Szold acted as the school superintendent until 1893. From the day it opened with thirty pupils, the Russian

Jewish Night School was an early cooperative where Germans and Russians worked in unison. Before the first season ended in April of 1890, one-hundred fifty Russian Jews were enrolled. In its second year, through the generosity of the Baron De Hirsch Fund, the Russian Jewish Night School occupied an entire house on Front Street. Its popularity was such that five-hundred pupils attended classes through the 1890-1891 school year; in the school year of 1891-1892, seven-hundred eager to learn paid thirty cents a month dues. The school moved to its final location at 1208 E. Baltimore Street. Except for male instructors in bookkeeping, women administered and taught in the Russian Jewish Night School. Those who attended learned to read and write English; they studied geography and American history in preparation for the goal of almost every immigrant, American citizenship. Eager as they were, Russian Jews had to overcome many learning blocks, an example being the confusion resulting from the twelve days difference between the Julian and Gregorian calendars. The Russian Night School in Baltimore, the first institution of its kind in America, became the national model for similar schools in other cities. It, along with the Jewish Educational Alliance founded at a later date also by German Jews to benefit Russian Jews, continued for years as the two most meaningful institutional contributors to the cultural Americanization of Baltimore Russian Jewish immigrants.

With concern for their children's education, Russian immigrant Orthodox Jews set a pattern of three basic levels of learning with some differences from those traditionally used in Eastern Europe. In Russia, classes at the cheder, an elementary school for very young children, some only three years of age, were conducted by the melamed (teacher) who received very nominal pay for his teaching. Courses were basic, and religion per se and Jewish history were rarely taught on this level. Study of the Torah and the Talmud was introduced in the Talmud Torah, the next higher school of education, usually a public institution. The third level, the Yeshiva, the highest institution of learning below the college level, followed a curriculum of courses that emphasized the Talmud and rabbinic literature. These studies were usually conducted under the direct guidance of a Ros Yeshiva, the head of the school.

In Baltimore, Jewish children started their formal religious education at an older age than old world Russian counterparts. Parents waited until the boys reached five or six years of age before sending them to the neighborhood cheder. There, different from the Russian schools, they began to learn about the Torah and were introduced to the Talmud. Russian Jews who taught in the American cheders were almost always of the immigrant generation and lacked understanding of American born Russian Jewish children, so they had difficulties keeping up with their students' pranks and subtleties. Scholarly studies of the Talmud began in the equivalent of the fifth grade, before boys reached the age of thirteen, when they became Bar Mitzvah in the synagogue. In the early twentieth century, boys who attended the schools of the colorful Hasidic orders studied and listened to the wondrous tales told by Hasidic rabbis who lived in the Eastern European shtetls of their fathers. The third level of education and the high school equivalent was the Yeshiva where non-secular teaching concentrated on advanced Jewish studies of the Talmud and rabbinic literature.

The Hebrew Society for the Education of the Poor and Orphan Children not only paid the students' tuition to the schools when needed, but the organization also supplied clothes for the students. Non-secular Hebrew schools became a function of individual shuls. Russian Jewish immigrants who were from the same shtetls and who worshipped together in the same synagogue sent their children to be educated in the schools conducted by their individual community synagogue. Parents who wanted their children educated within the tenet of each group had to become members of the synagogue of that group. Ukrainians differed from Litvaks and Romanians from Galitzianers; some had lived in large cities; some had lived in small shtetls. There were Hasidim and Mithnagdim (opposers of Hasidism), both of whom opposed the Maskilim.

In 1908, William Rosenau a prominent German Reform rabbi and Tanchum Silberman an Orthodox community leader joined in an effort to replace Yiddish with English in the Russian Jewish religious schools. Many Russian Jewish Orthodox parents objected and then rejected such a change. They were convinced that if this should happen, it would move the Russian Jews too close to assimilation with the Christian community.

Many of the schools supported themselves entirely by their tuition charges, and because of this, they had little money available for teachers' pay. Thus, most of the East Baltimore Russian Jewish religious schools were conducted by unqualified persons who, in addition to being ill equipped to teach, were ill equipped to do much else. Frequently, order was kept by an inch wide leather bookstrap with a knot on the end; at times some of these teachers didn't hesitate to use it. For an extra stipend, and for all it was worth, some of these teachers made house calls where they taught on a one-on-one basis.

Established in 1889, the Hebrew Free School, better known as the Baltimore Talmud Torah Society, was founded as the first large Hebrew School in the city. Located on High Street, the school drew most of its students from needy families. If warranted, tuition was waved and the school supplied the clothing needed to attend. Because most of the school's faculty considered speaking Yiddish almost as sacred as speaking Hebrew, for many years, Yiddish was the vernacular of the Russian Jews attending the Talmud Torah Society. Students at the school read a lot, and they benefited from a memorial library of over 1,000 Hebrew and English volumes in the school's building.

When the century turned, the remarkable Russian Jewish intellect flourished. As part of their education, immigrants visited Baltimore museums and viewed American curiosities never seen in the Pale of Settlement. No single constituency had a farther reaching influence than the public schools, and the Russian Jewish immigrants took full advantage of everything these schools offered. Public school teachers tried to ignore the tight little world in which the young children of Russian Jewish immigrants lived, as they taught the subject, America. In so doing, a striking feature of the scope of free public school learning brought about differences in the sociological mind-set of immigrant parents and their children. Public schools meant a great deal more to Russian Jewish women because in Eastern Europe, only males had the opportunity to go to school. American laws required that girls also attend school for the same number of years as boys. This factor prompted girls to visualize a potential to their lives more diverse than sitting all day facing a sewing machine in a garment factory.

In 1914, the Baltimore Jewish community recognized the need for a Jewish Board of Education; at its initial meeting, the board determined that approximately 2,000 Jewish children in Baltimore were not receiving a Jewish education. Conceptually, the board that was formed to supervise the Jewish schools was granted little authority to do so. They stumbled along with efforts to get rabbis and Jewish leaders together, and in doing so, felt certain they would make sure that all Baltimore Jewish children could have a proper Jewish education. The board helped to furnish classrooms, to train teachers in the curricula, and to select text books to support their program. They accomplished only a measure of success with the introduction of the curricula they designed to adapt to the needs and interests of a diverse group of pupils. A small 1921 census in a typical East Baltimore neighborhood revealed that the percentage of non-synagogue going Jews was quite high, and at least sixty percent of the children were growing up without a Jewish education.

Because of the high cost of education, at times parents had to make a choice between sending their sons to college as opposed to being able to afford to keep a daughter in high school. If parents favored the daughter remaining in school, it is likely she would become part of those young high schoolgirl graduates who found jobs as typists in offices. They worked in comfortable bright surroundings, heard and spoke English and were addressed as Miss. After work, they returned home to not so courtly or responsive parents and a gaggle of little brothers and sisters. Although typists made less money than factory workers, girls who worked in the refined settings of retail stores made less than typists. Both of the latter jobs were sought because they, had more yikhes (status).

Large numbers of Russian Jewish immigrant parents thought themselves to be too old, too set in their ways, and too depressed by their economic situations to even learn to speak English. Others worked extremely hard to learn about America and its language in order to live the fulfillment of their dreams. Though most immigrant men felt sure they did the right thing by coming to America, many of the women of these families were not so sure. They nevertheless seized the opportunities for free education for their children, and this they did with determination. As the years passed and some immigrants became financially able, in addition to their own children, many who could helped to send sons of their poorer relatives to college.

The propensity for immigrants and American born Russian Jews to learn helped to advance them in the city's secular world. The Jewish thirst for learning in turn created teachers, and this contribution to society played an important role then and now; the educated became the educators of Americans. Russian Jewish thought had great respect for intellectuals, as they did for medical doctors and lawyers.

While the Talmud Torah Society resisted the speaking of English, it did not forbid it. Some of the very religious faculty were opposed to this, and they could not be reconciled to such a liberal language expression. They withdrew from the Society in 1917 and were part of a group of fervently Orthodox rabbis who founded the Hebrew Talmudical Seminary and Parochial School, the Yeshivath Torah'Emunah Hebrew Parochial School of Baltimore City. The Seminary and Parochial School instituted high academic standards in a combination of secular and Hebrew education; it was the first school outside of New York to undertake such a venture. Beginning with an enrollment of six first grade boys in a rented room, a class was added each year, and in 1923, seven students graduated from the seventh grade. In that same year a merger was accomplished with the year old Talmudical Seminary of Baltimore, and the school became known as the Yeshivath Torah'Emunah Hebrew Parochial School of Baltimore City and Talmudical Seminary of Baltimore. With the merger, Yeshivath began classes for afternoon Talmudic studies. In 1934, the trustees changed the name to the Yeshivath Chofetz Chaim and Parochial School. Early in 1937, the charter was amended and the official English name became Talmudical Academy of Baltimore, Incorporated. The Talmudical Academy's secular studies program prepared students for the most demanding university requirements. In 1944, the academy added the Yeshiva High School and graduated ten students in 1947.

Named after a German born Jewish business man, the Isaac Davidson Hebrew School opened on Shirley Avenue in 1925; it operated for only 42 years. During these years it answered a need for a Hebrew school in the Northwest Baltimore area that differed from the Talmudical Academy. As the Talmudical Academy did not, the Isaac Davidson Hebrew School combined other activities with Hebrew studies. Many of its graduates entered into academic and professional life and the school developed good business people.

The Baltimore Hebrew College, founded in 1902, existed for a short period, disbanded, and in 1919 was re-established at 1038 Eutaw Street as the Baltimore Hebrew College and Teacher's Training School. Needing larger quarters, the school moved to 2102 Eutaw Pace until it followed the crowd to upper Park Heights Avenue in October 1958. The college trained teachers for independent studies of Jewish life. After its re-birth, the Baltimore Hebrew College grew academically; slowly at first, and then gathered momentum in recent years. In the early 1970s, through the joint efforts of its Board of Trustees, administrators, teaching staff, and students, the school moved towards accreditation as an under graduate and graduate school. In 1987, the Baltimore Hebrew College was renamed the Baltimore Hebrew University when it was designated as such through the accreditation of the Maryland State Board of Higher Education and the Middle States Association of Colleges and Schools.

Had the average man-on-the-street Russian Jewish immigrant been afforded the advantage of a formal education he, too, may have earned an advanced degree. They could not, so most educated themselves by satisfying their passion for lectures and reading almost to excess. As if to validate their revolutionary credentials, early Jewish

Socialists repudiated the use of Yiddish as well as their Jewish identity, tradition and culture; nevertheless the Yiddish Press played a vital role in the education and Americanization of the Eastern European. Thousands of Russian Jews were incipient intellectuals who joined hundreds of immigrant scholars, writers, and poets in forming a truly intellectual group in Baltimore for the first time. They crowded news stands and devoured the Yiddish publications that printed articles about American history, customs, short stories and sketches depicting immigrant life in America. The Yiddish press took a leaf from the American press in writing about crime, sin, and violence.[1] They fabricated non-Jewish stories by giving them a Jewish twist in a language their readers understood.

The popular weeklies, the *Jewish Messenger* published in New York and the *Jewish Exponent* published in Philadelphia, employed Baltimore correspondents to write Baltimore by-lines. In 1881, the *Jewish Messenger* editorialized on the importance for Jews to leave Russia after the riots in the Ukraine; however, most of the local news was lifted from German and English newspapers. By the 1890s, popular Yiddish weeklies *Der Baltimore Israelite, The Baltimore Jewish American* and *Der Weiser* began publication.

By the turn of the century, the Yiddish press matured and offered Yiddish writers opportunities to bring their prose and verse to the rapidly growing reading public. Hundreds of Yiddish books were published.[2] The flourishing years of the Yiddish Press were short lived, and it peaked in years between World War I and the Great Depression. The ability of fewer and fewer Jews who could read Yiddish diminished further, and so did the press.

Compared to other American cities with large Russian Jewish populations, Baltimore was typical in the number of its Yiddish publications. Some of them, *Hapisga* (1890-1914), the nation's only Hebrew weekly and the *Jewish Comment* (1895-1918) stood apart from the others. The *Jewish Comment* founded by Louis H. Levin, the most important local publication of its day, was published in Baltimore every Friday. It was Maryland's largest weekly publication, and the publishers claimed it to be the largest Jewish journal in the world. Regardless, the *Jewish Comment*, published as the area's first Anglo-Jewish oriented publication, was read mostly by German Jews though Baltimore's Russian Jews considered it their paper of record. In an era when most German Jews remained ambivalent about Zionism, the *Jewish Comment* supported the movement. In 1899, a single copy cost 3 cents, and the subscription rate was $ 1.00 per year, payable in advance.

David Alter, a Romanian immigrant businessman who lived in Pittsburgh founded the *Baltimore Jewish Times,* a far cry from the Yiddish Press,[3] written entirely in English, the publication later became America's leading Jewish weekly periodical. Though publication began in Baltimore in 1919, in its early years the *Baltimore Jewish Times* editorial writings originated in Pittsburgh. They were national in scope since there was much of Jewish interest to write about at the time. World War I had ended, Prohibition was about to begin, and many conflicts raged in Eastern Europe. *The Jewish Comment's* last issue was printed in 1918 so the 1919 starting date of the *Times* was an auspicious one to begin a Jewish weekly appealing to the interests of Baltimore Jews. In that year and of very special interest, the periodical published a historically important World War I commemoration issue. For years the *Baltimore Jewish Times* was widely read by German Jews mainly because its "personals" column covered German Jewish social events; announcements of their European travels and summer vacations in America. Its orientation gradually changed, along with the transition of Baltimore's Jewish population; it adopted a distinct Russian Jewish flavor, and in doing so, the publication lost almost all of its German Jewish readership.

Today's *Baltimore Jewish Times* is more editorially vigorous than it has ever been. It appeals to a younger readership by steering away from the Jewish oppression theme of earlier generations; nevertheless, it manages to be deeply committed to Jewish tradition and at the same time it remains independent of the clergy and the establishment. The *Baltimore Jewish Times* binds the community together by covering Jewish activity from orthodoxy to ads for steamed crabs. Published by the 4th generation of family ownership, on July 31, 1994, 10,000 people attended a 75th anniversary concert sponsored by the weekly that featured the Baltimore Symphony Orchestra. In March 1995, The *Baltimore Jewish Times* published a special anniversary issue that recounted much of its past seventy-five years and in the same week announced plans for a major expansion into other cities with large Jewish populations.

Possibly the last of the important local Yiddish-English weeklies, the *Baltimore Jewish Voice* enjoyed a wide readership and was highly respected. Immediately after World War II in August 1946, the *Northwest Suburban News* published for about one year and was replaced by the same owners two years later by the *Baltimore Beacon* that covered Jewish northwest Baltimore until December 1960.

UNCOMMON THREADS

1   *A classic article is one published by a popular Philadelphia Yiddish weekly that ran a headline, "The EMPRESS OF CHINA has come to America to look for a husband." The editor of the weekly had misinterpreted a headline in the shipping section of an American newspaper that read "The EMPRESS OF CHINA arrived yesterday on her Maiden Voyage."*

2   *Popular Yiddish writers and poets living in New York wrote in New York and published in Vilna; Yiddish writers in Warsaw published in American publications. Not until World War I did Yiddish fiction writers come into their own by writing Yiddish in the United States for this county's readers.*

3   *Published in New York City since 1897 and for many years edited by the eminent Russian Jewish author Abraham Cahan, the JEWISH DAILY FORWARD became the most widely read Yiddish daily newspaper in the world. Beginning with its social laborite founders, it was outspoken and paternalistic, anti-tsarist, socialistic, pacifistic, and until the March 1917 Russian Revolution, pro German. The FORWARD'S masthead carried the slogan "Workers of the World, Unite." Publication of the FORWARD was to make it possible for the Russian Jewish immigrants to read about life in the bewildering new world in his own language.*

After World War II, Isaac Bashevis Singer, the JEWISH DAILY FORWARD'S Nobel prize winning staff writer, wove the Yiddish language into intellectual respectability. He dedicated his writings to the preservation of this, the language of the Russian Jewish immigrant culture. Singer said, "Yiddish may be the only language on earth that has never been spoken by men in power." Fewer and fewer children of Russian immigrants read the FORWARD because they could not. Many, who once knew Yiddish, actually forgot how to read this curious cross of Hebrew and medieval German. In December 1962, in an effort to stay alive, for the first time in its sixty-five years the JEWISH FORWARD printed part of each issue in English. It now publishes weekly companion issues; one, in Yiddish; one, in English. Editorially secular, the FORWARD continues to keep its fingers tightly on the pulse of American Russian Jewry.

PART II-11

Zionist political zealots * Zionism traced to Russia * Zionist organization * Labor Zionists * American Jewish Committee * American Jewish Congress * Balfour Declaration * The Jewish Legion

Russian Jewish immigrants, while at work or in their homes, spent endless hours discussing their circumstances. Problems of living and working conditions, common to all, were actually not as far removed as they had expected they would be from those they had endured in Eastern Europe. Immigrants hoped for a much better way of life in America and in ways it was; at least, here they were free. In Eastern Europe, millions of Jews, who resided in the vast Pale of Settlement, suffered extreme poverty, tyranny and labor unrest. They dealt with this oppressive Eastern European confine by living as a community, and after they came to America, they tried to make similar communal living arrangements.

Living in the Pale produced fierce political ideals that spawned the revolutionaries of Russia. Many young Russian Jews became devout Socialists and yearned for the overthrow of the Tzars and for the leadership of Russia to be assumed by the workers. When they left Russia, hopefully they were not saying farewell to their homeland. Some carried with them to America the keys to "das alte heim" (their old home) even though they knew that home had been torched when their Russian shtetl had been erased from their area's map. They dreamt of returning to Russia after the new order was established; however, after the failure of the attempted revolution in 1905, they resigned themselves to the fact that there could be no return.

After landing in America, many Russian Jews continued to preach a form of anarchy; they did so in Yiddish, long considered to be the language of anarchists. Individuals who were active in workers' movements in Russia came to the aid of the garment workers through the Jewish Socialist Party, the Bund. As if to validate their revolutionary credentials, early Jewish socialists were hostile not merely to Yiddish as a language, but they also repudiated their Jewish identity and everything having to do with Jewish tradition and culture. Nevertheless, members of the Bund used Yiddish because it was the natural medium and the only way they could speak to the Russian Jewish proletariat. Russian Jews who threw themselves into revolutionary movements frequently returned to society repentant and shocked after they discovered anti-Semitism to be an active force against them. Fortunately, most of the newly arrived Russian Jews were grateful for being in America, wanted democracy and considered anarchy a danger to their existence.

Without doubt one of the most salient and most evident differences between German and Russian Jews revolved around the labor movement and their split over the issue of Zionism. The mission of Zionism was to create a publicly, legally secured home for the Jewish people in Palestine. Descendants of Abraham claimed that country as their promised land, and that claim framed the conditions and directly affected the ultimate

UNCOMMON THREADS

results. Russian garment workers' fanaticism embraced Zionism and its accompanying socialistic tendencies. The "here first" German Reform Jews considered Zionism a dual loyalty, and they told the Russian immigrant Jews that if they truly wanted to be Americaners, they would abandon Zionism; few listened. Toward the end of the nineteenth century, idealistic young Russian Jewish workers imbued with Socialist and Zionist doctrines held free-for-all open discussions. Some met at the Kibitzing Market at High and Baltimore Streets. Others with their katerinkas on their backs met to discuss their differences at the Hazir Market (Pig Market) at Exeter and Baltimore Streets. Progressive Russians convened but with more civility at the Young Men's Progressive Club.[1]

In 1895, the first bona fide Zionist group in America, founded in Baltimore, the Hovevei Zion (lovers of Zion), disseminated Jewish national ideals. In 1900, the Federation of American Zionists held its first national convention in Baltimore. At the height of the Russian Jewish migration, Zionist groups helped with their Americanization, thus swelling the ranks of their movement. Also in 1900, the Poalei Zion (workers of Zion) campaigned to spread Zionist propaganda throughout the world. Grown to be the world's largest Zionist organization, the Poalei Zionists held their first national convention in Baltimore in 1905; and this convention inaugurated the Labor Zionist movement in America. The convention was chaired by Dr. Herman Seidel, a Baltimorean who eventually held almost every important office of the National Labor Zionist's organization. For its part in the movement, Baltimore became known as the cradle of American Zionism. Many Russian Jewish pioneers in the movement were young, newly arrived fanatic socialistic immigrant fabrenta (red hot), who in 1903, founded the Ezras Hovevei Zion Kadina.

At first it was difficult for the Poalei Zion to become recognized by some members of Jewish trade unions who considered the movement too radical; however, in 1918 factional movements within the Poalei Zion, the labor unions, workmen's circles, and other like associations, organized the movement under a national umbrella, the First Jewish Labor Congress. Labor Zionism was a serious and revolutionary movement, and many members of the movement relocated in Israel. There, they were instrumental in founding the agricultural collectives, the kibutzim. After 1918, several branches of the Labor Zionists were formed within the Poalei Zion including the Jewish National Workers Alliance. In 1927, as part of the Labor Zionist movement, the Pioneer Women's Organization became an active group promoting the Palestine cause even though they were not locked into the idea that a Jewish homeland had to be in Palestine. For them, it could be located anywhere in the world.

Dr. Harry Friedenwald and a handful of well-known liberal thinking German Jews, some who had retained their orthodoxy and some who had not, actively supported the early Zionist movement. In fact, while most of the city's Reform Jews gave little thought to Zionism, those who did including Siegmund Sonneborn and his son Rudolph were a very important in erasing the barriers between German and Russian Jews. The great majority of Reform German Jews considered Judaism to be a religion free of nationalistic bonds, and they wanted to keep it that way. Starting in 1901, German Jews who believed in the movement, became instrumental in creating interest and raising funds for a Jewish University in Jerusalem. World War I brought a crisis to the Zionist movement because groups in both camps of the conflict lost touch with each other; this alone crippled the continuity of fund raising. Zionists persisted though it was not until 1925 that their long awaited Jewish University in Jerusalem was officially dedicated.

The Baltimore Chapter of the American Jewish Committee was formed in 1906 to prevent the infraction of the civil and religious rights of Jews in any part of the world. It was led by Dr. Harry Friedenwald and Dr. Jacob Hollander who believed themselves to be spokesmen for all of American Jewry. Though the American Jewish Committee in 1913 played an important role in abrogating the 1832 treaty between the United States and Russia, they in no way represented American Russian Jewry although both were ideologically supporters of Zionism. In fact, their leadership offended Russian Jews so much that several important Baltimore German Jews including Friedenwald resigned from the Committee. Because of their strong beliefs, they became leaders in a new and more democratic organization, the American Jewish Congress. The Congress was founded in 1917 and reorganized in 1922. Its first president was Simon Sobeloff who was very much committed to Zionism as were several of Baltimore's liberal German Jewish members of the Congress. The issues of Zionism and the anti-Semitism of the time played important roles in breaking the barriers between the German and the Russian Jews. High on the Congress' agenda was a united Baltimore Jewish community.

Dated November 2, 1917, the Balfour Declaration favored British support for a Jewish National Homeland in Palestine; it received enthusiastic support from American Zionists. The declaration was a simple single page letter from Lord Arthur James Balfour, the British Foreign Secretary, to Baron Edmond De Rothschild of Paris[2]. Between eighty and ninety Baltimore Labor Zionist zealots joined the Jewish Legion to be part of a Jewish army that would fight in Palestine under a Jewish flag. A group of Jewish volunteers who had already enlisted met at Baltimore and High Streets and another time at Baltimore and Exeter Streets, to play instruments and sing Hebrew songs. When a crowd gathered, a Jewish Legion member on a soap box spread the word of a Jewish homeland and made an appeal for volunteers to join his organization. The contingent enlisted in Canada, trained in England, and in 1918 they became the 38th Battalion of the Royal Fusiliers of the Egyptian Expeditionary Forces commanded by British General Allenby. None of its members had a criminal record, none drank, and most kept kosher. They entered Jerusalem with the British and helped free Palestine from Turkish rule in 1920. Supplementing this, a prominent Baltimore German Jew Louis H. Levin took charge of the international distribution of relief for Palestine war sufferers. His efforts were considered an outstanding tribute to the pre-eminence of Baltimore Jewry in the field of social work.

UNCOMMON THREADS

1   *In Baltimore, as far back as 1816, the well-known non-Jewish Hezekiah Niles, publisher of the NILES' WEEKLY REGISTER, wrote a lengthy article about the possibility of the Jewish people returning to their ancient homeland. Niles' article was prophetic and it concluded with, "The Jews were once a peculiar people of God, they are yet a peculiar people though scattered and dispersed in every country and in every clime their future state will no doubt be more glorious than ever. And he who led their fathers through the deserts has promised to lead them again to their native land. It is probable that the time is not too far distant when this great event shall take place, and the banners of Israel unfurled on the walls of Jerusalem the Holy Hill of Zion. The Jews will rebuild their ancestral homeland and those parts of the East so celebrated and sacred, now so degraded and lost to all that is good and great, may again be the seat of commerce and useful arts. The deserts of Palestine brought into cultivation by patient industry may again blossom as the rose, and Jerusalem miserable as it is, speedily rival the cities of the world for beauty, splendor and wealth."*

2   *Lord Arthur James Balfour had no Jewish connections whatsoever; no known Jewish ancestors nor Jewish friends. He was aware of the atrocities of Christians against Jews and he considered this conduct to be a disgrace. Balfour expressed an interest in Zionism as early as 1902.*

PART II-12

Jewish Educational Alliance * B'Nai Brith * Yiddish Theater

A love for music and theater pervaded the lives of Russian Jews. In the Pale of Settlement, itinerant "klezmorim" (musicians) brought news and performed for weddings and other celebrations. They traveled from shtetl to shtetl playing lively Yiddish folk music which originated in Alsace-Lorraine during the Middle Ages, including virtuoso solos for violin and clarinet. Eastern European Jews believe that music is education, and they neither pray well nor learn Hebrew without it. In Orthodox congregations, there is an adoration for brilliant cantors with outstanding voices. Within two or three decades after the beginning of the Russian Jewish migration, the Baltimore Jewish community offered musical programs as part of a wide range of cultural activities. Founded in 1908 and named after the famous German composer Giacomo Meyerbeer, the Meyerbeer Singing Society's forty all male voices sang in Yiddish, Russian and English. After merging with the female vocal Ensemble of Baltimore, the combined voices became the nucleus of the Baltimore Civic Opera Company. There is no way of knowing, but it seems reasonable that many Russian Jewish immigrant's sons became medical doctors at their parents urging while suppressing their true passion, the concert hall or the stage.

In an almost perfect amalgamation, the German founded Daughters in Israel, the Maccabeans who opened club rooms for boys in 1896, and the Hebrew Kindergarten and Day Nursery combined in 1909 to form the Jewish Educational Alliance to provide English instruction to Russian Jewish immigrants. In memory of their parents, two English Jewish brothers William and Julius Levy funded the erection of the JEA facility in 1914 on the site of the razed Princess Theater. At first, German Jews administered and staffed the JEA in a tangible effort to uplift, clean up, and quiet down the Russian Jews in preparation for citizenship. A true settlement house, the JEA was built in the pattern of but on a smaller scale than New York's Henry and Madison Street Settlement House and Chicago's Hull House. The gymnasium and general all around forum offered physical and mental outlets unavailable elsewhere for the young Russian Jews. The JEA bridged the old and the new worlds and stemmed the considerable growth of Jewish juvenile delinquency that began after the turn of the century. It was very important for the Baltimore Jews to keep their community's youngsters from being confined to state reformatories. There were at the time many too many Jewish delinquents confined in the Maryland School for Boys, candidates for becoming serious criminals.

The programs offered at the JEA made it difficult for Jewish boys and girls not to spend several hours a week in one or more of its activities. The comprehensive free constructive programs eventually dwarfed the institutions original purpose. The popularity of the JEA's outstanding theatrical groups, the debates and declamation contests vied with the great Eastern European Jewish sport, basketball. Jewish Educational Alliance basketball teams dominated Baltimore's other club teams; one former member Mike Bloom played professionally for the Baltimore Bullets now the

Washington Bullets of the National Basketball Association. Dedicated young adults, mostly German Jews and a sprinkling of Russian Jews, both thoroughly Americanized, considered volunteering at the JEA their contribution, their thing to do for society. They came as friends, not as aloof mench (upstanding person) to be advisors, guides, and teachers, and above all they were good role models for the young club members. Of the many clubs under the sponsorship of the Jewish Educational Alliance, The Pioneer Club, started in 1930 by a group of boys who had recently entered their teen years, was probably the best known.[1] Volunteers taught literary arts, classic English, reading, and the correct usages of written English. Other volunteers who possessed expertise in the subject gave courses in job training. They participated in stage, musical, literary and athletic programs. The Jewish Educational Alliance aided in shaping the lives of thousands of young Russian Jewish children as they aspired to Americanize their culture.

Operating a settlement house in a mixed neighborhood presented problems; Jews and Christians of the area attended the same schools and mingled in dance halls. Sponsoring dances on the JEA home ground became a potential social crisis because social intercourse between Jewish and Christian children was frowned upon. Addressing the dilemma, the board of the JEA stated, "We do not encourage and, in fact, seldom permit non-Jewish people on the floor." The word seldom failed to clarify the situation, and it was never resolved. After 1952, the illustrious JEA building at 1210 East Baltimore Street closed, and the Meyerbeer and other groups no longer performed free Sunday afternoon concerts from the stage of its auditorium. Functions of the Jewish Educational Alliance were incorporated in a lesser way in the programs of the Jewish Community Center and Y.M.H.A. and Y.W.H.A. facilities on W. Monument Street. JEA was no longer the same, no longer the charismatic settlement house of its former years in East Baltimore. By this time, the children of Russian Jewish immigrants were fathers and grandfathers and living uptown. The Jewish Educational Alliance, now the JEA Fellowship Association, with no gym and no stage is alive in the hearts and memories of some senior citizens.

Russian Jewish immigrant men had a great propensity to join, to belong, so they organized their own lodges and clubs. As the German Jews did years before, they became members of lodges of the Masonic Orders, the Elks, and the Odd Fellows. Within the Masons, Russian and German Jews joined separate lodges, the Amicable or the Blue. Brith Shalom, a parent organization of several lodges, was formed in 1902, and its members devoted much time and effort helping immigrants to become citizens. B'Nai Brith lodges have existed in Baltimore for many years; one, Jeshurun Lodge, founded in 1843 by German Jews, was the nation's third oldest. As far back as 1875, six B'Nai Brith lodges existed in Baltimore, but their social orientation allowed only a modest involvement as a help type organizations. In 1915, the Menorah Lodge of B'Nai Brith held its first meeting in the vestry rooms of the Oheb Shalom synagogue. Almost immediately after the end of World War I, Menorah Lodge, fueled with a large Russian Jewish membership and Zionist orientation, changed the image of B'Nai Brith by playing an important role in the affairs of the Young Men's Hebrew Association, the

Anti-Defamation League, the Jewish Big Brother League and the Baltimore Jewish Council. Founded in 1914, for youths in trouble with the law, the Big Brother League operated in a manner far removed from the direct relief concept of earlier organizations. Indeed, social changes for immigrants had progressed. With the Jewish community had institutions in place that dealt with almost every conceivable communal or individual problem.

Diversions were needed to relieve the tedium and to release the emotions of Russian Jewish immigrants. The Yiddish Theater as America knew it was a phenomenon with roots in Eastern Europe that bridged a gap between the past and the present. Non-existent until mid-nineteenth century Russia, it began at a time when the performing arts centered on groups of minstrels, singers, and acrobats who wandered from shtetl to shtetl where audiences half welcomed them as performers and half scorned them as ragamuffins. Here in America, the early days of the Yiddish Theater offered presentations to audiences in need of relief from their hours lost in the wretched darkness of sweatshops. Mostly raw talented, troops performed low levels of artless song, dance, and some foolery; all vivid trash. Though the early presentations skipped over realism, after a while a moderate increase in sophistication sought more structured performances that mirrored the lives of the immigrants. The audiences identified with the portrayal of life in the neighborhoods, the sweatshops, and the unions.[2]

For those immigrants who attended performances, they experienced their first secular outlet for communal emotion. Two separate traveling Yiddish repertoire companies played East Baltimore theaters in the 1890s. During the years of the traveling Yiddish Theater, all of the great Jewish thespians performed in Baltimore. Boris Thomashefsky,[3] Molly Picon, Maurice Schwartz, David Kessler, Fanny Brice, Sophie Tucker, Paul Muni, the Adlers, Celia, Jacob and Sarah became local household names. The Yiddish Theater[4] served as a training ground for writers, composers, producers, directors, and scene designers as well as for musicians and actors. Since show business was not considered a respectable calling, except for a few at the top, stage performers were not held in great esteem by the public nevertheless, after the Yiddish Theater firmly established itself in the early 1900s, the Jewish actors and actresses enthroned themselves as the aristocrats of the immigrant world.

Stage productions at the Front Street Theater, on Front and Low Streets, were largely those of the Yiddish Theater. On December 27, 1895, the theater was packed to capacity with at least 1,300 patrons including those seated and the standees in the rear. All were awaiting the rise of the curtain for a Yiddish presentation of the opera *Alexander, Crown Prince of Jerusalem*. In 1895, before the wide use of electric lights, most theaters were illuminated by gas lamps, and some in the audience that night complained of the smell of gas. A search for a leak began; a match was lighted near a faulty valve and a small flame flared with the sound of a slight poof. Though there was no actual blaze, a cry of fire was heard from the balcony. The gas lights throughout the theater were turned off; the audience panicked in the dark precipitating a mad rush through the aisles to the staircases. The stampede crushed hundreds of patrons; twenty-three men, women and children were killed, twenty-eight seriously injured and perhaps seventy-five less seriously. The following day, the *Baltimore Sun* described the audience as consisting of Russian and Polish Jews, mostly from the neighborhood and "they were naturally of a very nervous and excitable temperament."

The Yiddish Theater presented melodrama, comedy, opera, and historical and religious plays but the audience favored light opera and operettas. The laughing and crying of the audience at excessively sentimental performances was both contagious and cathartic. Some writers wrote on a higher literary level adapting to Jewish life such plays as *Romeo and Juliet* and *Hamlet*. Shakespearean productions pleased the audiences as did plays by Jacob Gordin who wrote *The Jewish King Lear* and whose writings occupied a central presence in the Yiddish Theater for two decades. The Yiddish Theater was a closed corporation to only those who spoke Yiddish because many of its idioms cannot be communicated in any other language.

In 1906, thousands of Baltimore Russian Jews crowded the in-person appearance of Sholem Aleichem, and they thrilled to the readings of this outstanding Yiddish author. Sholem Aleichem, the pseudonym of the Russian author Solomon Rabinowitz, transformed the humor that was inseparable from Yiddish speech into the lives of the immigrant. Some shows were flashbacks to life in the viewers' Russian shtetl and were an emotional bridge between the past and the present. Jewish humor had its roots in 18th century Eastern Europe where it was a response to persecution and an escape mechanism in their challenge for survival; the logic in the shtels was that things could always be worse. The heroes of Rabinowitz stories, usually pursued by bad luck, their quarrelsome loving wives and the ignorant yet wise dairyman, Tobias (Tevya), became a centerpiece of Yiddish literary types.

Yiddish curses were humorous and ridiculous, vivid and to the point. Many were the narratives about the *Wise Men of Chelm*,[5] a small town in Poland where Jews had lived since the 12th century until the Holocaust. Much 20th century popular Jewish American humor centered on the JAP, the Jewish American Princess, but there was never a Jewish American Prince. Jewish humor continues to be alive, strong, and distinctive.

Performances needed to be long, usually lasting until midnight, because only then did the audience feel satisfied that they were getting a full evening for their money. Yiddish Theater was a people's theater that reflected the cultural passions of the immigrants who delayed shows by demanding a repeat of songs they liked and by unabashed hissing and shouting "shaddop" at the villains. Frequently patrons yelled out advice to the actors, particularly during plays about family conflicts. On the Sabbath, the audience jeered actors who lighted cigarettes on stage although the audiences were obviously not observing the Sabbath themselves. The theaters did not charge for children under six years of age because they considered them to be lap sitters; they and a parent occupied only a single seat. Sold out performances tested the weight ratings of theater balconies, as the rear ends of most of the six year old lap sitters exceeded the girth of parental laps.

The Yiddish Theater depended largely on benefit nights when Jewish organizations bought large blocks of tickets at reduced prices. In the smaller houses, the aisles were crowded with patrons and candy vendors; babies cried, unruly Yiddish Theater audiences exchanged loud remarks, read newspapers, ate sandwiches, munched fruit, cracked peanuts, and shouted greetings to landslayt (those from their same Russian area or shtetl). It was not unusual for some of the men to remove their shoes as they did in shul in the late afternoon of Yom Kippur. At times, popular sold out performances presented problems for the management when patrons who paid for standing room only took seats. Others occupied seats as they found them and refused to move for the rightful occupants who held tickets reserving those seats.

The end of World War I was the turning point of the Yiddish Theater's performance of serious productions. By the early 1930s, the theater drifted towards the scintillating, titillating, and shund (slightly obscene) theatrical expression of burlesque centered in Baltimore's Block. The former offices and stores of this east Baltimore Street area had been leveled in 1904 by the Great Baltimore Fire and rebuilt. Eastern European Jews became owners of burlesque houses such as the Gayety built in 1906 and the dowdy Clover Theater known as the scratch house. The Gayety was one of a group of large well-known American burlesque theaters that booked The circuit, the shows that moved from city to city. Along with the Catskill Mountain resorts and the Yiddish Theater, the burlesque houses had long been the training grounds for the long list of hundreds of America's most famous performers and comedians.

Burlesque humor, purely Eastern European, spawned night clubs, and during the peak of their popularity in the 1950s there were over 60 on East Baltimore Street. Owners promoted a display of dancing performers' bodies that, at times, edged mighty close to just this side of the law but more frequently just outside the law. Popular clubs such as the Two O'Clock Club and the Oasis Night Club usually featured strippers not quite so artistic and comedians not quite so funny as those on the circuit. Many years later, the Oasis advertised that its floor show was the World's Worst Show, and no one contested this. Burlesque houses proved without doubt that a sucker is born every minute. At intermission, first from the stage and then from the aisles, hawkers sold candies; they guaranteed that each and every box contained a valuable prize. For a relatively high selling price, the boxes contained a few cheap overly sweet chocolates and a nothing trinket. The Cracker Jack company's slogan that promised a prize in each and every box remained the better buy.

Starting a little before the 1920s, Jewish immigrants enjoyed the movies and even in the industry's infancy, most of the important Hollywood producers and owners of Baltimore theaters were Russian Jews. Masses attended film productions with regularity; they could do this for only a five cent admission charge. Even after the Jewish migration to northwest Baltimore, the five cent charge held for a while. Those who owned the theaters made sure that they could exploit the local market to their advantage by screening at least four different productions each week. A new title was shown on Monday and Tuesday, changed for Wednesday and Thursday, changed again on Friday and again a different show on Saturday. On Sunday, no one went to movies, the theaters dark in compliance with local Blue Laws designed to sanctify the Christian day of rest

---

1   *At the date of this writing, the six remaining members meet on the first Wednesday of each month, the traditional day for Pioneer Club meetings. They discuss club business on that day and they gather on the other Wednesdays of the month to eat out.*

2   *The first performance of a professional Yiddish production was staged in New York in August 1882, and the Russian-Jewish Opera Company landed there in May 1884, ready to perform.*

3   *A young Baltimore girl, Bessie Kaufman, daughter of a failed short-time immigrant farmer in the Pisgah Colony, fell in love with Boris Thomashefsky when his theatrical troupe played in Baltimore. They married, and she joined her husband and became a renowned Yiddish actress.*

4   *The Yiddish Theater played the ORPHEUM on Baltimore Street near the Jones Falls, the ODEON on Frederick Street near Baltimore and the BIJOU in the 1100 block of East Baltimore Street. Yiddish players performed at the HOLIDAY STREET theater, the MONUMENTAL and the PRINCESS. The Yiddish Theater played the FOLLY full time in the 1920s. These theaters, mostly Jewish owned, were part of a legacy of Jewish theater involvement that began in Russia and continued throughout America. As the Yiddish Theater matured, it played the uptown FORDS on Fayette Street, the MARYLAND on Franklin Street, the LYRIC on Mt Royal Avenue and the ACADEMY OF MUSIC on Howard Street near Center.*

5   *An example of this vein of humor is of a Chelm wise man who said to another as it started to pour, "My umbrella is full of holes." The second wise man: "Then why did you bring it?" First wise man, "I didn't think it would rain." Popular jokes focused on women. Yankel tells the matchmaker, "I am very disappointed with your choice for me. She's old, she's ugly, she wears false teeth and she can't see." Responded the matchmaker, 'Why are you whispering? She can't hear either.' " During the Passover service, a traditional question is asked, "Why is this night different from all other nights?" A Baltimore lady preparing a Seder for 90 family members, wore an apron with this question imprinted on the front. She also had the answer imprinted: "Don't ask."*

PART II-13

World War I and the Pale * Bolsheviks * Social conscience * Anti-Semitism * Socialism * Hooliganism * Jews in politics

*O*n August 1, 1914, Germany declared war on Russia and though Jews in Russia had less reason to dislike Germany and its people, they remained inseparably allied to their mother country. The numbers of Russian Jewish men in Russian army uniforms were disproportionately larger than the Jewish population of the country, and during the fighting, a constant stream of battle weary and wounded Jewish soldiers returned for care to their homes in the Pale of Settlement. When battle grounds moved east into Russia's territory, the Pale's boundaries crumpled, and the entire area fell under the control of the Central Powers. Masses of Jews fled to the interior of Russia seeking safety.

With the overthrow of the Tsar Nicholas II in March 1917, groups of Russian Jews in America felt the air had cleared enough for them to fully endorse the war with Germany because of that county's violations of the United States neutral rights. Casting aside their past sufferings and the reason for their leaving Russia, they now felt comfortable with an allegiance to mother Russia no longer ruled by a Tsar. Some Baltimore Russian Jews who were involved in the needle trades had an affinity with the Bolsheviks, and they participated in meetings and organizations closely related to the left wing Russian movement. Concerned over this potentially explosive issue, the United States, wary of an infiltration of undesirables, passed immigration laws in 1918 that specifically excluded anarchists and subversives from entering the country. These laws aimed to undermine and suppress additional support for extreme radical movements from new Russian Jewish immigrants.

Along with St. Louis, Cincinnati and Milwaukee, Baltimore was one of the few major American cities whose large German populations played leading roles in those city's social, political, and economic life. So strong was the German orientation and influence in Baltimore that for years state laws required announcements of new legislation be published simultaneously in at least one Baltimore English language and one German language newspaper.

The arousal of social consciences and increased educational awareness are positives that surround times of war. The atmosphere in America during World War I partially spelled the end of German Jews as German Americans for they were now without any doubt American Jews. In defense of fanatical anti-German feelings of some Americans, most German Jews did not want to give any reasons for others to suspect that they professed any allegiance whatsoever to the fatherland.[1] This set Baltimore's German Jewish community apart from groups of Christian Germans, many of whom continued to quietly support pro German attitudes; nevertheless, perceptions within the Baltimore non-German Christian community varied in their views towards German Jews. Most clearly saw those of a lower social and economic strata to be completely apart from Germany, but they were not so sure of the prominent and wealthier German Jews.

Suspect Christian Germans, mostly well to-do, lost important political and business standings as their society entered a state of flux for the duration of the war. Unsure of themselves, many German Jews did not know exactly where they fit into the scheme of Baltimore society during this time, and they probably never found out.

In September 1914, a massive rally filled every seat of the Lyric Theater. They came to hear Louis Dembitz Brandeis, later to become an associate justice of the Supreme Court of the United States. The subject of Brandeis' speech was *The War as it Affects the Jewish People*. There was no question that it did. Although America had not as yet become actively engaged in the conflict, German and Russian Jews had given financial help to suffering Europeans. The rally captured the imagination of the administrators of the German Jewish Federated Jewish Charities. That organization raised $32,000 to be given toward the relief of the severe sufferings of 2,000,000 Polish-Russian Jews caught between the onslaughts of warring European nations. Another 1,000,000 Jews lived in Galicia and 4,000,000 in the Pale of Settlement. In 1915, Baltimorean Louis H. Levin was sent abroad by the American Relief Committee to secure food for the starving Jewish refugees in Palestine

When the United States entered World War I militarily, German and Russian Jewish boys joined the armed services; many were wounded, others gave their lives. Jewish owned businesses, particularly the needle trades, profited handsomely as they fulfilled contracts awarded them for uniforms, caps, blankets, and other needs of war. When the shooting ended, numbers of German and Russian Jewish servicemen returned to a world that had changed. In a sharper focus than before they left for war, they perceived that their future would be tied closely to advancing their education. Applications from Jewish would be students flooded colleges and universities many of which recoiled, and then put into practice their already in place restrictions on Jewish admissions.

For the Russian Jews, anti-Semitism specifically directed toward them flourished because of the Red scare of 1917-1919 and the Russian Jewish connection with Bolshevism. There were at this time a combined 65,000 German and Russian Jews living in Baltimore, a force that could not put aside the momentum they had established. True, many politically active, newly arrived Russian Jews could be found in socialist and anarchist camps. Although they had been trained for leadership in the revolutionary organizations of their native land, living in America greatly defused their fervor. In short order after the war, revolutionary types began to understand that Americans simply did not react to every offensive incident and that some issues actually solved themselves or agreements could be reached with discussions around a table. As prosperity loomed, many Russian Jews heretofore active in the Socialist Party, gradually drifted away and into temporary political obscurity only to reappear as supporters of less than fanatic Republicans and Democrats who ran for public office in the teen years and early 1920s.

Congress enacted and passed the Volstead Act into law in October 1919 to enforce the Constitution's 18th amendment.. For Jews, normally indifferent to the use of alcohol except for ceremonial wine, the law had little consequence except to create entrepreneurial possibilities. Article 7 of the Volstead Act was a gray area that allowed the production of sacramental wine and some self ordained rabbis did a thriving business, but dealing in sacramental wines was small potatoes compared to the profits made by those dealing in hard liquor.[2] For Baltimore, a port city, bootlegging was an active occupation. The general knowledge that so many Russian Jews were involved in the illegal trade of bootlegging produced fears of increased anti-Semitism. This knowledge, a source of extreme discomfort on the part of most Baltimore Jews, widened the gulf between Jewish groups. In 1922, the Reform Central Conference of American Rabbis petitioned the Commissioner of Internal Revenue to Revoke Article 7 of the Volstead Act.

In the 1920s, disputes in the misrepresentation of meat not slaughtered in accordance with Jewish law became a fertile ground for Jewish criminals and prosecutors working on both sides of the law to stabilize the issue. The kosher problems in Baltimore always existed but on a smaller scale than elsewhere in the nation. In Baltimore, a small segment of the garment industry knuckled down to hooliganism involving a subsidiary of a New York men's clothing manufacturer incorporated in Maryland.[3]

German Jewish interests in politics waned until a decade or so before World War I. Before the establishment of the People's Court in 1914, German Jews served on a variety of minor city courts and continued to do so through the years until Russian Jews eventually replaced what was left of the ineffective German Jewish political sphere.. German Jews kept the little political influence they had, and after 1914 and through the years, a few German Jews have served in high judicial positions in Baltimore City. Men like Joseph N. Ulman and Herman Moser served with dignity and respect on Baltimore's Supreme Bench, as did Morton P. Fisher as Judge of the U.S. Tax Appeal Court and Lee I Hecht, Chief Judge of the Orphans Court. Presently, Frank A. Kaufman is a Senior Judge of the United States District Court. German Jews have had no presence in recent years in the Maryland State Senate or House of Delegates. Many of the overwhelming numbers of liberal Eastern European Jews in Baltimore, some influenced by previous socialistic tendencies, had strong Democratic party affiliations.[4] Since the 1980s, primarily because of the exceedingly large growth of the value of equities and other financial gains made during recent Republican administrations, numbers of well to-do Eastern European Jews have voted the Republican Ticket along with the more conservative German Jews. Conjecture only, it may be they remain liberal in their hearts so it is presumed they see it as bad business to support Democratic candidates in national elections. Though most Jews continue to vote for Democrats, the theory that there is a positive Democratic Jewish vote in national elections is increasingly suspect..

In the 1920s, the years of the great migration of Jews from East Baltimore to the northwestern Fourth and Fifth Districts, E. Milton Altfeld was elected to the State Senate after serving in the Maryland House of Delegates since 1914. Harry O. Levin became a state senator in 1923 and later so did Melvin L. Fine, Jerome Robinson, Maurice Soypher, Marvin Mandel and others along with Albert L. Sklar who later served on the Supreme Bench of Baltimore City. Some of the household names in the Maryland House

UNCOMMON THREADS

of Delegates included Leon Abramson, Irvin Adler, Carl Bacharach, Paul Berman, Meyer M. Cardin, Morris Carden and Paul Cordish. Many others were appointed to the Liquor Board, Board of Movie Supervisors, and as Police Magistrates. Others were appointed to the Housing Court, the Public Service Commission, the State Tax Commission and elected to the Baltimore City Council.

Those Baltimoreans who voted in the City Fire House on Glen Avenue and Cross Country Boulevard endured long lines in order to cast their ballots. Year after year this precinct was the busiest in Baltimore and the percentage of those registered to vote, who actually voted and some more than once, was the highest. If a voter near or at the end of the line was recognized by a certain Maryland State trooper, he or she was escorted to the front of the line. The author clearly remembers an incident where a candidate for public office passed personal hand outs to voters as they entered the curtained booths and when the author who witnessed it reported it to the policeman on inside duty, he said "I didn't see anything."

Philip B. Perlman and Simon E. Sobeloff two Baltimore born first generation Russian Jews were appointed by presidents of the United States to be Solicitor General of the United States; Perlman in 1947 and Sobeloff in 1954. A city-wide powerful Russian Jewish political boss James H. (Jack) Pollack established Baltimore's most active and powerful Trenton Democratic Club. His political savvy and clout practically assured the election of Russian Jewish Marvin Mandel to the office of Governor of Maryland. Another Russian Jew, Philip Goodman President of the City Council, briefly served out the term of Mayor Harold Grady who resigned to become Chief judge of Baltimore's Supreme Bench.. Elected for several terms as Baltimore City Comptroller, Russian Jewish Hyman Pressman guarded the city's funds and while at it managed to become a colorful clown and bad poet. In segments of the city with large concentrations of registered Jewish voters, Russian Jews, by shear numbers, have played an important role in influencing and bringing out the local vote. For this, several have been appointed to petty political offices such as magistrates in police and traffic courts. Both German and Russian Jews have been placed on numerous prestigious city and state boards and commissions.

1 Some Baltimore Christian Germans supported Germany from 1914 to 1916. They changed their thinking after the "Fatherland's" U-boats attacked American ships carrying war supplies to England.

2 Between 1924 and 1932 when the Jews were 3% of the nation's population, 12% of those indicted for bootlegging were Jewish.

3 The two stockholders of record were the wives of underworld gangsters doing business as Murder Incorporated. Both the New York and Baltimore problems with Murder Incorporated revolved around union organizing activities.

4 Jews of Eastern European extraction profited very well during the Roosevelt and Truman presidencies.

UNCOMMON THREADS

PART II-14

Northwest Passage * Great neighborhoods * Easterwood Boys * Synagogues follow * Changing life styles * Regressive Reform * Family Circles * Yiddiskeit * East Lombard Street

A few years before, during and after World War I, thousands of Russian Jews were financially able to move away from a decaying and crowded East Baltimore. A surge of people left and the exodus continued well after World War II until the old neighborhoods were well drained. The attachment of Jewish parents and their children to each other was such that when married sons and daughters moved uptown, most likely pappa and momma also moved; many parents lived with their sons and daughters. While the mass Russian Jewish relocation diluted the old world flavor of and the crowded living in East Baltimore, more importantly, it precipitated a momentous and serious social upheaval that carried a strain of self-consciousness. Russian Jews reached for a higher comfort of living and at the same time tried to hold fast to their religious and social East Baltimore base.

For the most part, those who left did all but abandon the East Baltimore institutions that for years had been the heart focus and lifeline of their social and cultural being. The sheer numbers sent a message that affiliation with the East Baltimore social agencies was no longer needed. These moves fractured the neighborhoods and were a precursor of an eventuality; that the existence of a charismatic East Baltimore Russian Jewish community would disappear completely. In retrospect, many East Baltimore Russian Jews were actually only long term transients because only a few owned the houses in which they lived. Many had refrained from buying housing after they came to America not only because they couldn't afford to, but also because they had memories of life in Russia where Jews suffered the indignity of loss when the Russian government confiscated their houses and other property.

The move from East Baltimore in the 1820s and 1930s represented a significant climb up a rung of the American ladder. Many Russian Jews moved into newly developed areas adjacent to the southern boundary of Druid Hill Park where spacious and comfortable row houses had been built. Others moved into houses vacated by German Jews who had moved to upper Park Heights Avenue, Mt. Washington, Windsor Hills, Pikesville, and to large properties that touched the estate lands of the largely Christian estates of Baltimore County. Numbers of Russian Jews moved into a concentration of row houses south of North Avenue and west of Fulton Avenue and in the Walbrook and Garrison Boulevard areas. Others bought row houses and duplexes on Park Heights Avenue from Park Circle to Pimlico and on Reisterstown Road from Fulton to north of Belvedere Avenue. This vast section of the city known as lower Park Heights was the most popular area to move into from East Baltimore. Sections of Forest Park, a middle class nicer neighborhood had long been long restricted to Christians due to a gentlemen's agreement, an obstruction that collapsed rather quickly. These not too expensive properties in Forest Park became attractive to Jews, both German and Russian. Because so many Jews at the time worked in jobs in the downtown garment and retail districts, good public transportation was a criterion for the areas in which Jews moved.

At Bentalou and Baker Streets in northwest Baltimore, the seven acres of Easterwood Park was the site of a unique facet of Baltimore Jewish history. In Easterwood Park, through the auspices and supervision of the Playground Athletic League (the PAL), the Easterwood Park Boys was spawned. From the 1920s through the 1950s, the name Easterwood Park was synonymous with competitive sports. Jewish and Christian clubs teamed against each other; both produced some excellent athletes. Neighborhood bakeries, pharmacies, and eateries sponsored club teams and furnished uniforms and equipment. Camaraderie of Easterwood Park Boys continues; their well-attended annual reunions raise funds for charities and scholarships. A junior group, Easterwood Boy's Club is socially oriented. Both clubs take pride in the fact that not a single Russian Jewish boy who played on an Easterwood team has been known to have been arrested or convicted of a criminal act.

Almost all of the Russian Jews retained their orthodoxy after leaving East Baltimore though some, for a short time only. Had Orthodox Jews not been able to locate within walking distance of a shul, their moves would have presented a problem. Shortly after the large northwest movement, several Orthodox congregations were formed, and until they were able to erect synagogues, services were held in single family houses slightly remodeled for this use.

By the early 1920s, roughly one half of the Russian Jews who lived in East Baltimore had moved away; most of those remaining were extremely Orthodox. For the year 1920, Polk's City Directory listed over thirty Russian Jewish Orthodox synagogues in East Baltimore. The move of so many Russian Jews was sad and painful for smaller synagogues that lost so many members it became increasingly difficult for them to assemble ten men for a minyan, an essential to conduct a Jewish service. Small East Baltimore congregations either merged with larger ones remaining in East Baltimore or with those that moved to Northwest Baltimore. During the transitional years that spanned the move, some established East Baltimore congregations could not re-establish their existing synagogues in Northwest Baltimore while their members lived with a foot in each area geographically so far apart. Some of the very small congregations that ceased to exist had never incorporated, appeared on no synagogue lists, left no records, and their existence became hearsay.[1]

In a few instances, services were held in private homes to cater to those Russian Jews whose conscience allowed them to observe only the high holidays; nevertheless, formal Orthodox Jewish worship continued on a large scale, so much so that Baltimore attained the highest percentage of Orthodox Russian synagogues than any other American city. Baltimore has been called by outsiders the Yerusholaem D'America (The American Jerusalem).[2]

For most Russian Jews, their religion served as a co-extension of their lives, so entwined with their existence that the laws of the Talmud regulated every movement of their being. Until the time of the mass movement from East Baltimore, when some religious fervor eased, Orthodox Russian Jews did not question the authority of religion. The 1920s clearly marked a change in the immigrant parents' children who had come of age, married, and had children of their own. A large segment of the new families believed the ceremonies and restrictions imposed upon them by Orthodox Judaism hampered their freedom and Americanization. Hebrew chants and ceremonies in the synagogues and symbolic rituals in the homes had an ever decreasing meaning, so many began to affiliate with the older established Baltimore congregations, Orthodox and Reform. In a show of Americanization, many frequented vaudeville theaters and dance halls. Inveterate gamblers, many Russian Jews attended and bet on prize fights, played cards, and shot craps. Worse than just engaging in these activities, they did these during the leisure hours of the Sabbath. This was distressful to many older Jews who faithfully spent their energies making sure that their shuls could gather a minyan.

Eating kosher became threatened when a new word was introduced into the Yiddish language. Oysesn (to eat out) specifically referred to having meals in a restaurant, not in the home of friend or relative. Eating out became a status of a sort that developed into the super status of a vacation away from the city at which time all meals were eaten in a restaurant.

Regardless of the religious fervor built into the lives of Orthodox Jews, attendance in the synagogues increasingly lagged. The concerned board of Shomrei Mishmereth Hakodesh Congregation, levied fines on members who did not attend services at least once a month. It took a while, but most Orthodox parents eventually came to terms with their children's new life styles; styles that were no longer compatible with the intensity of orthodoxy. In 1924, the Council of Orthodox Jewish Congregations of Baltimore was chartered. Aimed at both adults and children, the purpose was to strengthen Orthodox Judaism and its Baltimore institutions.

Apart from other orthodox groups, White Russian Lubavitcher Hasidim converted and enlarged a Quantico Avenue house for use as a synagogue. The members of Lubavitz Nasach Ari Congregation, founded in 1931, had been Chernigover Landsleit (former residents of the Polish community of Chernigover). Previous to their move, they worshipped in the Agudas Achim Shul on south Caroline Street. Hasidim venerated certain rabbis whom they regarded as miracle workers. In their homes and in their shuls, in accordance with their religious rituals, a few Baltimore Hasidim made merry by ceremonially drinking and performing dances of unusual whirls and gestures.

Shortly after the German Jewish Chizuk Amuno Conservative Congregation constructed their large synagogue in 1920 on Eutaw Place and Chauncey Avenue, large numbers of Russian Orthodox Jews became attracted to it. The new synagogue was Romanesque-Byzantine style, designed by Baltimore's foremost architect of the day, Joseph Evans Sperry. Chizuk Amuno was to have been topped by a dome, but the congregation ran out of money. Before drawing plans, the congregation's board sent Sperry to Europe to gather design ideas, some of which are incorporated in the synagogue building. A few years earlier, Sperry had been the architect for the

UNCOMMON THREADS

Emersonian Apartments, built on the west side Eutaw Place, one block closer to Lake Drive than the site of the future Chizuk Amuno Synagogue.

For sabbath and daily worship the location of the shul, within easy walking distance from the new homes of Russian Orthodox Jews, was a great attraction. Chizuk Amuno[3] became the first of the Baltimore German Jewish founded congregations to embrace a majority of Russian Jewish members and to introduce them to services conducted in Hebrew and English with nary an utterance of Yiddish spoken from the pulpit. German Jews retained control of the synagogue's customs, business, and manner of worship for many years.

To keep abreast of rapidly changing social and religious practices during these years, several American born rabbis of Orthodox Russian shuls infused English into their Yiddish and Hebrew services. While an earlier assumed requirement was that rabbis who occupied German Jewish Synagogue pulpits be fluent in German, this language was no longer spoken in the services.

Post World War I through the 1930s, liberal Reform Judaism as practiced overwhelmingly by German Jews fell into a regressive religious meaning for a large number of its constituents. The teaching of Hebrew continued in the Sunday Schools, but many students and parents no longer considered Jewish history and culture to be a priority in their lives. Bar Mitzvah[4] and Confirmation continued in the Baltimore Reform temples and the accompanying services remained sanctimonious.

When families of Eastern European Jews came to America they formed Family Circles; of which the criteria for membership were blood relationship, legal ties such as marriage, or in some cases a geographic proximity. The Jewish family is one of constant spirituality in which the men are dominant in the public sphere and the women control their domestic world; this was well practiced in their weekly gatherings. Family Circles were originally formed because within their unity the family found strength and they used this strength. The circles kept the family together by helping one another in need and at times they shared in a member's good fortune. Members of the circles recognized that acting as a group they were able to send help to relatives remaining in the old country and in many instances they brought them to the United States.

For Russian Jews remaining in East Baltimore, social customs remained "Old World" within the Family Circle. On Sunday afternoons, families and friends, usually from the same Russian shtetl, gathered in homes with a narrow prescribed social agenda -- a repetition of the week before and all the weeks before that. The important issue was the selection to be made of whose home would be visited the following week. Families walked together to the weekly gatherings, arriving within a short while after the completion of the host's traditional Sunday dinner. While the children played, adults drank steaming hot tea from glasses. If the tea was too hot, they poured it into a saucer and drank from that while they exchanged views and ideas and confidences they heard in the work place during the week. They compared their ideas on charity, and some family circles made joint decisions and family circle charitable contributions. Russian Jewish immigrants talked and talked, and they continued to drink their tea until late afternoon when the host family spread delicatessen on the kitchen table accompanied by bottles of seltzer water. For most families who moved away from the tight quarters of East Baltimore, the family circles continued to exist but in a more mundane way. Although some families continue their family circle meetings to this day, the concept has disintegrated with the scattering of families.

Saturday afternoon visits were for the social gathering of a few neighborhood women at the home of a friend. Discussions were on an intellectual level, centering on world news pertaining to the Jewish people. True, the women gossiped, but they also talked about subjects from articles that appeared in Yiddish publications during the week as well as matters of the lovelorn. These women for the most part had an expertise second to none in matters of the heart. After all, many married their husbands by arrangement through matchmakers when love was a distant runner-up in their emotions. There were problems about problems between relationships to delve into, problems of aged parents, problems of in-laws, and problems of marriage possibilities for children. They exchanged individual home remedies for common health problems. Quite naturally and without fail, all discussion ended with affirmative nods in agreement on the power of the common denominator of all cures, chicken soup. Many of the older women's education took place in their homes, and their knowledge was limited to domestic arts and religious observances. Unlike the boys, Jewish girls received very little education in their Russian shtetls. They were raised and trained to cook, wash, sew, care for the house and by age sixteen or seventeen, made available for an arranged marriage. On the occasion when the gathering in the home included a woman who had received an education away from the home, she became a source of wisdom and information, the validity of which neither could nor would be questioned.

On the surface, East Baltimore Russian Jewish life appeared to be passive, and perhaps it was to an outsider who had not as yet sensed the ever presence of Yiddishkeit (can't be fully explained}. Yiddishkeit is a deep inner feeling that can neither be seen nor heard; nor easily explained and it flourished in Russian Jewish East Baltimore. Yiddiskeit fueled Budd Schulberg's novel *What Makes Sammy Run*. Yiddishkeit, the undefined drive inborn in the Russian Jew, manifested itself in ideas, styles, and mannerisms. It absorbed itself into an improvised culture of its own, and its language was Yiddish. With no conscious intent, Russian Jewish children learned Yiddishkeit at the knees of their parents, and they were not alone because German Jews had their own version of Jewishness called Yehudishkeit.

Yiddishkeit supported networking that exchanged information on the dealings of others; they developed a sixth sense that put Yiddish speaking Jews in synch with the market place. Yiddishkeit imparted confidence and aroused energies needed to handle situations such as transforming themselves from worker to manufacturer. For a former worker and union member, Yiddishkeit allowed a manufacturer to deal with the friction of having discarded union affiliations, feelings, and friendships towards relatives and others who remained as workers, and at the same time, be comfortable sitting as boss on the other side of the meeting or bargaining table. Yiddishkeit made it OK for an employee to go on strike against his employer who may be his father-in-law. Yiddishkeit became evident early in the lives of American Russian Jewish boys who sold newspapers on the streets or hustled as gofors for business people. Yiddishkeit worked for young boys who worked the telephone booth in the corner drug store. They answered incoming calls and performed a neighborhood service for tips by racing down the street and up the steps to notify a party that the phone call was for them.

As America moved from the nineteenth to the twentieth century, the country passed through its initial phase of modern industrialization. Factors were in place that allowed many Russian Jews to begin their own businesses where they could use their Yiddishkeit to good advantage. Between 1890 and the depression of the 1930s, the country needed manufactured low unit cost goods that could be made in large enough quantities to be profitable and did not require a huge capital investment. Russian Jewish Yiddishkeit worked well in this market challenge. Mostly as a by-product of education, Yiddishkeit exists today but in a limited way. How strange it is that a people who have repudiated so many aspects of their lives; some continue to cling at all to the rudiments of Yiddishkeit!

Orthodox Judaism is difficult to faithfully adhere to unless a family lives in a defined community large enough to provide the basics of a kosher butcher and a shul within walking distance. This was partly the reason for the 1000 and 1100 blocks of East Lombard Street. When German Jews lived in East Baltimore, Lombard Street[5] was in its commercial infancy. The Lombard Street remembered now was almost entirely the product of Eastern European Jews shortly after the turn of the century. A few Greek grocers sold olives, feta cheese, and grape leaves, and Italians sold ricotta and prosciutto ham.

Russian Jewish immigrant merchants, most of whom lived above their stores, catered to almost every human and kosher need. Their stores lined both sides of the 1000 and 1100 blocks of East Lombard Street from Central Avenue to Exeter Street and sparsely west to Albemarle Street. Every building displayed goods for sale; some had store fronts and stalls; others had only improvised stalls that extended two feet from the building line, the legal restriction. Merchants sold pots and pans, toys, and new and second hand ready made clothing from racks that hung outside the stores. On Thursday afternoon and Friday morning market days, vehicular traffic was impeded but not stopped as it slowly passed peddlers' wagon-wheeled pushcarts that lined the curbs, laden with fruits and vegetables or notions, sundries, and cloth. To bargain, Yiddish was the language of the turf, as most likely the participants could not speak English well enough to properly express themselves. Aged women begged for charity, and sometimes these same women sold fish from children's go-carts. Short heavy immigrant women carrying market baskets contrasted with well-dressed uptown ladies who, a few years ago, had lived in East Baltimore. Ladies named Reba at birth now answered to Rebecca.

Although many Russian Jewish women in accordance with the Talmud baked their own cholla, the ceremonial egg bread for the Sabbath, there was a sizable market for those who didn't. Lombard Street bakeries also sold bagels, Jewish ryes, dark and light, Russian black bread, and chocolate macaroons. When purchasing fish, to determine its freshness, buyers checked the eyes of fish that laid iced on sidewalk stands. Those not sure bought live carp and other fish that swam in tanks inside the stores. For a customer who bought a live fish, the store owner wrapped it in a newspaper. The purchaser returned home quickly to immerse the fish in a tub of water so that it could swim until the time it would lose its head, usually the following day.[6]

Chickens, ducks and geese in stacked wooden crates squawked loudly and smelled to high heaven. Buyers, recent residents of Warsaw or Kiev and mavens (experts) on fowl, reached through the breast feathers under the wing to feel if the hen were a fat one. The chosen chicken was a very special bird that let the buyer know it by frantically flapping its wings when handed over to the Lord High Executioner, the kosher schohet. He used a small un-notched special challafim (knife) to mercifully sever the trachea and esophagus of the bird, and allowed its blood to run into the alley gutter and on into the sewer. According to Talmudic Law, if the fowl's neck was not cut in the exact proper place, the bird could not be eaten. The fowl was then dipped into an old potato chip tin filled with scalding water and plucked. No charge, or a nominal charge only, was made for slitting the neck though there was a small charge for plucking. The plucker put feathers of ducks and geese in a separate pile as they had a commercial value. Sometimes a few chicken feathers wound up in the duck or geese pile, just enough of them to go undetected. (Hey, a guy's gotta make a living). The store owner sold the duck and goose feathers to a jobber who resold them to featherbed and pillow makers.

The schohet was required to be a student of Talmudic Law and was always approved and appointed to his position by a rabbi. He began his work with prayer before slitting the neck of the first chicken of the day. If he failed to pray, the chicken was considered terefah (non-kosher). Traditionally, chickens bought for the erev (evening before) Yom Kippur (The Day of Atonement) received a special rite. Before killing, the schohet held the chicken by its feet and swung it in a circle over his head three times while reciting a prayer. The chicken is symbolic of the human body, and the ritual is to cast away the sins of the old year and to begin anew.

Delikatessengeschaft (delicatessen) was of German origin but its Eastern European Jewish version in America was unique in itself. Inside a deli, customers endured and participated in a constant chatter of Yiddish and broken English. A melange of aromas of corned beef, pastrami, and kosher hot dogs vied with hanging salamis, sausage by the yard, and home barreled dill pickles, sauerkraut and pickled herring, smoked and dried fish. In the Jewish diet, much emphasis is on fish, especially for those who lived in the Baltic Sea area. Thursday night before Shabbat and Saturday night after Shabbat, the busiest times on Lombard Street, Yiddishkeit and the concentration of ethnicity generated an energy of its own.

On Baltimore Street, restaurants, community centers, schools, societies, and agencies lined two blocks parallel to the Lombard Street activity. On Saturdays, a large number of dories and moving and transfer companies' vans parked on Central Avenue at the end of the 1100 blocks of Baltimore and Lombard Streets. For visitors to Lombard

Street from Sunday to Friday, rest room facilities were available in the basement of the Shomre Mishmereth Hakodesh Shul on Lloyd Street. It was too expensive for the congregation to provide toilet tissue for the rest rooms, but they felt a certain responsibility. They always had available, an ample supply of orange paper usually used as individual fruit wrappers.

After World War II, Lombard Street changed. With only a comparatively few Jews continuing to live in old East Baltimore, merchants depended on northwest Baltimore Jews to return to their old neighborhood to buy. This they did until they learned they could buy the same dill pickles and pastrami in their uptown neighborhoods without succumbing to the psychological justification of traveling all the way downtown to Lombard Street. The Lombard Street of Jewish life had been all but destroyed by the upward mobility of former East Baltimore Jews.

A partial new life breathed into Lombard Street, however, when after World War II, northwest German and Russian Jews discovered that it was considered a minor expression of sophistication to return to their Lombard Street roots to buy corned beef. They, a rather persnickety lot, at first requested lean, but as time passed and they heard more and more medical reports, they asked for extra lean. For this request, the merchants countered by charging more per pound; still, on Sundays, the uptowners kept coming back to Lombard Street for a period of years. They came partly for the food and partly to banter with the brash, wise cracking delicatessen Jewish countermen; humorously insulting for the most part and always the masters of Yiddish expression. As the days neared when the uptown trade stopped coming, owners of the few stores left allowed them to become tacky and the awnings over the store fronts not repaired nor replaced, became noticeably more shredded.

---

1 *Formed in 1917, Shaarei Zion (Gates of Zion) (Orthodox) Congregation became the first synagogue on lower Park Heights Avenue, later to be euphemistically referred to as "Rue de la Synagogue." A cottage in the 3400 block was remodeled for use as a synagogue in 1920; in 1926, Shaarei Zion completed the erection of a grand synagogue in the 3400 block of Park Heights Ave, midway up the hill from Park Circle. In 1954, the congregation built educational facilities in the 6600 block of Park Heights Avenue where a new Shaarei Zion synagogue was consecrated in 1964. Adath B'nei Israel (Congregation of the Children of Israel) (Orthodox), founded in 1919 in East Baltimore merged about 1960 with the Chofetz Chaim (named after a Polish rabbi) (Orthodox) Congregation. Chofetz Chaim founded in 1934 by members who left the Har Zion Congregation occupied a synagogue in the 2100 block of West North Avenue. The combined congregations moved to the 3700 block of West Rogers Avenue in 1949.*

The Beth Jacob (House of Jacob (Orthodox) Congregation founded in 1938 held their first uptown service in a house on Park Heights Avenue and Pinckney Road. In 1945 they bought what they thought at the time to be a prime lot on the northwest corner of Park Heights and Manhattan Avenues; it has proven to be otherwise. In 1953, they dedicated a handsome synagogue on the property. Anshe Sphard founded in 1887 and Ohr Knesseth Israel, two venerable East Baltimore Orthodox Congregations, merged in 1950 to become known as the Rogers Avenue Synagogue. The ground level base in the 3900 block of West Rogers Avenue was dedicated in 1953 and the synagogue completed in 1958. Membership in both the Rogers Avenue

Synagogue and the Beth Jacob Synagogues declined in recent years so they merged in 1993. The Rogers Avenue Synagogue closed, and the combined membership worshipped at Beth Jacob, making it the second largest Orthodox congregation in Baltimore. In a grand procession, the seven Torahs of the Rogers Avenue Synagogue were transported eight blocks to Beth Jacob in seven convertible automobiles with their tops down. Traditionally they should have been carried on foot under a hupah.

Organized in 1918, Har Zion (Mount of Zion) (Orthodox) Congregation worshipped in a synagogue in the 2000 block of West North Avenue until 1956. In that year, they merged with the Tiferith Israel (Beauty of Israel) (Orthodox) Congregation founded in 1926. In 1948, Tiferith Israel built on Garrison Boulevard and Forest Park Avenue what was said to be Baltimore's first air-conditioned synagogue. In 1970, the combined Har Zion-Tiferith Israel merged with Petach Tikvah (Door of Hope) (Orthodox) Congregation which was founded in 1921and had occupied a synagogue in the 5100 block of Denmore Avenue since 1937. The combined congregations became the Pickwick (Orthodox) Jewish Center located in the 6200 block of Greenspring Avenue. Almost unheard of for a supposedly well established suburban synagogue, the Pickwick Jewish Center disbanded in 1988.

The congregants of Beth Tfiloh (House of Prayer) (Orthodox) Congregation founded in 1921, worshipped in cottages until they dedicated a synagogue on Garrison Boulevard and Fairview Avenue in 1927. Membership grew quickly and Beth Tfiloh became Baltimore's largest Orthodox Congregation. They purchased ground in 1929 for their own cemetery on Windsor Mill Road. In post World War II, the neighborhood changed and a diminished congregation continued to worship on Garrison Boulevard until 1966, much too long after many of its members had moved to other sections of the city. The lost was temporary as most of their former members rejoined after they erected an enormous synagogue center in 1966 on Old Court Road, the sanctuary topped by a spectacular stylized golden crown.

Founded in Walbrook in 1923, the Anshe Shalom (People of Peace) (Orthodox) Congregation opened a temporary, and in 1934 a permanent synagogue in the 1900 block of Poplar Grove Street; in 1956, it closed. The Shaarei Tfiloh (Gates of Prayer) (Orthodox) Congregation, founded in 1920, built the lower structure of their synagogue in 1921 and completed the upper structure in 1925. The impressive high domed synagogue on the top of a hill overlooking Druid Hill Park at Liberty Heights and Holmes Avenues is called the Park Shul or the Auchentoroly Terrace Synagogue. In 1995 only seven Jews remain living in this drastically changed neighborhood and the membership of about seventy families celebrated its seventy-fifth anniversary.

2   *An ad in the September 29, 1995, BALTIMORE JEWISH TIMES claimed Rabbi Avrum Nachman Schwatrz of the Lloyd Street Shul when it belonged to the Shomrei Mishmeres Hakodesh between 1910 and 1937 made the city the "Yerushalayim of America."*

3   *Founded as an orthodox congregation, though conservative since 1886, descendants of Chizuk Amuno's orthodox German founding fathers, the Friedenwalds remained members. Always "Pillars of the Shul," they continued to worship as orthodox in this conservative synagogue. On Yom Kippur, male members of this elegant family attended services wrapped in the customary "Kitel" (shroud) and wearing custom-made white prayer slippers. Some conservative and many orthodox Jews follow this custom and today non-leather white tennis shoes are acceptable for Yom Kippur services.*

4   *In several mid-western and southern parts of the country, the tradition of Bar Mitzvah was dropped and although the teaching of Hebrew was continued in the Sunday Schools, few children bothered to learn it. A stranger attending a Bar Mitzvah service in a Reform temple in the 1930s might observe how pious and knowledgeable the congregants appeared to be. What they would not know is that the Bar Mitzvah candidate most likely read his Torah portion in impeccable Hebrew from phonetics written on a sheet of paper inserted in the scrolls. In December 1994, the 58 year old Rabbi Floyd L. Herman Of the Har Sinai Congregation, after spending 30 years as a rabbi and teacher, had his own Bar Mitzvah. The Reform Temple he and his family attended did not observe the tradition.*

5   *Lombard Street was unlike New York's Hester, Orchard or Canal Streets because Baltimore lacked the concentration of Jewish people who lived in the five and six story tenements of New York's East Side. Lombard Street was Baltimore without tenements. Nevertheless, both had in common the fact that the ambiance of both was brought to the respective cities by Eastern European Jews.*

6   *A fish does not have to be killed by a schohet as Halacha states that as soon as fish are removed from the water they are as good as dead, and so may be killed as the fisherman, fish seller or the customer sees fit.*

In the early 1880s-Jews began a mass migration from Eastern Europe to America. Illustrations in the following four pages depict a way of life in the shtetls of Eastern Europe; a way of life that greatly affected the Jewish way of living in America.

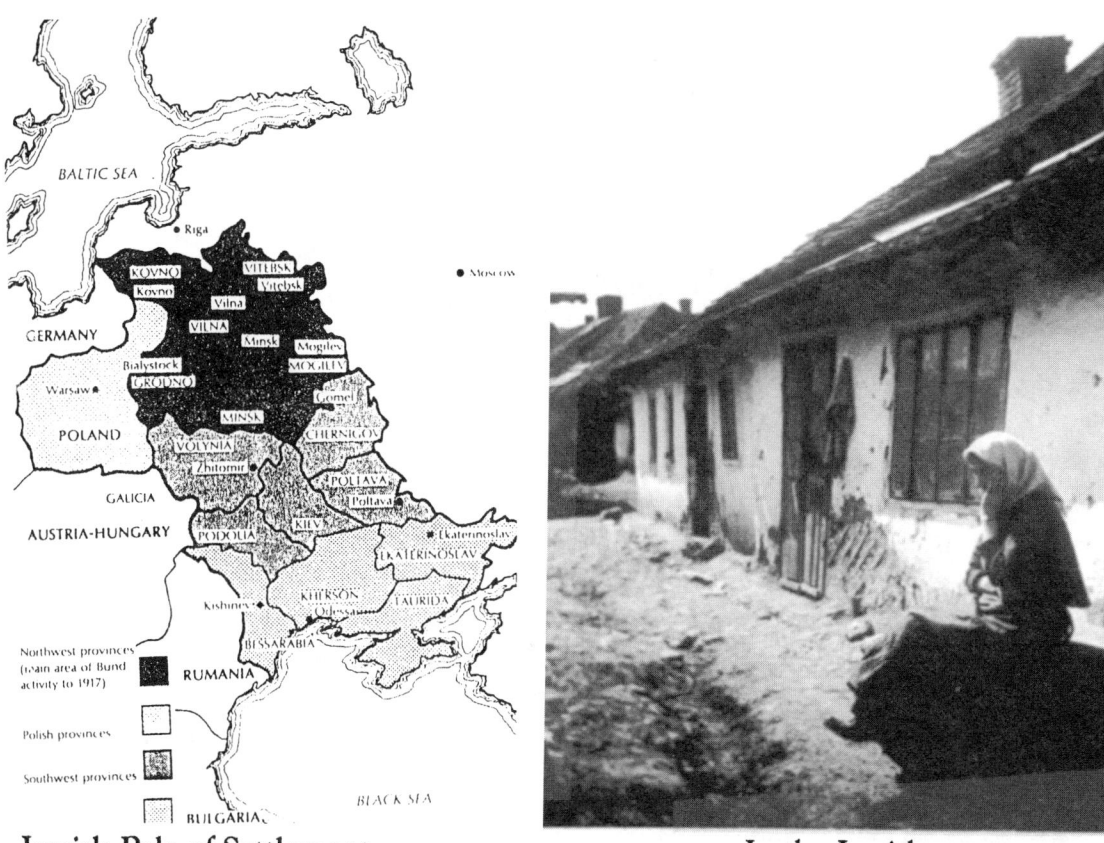

Jewish Pale of Settlement
Late 19th century

In the Jewish quarter
Zborow, Poland - 1915

Peasants in the Ukraine - early 20th century

HOME - SYNAGOGUE - MARKET

Jewish poverty Eastern Europe. Note condition of roofs.

17th century wooden synagogue of a type used in the area. Gwozdziecz, eastern Poland

Market day Kasimierez, Poland Early 20th century

Mobile coffee vender
Prague - 1905

Passover in Galicia - 1915
Note 2 soldiers in the
Austrian Imperial Army

Yehuda Penn, the watchmaker
Minsk/ Byelorussia - 1914

Klezmer band
Russia - 1910

Advertising Yiddish Theater
Warsaw - 1908

Carpentry shop
Galati, Romania - 1922

Destruction in a Jewish Street after a pogrom - Ukraine - 1881

After the riots, Kishinev, Bessarabia - Easter and the last day of Passover
April 19, 1903

After a battle, Jewish villagers trek back to their homes
1914 - 1915

The JEWISH WORKER - organ of the Poalel Zion, 1904

A red flag flown during the first Russian revolution in 1905 reads "Down with the Tsar's Constitution, long live the democratic Republic"

This Statement of Russian pogrom - October, November, 1905 is on a wall at Ellis Island, N. Y.

To reach European ports, Eastern Europeans boarded trains in Russia and transferred to German trains at the border.

Polish Jews sought emigration advice at the HIAS desk in Warsaw

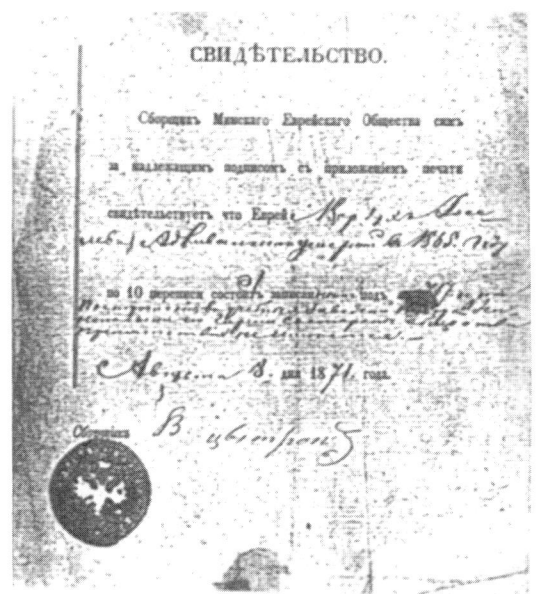

Russia required travel

The "Baalagoleh" (wagon driver) carted emigrants and their baggage from the shtetls to the railroad stations.

Russian train circa 1909

Emigrants registering in the large hall of a German steamship line - circa 1909

Morning prayers aboard ship

Huddled masses during an Atlantic Ocean crossing - circa 1890

The North German Lloyd steamship BALTIMORE docked at the Baltimore & Ohio R. R. Pier # 9 - North Locust Point - circa 1880

Hansa Haus - Baltimore headquarters of the North German Lloyd Steamship line - N/E cor Charles & Redwood Sts.

EUROPEAN IMMIGRANTS LAND AT NORTH LOCUST POINT. BALTIMORE

Arrival at North Locust Point circa 1904

Holding pen Pier 8 Locust Point

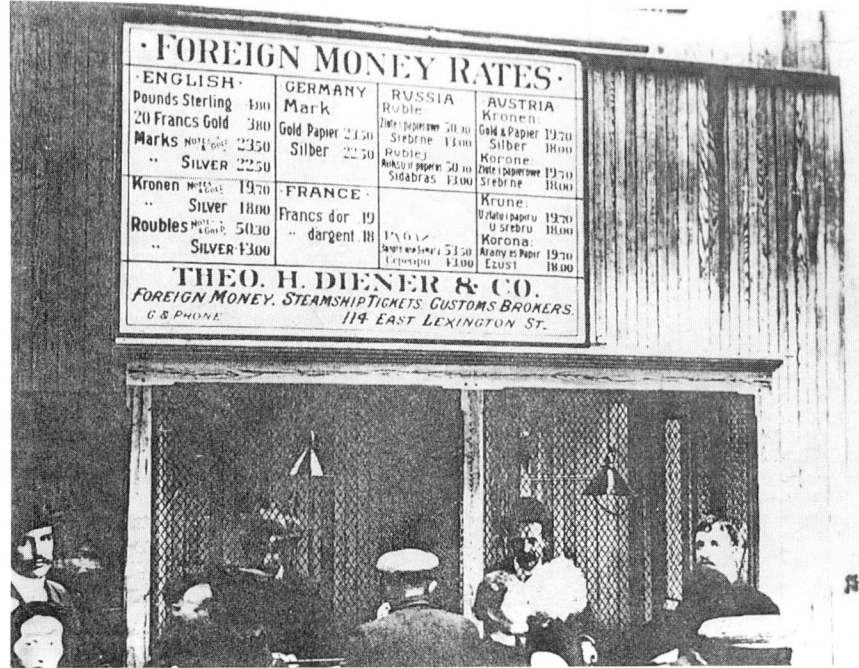

Currency Exchange E. Lexington Street circa 1904

Wall Exhibits - Ellis Island Museum

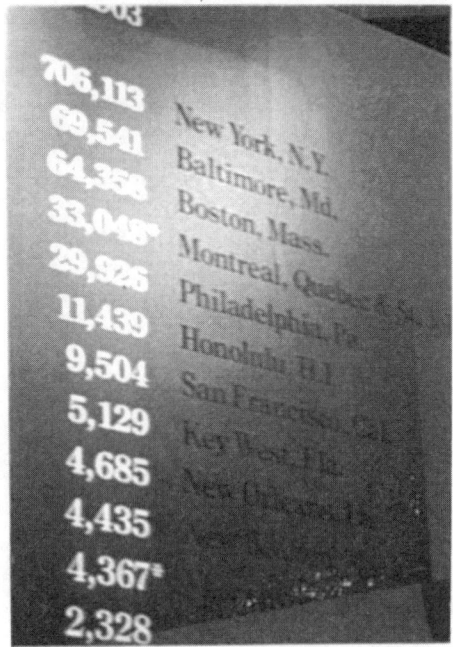

In 1903, and in other years,
Baltimore was the 2nd
largest United States port of entry

Since the first quarter of 1800s
there has been opposition
to immigration

Table 4. Jewish Population in Selected American Cities, 1878, 1907, 1927

City	1878	1907	1927
New York	60,000	600,000 (33.0)	1,765,000 (44.0)
Chicago	10,000	100,000 (5.6)	325,000 (8.0)
Philadelphia	12,000	100,000 (5.6)	270,000 (6.7)
Boston	7,000	60,000 (3.3)	90,000 (2.3)
Cleveland	3,500	40,000 (2.2)	85,000 (2.1)
Detroit	2,000	10,000	75,000 (1.9)
Newark	3,500	30,000 (1.7)	65,000 (1.6)
Los Angeles	330	7,000	65,000 (1.6)
Pittsburgh	2,000	25,000 (1.4)	53,000 (1.3)
Baltimore	10,000	40,000 (2.2)	48,000 (1.2)
San Francisco	16,000	30,000 (1.7)	35,000
Milwaukee	2,075	10,000	25,000
Cincinnati	8,000	25,000 (1.4)	23,500
New Haven	1,000	8,000	22,500
Rochester (N.Y.)	1,175	10,000	22,500
Minneapolis	172	6,000	22,000
Providence	375	10,000	21,000
Denver	260	5,000	17,000
Louisville	2,500	8,000	12,500
Portland (Or.)	635	5,000	12,000
Atlanta	525	3,000	11,000
Houston	461	2,000	11,000
Indianapolis	400	5,500	10,000
New Orleans	5,000	8,000	9,000
Columbus (Oh.)	420	4,000	8,000
Norfolk (Va.)	500	2,000	7,800
Montgomery	600	1,500	3,000

Source: Adapted from Lee Shai Weissbach, "The Jewish Communities of the United States on the Eve of Mass Migration," *American Jewish History* 78 (September 1988): 79-108.
Note: Figure in parentheses is the percentage of the total population of American Jewry.

Table 3. General and Jewish Immigration from Eastern Europe to the United States, 1871-1920

Year	General	Jewish	% Jewish
1871-80	2,810,000	15,000	0.5
1881-84	2,580,340	74,310	2.9
1885	395,350	19,610	4.9
1886	334,200	29,660	8.8
1887	490,110	27,470	5.6
1888	547,000	31,360	5.7
1889	444,430	24,000	5.4
1890	455,300	34,300	7.5
1891	560,320	69,140	12.3
1892	579,660	60,325	10.4
1893	440,000	33,000	7.5
1894	285,630	22,110	7.7
1895	258,540	32,080	12.4
1896	343,270	28,120	8.2
1897	330,830	20,685	6.25
1898	229,300	27,410	11.9
1899	311,715	37,415	12.0
1900	448,570	60,765	13.5
1901	488,000	58,100	11.9
1902	648,745	57,670	8.9
1903	857,050	76,205	8.9
1904	812,870	106,240	13.1
1905	1,026,500	129,910	12.7
1906	1,100,735	153,750	14.0
1907	1,285,350	149,180	11.6
1908	782,870	103,390	13.2
1909	751,790	57,550	7.7
1910	1,041,570	84,260	8.1
1911	878,590	91,225	10.4
1912	838,170	80,595	9.6
1913	1,197,890	101,330	8.5
1914	1,218,480	138,050	11.3
1915	326,700	26,500	8.1
1916	298,825	15,110	5.1
1917	295,405	17,340	5.9
1918	110,620	3,670	3.3
1919	141,130	3,055	2.2
1920	430,000	14,290	3.3

Sources: Based on data from U.S. Bureau of the Census, *Historical Statistics of the United States to 1957* (Washington, D.C.: Government Printing Office, 1976); Samuel Joseph, *Jewish Immigration to the United States From 1881 to 1910* (New York: Arno, 1969); Simon Kuznets, "Immigration of Russian Jews to the United States: Background and Structure," *Perspectives in American History* 9 (1975): 35-124.

East Baltimore row houses in the late 19th century were shoulder to shoulder with late 18th century wooden houses.

Before the many sno-ball stands, neighborhood ice wagons served the purpose

Waiting their turn for a shower at one of the Baltimore public baths

Yaazor farm community - Baltimore County

Jobs in garment factories were plentiful for young women.

And available for many men who had tailoring experience

Immigrants, avid readers, read dailies, weeklies, monthlies, locals, and nationals published mostly in Yiddish

Editorial office in a small Jewish press

Adult English class at the J.E.A. - 1919

English class in a public school

The Baltimore Talmud Torah Class of 1916

The goal for immigrants - American citizenship

Jewish Educational Alliance

East Lombard Street - "Just us chickens"

And vegetables too

Ritual killing

Yiddish Theater poster - 1892

Early Baltimore movie house

Holliday Street theater - popular for Yiddish Theater

The Gayety Burlesque Theater

Shaari Tfiloh Synagogue
Liberty Heights & Holmes Ave. (1921)

Beth Tfiloh Synagogue
Garrison Blvd. (1927-1966)

Second Zionist Congress
Basel Switzerland - 1898

Theodor Herzl stamp

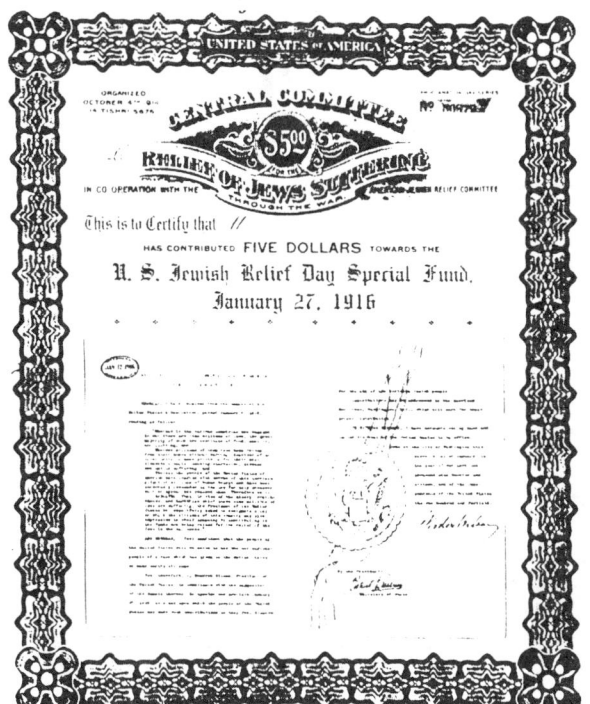

Certificate - Central Committee

Rev. Dr. Schepsel Schaffer, rabbi of Baltimore's Shearith Israel Congregation, was the only American to attend the Congress in Basel, Switzerland

DOCUMENT 1.
THE BALFOUR DECLARATION.

Foreign Office,
November 2nd, 1917.

Dear Lord Rothschild,

I have much pleasure in conveying to you, on behalf of His Majesty's Government, the following declaration of sympathy with Jewish Zionist aspirations which has been submitted to, and approved by, the Cabinet.

"His Majesty's Government view with favour the establishment in Palestine of a national home for the Jewish people, and will use their best endeavours to facilitate the achievement of this object, it being clearly understood that nothing shall be done which may prejudice the civil and religious rights of existing non-Jewish communities in Palestine, or the rights and political status enjoyed by Jews in any other country"

I should be grateful if you would bring this declaration to the knowledge of the Zionist Federation.

BALFOUR DECLARATION
This brief British document laid the foundation for the eventual establishment of the State of Israel.

Baltimore members of the Jewish Legion who fought with the British against the Turks for the liberation of Palestine in 1917.

PART III-I *COMMON CLOTH*

Mount Pleasant * The United and the Federated form the Associated * The Passing Years * Levindale

*T*he German Jewish community recognized that the dual costs of raising funds and administering charitable agencies for the same or similar purposes wasted money. As an initial step to address this issue, at a meeting of representatives of ten German Jewish charities in 1902, they attempted to organize and coordinate their activities. After numerous meetings and discussions, in 1906 Baltimore's German Jews organized twelve independent charities into a consortium -- the Federated Jewish Charities with Dr. Jacob Hollander, a liberal thinker, prolific writer, and a professor at the Johns Hopkins University, its first president. Two years later, Jacob Epstein,[1] a Lithuanian immigrant who attained great wealth was honored for his magnanimous gift to the Jewish community of Mount Pleasant, The Jewish Home for Consumptives. At Mount Pleasant, patients suffering from Tuberculosis could receive the treatment of long periods in the fresh air that physicians recommended. A communicative infectious disease, Tuberculosis, more commonly known as consumption, affects the lungs. As previously mentioned, Russian Jews were particularly susceptible to this illness because of their employment in sweat shops where untenable squalid conditions became incubators of the disease. Although Orthodox Jews could be fed kosher meals at both Mount Pleasant and the Hebrew Hospital, the latter lacked facilities for the months of special care needed to cure this illness

Within three years after the German Jews organized their federation, Russian Jews brought seven of their charities under a single umbrella; the United Hebrew Charities. Prior to this, Russian-Jewish administered downtown charities were foundering in disorganization so this amalgamation strengthened their purpose and added professionalism.

In a December 1910 issue of the *Baltimore Sun,* an article stated that a group of Baltimore German and Russian Jews met and expressed their distress at the existing schism between English speaking German and Yiddish speaking Russian Jews.. Members of the group urged that the Federated Jewish Charities and the United Hebrew Charities merge and serve the community as a single strong charitable force. Although there was no longer a need, if there ever really was, for separate uptown and downtown charities, the present separation was a comfortable buffer which many German and Russian Jews desired.. In 1910, neither charitable group was ready to deal with such a sensitive issue as the merging of German and Russian individually controlled interests. Though the meeting produced nothing concrete, it was far from a failure as it laid the ground work for future discussions of the feasibility of bringing together the common concerns of German and Russian Jews.

Even though the United States did not enter World War I until 1917, on-going combat since 1914 created conditions of starvation for thousands in several European countries. International relief agencies, with America playing a leading role, responded to the European needs, leaving local charities to deal with the communal needs in American cities. It was not until the war ended that German and Russian Jews actually felt secure enough to lay their animosities aside and make a sincere effort to combine their charities. Though they didn't arrive in America on the same ships, in this country they were for certain in the same boat. The decade of the twenties lay ahead, and it was a promising one as Baltimore rode the crest of temporary post-war prosperity. 1920 emerged as the year for Baltimore Jews[2] to take steps towards mutual understanding and to start the process of spinning their interests into a common thread. Needs after the war grew and charitable institutions were on their way to becoming big business. This thing of giving, stamped in the minds of both German and Russian Jews, particularly those who benefited financially during the war, stimulated both groups to unite.

In their generosity and with an awareness of the community's needs, those Jews who had gained considerable wealth had an uneasiness about how the charities' monies were going to be spent. They demanded prudent administration of the funds. In post World War I, the majority of the Baltimore Jewish community could not be described as affluent because there were large numbers of immigrants who had landed at Locust Point just before the war, and who as yet, were not able to rise above the poverty level. For the most part, the contributors to both German and Russian charities lived uptown; the recipients lived downtown. Interestingly, an odd juxtaposition occurred when members of the amalgamation committee came to the table. They had become partially entwined and didn't realize it. The Lithuanian Jacob Epstein, who had been so generous to the German charities, was among the representatives of the German uptown Federated Charities; a German Jew William Levy, a brother of Julius Levy one of the Federated representatives, was an important representative of the downtown United Charities.

The accomplished merger included thirteen Federated agencies[3] and nine United agencies. Two months before the Associated's formal incorporation, in November 1920, a gala dinner at the Lyric Theater launched a $500,000 fund raising campaign. All the boards of the individual constituent agencies finalized their achievement by voting independently to approve their inclusion in the combined Associated Jewish Charities. At first, the charismatic Jewish Court of Arbitration was not included because at the time it was immersed in labor problems in the men's clothing industry. The court was bearing the brunt of divisiveness between the mostly German Jewish owners and the Russian Jewish workers; it became a member a short time later.

The amalgamation of the two charities began as a legal corporation on January 16, 1921, when the Associated held its first meeting in the Veteran Corps Hall on Madison Avenue. The new board of the Associated elected the current in-office president of the Federated Jewish Charities, A. Ray Katz, Jacob Epstein's son-in-law to be the president of the combined organization and Louis Levin the Director. Within a few years, Epstein's other son-in-law Sidney Lansburgh became president and his youngest son Richard served as Chairman of the Board from 1992 to 1994. At the time of the founding of the Associated Jewish Charities, the majority of the greater Baltimore's sixty-five thousand Jews were of Eastern European heritage. Baltimore's German Jews, outnumbered by the thousands, would never again financially or otherwise dominate the city's Jewish community, even though Congress passed and the president signed the Johnson Act in 1924 that effectively restricted Russian Jewish immigration. Baltimore's German Jewish population, including the numbers that later fled Nazi Germany, continued to fall well behind the numbers of Russian Jews living in the city.

There is no exact date that marks the psychological beginning for weaving the threads of the two separate Jewish communities. It was a gradual happening that continuously tested the comfort level of both groups, but without doubt, the merging of the charities was the major happening of its day towards unification. There was the expected unorganized opposition to change which came from both Germans and Russians. Egos clashed when some members of each group considered themselves to be superior to the others. Russian Jews feared that they would be intimidated by the Yahudim (German) who were much wealthier than they, who spoke good English, and who reveled in their importance in the community. German and Russian Jewish leaders knew they had to continue to work in unison for the common good of the Baltimore Jewish community; however, because of their greater community influence and wealth, the Germans dominated the Administration and the board during the early years of the Associated Jewish Charities

In late 1922 with the Associated in existence for only two years, Baltimore's Jewish community flocked to Ford's Theater to witness a play written for the Associated by Louis H. Levin. It has been recorded that the theater was "packed to the chandeliers" and had the air of a Broadway first night and the anticipation that it would be a hit. Reviews said that the play which possessed a theme close to the hearts of the audience was extremely well performed.[4] Presented on two successive Sunday nights, the purpose of the *The Passing Years* was to dramatize the philanthropic history of the Baltimore Jewish community. The first presentation on Sunday, November 26th, was for those subscribers whose last names began with the letters A to K; those with L to Z attended the second performance on December 3rd. The first act of the three act play featured charity work during the Civil War; the second act focused on help for the Russian Jewish immigrants in 1890 by the German Jewish Hebrew Benevolent Society. The third act addressed the charity programs of the Associated in 1922. Very few Russian Jews had parts in the cast or were listed in the production staff. The audiences praised the production to such a degree that egos were well stroked, and those who participated rejoiced and believed the kudos received. Overwhelmed by such success, the play was taken to Philadelphia for a one night stand, and there before a small audience, the play flopped.

1923 became an auspicious year for the Associated Jewish Charities. A campaign to raise $700,000 to enlarge and improve the Hebrew Hospital and Home for the Aged fell slightly short, but the board nevertheless was elated with the results. After the campaign, they proceeded almost immediately with the construction of the hospital without scaling down the previously approved plans. The present amount of money raised was enough for the institution's immediate needs; later they raised the necessary funds.

The Associated made good progress in eliminating duplicity and overlapping of agencies and defining and re-defining the missions of the remaining ones. They launched a campaign to raise funds to build an orphanage on the present site of Levindale. Before the building was completed in 1923, the administrators of the Associated did an about face on their thinking because the number of Jewish orphans to be housed in the home was becoming fewer and fewer. Until all Jewish orphans were placed in private foster homes, Levindale functioned as an orphanage for a few years. The Baltimore Jewish community became the first in America to adopt a more humane solution to the problem of emotionally fragile orphan children.

The decision was more fortuitous than they knew at the time. Funds for the education of the orphan children had accumulated and the question arose what to do with this money. The Central Scholarship Bureau was founded in 1924, and the educational funds originally designated for the planned orphanage were made available to the Bureau for counseling and funding deserving Jewish children who lacked the wherewithal to continue schooling past high school. In 1940, restrictions were lifted to allow all children regardless of race or faith to be eligible for assistance. Depending upon the circumstance of the individual applicant, outright grants or interest free loans are available.

There can be little argument over the fact that the strength of the leaders of the Associated Jewish Charities, regardless of where they were born or their religious affiliation, established the oneness of Baltimore Jewish community.

UNCOMMON THREADS

1   Jacob Epstein was not a very religious man, and he never wore a yarlmuke in the synagogue though he carried one with him. He donned it in movie houses to protect his head so he wouldn't catch a cold

2   Compared to several other cities, Baltimore was late in planning the Jewish charities' merger. As early as 1864, Memphis established a single umbrella organization for that city's Jewish charities; Boston did so in 1895, and Cincinnati, in 1896.

3   The Board of the Jewish Children's Bureau, one of the thirteen agencies of the Federated and forerunner of the present day Jewish Family Services, had a problem agreeing on whom should be president of their agency. The German Jews thought that inasmuch as they had been in America longer than the Russian Jews, one of them should be made president The Russian Jews felt that the new president should be one of them. After all, they were much closer to, and understood the needs of the immigrants, more so than any German. A German Jewish community leader Sidney Hollander stood apart from the Germans on the board because he was considered by most German Jews to be much too liberal. When as a dinner guest in their homes, this gentleman chided the German Jewish clothing manufacturers for the low wages they paid their factory workers. Although well qualified, Germans on the board did not want him to be president. The Russian Jews didn't want him either, simply because he was German; so they compromised. Inasmuch as neither group wanted him to be President, and inasmuch as he was the only person both sides objected to, at least they were in agreement on the objection. So they voted and elected Sidney Hollander, the man neither faction wanted as President.

4   A young professional, Ed Wynn, the Broadway comedian of many hats, was booked to supplement the acting of the local non-professionals, starring Malcolm Lowenstein.

PART III-2

1920s Anti-Semitism

*D*uring the Roaring Twenties (1920s), the decade that spanned the years of prohibition, bobbed hair, short skirts, long dancing, bathtub gin, Model "T" Fords and making lots of money in the stock market, the most unfettered social period in American history took place. Russian Jews, very much involved in the intensity of these years, broke forth into the mainstream and began to share in the prosperity of Baltimore. Forty years had passed since the beginning of their migration and most of their children had been born in this country. In the period between the two World Wars, American culture changed drastically; the intellectual energies and improved economic resources of the Russian Jews fed upon each other and created an increased appetite and appreciation for all that America had to offer. Until this time, many Russian Jews worked day and night in Baltimore's garment industry and, by desire or otherwise, remained almost completely removed from everyday city life. Parents counseled their children not to follow their footsteps into the land of the sewing industries; it was way too difficult to earn a living.

German and Russian Jews realized that it was a psychological necessity for them to function in the community as a unified group in order to live with and to combat waves of anti-Semitism which swept the country in the 1920s. Never before or since in American history had 100% Americanism been so rampant. Prejudice in many forms ran high against most minority groups and an atmosphere of mistrust created a climate somewhat analogous to the days of the Know Nothings, but without the street fighting. It was almost impossible for Jewish boys to become bank tellers or for Jewish girls to get jobs as sales clerks in non-Jewish owned retail stores. Many newspaper want ads were so wanton as to specify that the prospective employer sought applicants with blonde hair and straight noses. The frightening presence of the Ku Klux Klan was revived in the south in the name of red-blooded Americanism; their act also reached into the north. The Klan philosophy, however, was not as anti-Semitic as it was anti-Catholic and anti-Negro.

Adding to the discomfort of Jews, the personal weekly newspaper of Henry Ford, the Dearborn, Michigan, *Dearborn Independent* began a series of articles on May 22, 1920 entitled, *The International Jew*. Kinship between the articles published and the *Protocols of the Learned Elders of Zion*[1] were far more than just co-incidental. At the same time the Ford publication appeared in America, like documents appeared in France, England, Germany and other European countries. Without doubt, Jews of the 1920s encountered a world wide wave of anti-Semitism. Non-Jewish readers who believed the trash published by the *Dearborn Independent*, never stopped to think how plans brought forth in the *Protocols* could possibly be realistic. No Jew, world wide, headed a government or military force or was even close to doing so. The *Protocols* insisted that Jewish wealth and intellect financed and advised those who shaped public opinion through domination of the press and that Jewish power was invisible, therefore more dangerous. The *Protocols* tried to convince readers that Jews planned to undermine existing political structures by their advocating free speech, atheism, and other shocking activities.

In the 1930s, due to the economic crisis in the United States and the rise of fascism in Europe, there was a sharp increase in anti-Semitism. The masses of unemployed became fertile ground for hate groups who perceived the Jew to be largely responsible for the depression. The largest and most influential of the hate groups of the period again came from the Detroit; the Christian Front. Baltimore radio listeners tuned their sets to hear the outspoken Father Charles C. E. Coughlin of Royal Oak, Michigan. Coughlin who published *Social Justice* spoke a mild form of anti-Semitic rhetoric from his church the Shrine of the Little Flower. Although the Jewish press spoke out against the Father, the conservatives of the Catholic Church appeared to be unaware or disinterested in Father Coughlin's message and activities; certainly only a few chose to speak out against him.[2]

In America by 1939, there were 80 known cells and 22 youth camps embracing the philosophy of Adolf Hitler. The National Conference of Christians and Jews founded in 1928 helped a great deal in stemming the spread of all types of organized anti groups.. Purveyors of anti-Semitism will not put the *Protocols* to rest. As recently as November 1993, in Kansas City, a hate monger quoted from the *Protocols of the Learned Elders of Zion* in a pamphlet he wrote stating that Federal child immunization was a plot to "harm and destroy the children of God's people."

---

1   *First appearing in Russia between the years 1903 and 1905 and a product of the Tsarist secret police, the PROTOCOLS OF THE LEARNED ELDERS OF ZION was later proven to be a forgery. Believers, and there were thousands, claimed the PROTOCOLS to be the minutes of a secret session held at the First Zionist Congress in 1897 in Basel, Switzerland. The truth was that secret police of the Tsar used a brochure written by a Frenchman as an attack against Napoleon III, and those anxious to spread anti-Semitism simply substituted the name Jews for Napoleon. The PROTOCOLS falsely claimed that THE LEARNED ELDERS OF ZION, Jews of great wealth, power and intellect, debated how they would rule the world and control its money. The PROTOCOLS said the Elders discussed the international conspiracy that they formed to accomplish this goal and that they came close to achieving it. In 1934 and 1935, ten articles appeared in the BALTIMORE MORNING SUN referring to trials in Switzerland regarding the validity of the PROTOCOLS. The Swiss judge ruled that they were forged and faked.*

2   *Father Coughlin got more than anyone's share of print. Between 1934 and 1941, the BALTIMORE MORNING SUN published over 400 articles about Father Coughlin who was an ardent supporter of President Franklin D. Roosevelt during his first term. Eventually he turned against Roosevelt, bitterly opposing his New Deal. Coughlin addressed a myriad of subjects from Communism and unemployment to birth control and the Russian-Japanese conflict. In 1936, he opened a Maryland headquarters for his National Union of Social Justice at 3 N. Calvert Street in Baltimore.*

PART III-3

2nd Mercantile Club * Woodholme Club * Demise of men's clothing manufacturing * Brooks Lane * John Eager Howard School No. 61 * Robert E. Lee School No. 49

Socially, Baltimore's own Jewish caste system was still in place in the 1920s; lines were firmly drawn. A much discussed event, before, during, and after World War I was when a German and Russian Jew became husband and wife; thus threatening the social equilibrium and quality of Baltimore Jewish life. Actually, it was not until after the end of World War II, that German and Russian Jews married without prompting some nifty comments from both camps.

Except for a handful of Russian Jews who had penetrated the German Jewish social circles and clubs, the Russian Jewish community was socially left to their own devices. For the most part, German Jews rejected associations with the Russians while they formed the perception that, though the Russian Jews were very enterprising, self sufficient and independent, they came across as loud, arrogant, brash and aggressive, plus a few other choice adjectives. The German Jews felt that Russian Jews were a long way from acquiring the fine social sheen that for a hundred years the Germans had strived to achieve. Russians, not permitted membership were seldom invited as guests to play golf at the Suburban Club, and they just didn't play pinochle at the Phoenix Club. Nevertheless, between 1919 and 1920 changes began to occur that threatened to dull the sharp division and status quo of two separate and unequal Baltimore Jewish communities. Not only with the instigation of, but also with the approval and participation of the German Jews, the Baltimore Hebrew College was founded, and the Baltimore Jewish Times began to publish. These were products for the mind that helped each group understand or at least be exposed to one another.

A 1920 reorganization of the social Good Fellowship Club resulted in three civic minded Eastern European Jews founding the Amity Club. Irving Blum, a son of one of the founders in later years became president of the Associated Jewish Charities. After a few years, The Amity Club was reorganized, and its members founded the Mercantile Club. In 1926, the Mercantile club purchased the former home of the Chauncey Brooks Family, a magnificent red sandstone mansion, that stands at 2500 Eutaw Place. Built on the highest ground of the original Brooks' estate, the mansion faces west and overlooks what was once the gentle slope of the estate's lawns. Mercantile Club members were more interested in an in-town club that offered card and recreational rooms and good dining than one that offered sunshine, although the Woodholme Country Club founding was underway at this time.

Mercantile was more than a private club. Their doors were open for meetings and affairs of Jewish causes and organizations, and the members were dedicated to their involvement with Jewish charities and community services. After World War II when the fading and eventual demise of Eutaw Place as a fine residential area took place, the Mercantile Club followed its members northwestern movement. In May 1956, they

183

moved to a quasi suburban setting at 4801 Greenspring Avenue, a short distance south of the Cylburn arboretum. After several years the city needed the club's property on the rim of the Jones Falls Valley as part of the site for the proposed Coldspring housing project. In October 1975, the Mercantile Club dedicated a new clubhouse at Old Pimlico Road and Pheasant Cross Drive in Baltimore County. The new, expensive facility featured a restaurant and a ballroom that overlooked an outdoor olympic size pool. Members played on ten first class tennis courts, but no golf course was planned for the club. By June 1987, as a result of the loss of quite a few young members, Mercantile's membership dropped to a mere two hundred families. The sixty-seven year old Mercantile Club filed for protection under Chapter 11 of the Bankruptcy Law, and in an attempt to pay off their mortgage debt, the club sold one third of their ten acre property to a housing developer. In 1978, the Jewish National Fund Council of Baltimore honored the Mercantile Club, and the proceeds of the event were used to plant trees in Israel, trees needed to drain swamps, curb erosion and create fertile land. The Mercantile Club had for years been a tower of charitable strength in the Jewish community and for the Israel Bond Program. It was particularly sad in October 1987, when a scheduled Saturday night State of Israel Bond event at the Mercantile Club had to be canceled. Speculation was that the club was bankrupt and in the process of closing; others said it was because of poor ticket sales.

  The reason for the founding of the Woodholme Country Club had a direct connection to social lines drawn by the German Jews. The Russian Jewish Woodholme founders reacted to the German Jewish social structure that adhered to a hold the fort and thou shall not pass attitudes of exclusivity of membership in their Suburban and Phoenix Clubs. Quite a number of new to uptown Russian Jews had become very well to-do; some wealthy by Baltimore standards. Until this time, it was unthinkable that Russians wanted or could afford to join the German clubs, and because of this, the schism between the two groups widened; wealth itself was not a reason for German Jews to accept Russian Jews in German Jewish clubs. In 1926, forty-nine founding fathers, many of them former Amity Club members, primarily immigrants and first generation Russian Jews, bought a large tract of hilly land in Baltimore County on Woodholme Avenue adjacent to Reisterstown Road. They retained the name Amity Club until they inducted fifty new members in 1927, at which time they adopted the name Woodholme Country Club. Members played on a nine hole temporary course until the Spring of 1930, when after three years of golf course construction and the remodeling of a house on the property, the club opened a championship eighteen hole golf course. As German Jews did on their undulating Suburban Club property on Park Heights Avenue, Russian Jews played tennis and golf on their own equal but hilly and separate turf.

  Members of the Suburban and Woodholme Clubs differed in several ways. Politically, for sure, the vast majority of Woodholme members voted as Democrats and were Zionists; not so for many of the Suburbanites. Though in 1927 German Jewish golf scores were lower than those of the Russian Jews, many Russian Jews felt confident that, as they had done when they competed in business, in time they would score better in golf. Although the Russian Jewish appetite for business sometimes overpowered their cultural leanings, they began an involvement in the musical and fine arts activities of Baltimore.

Though Jews who owned their own businesses appeared to be well off, this was not true for those employed by others. As previously mentioned, large numbers of Jews worked as tailors, sewing machine operators, pressers and cutters in Baltimore's garment industries. In early 1920, twenty-seven thousand workers earned their living in Baltimore men's clothing factories and shops, but by the end of that year, ten thousand jobs were lost. Due partly to unusually bad conditions in men's clothing manufacturing and partly to a postwar depression that began in autumn of 1920, the downturn in men's clothing manufacturing in Baltimore lasted through most of the 1920s with ups and downs through much of the following seven decades; it has now all but disappeared.

When the Baltimore City engineers planned the layout for the development of the Chauncey Brook's estate, Eutaw Place was drawn in only a few yards from the front steps of the Brook's mansion, and a couple hundred feet south of a planned entrance to Druid Hill Park. The lane that led from the mansion's entrance to the east was appropriately named Brooks Lane; and a parallel street south of it was named Chauncey Avenue. The developer for this entire plat was the Abell Building Company, whose principal owner was Arunah S. Abell, publisher of Baltimore's newspaper, The *Baltimore Sun.*

Many of the differences between German and Russian Jews centered in the neighborhoods in which they lived, and the 900 block of Brooks Lane was typical and atypical at the same time and it became legendary. Spacious three story row houses of eleven rooms, two baths and front and back porches were built between small apartment buildings erected during the decade of World War I.[1] Those living in the houses were young married Jews with lots of children, and the families were financially well off. A few of the German Jews were socially well connected; their parents listed in the turn of the century Baltimore German Jewish Social Register. In their mid teens, some of the girls of the 900 block made their debut into German Jewish society at the Harmony Circle balls. Though the 800 block of Brooks Lane and both blocks of Chauncey Avenue were occupied almost entirely by Eastern European Jews, the 900 block of Brooks Lane was mixed though German Jewish Reform families predominated. By the mid 1920s, it was jammed with children. It was difficult for the lesser number of Russian Jewish playmates living in the 900 block to understand the decorated Christmas trees in the homes of the German Jewish children. Parents of the Orthodox Russian Jews tried to explain, but the fact was and still is that decorated Christmas trees are a pure and simple symbolical representation of Christianity with a big German accent. Unfortunately, German Jewish parents made little effort to have their children understand the religious practices of their Orthodox Eastern European Jewish neighbors, so there was an underlying current of snobbishness or standoffishness. When black bearded shnorers (door to door charity collectors) rang the doorbells on Sunday mornings, they always asked of whoever opened the front door, "Are you Jewish?" German Jewish Brooks Lane children, with a disrespect they now know was wrong, answered "no Jewish live here."

Though German Jews 900 block Brooks Laners eventually moved from the neighborhood to other Baltimore areas and to distant cities, friendships formed there have remained firm and in some manner some former residents continue to network. Words do not explain Brooks Lane very well, and it can be fully understood only by the fewer and fewer remaining who lived through this unique Baltimore Jewish experience.[2]

Many 900 block German Jewish parents sent their children to Miss Jones' private school. Conveniently located on the east side of the 2300 block of Linden Avenue, the school's curriculum extended from kindergarten through the second grade. Each school day morning the diminutive stone-faced Miss Jones, on foot, stopped on the sidewalk in front of a pupil's home and blew a whistle. Each child took his or her place at the back of the ever growing line; Miss Jones proceeded to her next stop to pick up another child or two. When the long line of six, seven and eight year olds arrived at the school, they were greeted by Miss Burgess, the schools 2nd grade teacher and second in command.

Ready for the third grade, several 900 block parents sent their children, mostly the girls, to the Park School on Liberty Heights Avenue while others attended the John Eager Howard Public Elementary School No. 61 on Linden Avenue and Koenig Street. No. 61 was a melting pot for German Jews, Russian Jews and a handful of Christians kids whose families lived for years north of North Avenue on Park Avenue and on Bolton Street. After school, mobs of children pushed and shoved each other down the steps to the subterranean entrance of the small basement store of Schwartz opposite the school on the north side of Koenig Street next to Mason Alley. When they reached the counter, they purchased either an enormous five cent pickle (surely cucumbers grew larger in the 1920s), or for two cents a coddie made with a limited touch of cod fish and plenty of potato filler carefully laid on a mustard slathered saltine. A box of Ju Ju Bees at five cents was considerably more expensive than assorted penny gummies or sugar dots affixed four abreast to long white paper strips. At school, the German and Russian Jewish kids joined in outside play activities, along with, but always slightly apart from the minority Christian children.

After the completion of the sixth grade at P.S. No 61, students were assigned to either the Robert E. Lee school No. 49 or to P.S. No. 79. Public School No. 49 was Baltimore's single accelerated three-years-in-two junior high school. Centrally located on the east side of Cathedral Street, between Preston and Biddle Streets, the school faced the exclusive Bryn Mawr girl's school, later occupied by the Deutsches Haus, a public Christian German pub and dining facility that made Germans Jews feel uneasy. More students were sent from P.S. No. 61 to P.S. No. 49 than from any other grade school in Baltimore City. The School Board closed School No. 49 after World War II. The school building and its small ornate gymnasium across the school yard facing Maryland Avenue has been renovated to house the functions of the Medical and Chichurgical Society of Maryland, the school's long time neighbor.

1   *In the spring, heavy canvas awnings were affixed to the front porches of the houses and at the first sign of winter they were removed and stored by the awning company. Stored in the basement of the homes during the warm weather, portable 4' X 8" wooden glass windowed vestibules were erected around the front entrance door of several of the houses. During hot summer evenings, porch sitting was a way of life for Brooks Laners. Every family had sturdy metal porch furniture with cushions that offered varying degrees of comfort, usually matching those on a glider that made a low key swishing tranquilizing noise as it rode back and forth. A recent article in the BALTIMORE SUN stated that antique dealers in New York have a waiting list for persons wanting to buy porch gliders manufactured in the 1930s, 1940s and 1950s.*

2   *At the funeral service for Philip Kahn, the author's father, Rabbi Abraham Shaw described Brooks Lane as "Gemutlich," (comfortable and congenial) whereupon a neighbor Morton Lazarus, a man of great humor said, "I always thought it was "high class." Incidentally, the Lazarus family, except for Grandma Lazarus, notoriously poor porch sitters had the neighborhood's most comfortable porch furniture.*

PART III-4

1929 Stock Market crash * Rise of Chancellor Hitler * The New Deal

During the 1920s, the German Jews remained the social and financial kings of the Jewish hill regardless of the fact that their men's clothing factories were experiencing poor business. A number of these manufacturers dealt with their financial reversals by cashing in their chips. Some closed their factories while others were able to sell them to Russian Jews. Along with this, several large German Jewish owned wholesale dry good houses, popular since the Civil War, saw their businesses shrink as marketing methods changed during the 1920s. Since the 1860s, and before, most merchandise sold in retail stores was distributed through middle-man wholesale merchants, and except for a few items such as domestics, underwear and hosiery, this was in the process of change. More and more large retailers traveled to the New York garment merchandise centers where they bought their seasonal requirements directly from manufacturers' showrooms. Those in small towns most likely selected their needs from traveling factory representatives.

A number of German Jews with large amounts of capital to invest became enamored with the money they could make in the stock and bond markets. During the decade, values of issues on the financial markets rose steadily and good, secure returns could be realized by investing in them. Each day many visited their brokers and sat in comfortable lounge chairs in a special customer's room. There, up to the minute quotations on issues were posted from ticker tapes to large boards, and there the customers watched their investments grow. Considered at the time to be a small gamble, investors were able to buy on margin, an appealing but treacherous way of purchasing stocks without actually having to put up all the cash needed to pay for them.

The euphoria of Baltimore German Jewish life was only slightly disturbed by problems away from home, surely not enough by happenings in the mid-east, so only a few attended a 1928 mass meeting held for Palestine relief. The meeting netted over $30,000; the contributions came primarily from Russian Jews. Reform Judaism, still mostly popular with German Jews, was no where near changing its position on Zionism, and there was every reason to think they would never embrace the movement. Well-to-do Baltimore German Jews had their own relief interests; their clubs, foreign travel and the New York Stock Market.

The road to wealth seemed quiet and smooth for investors who ignored or didn't understand or believe the ominous danger signs lying ahead. In October 1929, the sky fell in. Prices on the New York Stock Exchange crashed, and investors panicked as the values of prime securities tumbled. Along with tremendous buying on margin by some, there were frantic rushes to sell. No one really understood what to do or what they were doing. Though they probably sensed otherwise, national political and financial leaders treated the market crash as a mere spasm; they reacted and preached optimism. For those with heavy holdings of stocks bought on margin, it was no spasm. Lifetime savings disappeared when brokers called for funds from the investors to cover securities bought on margin. Stocks now greatly devalued were signed over to banks as collateral on loans secured to buy more and more stocks. The losses sustained by wealthy German Jews were disproportionately greater than they were for Russians Jews, many of whom had most of their resources invested in their growing businesses rather than in the financial markets. President Hoover optimistically predicted that the situation did not warrant pessimism, but as the months passed, everyone knew America had entered a depression; its economy heading for unprecedented depths.

Not only for Americans, but for people everywhere, the first half of the 1930s was economically and psychologically difficult. The economic conditions brought world wide discontent and fear. In Germany, the depression helped nurture and hasten the emergence of probably the most evil demagogue ever to set foot on this earth. Adolph Hitler became Chancellor of Germany in 1933; although it was at a much earlier date that he signaled the politics of the path he would walk. Ten years before while in prison, Hitler completed the first volume of his book *Mein Kampf* which described an anti-Semitic ideology far too remote for most of the world to understand at that time. The most ominous statements made in *Mein Kampf* addressed the *Protocols of the Learned Elders of Zion. The Frankfuter Zeitung* charged that the statements in the *Protocols* were untrue. Hitler convinced many people that the refutation of the *Protocols* by a Jewish owned newspaper was the best proof of their validity.

In 1933, Franklin Delano Roosevelt was elected to the presidency of the United States and in a short period of time offered a New Deal to the American people. During this era, citizens of the United States were presented with the most powerful movement for ethnic democracy ever seen in this country. Opportunities opened for aggrieved minorities to combine forces against a common enemy, the conservative bigots, the 100% Americans. When the government revealed a new vista attracting liberal thinking participation to federal jobs in Washington, it was particularly good for Baltimore Russian Jews who lived a short distance down the road. These jobs were a gift to a host of well-educated Russian Jews who because of selected hiring in private business had been thwarted from being able to work productively for themselves in the private sector. The Department of State, however, remained apart from other government agencies in that it held fast to good old boy policies, particularly in the immigration section.

During the depression years,[1] a number of uneducated but enterprising Russian Jewish immigrants found their niche in the middle range of businesses as proprietors of small garment factories and as footwear, glove, or millinery jobbers. Many first generation Russian Jewish men became factory representatives rather than tailors. The surge of the Russians Jews to become middle class was well under way, and most surprising was the speed with which the first American born generation of Russian Jews entered the middle class. This upward surge did not ensure that Russian Jews would continue to dominate businesses developed by the preceding generations of German Jews. The tendency for Jews to own their own businesses reduced their numbers within the blue collar class. Some surveys of the mid 1930s indicated that Italian workers in the garment industries outnumbered Jews.

---

1   *In a survey taken in Baltimore in 1940 of 400 Jewish youths of Russian heritage, only 4.7% of the fathers of these youths who had reached maturity during the 1920s could be classified as professionals or technicians; 13.4% of their sons were aspiring for much the same careers as their fathers. By the mid 1930s, a new Jewish occupational profile emerged. Almost 35% to 40% of the Jewish work force was engaged in non-manufacturing commercial occupations compared with 13.8% of the general population.*

PART III-5

Roland Park * Educational quotas * Barrier fraternities * Johns Hopkins University * The University of Maryland * Atlantic City * The Catskills

When Jewish families contemplated moving to better neighborhoods, they were confronted with outrageous restrictions. Jews were not welcome in several residential areas of the city due to gentlemen's agreements between white Christian home owners.

In the mid 1930s, a prominent Jewish Baltimore straw hat manufacturer and philanthropist, Julius Levy, of English heritage, highly respected in business circles by both the Jewish and Christian communities, bought a house on Ridgewood Road in restricted Roland Park. The reason he and his family wanted to live in a neighborhood that didn't want them is obscure, but the family moved from their northwest Baltimore town house, well aware of the possible consequences. Instead of the expected objections to their presence from Christian Roland Park neighbors, the objections came from an unexpected sector, and the repercussions were as subtle as a brick falling on their heads; only because they were Jewish heads. There were no rocks thrown through windows or threatening letters received; that would not have been the style of Roland Parkers. The Levy family was made to feel uncomfortable and unwanted in the neighborhood by the bread delivery person, the milkman, and the newspaper delivery boys, all of whom would not include the new family in their routes.

There was no attempt on the part of this family to hide the fact that they were Jewish. Anglicizing their name was completely out of the question; it was almost unheard of for an English or German Jew to change his name. Theirs was a proud name, and they were a proud family, secure in their orthodox religious practices. Julius Levy and his family lived in their Roland Park house for several years, and at his death, the funeral took place from this house rather than from the Sondheim Funeral Home, the Eutaw Place undertaker of choice of German Jews.

In the early to mid 1800s, many German Jews upon entering the United States took the name of the German city or state from whence they came. Those from Hamburg became Hamburgers, and those from Frankfurt became Frankfurters; none became "hot dogs." German Jews were quite proud of their names because they represented who they were in their German homeland and in America. In many instances theirs were the same names as those of Christian Germans. There were Christian Thalheimers in Baltimore and there were Jewish Thalheimers; both of whom came to America from Thalheim, possibly on the same boat.

For Russian Jews it was quite different. Many received assigned names before or aboard ship; some were the creations of an American immigration station agent. For the most part, English speaking immigration officers could neither understand the Russian Jewish pronunciation of their birth names nor could the immigrants spell those names This was not true for all because some Jews from Moscow entered the United States as Moscowitz and some from Minsk as Minsky and so on. There were a few who had no names. As Russian Jews hastened toward mainstream America beginning in the 1920s, quite a few legally anglicized their names for ease of use or to obscure their identity. The Christian community did not always look favorably upon name changes when the proposed new family name of a Russian Jewish family was the same as that of an old line local Christian family.[1]

During the little over twenty years between the two World Wars, two unrelated and at the same time unrecognized forces worked to better German and Russian Jewish relationships. One was higher education and graduate studies for the professions, the second of lesser or higher force, depending on one's view was Atlantic City, New Jersey.

It was not until after World War I that certifications, procedures, and educational requirements were formalized by associations and institutions and professionalism came into its own. Though university quotas were designed to restrict Jews from studying law at the University of Maryland or medicine at the Johns Hopkins University, this did not stop determined Jews from trying to enter these fields. Again, using the mid 1930s as a time line, 50% of the national entrance applications to medical schools were from Jews. For those rejected, dentistry and pharmacology became the closest acceptable substitutes for would be physicians. In Jewish communities, D.D.S. was jokingly spelled out as Disappointed Doctor or Surgeon. In 1940, only 2% of America's college professors were Jewish, but by 1970 10% were. Post World War II American Jews sought and entered the intellectually demanding fields such as anthropology, mathematics, physics and history. As expected, Jews were not known to be interested in agriculture, home economics nor physical education. There was, and still is, the fact that Jews are attracted to abstract and theoretical endeavors. Interestingly, an amazingly few Jewish professionals are deeply religious so their names are few and far between on synagogue membership lists.

Children of Russian Jewish immigrants were not disposed to spending their lives as tailors or small shop keepers. Education beyond the secondary schools was an attraction for them, and thousands after completing the "A" course at Baltimore City College (a high school) sought to enroll in colleges. Between 1890 and 1920, the Jewish enrollment in undergraduate schools was large but very much less in many graduate schools that traditionally controlled their admission.

After World War I, college policies shifted to outright rejection of Jewish students who applied to some elite private colleges and universities in or near large Jewish population centers. As for graduate medical, law, and engineering schools it was extremely difficult for Jewish students to be accepted because of established quotas. Hundreds of bright young Jews who could not be enrolled in the graduate schools of some of the better rated universities obtained graduate degrees from lesser institutions. A 10% quota was too low to accommodate anywhere near the numbers of Jewish students anxious to enroll, and the desire of so many Jews for higher education was cited by university officials as the justification for their quotas. This rationale failed to take into account that the Jewish people, for whatever reason produced a higher percentage of potential college students nationwide than did non-Jews. Eastern European immigrant parents understood better than German Jews that a diploma from a top rated university was their passport in a forward moving America. Certification for their children would yield dividends, and an investment in them was the best investment they could make for their hard earned dollars.

In the undergraduate schools, in the 1920s and 1930s, conflicts between German Jewish and Russian Jewish students were quite apparent. Many German Jewish students, sons of well-to-do parents, snubbed the less affluent Russian Jewish students.[2] The Germans were concerned that they were being painted with the same brush as the Eastern Europeans. Same brush or not, undergraduate Christian Greek letter fraternities and sororities were exclusively Christian. German Jewish students answered both problems by distancing themselves from both groups; founding their own Jewish Greek letter fraternities. The German Jewish Zeta Beta Tau (Z.B.T.s) and the Phi Epsilon Pi (Phi-Eps) did to the Eastern European Jewish students exactly what the Christians did to the German Jewish students: They barred them from membership and more importantly, fellowship. To counter, Jewish students of Eastern European extraction founded the national fraternity Tau Epsilon Phi. Attending graduate schools together, more mature German and Russian Jewish students philosophically and practically overcame their prejudices. As they headed for their professions, they developed great admiration for their respective intellect.

For years American Jews suspected they were being discriminated against by prestigious universities. Their suppositions were proven to be true when a paper was found in the files of one of the top three Ivy League Universities,[3] bearing out the fact that until 1945 they, and several smaller but highly regarded Ivy League type eastern universities enforced a 10% quota cap on Jews entering their schools. Johns Hopkins, a top ranking American university, and the nation's first true research university, is Baltimore's most prestigious institution. During the depression years, parents of Jewish boys were happy that their sons could receive a top quality education at the Hopkins undergraduate schools without having to pay the residency fees of out-of-town institutions.[4] In addition, hundreds of Baltimore Jewish students attended the high ranked medical, dental and law schools of the University of Maryland, located in downtown Baltimore.

The University of Maryland's Dental School is the oldest in the United States. The first American lectures in dentistry were delivered at its School of Medicine, and the College of Dental Surgery was opened in 1840. There could not have been a better match; all those bright young Jewish boys eager for professional careers and the nation's number one dental school a street car ride away from their homes. Being a state institution, there has been little overt anti-Semitism surrounding admissions but Jewish boys were barred from joining the Christian dental fraternities. Alpha Omega, the first international dental fraternity, was founded in 1907 by a group of Jewish dental students. About 40 years ago, the administration of the fraternity moved to New York; in 1994 it returned to its new and rightful medina (domain), Pikesville. The fraternity is strong on philanthropy, and in recent years its foundation has contributed over $10,000,000 to scholarships and for dentistry research.

For many years, the medical school of Johns Hopkins cheated itself by imposing entrance limitations on Jews. They were careful to admit between six and twelve prospective Jewish doctors when during the 1930s admissions totaled seventy medical students each year. By appointing only a token representation of illustrious Jewish medical doctors to their teaching and hospital staffs, they inadvertently contributed to the fine quality of Sinai Hospital which absorbed Hopkins turn downs.[5] During these same years the University of Maryland Medical School admitted about one hundred medical students including between twenty-five and forty-five Jews. In 1936 the numbers dropped to about fifteen Jewish students each year for a period of ten to twelve years. Under threat of suit, admissions jumped to between twenty and twenty-two.

Things have changed.[6] Recently, a Baltimore Jew Dr. Louis Kaplan, chaired the Board of Regents of the University of Maryland. The most recent past President of Johns Hopkins University Dr. Steven Mueller is Jewish as is today's Interim President Dr. Daniel Nathans, a Nobel Prize winner in medical research. Until he left the school in mid-September, Jewish Dr. James E. Block was president of the Johns Hopkins Hospital and Health System. Several Jewish scientists, almost all of Eastern European backgrounds, head research teams at both institutions.

Baltimore is vying with five other major American cities in taking a leading role along with San Francisco and Boston in the biotechnical industry, the development, sale and distribution of new drugs and medical devices. The presence of the Johns Hopkins medical complex and the research being done at that institution are important cogs in the biotech plans for Baltimore. Many of those taking leading roles in this development are descendants of Eastern European Jewish immigrants.

The Johns Hopkins University has reaped enormous benefits from former Baltimore Jewish students. In the 1980s, Dr. Steven Mueller, teaming with the New York based Jewish financier Morris W. Offit and others, played a dominant role in a $400,000,000 campaign to expand the university's endowment fund and facilities. Generous sums of Jewish money were pledged by a large number of former Jewish students who graduated in the 1920s, 1930, and 1940s; this was their pay back to their alma mater. In 1994, The Johns Hopkins University announced plans for raising another $900,000,000, and as expected, Baltimore Jewish money will be liberally given. The recent gift from Baltimore's Zanvyl Krieger of $50,000,000 for the Arts and Sciences endowment was followed by Michael Bloomberg's gift of $55,000,000. Both are graduates of the Hopkins though Bloomberg is not a Baltimorean. He is Chairman Elect of the Board of Trustees to replace Morris W. Offit in June 1996. In 1995, the Harry and Jeanette Weinberg Foundation gave the Johns Hopkins Hospital $20,000,000 although the Weinbergs had no connection with the hospital. Stewert J. and Marlene Greenebaum chose the University of Maryland Medical System and School of Medicine for their $10,000,000 gift, the largest private contribution ever given to the hospital or school.

Atlantic City attracted Jewish vacationers as far back as the mid 19th century. The Atlantic Hotel, queen of the era, catered exclusively to Jewish people, and in 1867 advised Christians seeking reservations that they could not be accommodated. Managers advised them that the hotel was chiefly if not entirely for the use of persons of the Hebrew faith, mostly those of much wealth. In the three decades of the early twentieth century, slightly disrupted for some by a major depression, German and Russian Jews visited Atlantic City. The lure of the ocean, a wide assortment of accommodations, the boardwalk, the amusement piers, elegant or typical seaside shops, the auctions, the sun, the sand and the surf attracted hundreds of thousands of Jews from Baltimore and other East Coast cities.

In the early 1900s before the erection of the fine hotels on the Boardwalk, German Jews vacationed at the Royal Palace Hotel on Pacific Avenue and the beach near the Absecon inlet and lighthouse, or at the Pierepoint, or the Rudolph (renamed the Breakers) on the Boardwalk. Though some were able to afford fine hotels in the early 1900s, because of dietary restrictions, the probability of Russian Jews registering in them ranged from nil to a very few. In Ventnor and south to Margate, communities of a mixture of Jews and Christians, rented cottages were particularly popular with a few Baltimore German Jewish families who continued to keep kosher. Later, unwittingly, vacations in Atlantic City became a common denominator for thousands of Baltimore Jews who flocked to this attractive and resourceful resort. For some it didn't matter where they stayed, but for others it did. Where they walked, the Boardwalk was the same for all, but not for the few who rode. They could walk, but they could also afford to be pushed;[7] a sign of having "arrived." Beginning in the early 1920s, Baltimore German Jews frequented the grand and expensive Boardwalk hotels such as the Ritz, the Ambassador, the Shelburne, and the Traymore. These elegant hotels were built with huge lobbies and several ground floor social rooms, and their dining rooms served the finest cuisine. Other fine hotels in Atlantic City of the genre of those preferred by the German Jews were either off limits to Jews or simply not considered to be places they wanted to stay. Shoulder to shoulder, lesser wooden structures with fewer and smaller rooms such as the Britain, The Esplanade, Kaufman's and Berman's Bayle Hotel lined the side streets that dead ended at the boardwalk. Rooming houses extending inland for one or two blocks attracted hundreds of less affluent vacationing Russian Jewish garment workers. The fact that Russian Jews tended to patronize the smaller side street hotels was not only because they were less expensive but also because many of them had kosher kitchens and a resident rabbi, who usually shared his services with other hotels. The smaller hotels tended to be "gemutlich" with lobbies and large front porches with wooden rocking chairs. Russian Jewish families who acquired wealth and no longer kept kosher while on vacation, flocked to the boardwalk hotels. It became increasingly common for Jews who kept a strict kosher regime in their homes to eat non-kosher food outside. Rationalization for eating such while on vacation was a personal choice that they did not allow to interfere with the moderate religious principles of their orthodoxy.

In the morning and afternoon, bathers flocked to the wide sandy Atlantic Ocean beach, and in the late afternoon before the dinner hour, a popular pastime for the younger German Jewish set were "tea dances" held at the better hotels. After dinner and after time spent on the Boardwalk with their families, hundreds of young German Jews congregated at the Ambassador Bar to listen with rapture to the music of the Isham Jones orchestra.

Evening brought a change in the complexion of Atlantic City. After dinner, as the sun set, thousands of vacationers descended upon the Boardwalk. They walked and enough shopped to make store-keeping on Atlantic City's Boardwalk quite profitable. The auction houses were jammed with bidders and on-lookers; the Atlantic City house auctioneers, without doubt, were the best of their trade; the quintessence of professionalism. With a fifth sense and good humor, they insulted those who gathered for the sale and at the same time kept in touch with their instincts that enabled them to separate those in the audience who would be top bidders from those who were non-bidders. One auction house used a formula to help their auctioneer zero in on a probable buyer. The auctioneer[8] would ask the bidder if he or she knew the well known Baltimore ice cream manufacturer L. Emanuel (Mannie) Hendler; they alluded to his having been an important customer of the auction. If the answer was no, they no longer directed their spiel to that person. If the answer were yes, they and their assistants worked hard on this potential buyer.

All of this is merely background for the German-Russian relationships that began in Atlantic City. For the upper and middle income vacationers Atlantic City was dressy, and couples or families donned their best for the daily social event, walking the boardwalk or renting wide rattan wheeled chairs that rode the boards. Propelled by sweating middle-aged to elderly black men possessing unusual strength, the pushers guided the chairs along the right lanes of the Boardwalk. Pushing a Boardwalk chair was probably more strenuous than pulling a rickshaw, but like rickshaw drivers, this was the only way they were able to make a living in Atlantic City, a city with little industry. Chair pushing was hard work so the pushers sought regular customers who tipped well, and in turn customers sought their preferred pushers. Whether the chair was pushed or was parked the rate was by the hour, so chair renters were considered to be quite well off if they could psychologically afford to pay the rate to be pushed but remained parked. Boardwalk benches were free; everyone knew that. This is the way it was in Atlantic City. Usually the chair, some seated up to four occupants, was placed against the boardwalk rail with it's back to the ocean and in front of one of the fine hotels in which the riders were guests. From this vantage location, occupants could see up and down the boardwalk, watch the passing parade, and be seen by those passing. Vacationers did this in summer, and in winter tucked under a blanket. Though not the crowds of summer, hundreds of Jews visited Atlantic City in the winter; the temperatures were more moderate than inland, and the air from the sea, invigorating and clean. Where else could a lady show the others their minks and karakuls and for a few, their sables. With a propensity for gambling, many Russian Jewish men spent their days and nights at the tables of Atlantic City's illegal gambling houses, condoned by city fathers long before gambling was legal in Atlantic City.

Those who walked and those who sat recognized and greeted each other, not because they were friends; most likely they had only a nodding acquaintance on the streets of the lofts, Baltimore's garment making area. On the part of each, these were people who would pass on the streets of downtown Baltimore with or without a tip of a hat to acknowledge their passing. *On the Boardwalk in Atlantic City* they stopped, and they talked. On the Boardwalk, Baltimore Russian Jews, who had become manufacturers or store owners, introduced their wives and families to German Jewish families, the father of whom may have been his employer a few short years before. They exchanged pleasantries and later, at home, on the streets of Baltimore, instead of tipping a hat and walking by, German and Russian Jews stopped and chatted. Their Atlantic City chance meeting had broken the ice. Of utmost significance for their future, German and Russian Jewish boys and girls met each other in Atlantic City. There they laughed, and they loved through fleeting summer romances.

In addition to the large numbers of Baltimore Russian Jews who were lured to Atlantic City by the Boardwalk, the sound of the waves and the sniff of the air, others traveled north to a world of its own, the Jewish resort hotels of the Catskills; New York State's Borscht Belt. There were few chances for Russian Jews to meet German Jews in the Catskills where the American Plan hotels featured obscene amounts of kosher food and huge scale entertainment. The moderately indelicate humor of stand-up comedians, stars, those destined to become stars, and those destined to be flops was not especially enticing to non-Yiddish speaking German Jews. The humor of the Catskills was a comic expression and combination of Old World Yiddish culture and the New World culture of the Russian Jews. Catskill resort advertising purposely did not direct their virtues towards a German Jewish clientele.

By the 1960s, the phrase Borscht Belt was no longer appropriate as Beet Belt would have been more so because Catskill hotels began to list borscht as beet soup. The emphasis on vast quantities of Jewish foods in the hills changed as many Catskill resort guests' tastes opted for the more delicate French and Chinese cuisine. The Catskills, as well as Atlantic City, fell victim to jet planes that flew vacationers to Europe, Israel, Asia, and the Club Meds of the Caribbean. Regardless of the competition of other vacation spots, the Catskills were self defeating. The children of the former clientele of the Jewish resort hotels were less Jewish and less enthusiastic about the humor of Jewish entertainers and the built-in ambiance of Russia in the Catskills. The Catskill hotels had long been a favorite spot for religious Jews, some without synagogue affiliation, as a place to spend the Jewish high holidays. Rabbis, other than those hired by the hotels for the holidays and the Sabbath, had their say by questioning observance in resort surroundings. How could religious services be held in converted night clubs where the whole congregation danced the watusi the night before? Many rabbis felt that Jewish guests of the resort hotels were observing the Jewish holidays in pagan surroundings. By 1985, the hey days of the best days of the Jewish borscht belt had ended.

UNCOMMON THREADS

1. Much verbiage was printed by the daily Philadelphia newspapers when the Kobatchniks of that city petitioned the court to change their name to Cabot. In Baltimore in 1941, "Dr. H.L.S." a dentist wanted to change his family name to "S"; the "S" family, wealthy fuel dealers, appeared in court to block the change. After five appearances before a local judge, "H.L.S., Jr." was permitted to change his name to "S." The petition of "Dr. H.L.S.," his wife and two daughters was disallowed because they failed to appear in court for the last hearing.

2. In April 1996, The Baltimore Jewish Times reported conflicts at the Pikesville High School between some American born Jewish boys and Russian born Jewish boys who have recently come to America.

3. In 1922, President A. Lawrence Lowell of Harvard University broke his silence relative to his recommendation for a quota at his undergraduate Harvard College. He truly believed that a 10% quota was a contribution to the prevention of anti-Semitism and would solve the school's "Jew problem." Lowell stated that if Harvard would enroll as many as 40% Jews, the feelings of Christians would be intense and a cause for anti-Semitism. Dr. Lowell, however, was silent about the fact that along with Columbia, Harvard had no difficulty absorbing the sons and daughters of wealthy German Jews. Indeed, Harvard eventually had its "Jewish problem" when hundreds of bright Russian Jewish boys from the Boston public schools enrolled. A disturbing problem with undergraduate Russian Jewish students in the colleges located in the big cities with large Jewish populations was their lack of participation in campus activities, athletic and otherwise. The Russian Jews of New York and Boston were "subway" commuter students, most of whom headed home after class.

   In 1930, when Jews were 3.5% of the United States population, the national total of Jewish enrollment in American colleges was 10%. In the big cities with large Jewish populations, the percentage was considerably higher. In this same year in the Washington Square campus of the New York University, 93% of the students were Jewish. In the tuition free City College of New York for men and Hunter College for women, Jewish enrollment varied between 80% and 90%.

4. Some of the better known Jewish professors of the Johns Hopkins University's Homewood school were Dr. Jacob Hollander, Professor of Political Economy; Dr. George Boas, Professor of History and Philosophy; Dr. Florence Bamburger, Professor of Education; Dr. N. Bryllion Fagin, Professor of English Literature, Dr. Ferdinand Hamburger, Professor of Electrical and Computer Engineering, Rabbi Dr. William Rosenau, Professor of Semitics, Dr. Abraham Cohen, Professor of Mathematics, and Dr. Abel Wolman, Professor of Environmental Engineering.

5. Both Dr. Harry and Dr. Jonas Friedenwald were Professors of Opthamology at Johns Hopkins medical school; Dr. Simon Flexner, Professor of Pathology and Anatomy and Associate Professors Dr. Jonas S. Friedman, Dr. Charles Austrian and Professor Dr. Arnall Patz.

6. Quoting a recent Johns Hopkins University School of Medicine brochure, referring to their updated billing system, they said there are 30 physicians named David, 4 named Lee, and 10 named Nancy but starting February 1, 1995, there will be only one bill.

7. Some years ago, the wife of a couple arriving at an Atlantic City hotel asked the bellman to obtain a wheel chair to take her husband to their room. The bellman remarked that he was sorry the man was unable to walk; her reply, "He can, but he can afford not to."

8 *Years ago, the author, usually a $1.00 bidder, responding to wifely pokes in the ribs, found himself to be high bidder on a diamond ring. On second thought, he felt he was "taken." The next morning he registered a complaint with the Atlantic City Commissioner of Auctions. The auctioneer was summarily summoned; the Commissioner arbitrated the complaint on the spot; compromises were made, and the author ended up with a very substantial bargain; no ring but a fine solid gold case watch.*

PART III-6

Pre-WW II Germany * The Roosevelt Administration before and after Kristallnacht * United Jewish Appeal * 2nd German Migration * World War II

*T*hrough generations of Jewish oppression, there has never been anything like the ultimate resolve of the Jewish people of twentieth century Germany, Poland, Russia, and other European countries. Compared to the numbers who lived in Eastern Europe, German Jews were few in numbers, representing only 4% of Germany's population. Granted full civil rights by the National Constitution after the Franco-German War in 1871, German Jews played a disproportionate role in German culture. They contributed heavily to their country's arts, sciences, and education; their capital controlled immense retail, industrial, and shipping interests. At varying times, Jews in Germany owned from 75% to 90% of the nation's banks. In twentieth century Germany, they reached and sustained a culture, class, wealth, and productivity far in excess of any Jewish Community in history, and in some ways the least typical. Along their way in Germany, many soft pedaled their Jewish heritage and embraced the German culture as if it were their own.

Large numbers of Jews living in Germany believed that by accepting their country's culture they could become more German and thereby overcome their own traditional insecurity living in an overwhelmingly German nation with a long history of anti-Semitism. They tried hard to penetrate the Christian community with success on some levels but never with full acceptance; that was an illusion. Due to their association, Jews of Germany were solidly Germanic in their personalities and their attitudes but interestingly, even though they sought assimilation, Jews rarely crossed the line of intermarriage. Most were passionately attached to what they believed to be their Fatherland only to eventually suffer disillusionment when this parent turned on them, reviled them, ostracized them, expelled them, and in the end almost exterminated them.

A century after the beginning of the German migration to America, political unrest in Germany seeded a second Jewish migration. Blame for the bad economic conditions of the late 1920s became focused on the Jews. Physical attacks on Jews in Germany took place as early as March 1933, when bands of Nazis feeling their oats insulted them, in some instances, assaulting them by slapping them and hitting them in the head with blackjacks. A few Jews were taken from their homes in their night clothes and jailed but the majority could not and did not want to believe these events were happening. They looked upon this activity as random violence associated with the Nazi struggle for political power. After all, Jews lived in a modern enlightened Germany, a world cultural center where violence was not part of its way of life. Most, but not all, German Jews rationalized that this kind of sporadic annoyance on the part of the Nazis would in time exhaust itself. A small number of Jewish students of German history, heeding the line from Shakespeare that the "Past is Prologue," faced the possibilities and the probabilities of having to leave Germany.

UNCOMMON THREADS

In September 1930, President Herbert Hoover called for strict enforcement of the loophole "likely to become a public charge" (LPC) provision in the 1924 Johnson Act. This action, though it caused little havoc at the time, created an impenetrable wall down the road for Eastern European immigrants. The 1933 annual quota set by the United States immigration authorities for Germans who might be permitted to migrate to America was 26,000 but only about 1,450 took advantage of this quota. This is not indicative of contentment of Jews living in Germany; more likely it was because of the depression in America where job opportunities were scarce. A year earlier, in a move to protect American jobs, President Hoover ordered American consuls world wide to limit the number of immigrant visas granted, though these limitations had only a minor effect on immigration. Politicians are born with the ability to find quirks in laws; one wonders if legislation is purposely designed with built in loop holes. Even after the March 1933 assaults on German Jews, the Roosevelt Administration adhered to its inherited foreign policy towards Jews, a policy of appeasement to those opposed to additional Jewish immigration. This policy was formulated by those who thought Jews, entrenched in the vanguard of international movements such as Communism and Zionism, were the reason for every American ill. They were certain Jews tended to undermine the cohesion of national states, and therefore could not as a rule be trusted to be loyal citizens of their respective countries of residence.

From 1935 to the end of 1941, when the United States entered World War II, 150,000 German Jews came to America. Had limitations not been in place, it is pure conjecture how many more Germans Jews would have been able to come to America then and in the ensuing years. The fact that an estimated 43,000 Jews left Germany for settlements in Palestine during the years of 1933, 1934 and 1935 is a hint but makes no positive conclusions. In 1933, Baltimore German Jews could not have foreseen how the ensuing events of history would affect their well-being and what effect these events would later have on German/Russian Jewish relations.

Some American German Jews realized that a crisis was upon Jews in Germany, and had been upon them as early as the date Adolph Hitler became Chancellor and the passage of the Nuremberg Laws in 1935. True, some Baltimore German Jews were alarmed at the news from Germany, as were most Jews actually living there, but a large measure of disbelief continued on both sides of the Atlantic. A group of Baltimore Jews including the Friedenwalds and the Strauses with important German connections had a reasonably accurate line on what was planned for Jews in Germany. They beseeched Congress to ease immigration bars and to allow 10,000 German Jewish children to enter the United States, assuring authorities that these children would be neither a financial nor a social burden on this country. Their pleas were ignored.

The Roosevelt administration buried its head, failing to be cognizant of what was happening. Many historians of the 1930s severely condemn the Roosevelt Administration for its alleged indifference and complicity with respect to Nazi Germany's persecution and murder of the European Jews from 1933 to 1945. Some historians have said the complicity was a "conspiracy of silence" among the Allies to avoid calling attention to the special plight of the Jews both before and during the war years. Its purpose, they said, was to reduce popular pressure for rescue activity which was opposed by Allied military and political leaders as inimical to their basic goal of defeating the Axis as quickly as possible. In 1936 President Roosevelt instructed the State Department to extend "the most generous favorable treatment" to Jewish refugees. In 1938, Roosevelt verbally blasted Hitler and the Nazis although Jews hoped Washington would do more than just condemn them. In March 1938, President Roosevelt asked the State Department to see to it that the immigration quotas be filled for the entry of Germans and Austrians. Nationals of these countries were permitted to apply for visas from wherever they were living;

Kristallnacht (The Night of Broken Glass), November 9-10, 1938, when the Nazis went on an out of control rampage took the world by surprise. German storm troopers destroyed synagogues and smashed the shop windows of Jewish merchants. These atrocities confirmed all conjectures of what the Nazi were up to, the beginning of Nazi pogroms across Germany, the evil and final extent of which exceeded the worst assault on humankind in recorded history. Even after Kristallnacht, the majority of American Jews were unaware or failed to grasp the dire situation of their German co-religionists, and many remained unenthusiastic about subsidizing their migration to America. Regardless, German Jews had to leave Germany and by the spring of 1939, ships loaded with Jews steamed to ports of the countries that would allow them to take refuge. Germany invaded Poland on September 1, 1939, and two days later England and France declared war on Germany. By early 1940, all Jews in Europe were potential refugees or captives. In Poland, millions of Jews remained as only an infinitesimal number had left that country. In Germany and Austria with a pre-war Jewish population of well over half a million, approximately 300,000 remained; the others had escaped.

It was not until 1939 that the joint German and Austrian quotas were filled; in that year, applications from Germany and Czechoslovakia were six times the year's quotas. It is not the purpose of this book to defend or condemn the Roosevelt Administration; in retrospect, his, like all administrations, was sensitive to the thinking of the majority of the American people at the time.[1] Between 1933 and 1940, 140,000 German and Austrian Jews came to the United States. An American sponsor was required for each person; sponsors produced financial statements attesting to the fact that the refugee would not be a public charge. Arrangements for Germans who came to Baltimore were made through the Jewish Welfare Agency. Sadly, the Wagner-Rogers bill that would have allowed 10,000 children to come to the United States in 1939 and another 10,000 in 1940 never reached the floor of the House or the Senate. Politicians, bowing to the opposition of over 100 American organizations, killed the bill with amendments while it was still in committee.

From the late 1930s to the date that the United States entered World War II, Jews accounted for over one half of the immigrants who entered the country. Beginning in June 1940, fearing that Nazi spies would infiltrate the United States along with refugees, there was no burst of enthusiasm to receive German Jewish refugees. In fact, the State Department cut the flow of refugees in half by banning most immigration from Germany,

Central and Eastern Europe. The Roosevelt administration issued guidelines to United States consuls for their use in curtailing immigration. In 1940, the President's Advisory Committee on Political Refugees drew up a list of 3,200 anti-Nazi cultural carriers, prominent Christian German political and cultural personages who were to be allowed to enter this country.

After France crumpled under the heel of Germany, the northern and central sections were occupied by German troops; in July 1940, the Vichy puppet government of southern France was formed. Answerable to the Germans in control of their section of the country, the Vichy government enacted its own anti-Semitic agenda, one the French Jews were no strangers to. Fortunately, the French were in no way as cruel to the Jews as were the Germans. Eventually, Vichy-controlled southern France became the largest European concentration of Jews who had fled Germany. The United States State Department authorized the American consul in Lisbon, Portugal, to supervise the immigration quotas from the low countries Belgium, Luxembourg and the Netherlands and for part of the British, French, Italian and Swiss entry quotas. HIAS (Hebrew Immigrant Aid Society) and the JCA (Jewish Colonization Association) combined to form the HICEM (HIAS-JCA-Emigdirect) to aid refugees.

After pledging and furnishing a tremendous amount of aid to England in its effort to fight the war and survive, President Roosevelt asked the Congress of the United States to declare war on Germany and Italy shortly after the December 1941 Japanese attack on Pearl Harbor. Baltimore's German and Russian Jewish sons and daughters participated to the fullest in the military and civilian facets of the war effort. In the early days after the United States entry into World War II, in active anti-Semitic circles, Jews were called a threat to America. When the full horrors of the Nazi concentration camps became known, there was a marked lessening of public anti-Semitism.

Greatly due to active warfare between 1941 and 1945, only about 21,000 Jews were able to escape from Nazi Germany. Passivity continued in the Roosevelt Administration despite the entrance of the United States in the war. Even if Jews could have gotten out of Nazi Germany, the United States immigration gates were basically closed during the war itself except for approximately 400,000 German Prisoners of War. Few Jews could get out of Eastern, Central or Western Europe to even attempt to come to America.

Founded during World War I to establish soup kitchens for refugees in Eastern Europe, the Joint Distribution Committee, no longer confined to providing food, at the beginning of World War II arranged for the rescue of some few Jews when the American consuls in Germany were still issuing visas. In the wake of "Kristallnacht," the Joint Distribution Committee and the United Palestine Appeal joined to become the United Jewish Appeal; huge sums of money were raised to help European Jews. In Baltimore, funds flowed primarily from German Jews who headed the UJA campaigns from 1941[2] through 1950.

When fighting began on the Eastern Front in June 1941, about 8,000,000 Jews, roughly one half of the world's total, lived in the battle zones between the Baltic States and the Black Sea. The situation allowed the Soviet government to prove that on their own they could be as astute murderers as the Nazis. Along with the continuation of the Nazi campaign for annihilation, by the end of 1942, at least 2,000,000 European Jews had been killed. Unlike the Germans, the millions of Polish and Russian Jews, who were eventually killed, were spared one last tragic torment with no solace. They were killed by nations to which they never really belonged.

Baltimoreans did not consider those who came to the United States from Nazi Germany to be immigrants in every sense of the term; a connotation many Americans associated with those of cultural and financial inferiority. They were too refined for that designation, and they did not replicate or resemble in any way the bearded men and shawl draped women who, in earlier years, carried bundles and pasteboard suitcases down the gangways. The German government limited the Jews to what they could carry on their person when leaving the country so most of the refugee's chattels remained with families who stayed behind, The German Jews of the 1930s who managed to come to America were well educated, and many, particularly from the great urban centers, had been well to-do. Thousands were physicians, educators, attorneys, and businessmen from cosmopolitan cities such as Frankfurt, Coblenz, Berlin and Heidelberg, Hanover and Hamburg and from the smaller communities of Willmars, Bamburg and Wurzburg. Those who came from rural areas lacked the sophistication of urban Germans, but not the refinement and education. Most who came were young people because many older people, unwilling to start over in a strange country, chose to remain in Germany and unknowingly faced extermination. For the most part, German Jews lived in the same cities, towns or rural areas as had their fathers and their fathers before them. Adding to their reluctance to leave their homeland was the comfort of friendly relationships with their Christian neighbors who assured them that no harm would come. Jews in Russia were prevented from leaving their country at this time, and unlike the Germans, they faced only the usual anti-Semitism they had lived with for generations. So, the rank and file of Baltimore's Russian Jews were not overly concerned with what they perceived to be a German Jewish problem.[3]

It was difficult for German Jews to leave their homes and families in such an atmosphere of fear, dealing with the uncertainties of the Nazi government, waiting for clearance and postponing plans frequently. Those who stayed and those who left shared the terror and suspicions of their government as families gathered in their homes prior to a member's leaving. The emotions of those families probably resembled, but with much more trauma, those of the mid-nineteenth century Jews of Hesse and Bavaria.

Upon leaving, Jews were almost consumed with anxiety and uncertainty about the actual voyage to America, the sponsors they would meet on arrival, and those with whom they would probably live. Boys and girls of school age adjusted as best they could to their new way of life. Most completed their education by attending Baltimore public schools, and when not studying, worked in the businesses of their sponsors or friends of their sponsors. Because of German family attitudes and the natural tendency of males to venture forth, many more boys than girls came to America. Quite a few of those who completed their pre-university education in Germany worked full time in Baltimore while continuing with higher education studies in night schools. During World War II, male German refugees in good health were required to serve in the United States armed services, and when the war ended, many of those who served in the military were valuable assets to the United States at the Nuremberg Trials.

Those German Jews who came to Baltimore during these years assimilated well into the Baltimore Jewish community and at the same time retained their German characteristics and friendship with their fellow German refugees. A camaraderie exists to this day between members of this tightly knit group. Aided by existing community agencies, the new Americans formed social associations that frequently led to marriages with one another. This was exactly the same as immigrants did one hundred years before.

Two hundred Baltimore German Jews formed the Chevra Ahavas Chesed in January 1942, a brotherhood committed to fulfill the commandment to love mercy. The model for the organization was the Chevra Kadisha, the holy brotherhood, maintained by the Jewish communities in Germany as far back as the fourteenth century. At the death of a member of the Chevra, others carry out the rituals of burial preparation prescribed by the *Schulchan Aruch* (The Code of Jewish Law). They supervise the Shiva, the seven day period of mourning observed by the family of the departed. Because of this, funerals for members of the Chevra are handled by Orthodox undertakers, and the deceased are buried in the traditional six board unadorned caskets. At the time of the death of a Chevra member, telephone squads spread the news so that as many members as possible attend the funeral and visit the family of the deceased. The Chevra is active for the living through social functions and sponsorship of educational courses. In the past, and occasionally now, they help German Jews in financial crisis and coach others with their English. Chevra members participate in birthdays, weddings, anniversaries and the birth of new babies, since the association is not entirely concerned with the sorrows of life. In recent times, the Chevra's 1,800 members in the Baltimore area have been active in helping Jews who have wanted to come to America from the Soviet Union.

UNCOMMON THREADS

1   *In its July 1938 issue, FORTUNE magazine published the results of a Roper national public opinion poll that determined that in the Spring of 1938, 4.9% of Americans were willing to suspend immigration quotas to make room for Hitler's victims. 18.2% thought the United States should admit refugees under existing quotas; 67.4% of those polled wanted to keep refugees out of the United States altogether, and the balance had no opinion. One year later, with the passions of the people still not ignited, 83% opposed admitting any refugees above the established legal quotas.*

2   *By 1941, twenty years after the merger of the United and Federated Charities into the Associated Jewish Charities, German Jews controlled the Associated. With the exception of three persons totaling nine years in office, German Jews headed the organization for thirty-nine of the forty-eight years between its 1921 founding and 1969. The Associated Jewish Charities conducted fund raising campaigns in alternate years until 1950, at which time they were joined by the Jewish Welfare Fund in joint annual fund raising campaigns. Today, about one third of the funds distributed by the ASSOCIATED: Jewish Community Federation of Baltimore is granted to the United Jewish Appeal for overseas needs.*

3   *A well to-do childless Baltimore German Jewish family, Myer and Julia Strauss, "took the bull by the horns." For many years, Julia's family the Friedenwalds had been one of the city's most ardent and active advocates and supporters of Zionism. During many summers, she accompanied her father Dr. Harry Friedenwald on trips to Palestine where, because of their influence and affluence, they became close friends with most of the future leaders of Israel. Both Julia and Myer spent endless amounts of energy and much money to bring children out of Germany and to send them to Palestine. They signed more than two hundred personal affidavits that enabled German Jews to come to the United States. The couple worked day and night on the details of securing these visas and preparing the affidavits, and they greeted their sponsored refugees when they arrived at piers or railroad stations. They located housing for them, bought furniture, provided other necessities and most important, they acted as moral and spiritual mentors and advisors. The couple adopted two boys, the sons of a German woman, who, many years before, had been Julia's classmate in a private school they attended in Switzerland.*

PART III-7

Post-WW II * United Nations * Meetings and conferences * Zionists * The British and Palestine * The Jewish Agency * German-Eastern Europe refugees * The Poles still at it * *President Warfield/Exodus 1947*

*T*he Emergency Committee to save the Jewish People of Europe was formed at a July 1942, conference in New York City, and they presented to and urged a twelve point program upon the governments of the recently formed United Nations. The Declaration of the United Nations was signed on January 1, 1942, to set forth war aims of the Allied Powers though it was not until April 1945 that the charter of the organization was drafted. Baltimore philanthropist and industrialist Jacob Blaustein was a consultant to the United States delegation that met in San Francisco for this purpose. In 1949, President Harry Truman appointed Blaustein to be a member of the United States delegation to the United Nations. The activity of Zionists during this period increased, and almost every major move to save Jews revolved around the founding of a Jewish State. As written in Chapter 26, Zionist activity goes back to the late 1800s and has been a continuous issue for the well being of the Jews in the Middle East ever since. At the Paris Peace Conference held in May 1919, that framed the treaties that ended World War I, United States President Woodrow Wilson thought the question of Palestine would be especially difficult to solve owing to the Zionist question; he was correct. The British, the United States and, he thought, the French government were to some extent favorably committed on the question of a homeland for the Jews, but timing was not for then.

A world wide conference of Jewish leaders in May 1942 repudiated the British White Papers and called for an immediate establishment of a Jewish State and a Jewish Army. Impressed by the Arab opposition to a Jewish homeland in Palestine years before in June 1922, the British government issued its interpretation of the concept of a Jewish national home. The White Paper agreed to the establishment of a Jewish home in Palestine, but it did not agree that it should be considered for the entire area of Palestine. A most important British White Paper of May 1939 made a unilateral statement of policy based upon the assumption that the Jewish national home pledge had already been substantially filled. Indefinite Jewish immigration and transfer of Arab land to Jews were contrary to the spirit of Article 22 of the Covenant of the League and to British undertakings to the Arabs under the Mandate. Within each of the next five years, 15,000 Jews would be allowed into the country. Thereafter, Jewish immigration would be subject to Arab acquiescence. Land transfers would be allowed only in certain areas of Palestine, and an independent Palestine State would be considered within ten years. Just as Sweden saved the Jewish population of Denmark by simply opening its doors, the Emergency Committee believed that by simply opening the doors of Palestine, thousands of European Jews would be able to save themselves. American Zionists claimed and Washington rejected the idea that the United States' policy was contrary to the provisions of the 1924 Anglo-American Conference on Palestine. That agreement bound the United

States government to hold the British to its pro-Zionist commitment under the League of Nations Mandate for Palestine.

Returning from the Three Power Conference in Teheran, Iran, in December 1943, President Roosevelt at last seemed to comprehend the problems of Jewish refugees when he issued an executive order that created the War Refugee Board. The Board's policy was to "take all measures within its powers to rescue the victims of enemy oppression who are in immediate danger of death and to otherwise afford such victims all possible relief and assistance consistent with the successful prosecution of the War." This sudden action on the part of President Roosevelt was due to mounting pressures of public opinion and his own political plans to run for a fourth term in 1944. In that campaign, Roosevelt launched an increasingly vocal pro-Zionist position; however, discussions at the Yalta Conference in February 1945 deflated these hopes. There, FDR stated that he personally was a Zionist, and he asked Marshal Josef Stalin if he were one. Stalin replied that he was a Zionist in principle, but he recognized the difficulties of creating a Jewish state.

Without the British protection of the Jewish community in Palestine, the Jews would be helplessly exposed to physical extermination by the Arabs, particularly if the Arabs were aroused to action by the German Adolph Hitler. The American position on Palestine would have probably been more positive had the German Jews of America who supported the non-Zionist position of the relatively powerful American Council for Judaism, aligned themselves with the Russian Jews of America. The Council considered their anti-Zionist position a positive statement that helped them forge relationships with the Christian community, and they claimed the issue of Zionism to be a philosophy of defeatism. The Council viewed Judaism as a religion, certainly not a nationality. Separate and distinct from most of the rest of the world, the council looked upon Israel to be the homeland for its present citizens and not all Jews. Many of the prominent German Jewish Reform rabbis of America spoke out against Zionism, including Baltimore's most prominent and nationally known rabbi, Morris S. Lazaron of the Baltimore Hebrew Congregation.[1]

In June 1944, the Allied Forces successful invasion of France and the capture of Rome changed the refugee situation in Russia because it created a safe haven for Jews in southern Italy. Later, refugees brought into the United States from Italy and other places entered the United States, not as immigrants, but as temporary residents, uncomplicated by the formalities usually associated with the admission of people under America's immigration laws.

World War II ended in Europe in May 1945. For American Jews, Christians and atheists there was much rejoicing, but for the Jews, their happiness was tempered by the shadow of the Holocaust. When the numbers were fully known and the realization that so many relatives and friends had perished, it was difficult to be joyful. Almost every Jewish family was affected by the loss of at least someone. Jews questioned themselves as they always have; was the price for being God's chosen people too high?

Of the approximately 8,860,000 Jews directly affected by Hitler's "Final Solution," approximately 5,935,000 lost their lives. Several thousand were able to leave

Europe before the war but those that did not were the casualties, Allied soldiers found thousands of Jews still alive in the death camps of Poland and Germany; and those Jews and other displaced persons throughout Europe were unwilling to return to their homes in their countries of origin, as if they had any homes to return to. There was no question that these persons were aliens in the countries where they were born, mostly because of the political changes that had taken place during the war. Approximately 600,000 Poles; 100,000 Yugoslavs; 250,000 Baltic Nationals; and 50,000 Ukrainians were being maintained in displaced persons centers in Germany, Austria and Italy. Of the approximately 1,925,000 Jews not accounted for in the above figures, 200,000 German Jews remained interned in Denmark, 200,000 in Austria and large numbers in the Soviet Union, the Netherlands, France, the Ukraine, Romania and elsewhere.

The rehabilitation of the European Jewish Holocaust survivors rested primarily with American Jews. Children of immigrants, and children of the children of immigrants began to wear the mantle of world Jewish leadership. Several Baltimore Jews assumed the roles of the foremost leaders of world Judaism. In 1949, Harry Greenstein, then the director of the Associated Jewish Charities, was given the rank of Major General when he went to Germany as the advisor of Jewish affairs to General Lucius D. Clay, Commanding Officer of the American Occupation Zone. As for the choice of Jewish displaced persons where they would be sent to continue their lives, only about 15% wanted to come to the United States or England. Another 15% were indifferent as to where they would be sent, and interestingly, 70%, mostly young people, requested to go to Palestine.

The Anglo-American Committee of Inquiry, charged with investigating the problems of Jewish displaced persons, and backed by the request of the Jewish Agency, issued 100,000 certificates in 1946 for entrance into Palestine. The Committee in a difficult situation suspended judgment on Zionist aspirations and recommended that, for the time being, Palestine continue under British mandate. The British government, not too happy with 100,000 additional Jews in Palestine, suspected that the Americans were self serving on this issue. They suspected that the United States wanted the 100,000 Jews sent to Palestine because "who needed them in New York City." The Jewish Agency took charge of transportation, placement in housing and jobs for Jewish emigrants to Israel. Many years after the major headaches of the Jewish Agency had passed, in 1983, Baltimorean Jerold Charles Hoffberger assumed the Board Chairmanship of the Jewish Agency.

Hopefully the troubles of Europe, except for repatriation in some few cases, economic adjustments, new homes for refugees and the contemplation of and activity surrounding the major task of physically rebuilding the damages of war were now behind the world, but not for Poland. On July 4, 1946, in the city of Kielce, Poland, the old rumors of a ritual-murder of a Christian boy set off a major riot in which 42 Jews were killed. About 150,000 Polish Jews who had taken refuge in the Soviet Union wanted desperately to leave, so they flooded into the Allied occupation zone of Germany. There they were although they did not want to stay in Germany either. The United States' immigration quota for Poles that year was 6,500; for Germans and Austrians combined, 26,000. This created the seemingly unreal situation of the prospects of such a large number of displaced persons unable to enter the United States, and on the other hand, an open quota that could not be filled by available Germans. When the United States' Johnson Act of 1924 was drafted and became law, the idea was not to consider each immigrant as a human being but to keep a balance in the country of the various nationals that wanted to come to America. Quotas were based on a percentage of each nationality living in the United States at the time of the passage of the act. There were possibly good reasons for this at that time, but it began to look like the legislators of the 1920s were well behind in their thinking for the future.

After the War, another 150,000 Jews who had escaped death in Eastern Europe and Germany found refuge in the United States; many came to Baltimore. Among the 150,000 were about 12,000 ultra Orthodox Hasidic Jews, completely in black with payes, beards, hats, suits or caftans, almost all of whom settled in the Williamsburg section of Brooklyn, New York. The entire world wide Jewish situation prompted increased Zionist activities and ardent clamoring for the birth of a Jewish State. Because Baltimore had long been a center for American and world Zionist factions, in January 1940, Dr. Chaim Weitzman, president of the World Zionist Organization came to Baltimore to address a mass meeting at the Lyric Theater.

Great Britain continued to be the bad guy in Palestine, and in Baltimore a Russian Jew Moses Speert and a German Jew Adolph Hamburger worked as brothers on a secret plan. In July 1945, Speert a very active Zionist and Hamburger a Baltimore business man met in the New York apartment of Rudolph Sonneborn, a former member of what was at one time, Baltimore's largest clothing manufacturing firm. Sonneborn arranged for a group of eighteen concerned national business men and Zionists to meet David Ben Gurion and to hear a report on Palestine. When the State of Israel was declared, Ben Gurion became its first Prime Minister, They made plans to raise needed funds from private persons in America in secrecy because whatever they did for Palestine would breach the mandated power of the British government.

In 1942, the United States took possession of an Old Bay Line steamer the *President Warfield* built to carry 200 passengers, and converted it to a troop ship to accommodate hundreds of men. After the war, she was moored for a year along with a cluster of old ships in the ship graveyard in Virginia's James River. In November, 1946, the aged and limping Chesapeake Bay liner was sold for $8,000 to a ship wrecking company, but before it could be scrapped, it was resold for $40,000 to a mysterious group known as the Weston Trading Company, a front for the Haganah Palestine underground organization.

The *President Warfield* was again converted, this time by the Weston Trading Company to accommodate five thousand persons. They requisitioned Ben Kolker, owner of the Maryland Lumber Company to deliver several truckloads of wood to be used for bunks. Kolker did not know at the time what the wood was to be used for. He asked the Weston Trading Company where to send the bill and he was told to charge and send it to

GOD. The Weston Trading Company registered the *President Warfield* in Panama, and in secrecy in Baltimore's harbor, loaded it with supplies. Dock personnel told inquisitive onlookers that the ship was being stocked with supplies for a trip to China. The *President Warfield* sailed from pier 5 Canton on February 25, 1947, with a twenty-one year old Palestinian skipper. The ship was manned by an incompetent crew, seventy percent of whom were adventurous young Jewish clerks and students. Others in the crew were mostly retired seamen. Each had been given a bottle of champagne, a sweater, a Jewish bible and a flag of the Haganah.[2]

The ship headed down the Chesapeake Bay and into the Atlantic Ocean, and then turned east in the teeth of a squall. Probably due to the inexperienced crew, the *President Warfield* ran aground, sent an SOS, and was towed to Hampton Roads. She was then taken to Philadelphia to be patched up and to replace thousands of dollars worth of supplies ruined in the storm. In Hampton Roads, questions arose regarding the ship's Panamanian registry so it was withdrawn; then *President Warfield* secured a certificate of registry from Honduras. Due to the mysterious aura surrounding the ship, this registry also was about to be withdrawn, but before the authorities could act, the ship sailed for Europe.

The *President Warfield* made port in Sette, France in the Gulf of Lyon. Under constant surveillance, four thousand five hundred passengers boarded the ship. Although pressure was brought upon the French government not to let the ship sail, it again escaped the grasp of the law. The ship headed for a narrow deserted strip of beach north of Tel Aviv where plans had been made for a secret unauthorized landing in Palestine.

British Intelligence is not easily fooled; the British Foreign Office knew for some time what was going on so when the *President Warfield* sailed from France, a British warship followed in her wake. Near the site of the planned beach landing, other British ships pulled alongside the ship to forcefully prevent her from going in; they demanded that the ship proceed to Haifa. As the British warships turned their searchlights on the large *President Warfield* name boards, the crew dramatically flipped them aside revealing her proper re-name painted on two canvas banners, Haganah ship *Exodus 1947*. While The *President Warfield* sailed in the Mediterranean, crew members had painted the new name on banners and lashed them to each side of the bow under the name boards. *Exodus* raised blue and white flags of Zion as two British destroyers rammed the ships bow causing damage. With a British landing party aboard, British ships escorted *Exodus* to the port of Haifa, arriving on July 20, 1947. The passengers were ordered off and put on British ships to be returned to France. At Marseilles, the passengers refused to disembark so the British ordered the ships to proceed to Hamburg Germany, where the passengers left the ship. After the May 1948 establishment of the State of Israel, in 1951 the mayor of Haifa wanted to make the *Exodus* a floating museum; however, before the plans could be carried out, in 1952 she was destroyed by fire.[3]

At this time of world need, Eastern European and German Jews working together in America touched the lives of world Jewry. In Baltimore, both groups, well on their

UNCOMMON THREADS

way towards unity in the Jewish community closed ranks, Zionist and non-Zionist, German and Russian.

---

1   *A powerful national voice, Lazaron changed his position at a later date but because he split his congregation, the damage had already been done to his pulpit. The liberal Rabbi Edward L. Israel spoke the message of the State of Israel to his congregants*

2   *Amalie Sonneborn Katz remembers accompanying her husband Shakman Katz to a pier to deliver hundreds of sweaters to the PRESIDENT WARFIELD. The secrecy was such that she had no idea of the destination of the ship. A few other prominent Baltimoreans, sworn to secrecy, helped to get the ship underway; Reuben Levinson Ben Katzner, Elkan Myers, Joseph Allen, Samuel J. Kaiser, Herman Speert, Henry Kuntz, Samuel Shapiro and a few others.*

3   *In June 1996, the Jewish Historical Society was given a five foot wooden replica of the celebrated Chesapeake Bay vessel. At the reception for the gift, the ship's bell and whistle were on display; they had been obtained on loan by Baltimore dentist Dr. Barry Lever. Lever heads the World Zionist organization's campaign to commemorate the EXODUS 1947 fifty year anniversary.*

PART III-8

Roosevelt and Truman * Jewish underground * World Zionist Organization * State of Israel * Displaced Persons Act * Joint Distribution Committee

At the end of World War II, it became increasingly evident that an independent State of Israel would be created, and in the not too distant future. After the untimely death of Franklin Delano Roosevelt in Warm Springs, Georgia in April 1945, Vice President Harry S. Truman became President. American Zionists were elated as they now felt they would have a better friend in the White House, and truly they did. In October 1945, President Truman expressed his support for the Jewish Agency for Israel's plan for a Jewish state in Palestine.

During World War II, Zionists found themselves in the paradoxical position of having to oppose the 1939 British White Paper and at the same time fight on the side of the British against their common enemy, Germany. Before World War II, Jewish underground organizations actively worked against the Arabs. Led by David Ben-Gurion and sponsored by The Jewish Agency for Israel, the Haganah (defense) had unwittingly been trained by the British in commando tactics. Although its formation was without doubt illegal, the Haganah considered itself to be the legitimate Jewish army. Between 1943 and 1947, the Irgun Tzevai Leumi, a dissident group formed and headed by Menachem Begin, mounted violent attacks against the British and Arabs.[1] The World Zionist Organization held a World Congress in December 1946, and called for immediate Jewish statehood. Prospects moved rapidly into reality and in February 1947, Great Britain submitted the Palestine question to the United Nations. In May of that year, the United Nations established UNSCOP, the United Nations Special Committee on Palestine. Their report to the United Nations at the end of August recommended that Palestine be granted independence at the earliest practical date. They urged that the country be partitioned into three separate states; an Arab state, a Jewish state and the City of Jerusalem, to be governed by an international trusteeship.

The British acquiesced to this plan; the Americans and the World Zionist Organization agreed with it; the Arabs opposed it. In November 1947, a vote was taken and an agenda was adopted to terminate the British Mandate for Palestine effective no later than August 1, 1948. In any case, the British were to be out of Palestine by October 1948, at the latest. It was questionable if the resolution would be passed by the United Nations. If Great Britain and her friends planned to abstain, could the plan receive the necessary two thirds majority required for passage? The Soviet bloc surprised all when they cast favorable votes and the resolution squeaked by. The communists had always opposed Zionism before voting on this resolution, however at this time, the Soviet Union considered a Jewish state a price tag they had to pay in order to oust the British from the mid-east. On November 30, 1947, one day after the vote, Palestinian Arabs and volunteers from neighboring countries attacked the Jews.

On May 14, 1948, Israel officially became an independent nation, the first time in modern history that the Jewish people were in power in any recognized nation. On the same day, the United States recognized Israel, and eleven days later, on May 25, 1948, Israel's first President, Chaim Weitzman visited United States' President Harry Truman in the White House. He presented the American president with a beautifully adorned Torah scroll. This evoked an interesting response from President Truman, "Thanks, its just what I've always wanted." The Arab countries wasted little time as the regular armies of Iraq, Jordan, Egypt, Lebanon and Syria invaded the state of Israel on November 15, 1948.

Zionist accomplishment came to be a reality a half-century after the meeting of the Zionist Congress in Basel, Switzerland in 1897 in which Baltimore Zionist organizations played a role.[2] Israel showed the world that it had erased forever the historical image of Jews as restless lost tribes. Age old discussions as to whether the Jews constituted a race or a religion died because they was now a nationality in Israel. The old differences between Eastern European Jewish Zionists and German Reform Jews ended with a resounding beside the point. Every discussion on the subject now had to be after the fact, and for the first time on the question of Zionism, most German and Russian Jews thought alike. A handful of German American Council for Judaism members stubbornly remained holdouts, but why did they not accept that Israel existed. The emergence of the State of Israel dissolved immigrant ideologies between socialism and Zionism. American Jews, Orthodox and Reform, German and Russian, appeared to be proud of Israel's military accomplishments and the apparent genius of its Jewish field leaders. Many Jews hold views that question the political and international progress of Israeli governments that are unfortunately effectively restrained by factions at odds with one another. A danger exists in some archaic extreme nationalistic American Jewish thought, "Israel right or wrong, Israel." Of all the historical happenings that have brought Jews together, the greatest common denominator has been the State of Israel. In retrospect though, Zionism has not always been a force for the eventual unity of German and Russian Jews. For years before the founding of Israel, the leaders of Shearith Israel and Chizuk Amuno, the two German Jewish synagogues that rejected Reform, raised funds for Palestine.

For many refugees in the United States who escaped from Nazi Germany and Poland, the State of Israel had a symbolic meaning only; as it was not their new homeland. For them, Israel arrived ten years too late. While Israel spelled a homeland for others, it was not for them unless they pulled up their stakes to go to Israel. What did happen was that there were no longer the medieval and modern periods of wandering Jews. In June 1948, less than a month after the creation of the State of Israel, the United States Congress passed and President Truman signed the Displaced Persons Act. While there were discriminatory points to the Act, it accomplished its purpose at the time by easing the burden on Israel during the critical days of that nation's formation. HIAS handled the details that brought 205,000 displaced persons to the United States. In June 1950, additional federal legislation passed designed to allow another 150,000 displaced persons to come to the United States. By the beginning of 1953, European displaced persons camps were almost completely emptied so the immigration to the United States reverted to the parameters of the old 1924 Johnston Act, but not for long. In August 1953, new legislation provided for the acceptance over a period of three years of 214,000 new arrivals in the United States from Communist countries. They came mostly from the Soviet Union and Hungary and from non-Communist South Africa, Iran and some from Israel who at that time preferred to come to America.

The power of the government of Israel on American Jewry is enormous, and its ability to raise funds largely through bond sales is awesome. Although the government for most of Israel's years has been somewhat leftist, its impact on American Jews is conservative. Because Israel has been forced to defend itself, it has depended on American military advice and help, and this has been troublesome to some liberal American Jews.

Although the State of Israel's first prime minister David Ben-Gurion urged Jews all over the world to "return home," this has had little appeal for Americans so very few have done so; they consider home to be the United States. For the German Jews in America who did not support Zionism in the beginning and for the Eastern European Jews who did, why would they want to leave the United States? For a majority of them, whose fathers and grandfathers had come to America as huddled masses, here they wanted to stay. Where else in the world could their talents and energy be so recognized and rewarded? Since Israel's statehood, hundreds of thousands of American Jews have visited there and returned with glowing inner feelings. Theirs is a romance with the spiritual and physical, a pilgrimage that allows American Jews to identify with the people and the land of Israel. Nevertheless, like the old adage about New York City, it's a nice place to visit but not many American Jews want to live there.[3]

The American Jewish Committee in the late 1940s threatened to withdraw its support of the State of Israel if her leaders did not stop pressing for a massive migration of American Jews to Israel. At a meeting held in Jerusalem in August 1950, the president of the American Jewish Committee Jacob Blaustein met with David Ben Gurion. He released a statement that was loud and clear, "The Jews of the United States, as a community and as individuals, have only one political attachment, and that is to the United States of America." Baltimore Reform Jews significantly expressed their support for Israel when in July 1962, when an Israel Bond Dinner was held at the Har Sinai Synagogue, the first time in Baltimore's history that its Reform Jews identified themselves so closely with the State of Israel.

The major players in the field of Jewish refugee and rescue work were the Hebrew Immigrant Aid Society (HIAS), the United States Services for new Americans and the Joint Distribution Committee (JDC) of which the JDC was by far the largest. In January 1957, the three merged to form a single Jewish immigration agency, The United HIAS Service Incorporated.

UNCOMMON THREADS

---

1   Hardly two weeks after the Kielce Poland, pogrom, this Palestine Terrorist gang reacted with anger by planting enough T.N.T. in a wing of the King David Hotel in Jerusalem to produce a blast that killed 91 persons, Jews, Britons, and Arabs.

2   Rabbi Schepsel Schaffer of Baltimore's Shearith Israel Congregation was the only American representative to the Zionist Congress. In 1890, The first American Zionist Convention was held in Baltimore.

3   Several Baltimore families including those of Irving Abromawitz, an insurance executive and attorney Fred Weisgal moved to Israel. In August 1996, Rabbi Ira Schiffer resigned from the pulpit of the Beth Am Synagogue and moved to Israel with his wife and two children. The Schiffers are seeking a sense of comfort within the Israel culture and society and a sense of being home in an ancient land.

PART III-9

Economic emergence of Baltimore's Russian Jews * Suburban synagogues * Orthodox to Reform to Conservative * Liberty Road Judaism * Jewish foods * Suburban "Bars and Bats"

*A*merican nationalism generated by World War II had a positive effect on sealing relationships between Baltimore German and Russian Jews, and in the 1950s, they acted together as a buffer against widespread criticism from the Christian community. Jewish names appeared in the national press frequently, and not always in a complimentary way. In post-World War II trials and allegations, Jews were accused of being Communists and engaging in espionage and in unpopular involvement in the civil rights movement. Baltimore Jews worked together on the issue of residential restrictive covenants, and in 1948 these covenants were declared unenforceable by the United States Supreme Court; in 1953, the Court declared them to be unconstitutional.[1]

Though Russian Jewish business men flexed their muscles before World War II, it was not until the war ended that Germans Jews faced the reality that their numbers in and out of business were fewer. They were dying faster than they were being replaced while Eastern Europeans continued to generate larger families. While it was difficult for German Jews to accept, the facts were that they were on their way to becoming minor players in Baltimore's community and economy. The immense economic growth following the war enabled first and second generation Russian Jews to paddle up the tributaries of mainstream Baltimore where German Jews pulled heavy oars for many years. While most German Jews extended their hands to Russian Jews through their businesses and professions, some reacted introspectively, confirming their life long beliefs that German Jews were of a different and, in their own minds, a better class than their co-religionists. It was difficult for German Jews to acknowledge the awful truth to themselves that Russians Jews in Baltimore outnumbered them by the thousands. They reluctantly conceded that Russian Jews had out-paced them in business. They had caught up and were poised to overtake them in the professions and philanthropy.

Baltimore German and Russian Jews who had prospered in needles trade manufacturing began to live in a different world. They closed or sold their businesses because many lacked willing family successors, or they just wanted to be less active, maybe play a little golf. Russian Jews, mainly, invested heavily in real estate; some have reaped fortunes. Hundreds of sons and daughters of both groups attended graduate schools to further their education and to satisfy their intellectual interests in the arts, the law, science, and education. They have advanced well in these fields.

World War II opened new horizons for non-professionals, and though there appeared to be a surface social acceptance of Jews by more of Baltimore's Christian community, there were no standards by which this could be measured.[2] Multiple varieties of ventures diminished the distinctiveness of Jews. Russian Jews no longer had a need to continue to speak Yiddish in their homes and less reason to speak it in their work places. As business barriers crumpled, Jewish businesses and professional services grew quickly;

becoming increasingly important contributors to Baltimore's economy. On the surface, overt anti-Semitism waned, and Jews became more in control of their own destinies, but having been ostracized so consistently since the beginning of recorded history, Baltimore Jews stepped lightly into that which they long considered to be "The Enemy Camp." In the mid 1950s, about three out of four Baltimore Jews were second and third generation Americans. The huge move of Jews from East Baltimore was nearing its end and a large percentage of them sought better than working-class jobs. Older members of middle income families, a large number of whom were small retailers, continued to be involved in their businesses. Those sons and daughters who preferred associations with large commercial enterprises rather than the professions stepped up corporate ladders as best they could.

All was not peaches and cream. In the large corporate arena, particularly in finance and insurance, Jews continued to work shoulder to shoulder and face to face with those who would block their advancement. In the past fifty years, the impasse in these fields had changed ever so slightly, and there are many indications that the gentlemen's agreements of the past were still in place in some areas. Although not found in the minutes of board meetings, it appeared that only a handful of selected and carefully screened Jews can occupy top corporate positions and be given the opportunity to serve on important Baltimore City corporate boards.

By the end of World War II, the economic conditions in East Baltimore were much improved and the city's demographics began to show drastic changes. Large numbers of German Reform Jews moved into upper Park Heights from mid-town northwest and Jewish East Baltimoreans moved into these vacated residences. Now, again, it was the right time for the three venerable Baltimore Reform Jewish congregations to consider moving nearer to the residences of most their congregants living in Pikesville and Stevenson. The decisions to move were difficult, but they had learned a lesson from the post Civil War history of the Hebrew Friendship Congregation, then Baltimore's largest. Refusing to move from East Baltimore along with their congregants, they lost their membership and had to close their synagogue. Because of the high cost and the vanishing of fine craftsmen, synagogue boards could not dream of replicating the elaborate traditional interior ambiance and design exteriors of their present synagogues.

The Baltimore Hebrew Congregation became the first of the three Reform synagogues to relocate. In 1951 they erected a modern temple with little exterior adornment on the multi-acre property they owned on the southeast corner of Park Heights and Slade Avenues, catty-corner to the Suburban Club. When Baltimore Hebrew moved from Lloyd Street to Madison Avenue, they sold pews instead of seats to members and small silver plaques with the family name in script were attached to each pew. At the time of the move to Park Heights Avenue, individual seats replaced the pews so the plaques were removed from the Madison Avenue synagogue and stored with their archival material. After forty years in storage, the synagogue archivist uncovered a shoe box containing the plaques. A special service was held in November 1994 to honor those who owned family pews at the Madison Avenue Synagogue, and as expected, almost every name was that of a German Jew.

During and shortly after the Reform temples moved, leaders made efforts to eliminate or at least diminish their elitist image; otherwise, there was no way for them to continue the support of these large, elegant, and expensive complexes. Since the mid 1940s, well on target for the Reform synagogues, more and more prosperous Russian Jews perceived orthodoxy to be synonymous with poverty, and the continuation of their adherence to its time consuming practice an impediment to their social and economic progress. They did exactly what the German Jews had done a few years after the Civil War; they joined the "more American" Reform synagogues and also founded Conservative congregations. At this time, many Russian Jews felt ambivalent about their Judaism; perhaps in some instances, this had something to do with the way they earned their living, More and more, they had become identified with banking, insurance and practicing law; sewing factories and retail stores were for their fathers. Many orthodox rabbis tried to stem the exodus of their congregants, but those who chose to leave immersed themselves in their new religious life styles.

On Park Heights Avenue and Fords Lane in 1959, the Har Sinai Congregation erected a temple featuring a huge landmark dome.[3] Two years after Har Sinai erected their dome, Oheb Shalom, the last of the large Baltimore in-town German Reform congregations to move, occupied their new synagogue on the west side of Park Heights Avenue slightly north of Seven Mile Lane. Oheb Shalom engaged the internationally famous German-American Bauhaus architect Walter Gropius for this project.

The boards of the Reform temples no longer followed their decades old tradition, a preference that their rabbis be of German heritage. More and more bright Jewish scholarly males and females of Eastern European heritage attended the Hebrew Union College, the Reform seminary in Cincinnati, now merged with the Jewish Institute of Religion in New York and Los Angeles, to study for the Reform rabbinate. In 1956, the Baltimore Hebrew Congregation continuing a string of historical firsts, elected a woman, Helen Dalsheimer to be its president, the first major American Jewish congregation to do so. Dalsheimer was old line wealthy Baltimore German Reform. Then in 1979, the congregation engaged Baltimore's first female rabbi, a graduate of the Hebrew Union College. In a step nearer to female equality in Reform, in 1995, the names of matriarchs, our foremother has been added to communal prayers to the God of all Generations.

Not anxious to relinquish a hold on their Reform congregations, German Jews continued to control their boards for several years. They tenaciously held on to the Union Prayer Book, the traditional music which they had known since their first days of German Reform worship, and "brummeled" over former Russian Orthodox Jews attending their synagogues. Because they had limited board representation, the former orthodox made few attempts to revise the worship rituals of the Reform services until the 1970s and 1980s, well after they were entrenched in the Reform movement. Attending services, former Orthodox Jews heard less Hebrew in the orderly and structured manner of Reform worship, neither did they doven, nor wear yarlmuke or tallit as men and women sat in adjoining seats next to their families in the Reform sanctuaries.

With dwindling numbers of German Jews, more Hebrew has been introduced into the services and the present Reform congregational worship has become more akin to Conservatism. Bar Mitzvah has regained its importance, and Bat Mitzvah for thirteen year old girls has been introduced. Lifetime German members of Reform congregations worship shoulder to shoulder with former Orthodox Jews who have not shed all vestiges of their Orthodoxy. Presently in an increasing return to conservativism, a few yarmulkes and tallit are visible in the Reform temples.

Photographs of past confirmation classes on display at the Baltimore Hebrew Congregation clearly indicate that the size of these classes has decreased through the years, testimony to a diminishing role of this exclusively Reform Jewish rite of passage. Some present day Reform Jewish parents have made Bar and Bat Mitzvah the culmination of a thirteen year cycle of children's Jewish learning, and when those milestones are reached, their children's Jewish education ends. Former Orthodox and Conservative, newcomers to Reform Judaism, have little feeling for confirmation's objective to continue their children's religious education.

Temple Emanuel was founded in 1955 to accommodate Reform Jews living in the Liberty Road corridor who wanted to worship nearer to their homes and in a simpler manner than in the well-established Park Heights Avenue Reform synagogues. Temple Emanuel is presently building a new synagogue on Berryman's Lane in Reisterstown, again due to demographic change.

Along with the movement of Orthodox into Reform, the Conservative movement since its inception a supporter of Zionism with its own agenda presented a strong and simple appeal. An amalgam of Reform and Orthodoxy, Conservatism links the old traditions of Judaism to the modern world although its rabbis frequently omit religion from their sermons. A good bit of the post-war appeal for the Conservative movement can be laid directly to younger people.[4] This greatly strengthened a movement that allowed Jews to participate fully in secular life, and at the same time, retain a good measure of religious intensity. Conservative congregations allow degrees of latitude in their services; for instance, Beth El includes organ music but has no choir. They and some Conservative synagogues have made their services more meaningful by adapting the Triennial, a completion of the reading of the Torah on a three year cycle rather than Orthodox minyans who complete the reading in a single year.[5]

A substantial, and possibly the largest, percentage of affiliated Baltimore Jews are members of Conservative synagogues, the largest of which is Chizuk Amuno. Chizuk Amuno and Beth El have built enormous synagogue complexes in Baltimore County, a distance north of the upper Park Heights Avenue locations of the three major Reform temples. Beth El was founded in 1947 by twenty families who had become disenchanted with the ideologies of the Orthodox Beth Tfiloh synagogue. Beth El was originally to have been built in the Ashburton section of the city at Hilton and Dorithan Roads. Before construction started, the fabric of this neighborhood began to change so they chose a location on Western Run Drive near Taney Road. Neighborhood changes also became evident at this location; thus many Beth El members were on the move again to Pikesville and Stevenson, north of the city line. Beth El bought property on Park Heights Avenue in Stevenson and in 1960, erected a synagogue complete with a mikvah, unusual in a non-Orthodox house of worship.

Two newer suburban congregations accommodated the growing numbers of Jews who opted for Conservative worship. Young families who moved into the Randallstown section of Baltimore County, founded the Liberty Road Conservative Congregation in 1956. A month later, the congregation changed its name to Beth Israel to honor the State of Israel. Beth Israel dedicated its first synagogue in a remodeled house in 1957; in 1959, they consecrated a combination synagogue and all purpose building at 5900 Liberty Road; and in 1968, the congregation completed a new sanctuary in the 9400 block of Liberty Road. An old East Baltimore Orthodox congregation, Mikro Kodesh, founded in 1886, merged with Beth Israel in 1963. Kol Tikva, founded in 1984 and the Reisterstown Jewish Center founded in 1972 merged to form Adath Chaim (Conservative) in 1985. In October 1993, the merged congregation completed building a synagogue on Cockey's Mill Lane in Reisterstown. Incorporated in 1989, Chevrei Tzedek (Association for Justice), the most recently founded Conservative congregation, offers members, as do a few other congregations, a light break-fast at the end of Yom Kippur Services.

The legendary elder of Baltimore's Conservative synagogues is Chizuk Amuno that moved from Eutaw Place and Chauncey Avenue in 1961 to their present complex on Stevenson Road. Fifteen years after its founding in 1871, Chizuk Amuno's orthodox German congregation moderated toward Conservatism and in 1886 they and five other congregations founded the Conservative Jewish Theological Seminary of America in New York City. In 1913, Chizuk Amuno was one of sixteen congregations to organize the conservative United Synagogues of America. After Chizuk Amuno dedicated their new synagogue on the corner of Eutaw Place and Chauncey Avenue in 1922 their membership was increased by many former Russian Orthodox Jews living nearby, so Chizuk Amuno retained a strong Orthodox image. It was not until 1948 when men and women chose to sit together during services that Chizuk Amuno moved solidly into mainstream Conservativism.

Several suburban synagogues include the word center in their name which indicates they are more than a house of worship. Jewish congregations use their sanctuaries, religious school facilities and meeting halls for the multi purposes for which they were intended; learning and sociability as well as worship. Since the days of the First Temple, Jews have considered their synagogues to be the center of their Jewish lives. Makes one wonder, if down the road, will there be a shul with a pool.

By the end of World War II, Reform and Conservative synagogues became less politically and culturally isolated from the community. Rabbis of each supported and marched in demonstrations for civil rights in the 1960s; some were arrested for doing so. Recently, for ecumenical understanding and solidarity, Christian priests and ministers have spoken from the pulpits of Jewish sanctuaries and in a less formal atmosphere in synagogue social halls. In turn, Reform and Conservative rabbis have spoken in churches. Beginning in 1956 and continuing for several years, a popular Baltimore weekly television show *To Promote Good Will* featured discussions between Har Sinai's Reform Rabbi Abraham Shusterman, Rev. Dr. Frederick W. Heifer of the Christian Temple and Msgr. William Kailer Dunn of Notre Dame.[6]

Nationally by 1960 the Conservative movement began to decline. In 1965, 44% of American Jews affiliated with the Conservative movement and 27% with the Reform. Ten years later, the Conservative figures were 35% and the Reform 34%; however, in Baltimore the statistics for Conservative affiliation continues to be strong. Membership in Conservative synagogues in Baltimore has never reached the heights of the national affiliations, which probably has much to do with the city's very strong Orthodox presence. In 1990, according to figures published by THE ASSOCIATED: Jewish Community Federation of Baltimore, there were approximately 95,000 Jews in the metropolitan area. 22% were Orthodox, and about the same percentage for each, Conservative and Reform; the other third are not affiliated. In 1990, those in Baltimore with synagogue affiliation worshipped in 30 Orthodox, five Conservative, four Reform, one Reconstructionist, and two non-affiliated synagogues.[7]

Because of the large numbers of Jews who relocated away from East Baltimore in the 1950s and 1960s, new synagogues were erected in two suburban areas to which Jews moved. Though several were built in the Liberty Road corridor, more were built in the Park Heights-Pikesville-Stevenson area.

In 1956, the Anshe Emunah, founded in 1887 in East Baltimore, became the Liberty Jewish Center (Orthodox); they erected a synagogue in the 5200 block of Liberty Heights Avenue. In 1961 the Center merged with Aitz Chaim, also founded in 1887 on Eden Street; in 1963 the center relocated to Church Lane off Old Court Road. Tifereth Israel Anshe Sphard (Beauty of Israel) Congregation, founded in 1919 on Smallwood Street, merged in 1974 with the Liberty Jewish Center. The Suburban Orthodox Congregation Toras Chaim (Torah of Life), founded in 1956, dedicated a synagogue in the 7500 block of Seven Mile Lane in 1962. Shaarei Tfiloh (Gates of Prayer) of Auchentoroly Terrace planned a merger with Toras Chaim in 1964, but it did not take place; a small minyan continues to pray in this changed neighborhood.

Woodmore Hebrew Congregation (Orthodox) was founded in 1957. In 1962 they merged with the Moses Montefiore Emunath Israel Congregation which, since 1888, conducted services in southwest Baltimore. Woodmore built a synagogue in 1961 on Coronado Road off the 7800 block of Liberty Heights Avenue. The congregation of B'Nai Jacob (Orthodox), founded in 1883 in West Baltimore, in 1957 purchased property on Liberty Road and Patterson Avenue, and in the following year completed the building of a synagogue. In 1949, the Adath Yeshurin (Orthodox) Congregation, founded in East Baltimore in 1888, erected a synagogue in the 4600 block of Old Pimlico Road. They built a sanctuary in 1968 at Old Court Road and Marriott's Lane; in 1974 they merged with the Mogen Abraham Congregation, founded in East Baltimore in 1891.

The venerable East Baltimore congregation founded in 1875 as Anshe Chesed Bialystok (People of Kindness of Bialystok), changed its name in 1886 to Ohel Yakov Congregation (Bialystoker Polish Synagogue) They occupied the same synagogue building on Aisquith Street for fifty-five years until in 1958, they relocated to temporary quarters in the 3200 block of Glen Avenue and four years later built a permanent synagogue at this address. As was the custom in Poland, at their Aisquith Street address, officers of the synagogue wore formal clothing and top hats to Sabbath and high holiday services.

Randallstown Synagogue Center (Orthodox), founded in 1962 as the Old Court-Liberty Road Synagogue, merged with The Talmud Torah V'Emunah (Study of Torah of Faith) in 1965. Talmud Torah V'Emunah was founded in 1897 as a free school for study of Hebrew; in 1917 it became a part of the Hebrew Talmudical Seminary and Parochial School, now named the Talmudical Academy of Baltimore. The Ahavas Sholom (Love of Peace) Congregation, founded in 1905, joined the Randallstown Synagogue Center in 1966. In 1971, the Agudas Achim Anshe Sphard, founded in 1921, joined the center; a few years later the Randallstown Synagogue Center was close to being bankrupt but in March of 1995 managed to pay off their mortgage. The Winands Road Synagogue Center (Orthodox) emerged from a 1974 amalgamation of the Beth Yehuda Congregation founded in 1933, and the Beth Jacob Anshe Kurland Congregation, a product of other mergers. The dedication of a new synagogue at Winands and Carthage Road took place in 1969.

All of the suburban Baltimore synagogues suffer from lack of attendance except during the high holidays, at which time they are crammed with worshippers. Suburban synagogues are of contemporary design and depending upon one's taste are or are not architecturally pleasing.

Because there have been neighborhood changes and population shifts in the last ten to fifteen years, a large number of Jews have moved from the Liberty Road area and now occupy residences in and around the Owings Mills and Reisterstown areas of Baltimore County. Some Liberty Road congregations have moved or have plans to move. B'Nai Jacob moved in 1981 from Liberty Road and Patterson Avenue to the 3600 block of Seven Mile Lane in Pikesville. Temple Emanuel broke ground on December 12, 1993, for a synagogue on Berryman's Lane north of Church Lane in Reisterstown. The date they chose occurred during the week of Hanukkah, the Hebrew word for dedication and the holiday commemorating the rededication of the Temple in Jerusalem.

In 1988, The Liberty Jewish Center acquired the former property of the Mercantile Club on Rockland Hills Drive and Old Pimlico Road, and the move all but put them in bankruptcy. They survived five years of financial distress after being forced into Chapter 11 in 1990, and in January of 1995, the congregation celebrated ownership of their synagogue.

As a result of plans begun in 1986, in June 1994, the congregation of Randallstown's Conservative Beth Israel synagogue approved the purchase of 10 acres of land, improved by an 88,000 square foot commercial building on Crandall Lane in

Owings Mills. Before making the decision to move, Beth Israel's 1,000 family congregation dwindled to 750 as only about a third of their congregation remained living in the Liberty Road area. So it was the old story, synagogues must move into the area where their congregants live, or in time they will no longer have a minyan. Fortunately, the congregation was able to sell their existing synagogue building to the Colonial Baptist Church; since the move to Owings Mills, almost 200 new families have joined the congregation

Many worshippers living in suburbia look for a relaxed atmosphere for Judaism within their synagogues rather than a house of worship with a positive strict Torah philosophy of Jewish living. Along with this, a number of Conservative and Orthodox Jews have come to terms with the question of keeping kosher households and at the same time feeling comfortable when they choose to eat in non-kosher restaurants. Though there are several kosher caterers and carry-outs in northwest Baltimore, kosher restaurants are few, and they are glatt.[8]

There is much ado about food in the Jewish religion and there is much humor surrounding it. On a personal level, many Jews rationalize that as long as they keep kosher at home and not eat shellfish or pork products in restaurants, they can handle their conscience. Others keep kosher in their homes and eat anything they care to outside of their homes. These choices are personal ones that seem to work well for individuals and families.[9]

A group of Orthodox Jews who call themselves the Kosher Dining Club gather almost every six weeks in the Inner Harbor Sheraton hotel that maintains a kosher kitchen. The hotel's special chef prepares kosher dishes of styles served in countries throughout the world. Most Americans, Jewish and non-Jewish, are misinformed about Jewish food and its origins. Jews have usually adopted the foods of the areas in which they lived; so there is no such thing as Jewish food, Because American Jews are overwhelmingly of Eastern European heritage, such foods as chicken soup with knaidlach (matzoh meal dumplings), gefilte fish, borsht, chopped liver, corned beef brisket, pickled herring, latkes and the three Ks, kasha, kugel and knishes, are the foods of Russia and Poland. The German Jewish diet is akin to the heavy Bavarian foods such as gansebraten, kartoffel kloese, sausages, sauerbratten, braised meats and schnecken.

Nevertheless, Jews all over the world eat the representational foods, matzo and hamantashen. Matzo, a thin perforated wafer is made of flour and water. It is a representational food eaten by Jews worldwide as part of the ritual of Pesach (Passover). Baked in haste in the dessert, it was their mainstay when Moses led the Israelites from Egypt. Hamentashen is Purim's rectangular pastry made to resemble the three corner hat worn by Haman, an anti-Semite principal figure in the story of Purim who plotted to kill the Jews.[10]

A recent addition to the city is the Baltimore Schmurrah kosher matzo bakery, one of a very few of its kind in the country. With a limited production its product is very expensive because it is made one piece at a time. The bakery makes round Schmurrah (guarded) matzo by hand, completely free of yeast or leavening. Many Torah Observant

Jews will eat only Schmurrah matzo for the first night of Seder, but for the remaining days of Pesach, they eat less expensive kosher matzo.[11]

Jews have a propensity to eat Chinese food despite its heavy use of shellfish and pork; mainstays of the cuisine that are in violation of Talmudic dietary laws. Though Jews are almost addicted to Chinese food, the Chinese do not reciprocate and are rarely seen in a Jewish delicatessen. Customarily, Chinese cooks do not mix meat and dairy products and neither do kosher Jewish cooks.[12]

Suburban living is sensitive to keeping up with the Cohens. This tends to promulgate Bar and Bat Mitzvah reception excesses that are at times so lavish and extravagant they border on vulgarity. Those who believe in simpler receptions or those who cannot afford ostentation usually celebrate with friends and relatives in synagogue centers. Baltimore rabbis fight a losing battle in opposing these excessive and lavish celebrations as they are not in keeping with the traditional Talmudically prescribed manner of simple celebrations of Jewish life cycle events. Many Jews are not listening because of their social misconception that elaborate parties are symbolic of a high status and importance in the Jewish community. A rule of thumb cost: about one year's college tuition and board. It was not always thus when Jews were new in America and less affluent.[13]

A gentleman writing his memoirs in a 1962 edition of *The Menorah Journal* relates that on a Thursday, his father wakened him at 6:30 and took him to shul. About thirty persons who attended this early morning service witnessed him being called to the Torah for the first time in his life. After the service, some of those present came over to him and wished him "mazel tov" (congratulations), and his proud father bashfully put his arms around him and congratulated him. They both went for a little walk and then his father went to work. The young man wrote that he turned toward home feeling very lonely. He had become a full mature Jew on that morning while most of the city was still asleep and didn't care.

---

1   *While there was a definite move into formerly restricted neighborhoods, it was a small one. Though a trickle of Jews moved into the Charles Street corridor, most remained in and around Pikesville.*

2   *It appears that few Jews want to join Christian country and in town clubs. There is a psychological barrier on the part of both groups and an actual barrier on the part of some Christian clubs, though in increasing numbers, Christians and Jews and especially their children have good social relationships.*

3   *Har Sinai's property was formerly the Maryland Country Club. Several years before Har Sinai bought the property, the clubhouse had been partially destroyed by fire. The club membership was Christian so possibly they were happy to be able to move from a neighborhood that demographics of the time indicated it was on its way to become entirely Jewish.*

UNCOMMON THREADS

4   *During World War II, Jewish chaplains could not be all factions to all Jewish soldiers so most adopted middle of the road conservatism. Thousands of Jews who served in the armed services learned to prefer this ideology; and upon their return to civilian status, they joined or helped to organize Conservative congregations.*

5   *In Reform and Conservative synagogues, the Scrolls of the Torah are read from a reading desk in front of the Ark (repository for the Torah) on the bimah (raised platform) located along the Eastern wall of the sanctuary. In Orthodox synagogues, the bimah is in the center of the Sanctuary so that congregants may easily ascend to read from the Torah. The placement of the reading desk in Reform and Conservative synagogues was copied from Protestant churches long after the Reformation, in it symbolizing a moderation in the role of the Torah in Reform and Conservative worship.*

6   *The program was also carried by VOICE OF AMERICA. Through the years, the Christian clergymen changed but Rabbi Shusterman remained until the program left the airwaves.*

7   *Not to worry, if a Jewish family is one of the one third unaffiliated. In the near future, Baltimore Jews will probably be able to rent a rabbi for their sons' and daughters' Bar and Bas Mitzvahs along with the tables and chairs, the decorations and the reception hoopla. Presently in New York City, the Rent-a-Rabbi Agency will discuss the details; dial 1-800-RABBI-98. The charges for a Bar or Bas mitzvah are from $500 to $600 and this includes two to three meetings for preparation (just the blessings) since most of the children have had no religious training. For funerals the cost is between $400 and $500, no training needed; for weddings $450 to $1,500. The rabbi will be happy to come to Baltimore if his time and expenses are paid. This can amount to a big ticket. Although at one time Rent-A-Rabbi did a Bar Mitzvah in Montana, he encourages would be out-of-town clients to look for a rabbi in their area.*

8   *Heeding the bad advice of friends regarding the need for a kosher restaurant in downtown Baltimore, one opened in the 300 block of N. Charles St. After being in business for only a few months, the restaurant closed for lack of patronage.*

9   *Sunday is penciled in for Chinese; however in the summer on Saturday nights in Jewish neighborhoods, most likely it will be, "Lets go for steamed crabs." Though people communicate today by Bell Atlantic, such was not the case a couple of thousand years ago. The sound of the shofar, the ancient internet, would have told all from Randallstown to Pikesville to Reisterstown and all points in-between, which carry-out has "No 1 jimmies" (jumbos), the price for a dozen and when the best time was to pick up the crabs.*

10   *There is a curious juxtaposition of round and square matzoh shapes in Baltimore; interesting but of no religious significance. Matzo baked in the desert by Moses' crew were in all probability round as is Schmurrah matzo today. When it was readily available in past years, Baltimore Reform Jews ate only Goodman's lighter textured round matzo, the shape of the original. Eastern Europeans Jews in Baltimore, generally more religious, preferred the heavier cardboard type made by Manischewitz in the non-traditional square shape. Hamantashen is made from either a yeast or a cookie dough. The yeast dough is Eastern European in origin.*

11   *The making of Schmurrah matzo begins with wheat that is rabbinically supervised through its milling to make sure that the wheat and flour do not pick up moisture that could cause premature fermentation. The flour is stone ground in a small milling room and mixed with spring water from a well in Owings Mills. The water is rested overnight so that it reaches the proper temperature by morning. Since fermentation begins in exactly eighteen minutes after the flour and water are mixed and the matzo dough rolled, the matzo must be placed in a wood-burning oven before this happens. While the bakers need and form the dough, they chant a prayer, "I,'shem matzos mitzvah" which means "commanded for the purpose of matzo." After the dough for a batch of matzo is rolled, the wooden rolling pins are sanded down to make sure no bits of dough remain from the previous batch, and every surface, every apron, every pair of gloves is changed to make ready for the next batch.*

12   *Wontons on menus of some Chinese Restaurants catering to the northwest Baltimore trade are listed as kreplach (dumpling) Much humor surrounds American Jews and their love for Chinese food. A well known Jewish Comedian, himself trained as a rabbi, posed a question worthy of examination by Talmudic scholars, "If the Jewish civilization is 6,000 years old and the Chinese civilization is 4,000 years old, where did the Jewish people eat Chow Mein on Sunday night for 2,000 years?"*

   New York sets the stage for the unusual, Baltimore being ever the province. For authentic kosher Chinese food, New Yorkers traipse to Shmuel Bernstein's, Moishe Peking or Shang Chai. For kosher Japanese food they go to the supper club Shalom Japan. The club's Japanese owner, a convert to Judaism, tells the story of a Mr. Yaaki who also converted to Judaism. Mr. Yaaki built a succah, and during Passover, friends came to eat Sukiyaki in Mr. Yaaki's succah. Los Angeles Jews eat at Ghenhis Cohen's and Baltimore Jews who keep kosher eat in a much less fascinatingly named Pikesville restaurant.

13   *Photo sessions on the Thursday before the Bar Mitzvah insure that every hair will be in place. If the event itself is perchance not picture perfect, the pictorial memories will be. Services are fairly standard for the synagogue in which the event is held, so there is little variance except, depending on the family's wishes, members are invited to take part. Frequently a Kiddish luncheon by invitation follows the service. If a Saturday night party is given, it is usually quite elaborate and flashy expensive invitations herald the formal dress event. In one instance Invitations to a fancy Baltimore Bar Mitzvah wing-ding were hand delivered by a person being carted around in a stretch limousine. Keeping up with the Cohens means comparing the height and the complexity of the table arrangements, periphery decorations, the food and the entertainment. Parental imaginations and professional party planners are challenged to present such a memorable event that will surely be remembered long after the significance of the Bar or Bas Mitzvah has been laid aside. Themes are the in thing as are dazzling light shows with go-go dancers reminiscent of the TV show Laugh In of a few years back. THE BALTIMORE JEWISH TIMES in their March 8, 1996, issue answered all the questions of where, how, and what by publishing an entire pull-out section devoted to Bar and Bas Mitzvah. There were many, many ads by caterers, florists, entertainment specialists, gift shops, jewelers, video photographers, still photographers, camera ready make-up artists, and boys and girls fashion shops from Baltimore and Rockville. Missing were tatoo artists. In previous issues of THE BALTIMORE JEWISH TIMES, there have been ads for those who will install a stage and a dramatic back drop for dancing or for a Master of Ceremony. 4' X 4' cages can be attached to each end of a portable stage. The bars of the cages are lighted neon tubes and guests can enter for solo or intimate dancing with a partner. Costing big bucks, dialing an 800 number can bring an entire live New York show to town.*

PART III-10

Talmudical Academy * Ner Israel * Bais Yaakov * Baltimore Hebrew University * Hasidic Lubavitchers * Independent congregations

*E*xtreme Orthodoxy retains a strong national position in Baltimore. Earlier in this book there is a reference to the city being known as the Jerusalem of America. This position is not only supported by the city's synagogues but its institutions of learning as well. For each of the major manners of Jewish worship in Baltimore, at least one synagogue conducts a Jewish day school -- Beth Tfiloh (Orthodox), Chizuk Amuno (Conservative) and Baltimore Hebrew (Reform).

Established in 1917, the Talmudical Academy, the first Hebrew day school founded outside of New York City, has 650 students enrolled in its Old Court Road school in Baltimore County. Students attending the school come from a variety of places in the United States and from Europe. The over fifty year old Orthodox Bais Yaakov School on Park Heights Avenue in Owings Mills has an enrollment of over thirteen hundred students. It offers an outstanding educational curriculum to young Jewish girls.

Baltimore Jews have always considered the Talmudical Academy a huge rock in the Orthodox Jewish community, so the announcement on May 22, 1993, was a shocker though not entirely a surprise to those close to the school. For years the seventy-six year old private parochial school experienced financial difficulties, but in 1993 it faced a financial crisis that threatened its existence. The academy, struggling with debts and chronic cash flow problems, slowed payments on their mortgage and caused them to be late with pay owed to eighty teachers. In June 1993 the public press revealed that the teachers and administrators had not been paid since April 21st. The article also confirmed that no payments had been made on their mortgage loan for a year. Though not an agency of the ASSOCIATED: Jewish Community Federation of Baltimore, that organization accepted the responsibility of keeping the Talmudical Academy solvent. In an immediate response, The Associated stepped in, and on June 20, 1993, a new board replaced the existing one. On that same day, the Talmudical Academy announced that an emergency fund raiser had netted $265,000 of the $440,000 needed to pay their teachers through the balance of 1993. On July 16th, the Associated announced that it had brokered a plan whereby the Talmudical Academy's old mortgage would be paid off and a new one secured and guaranteed by the Associated. This was based on the supposition that the school would continue and could operate in the black. The problems of the Talmudical Academy were of such magnitude that, in December 1994, a New York City beit din (rabbinic court) came to Baltimore to sort out the future payments on the school's remaining $5,400,000 debt. In May 1995, they reported preliminary plans were in place that would assure the Academy's survival.

The campus of the Ner Israel (Perpetual of Israel) Rabbinical College occupies sixty-five acres on Mount Wilson Lane off Reisterstown Road north of Pikesville. Founded in 1933 and originally located on Garrison Boulevard, this highly respected

UNCOMMON THREADS

black hat traditional Lithuanian yeshivah on a university level is accredited by the state and the American Association of Rabbinical Theological Seminaries. Before World War II, Lithuania had been the center for rabbinic learning. A recognized world leader, Ner Israel has progressed well on its mission to replace the great Yeshivas of Europe lost during the war even though many Orthodox Jews doubted that the Lithuanian style of study would ever take hold in America. Ner Israel confers bachelor's, master's and doctorate degrees in Talmudical Law. Presently, 620 male students (no females allowed here) are enrolled; 200 attend its Mechina High School, 300 at the college level and 120 are enrolled in post graduate studies. Baltimore's Ner Israel is the largest institution for rabbinical training outside of New York City and has study agreements with the University of Maryland, University of Baltimore, and the Johns Hopkins and Towson State Universities. About one half of the graduate students of Ner Israel[1] are from scattered areas of the United States and after graduation, many of its students remain in the Baltimore community. Some become rabbis and others enter into the professions of law, medicine and education.

The transition of the Baltimore Hebrew College into a university was accompanied by increased interest in Jewish graduate studies in their day and night schools. A master's program was offered in 1972 and a doctoral program in 1980. The Baltimore Hebrew University parallels the best education offered in other American religious and secular schools to its approximately 1,200 students, about ten percent of whom are non-Jewish. Many graduates have contributed much to the community while others have gained international recognition. The library of the university houses one of the nation's outstanding collection of Judaica.

Akin though apart from most of the city's fervently Orthodox are Baltimore's Hasidic Lubavitchers, named for the late eighteenth century Lithuanian town of Lubavitch. It is important to understand though that all Hasidic Jews are not Lubavitchers; research for this book has not revealed that other Hasidic factions such as the Popo, the Spinka, the Munkatcha, the Siget, the Kasho, the Satmar, the Nicholsburg ever had a presence in Baltimore. Hasidism, taken from the Hebrew hasid (devout), arose from a movement that began in Poland and the Ukraine in the eighteenth century. By the beginning of World War II, one third of the Polish Jews were Hasidic. As do all charedi, full bearded Hasidic men with ear locks wear black suits and high crown black fedora hats. Underneath their upper garments they wear a tzitzit, a four corner small fringed shawl with a central opening for passing over their head. On special occasions, traditional old world kapote (caftans) and the distinctive round fur brimmed shtreimel are seen on the streets of upper Park Heights. Charedi women and their female youngsters wear long dresses with sleeves that cover their arms and shoulders. Women shave their heads on their wedding day, remain shaven, and from then on wear a wig of natural or artificial hair which is usually kept covered by a tichel (head scarf) when out of the home. The way charedi men dress is not biblically dictated nor spiritual; it is the ritualistic dress of the seventeenth century Polish upper class. The continuation of the dress of the ultra

Orthodox Jews indicates a difficult to describe cultural stagnation that exists even for those who are engaged in occupations away from their homes.[2]

Most Hasidim speak Yiddish in their homes, and they refrain from watching television and going to the movies both of which are considered by them to be objectionable forms of other cultures. They believe in their "Tsadikim" (spiritual leaders) and have great admiration for their rebbes (rabbis) and cantors. They take joyful delight in singing and dancing though the latter activity is usually segregated by the sexes, men dance with men, and women dance with women. Hasidic Jews talk about G-d and the meaning of life and other spiritual subjects. Torah observant Jews will not write the word G-d because the written word frequently winds up in a waste basket, thereby desecrating the name.[3]

Chabad, an acronym of the Hebrew word for wisdom, understanding, and knowledge is an 18th century philosophy of an intellectual Hasidic approach to Judaism and is the ritual of the Baltimore Lubavitchers. Maryland is not a stronghold of Hasidics; only about one hundred families are associated with the Lubavitch movement of whom eighty worship at the Levi Yitzchok-Bais Lubavitch synagogue; a converted house at 3402 Clarks Lane. All Torah Observant charedi, highly visible in the Park Heights Avenue corridor, are mistakenly labeled to be Hasidim by most onlookers. Through the Lubavitch Center for Jewish Education in Columbia, Md., Lubavitchers reach out into the entire Baltimore area Jewish community. Young students in synagogue day schools and Sunday schools have been invited to the center to make shofars, the ceremonial ram's horn. In Biblical times, the shofar was a means of communicating important happenings such as to warn of an attack, to proclaim important events and to usher in the Sabbath. Modern day Jews adhere to a tradition of sounding the shofar on the eve of Rosh Hashonah, the New Year Day of Judgment and again, a single blast during the concluding prayers at sundown on Yom Kippur, The Day of Atonement.

Hasidic Lubavitchers have been present in Baltimore for over one hundred years. The first Hasidic congregation, the Anshe Neisen Nusach Ari synagogue, was founded in East Baltimore in 1890. The Tzemach Tzedek Congregation (Lubavitcher) founded in 1913 merged in 1956 with Shomrei Hadath (Lubavitcher) to form the Tzemach Tzedek-Shomrei Hadath Nusach Ari Congregation. This combined synagogue in 1987 became part of the Khal Ahavas Yisroel Congregation whose synagogue today is in the 6800 block of Park Heights Avenue. Ner Tamid Greenspring Valley Synagogue and Center in the 6200 block of Pimlico Road was organized in 1955. In 1969, the Lubavitz Nusach Ari Synagogue became part of Ner Tamid. This congregation, founded in 1931, dedicated a synagogue a year later in the 2600 block of Quantico Avenue. It was an amalgamation of the Agudas Achim Anshe Chernigov Nusach Ari founded in 1896 and the Anshe Bobruisk Nusach Ari Congregations. The interpretation of Nusach Ari is that it is a distinctive form of worship associated only with Lubavitchers.

Beth Am Congregation, founded in 1975, holds eclectic services in the former Eutaw Place Chizuk Amuno Synagogue. Worship at Beth Am has become extremely important to modern thinking Jews. The non-affiliated Bolton Street Congregation, founded in 1986, in 1989 acquired the chapel of the Brown Memorial Church. They offer informal Judaism, popular with many young people, and their beliefs are close to those of the Reconstructionist movement. The rabbi of non-affiliated Beth Am considers himself a Reconstructionist. Stemming the Conservative tradition and qualifying completely as Reconstructionists, the Beit Tikvah Congregation conducts services in the First Christian Church building on Roland Avenue, but never on Sunday.

Reconstructionists advocate a reconstruction of American Jewish life. The authoritarian structures are the Jewish Reconstrucionist Federation and the Reconstructionist Rabbinical Association. Their rabbis attend their rabbinical school in Philadelphia, and their concept is that Judaism should embody language, literature, music and art with the enhancement of a meaningful religious life. The rabbi who doubles as the cantor is considered to be their teacher and authority, following the ancient and traditional concept of rabbi, that of being a teacher. Each generation of Jews inherits traditions of the religion and each generation wrestles with the concepts of these traditions in relation to their own lives. Reconstructionists face this by rejecting the supernatural origin of the Torah and the Covenant; they believe in the importance of the present day Jewish people establishing the authority of Judaism. Reconstructionists believe in the full equality of the sexes in the rights of Judaism so they celebrate the birth of a female child in a manner equivalent to a brit milah (circumcision ritual) for a male child. They have led the way in the movement to ordain female rabbis and to give to women the right, among other rights, to grant husbands a Jewish divorce. According to the Talmud that right rested with the husband with no equality of provision for the wife. The variety of thought is one of the true beauties of Judaism.

---

1   *Some graduate students at Ner Israel, not so observant while attending undergraduate Ivy League schools, changed immediately when enrolled at Ner Israel. In the fall of 1984, a Baltimore native Sofer (scribe) and full time graduate student at Ner Israel, using a turkey quill pen, began the task of inscribing a Torah on parchment. Parchment, usually cow skin for Torahs, must be made from ritually clean animals, although the animals need not have been ritually slaughtered. He completed the project in 1991.*

2   *Wearing a black hat indicates that the man is orthodox and a strict adherent of Halakhah. Orthodox Jewish boys receive their black hats at the time of their Bar Mitzvah and the quality of this rite of passage is discussed by Jewish boys the same as secular boys discuss their athletic shoes. A local Orthodox Rabbi operates a small hat shop in his basement.*

3   *In October 1994, THE BALTIMORE JEWISH TIMES inadvertently displayed the Hebrew name of God in an illustration. In the following week's edition, the JEWISH TIMES apologized for the error and suggested that readers cut the illustration out of the magazine and place it in a Hebrew text to be buried.*

PART III-11

Demise of Eutaw Place and the Phoenix Club * Country and swim clubs * Vacationing singles * Marriages and interfaith marriages * Violence in Jewish marriages

*T*he great depression of the 1930s quieted the Roaring Twenties and changed the lives of most people. The Phoenix Club continued to be financially strong until the mid 1930s when the club's professional manager absconded with several thousand uninsured dollars. Previously limited to three hundred members, the board opened the membership to the entire Jewish community. Quite a few Russian Jews who could afford to join applied for membership, and their acceptance reshuffled the memberships of Baltimore Jewish clubs. The numerical membership of the Phoenix Club remained about the same as Russian Jews replaced a number of German Jews who resigned. Several Russian Jews who joined the Phoenix Club during this period resigned from membership in the Mercantile Club, thus weakening that club's structure. During World War II, most members of the Phoenix Club of military age served in the armed forces, temporarily reducing the club's German Jewish constituency; after the war with a changed membership philosophy, it was permanently reduced.

During the war, thousands of Appalachian mountain people descended upon Baltimore to work in the city's war industries. Hundreds, attracted by cheap rent, chose to live in what were once the elegant mansions of Eutaw Place. Ahead and abreast of the arrival of the war workers, real estate speculators bought unoccupied Eutaw Place mansions for little money and, also for little money, remodeled their interiors into small apartments that nicely accommodated the incoming West Virginians. Colloquially known as hill billies, these folks changed the ambiance of Eutaw Place for the worse and hastened a movement of German Jews away from it and from adjoining neighborhoods, though during the war years there was no other justification for a mass movement from any section of the city. Used to living in fine neighborhoods, there were few places for Eutaw Place and Linden Avenue Jews to move to as new housing was confined to the critical needs of workers and built near industrial locations.

When World War II ended, it took only a few years for emerging social and demographic changes to seal the demise of the venerable Phoenix Club. The dwindling German Jewish membership was further accelerated by the movement to the suburbs of those who had continued to live in-town during the war. During the winter months, the Phoenix Club continued to schedule Saturday night dances in a losing attempt to prolong the club's survival. Although the Phoenix Club was open during the summer months, the Suburban and Woodholme Clubs offered golf, tennis, and swimming during the day and less formal and relaxed social activities at night.

Twenty-five years had passed since the combining of the Jewish charities, and good relationships continued to build between Germans and Russians. The closely guarded German Jewish social structure, an anchor of which had been the Phoenix Club, shook and began to collapse. The pre-war Harmony Circle Balls,[1] the Cotillion, and the

Junior Cotillion were not continued; there were no longer reasons for them. Then, too, there were Germans who were not really sure how they felt about having Eastern European Jewish girls join German Jewish girls in making their bows. Not only were the costs of these activities high, but there was no justification to propagate a social system that perpetuated a schism within the Jewish community. Make no mistake; German Jewish social events of the past played the roles and served the purposes of earlier generations of German Jews. It is interesting to note that in December 1994, the Associated Press reported that in Christian communities debutante balls were on the rocks. In Palm Beach, New York, and Baltimore as well, prospective comer outers were tossing in their long white gloves.

The Phoenix Club, named for the legendary Egyptian bird that rose from its own ashes, disbanded in 1960: its Eutaw Place property and building were sold to the Joint Board of the Amalgamated Clothing Workers of America. Ironically, many of the founders of the Phoenix club had been men's clothing manufacturers. All of the Jewish members of the Joint Board of the Amalgamated were Eastern European Jews who in earlier days were not welcome to walk through the club's portals and many who during labor disputes sat on the other side of the bargaining table from German Jewish clothing manufacturers. The Amalgamated razed the red sandstone clubhouse in 1963, and in its place, built a crass modern union hall, thus putting the kabosh on the legend of this German Jewish Phoenix bird.

By the 1950s, more and more Eastern European Jews relaxed on patios of country clubs, and with drink in hand, were mesmerized by the light blue rippling crystal waters of the club's swimming pool and the emerald greens of its golf courses. Here, with old and new friends, they put their struggles to succeed behind them and enjoyed the elegance their money had brought. New post war country clubs, Bonnie View founded in 1951, and Chestnut Ridge in 1957- easily filled their memberships, primarily with Eastern European Jews, while the older Suburban and the Woodholme Clubs were having problems. Both were extremely expensive and the Suburban's German Jewish membership dwindled through attrition. German Jews, who for many years bred small families, were becoming fewer, and the appeal of a country club was no longer an enticement and much too expensive for many young people. The salvation was to open the Suburban Club's membership to all, and in a relatively short time, the club that didn't know from bagels, lox and cream cheese began to understand and in fact enjoy. A recent Suburban Club history written collectively by a few carefully selected, almost all German Jewish members, presents few memories for much of its present 1996 membership.

To attract new members in the 1970s, both the Suburban and the Woodholme clubs reduced their initiation fees. The Woodholme, whose members nearly seventy years before had been looked down upon by the German Jews, now looked down on the changed values of their new young members who appeared to have lacked the refinement and taste of the older members. If Jews have the money, are properly sponsored, and contribute enough to the Associated Jewish Charities, they are most likely welcome as members in the country clubs. Membership committees rarely deny admission unless there is a serious reason to consider a blackball.

Except for jobs, Baltimore's country clubs, Jewish and Christian, offer little to the well being of the community and stand as symbols representing each club's specific social strata within the city's society. This is not new; it will probably always be. One reason for a club's being is to offer a form of social snobbery and comfort on a level dictated by their membership and for some, a partial tax write-off[2]

Today, the Suburban Club has a limited constituency of German Jews; a mix that the other clubs never had. All four Jewish country clubs are large and their members are from diverse backgrounds, none of whom could ever hope to be welcome as a member in almost all Baltimore Christian country clubs. Social cliques are part of all clubs, but they are most evident at the Suburban Club where vestiges of German Jewish families prefer to continue their close friendships with other German Jews, friendships they made when they were children and friendships they feel comfortable with.

In recent decades, the anthropometric data of the American Jew appears to have changed. Male and female Jews are taller, leaner, and better golfers. This is probably due to a combination of factors such as inter-married parents, improved nutrition, and being able to engage in athletics at an earlier age with the benefit of professional instructions. The Suburban Country Club's eighteen hole golf course is one of the least challenging in the Baltimore area. In 1987, the board of the club submitted plans to its members to sell their 129 acre Pikesville real estate and clubhouse and to relocate their facilities on between 300 and 350 acres of land far out in the suburbs. By vote, the 900 club members rejected the proposition, choosing to remain within their tight Pikesville enclave. According to published reports in August 1987, the U.S.F.& G. Corporation considered acquiring the Bonnie View Club's property for the recreational needs of their executives; however before serious negotiations were under way, U.S.F. & G.'s troubled financial condition introduced to that organization a new and sharp curtailment of executive perquisites.

In the early 1950s, young family oriented couples who wanted to be a part of the social and recreational activities of their children founded the Green Valley and Silver Birch swimming and tennis clubs. These smaller clubs located in rustic surroundings made little distinction regarding membership, and they attracted professionals and others with little propensity for snobbery and a much lesser association with wealth. The Summit Club founded in 1955, a swimming and tennis club, was not so deutlich (plain) as the swimming clubs. Their social activities are of prime importance to their members, possibly because they inherited a clubhouse with excellent facilities for dining and dancing.[3]

On October 7, 1977, the headline for the cover story in the *Baltimore Jewish Times* read THINGS YOU ALWAYS WANTED TO KNOW ABOUT COUNTRY CLUBS. AND MORE. The weekly took a look at Baltimore's Jewish country clubs; what they were like, who joined, and what they cost. Readers not belonging to country clubs thought the revelation fascinating. Many who belonged to the clubs were outraged, charging that the *Jewish Times* overstepped an imaginary line drawn between the public and private domain. Baltimore Jewish club members, in this attempt to hide their activities, instead displayed their 200 year old American communal insecurity. So the question of social relationships remains however, and the answer is not so much of a relationship between German and Russian Jews and their clubs, but one between Christians and Jews and barriers maintained by Baltimore area Christian country clubs.[4]

The numbers of young Baltimore working class boys and girls who had no access to country clubs was by far larger than those who did. They created their own social lives, and they crammed a lot of it into one or two week summer vacations. They became part of a vast arena where boy meets girl, and they did meet one another on a playing ground as reasonably level as they could find. Primarily girls were seeking a good marriage but first a bit of fun. Boys were seeking lots of fun with no entanglements, especially not marriage. By the hundreds, single Baltimore working girls spent week-ends and vacations at singles resorts, most of which were located in the Pocono Mountains of Pennsylvania. Some of the resorts were quite expensive, but the girls considered the time and money spent to be a worthwhile investment even though there was a chronic shortage of eligible males. Singles resort vacationers, boys and girls alike, spent lots of money for clothes that they hoped would hide their working girl status; all were keenly anxious to look affluent. Attractive college boys employed as staff purposefully to romance the girls furnished much of the social life. With no commitments of course, they tugged on the heart strings of young single girls assuring them that they and their friends would visit again in the following years. If perchance a relationship developed to the point that a young lady wanted to bring her summer boyfriend home to meet her parents, it could be difficult for some. With the Pocono Mountain's charade laid aside, an American Jewess could feel quite uneasy about the broken English spoken by her parents.

During post World War II enlightenment, the breakdown of social and religious barriers was hastened by inter-faith marriages and those between German and Russian Jews. Weddings between Reform and Orthodox Jews are quite memorable if the couple is married in the Eastern European Orthodox Jewish tradition. At the wedding, families of different backgrounds come together and the parents of the soon to be spouse can be a bit shaken by the large numbers of aunts, uncles and cousins seated on the opposite side of the room. After the Ketubbah is signed by the groom who has fasted all day, the ceremony begins. With no bridal procession nor music, the bride is brought to the chupah (marriage canopy) by her parents and the groom by his, where a black caftan robed, black hatted, black bearded rabbi wearing a talit (prayer shawl) waits to begin the ceremony.

A feature of an Eastern European Orthodox Jewish wedding is when the bride and groom are lifted high in separate chairs and danced around the room to the quick choppy rhythm of a klezmer band (popular in stage performances today and becoming popular for weddings), but more likely to a rock and roll band. Married, the bride must keep her distance from any man other than her husband; if she should dance with a male guest, she must hold one edge of a handkerchief and he the other. Dance has always been a component of Jewish festive and commemorative occasions, and at weddings, eventually all join in dancing the horah, a dance identified with the pioneer spirit of Zionism. Missing from present day Orthodox weddings is the old country merrymaker dressed in a harlequin costume and known as the Chupah Schlemeil. After a Torah observant wedding, the couple, forbidden to touch each other before marriage, enter a private room in seclusion for seven minutes. If both have courted according to the letter of the Talmud, this should be the first time in their relationship that the couple has been alone together. In this room, the marriage is symbolically consummated. Later outside the bridal chamber, and anxious for actual consummation, the groom may cool his heels because he can not enter until the bride feels comfortable about the marriage and impending consummation, and is ready to grant him permission to enter the room. This is a protective maneuver by the bride that keeps her from having intercourse the night of the marriage if she is not psychologically ready for it.

Reform Jews marry with less tradition,[5] less color, and sedate receptions. Reform and Conservative Jews continue some of the Orthodox marriage traditions such as the breaking of a glass stomped on by the heel of the groom to end the ceremony. Until recent years, few German Reform Jews were married under a chupah and all Conservative Jews were. Reform Jewish brides on the arm of her father, follow her bridesmaids and maid of honor in a slow procession to the tune of *Here comes the Bride*, the wedding march by Mendelssohn. Not unheard of is the German Jewish bride who has requested for the procession the wedding march from Lohengrin, composed by that ace of German anti-Semites, Richard Wagner.

Interfaith marriages are nothing new because from the date of their early settlement in Baltimore, German Jews and Christians have married each other. In fact, the Baltimore Hebrew Congregation marriage records show that their rabbi, between 1850 and 1861, listed 203 marriages performed, of which the first and last names of 20 partners suggest that they were Christians. As previously mentioned, in the re-interred Cohen family plot in Baltimore Hebrew's Belair Road Cemetery the names on several gravestones are unquestionably not Jewish.

Until 1950, fewer than 6 % of American Jews married non-Jews, and almost all Jews regarded interfaith marriage as calamity of a sort. Some Orthodox Jews even observed the laws of mourning for a child or sibling who interfaith married.[6] After 1950, marriage patterns changed rapidly as more and more Jews took partners of other faiths. In 1964, the rate of such nuptials was perhaps one fifth, and by the mid 1980s within the Reform group, about one third were mixed marriages. A report in the *Baltimore Jewish Times* in May 1964 stated the possibilities that 2.9 % of the nation's Jewish population would fade, attributed to a soaring rate of interfaith marriage and low Jewish birth rates. The report estimated that 70 % of the children of mixed marriages were lost to Judaism. More precisely, according to a 1995 Union of American Hebrew Congregation's estimate, 31% raise their children with no religion, 21% raise their kids in a religion other than Judaism and 20% raise their kids with a combination of religions. The Union is considering a proposal to bar youngsters from Hebrew school if their parents simultaneously give them schooling in another religion. Reform Jews who have a tradition of embracing interfaith marriages may have reached the limit of their tolerance.[7] The *Baltimore Jewish Times* flirted with widening the breech when they noted that they would no longer publish engagement and marriage announcements if both parties were not Jewish.

In a report of the Council of Jewish Federations released August 30, 1994, the 1990 National Jewish Population Study found that 52% of Jews were marrying outside of their faith. Statistics indicate a deterioration of the social complexity known as marriage as more and more unmarrieds, Jews and otherwise, lived together. The same survey stated that about 37 % of Jewish marriages today end in divorce, and about half of all interfaith marriages end in divorce. The study said that many, it did not say how many, re-marriages after divorce also are interfaith marriages. Divorce[8] and interfaith marriage frequently affect the common threads of three generations. Parents of the Jewish spouse in the mixed marriage often feel that they have failed to give their married son or daughter a solid Jewish identity; frequently there is the guilt of the marrieds, and that at times is shared by their children.

The Council of Jewish Federations report emphasizes that serving the Jewish intermarried couples is now an urgent matter. Baltimore's Jewish Family Services has been a pioneer in their outreach program with workshops and counseling, programs for congregational schools, and support groups. As for many Jewish issues there are differences of opinion on outreach with the Conservative and Reform taking a more liberal view. If we did nothing to reach out to interfaith married families, the future of the Jewish community would be more threatened. This is a concern about the reality of life and not a blessing on interfaith marriage.

The economic gains of Jews after World War II helped produce a generation of young Jewish boys, quite attractive and socially quite like their Christian private school mates. No longer do Jewish boys marry Christian girls of lower intellect and social standing. Instead, they are attracted to the upper circles, who in turn have found in Jewish boys a profoundness and a genuine interest in them as a couple. Perhaps Christian girls are proving to themselves an age old adage that Jewish men make better husbands.

Some published figures indicate that in interfaith households, only twenty-five % raise their children as Jews. More often, Jewish men have sought Christian women to marry, while Jewish women have not been as prone to marry Christian men. Interfaith marriages present a frightening course because they reaffirm Jewish concern for the continuity of its people and their religion. Can we Jews actually self destruct; accomplishing in time that which despots of history could not achieve? The possible loss of Jewish identity of one of the mixed religion couple, and more importantly, the loss of identity of their children, must be considered a real problem. Some Jews find it difficult to retain their heritage in the popular culture in which they live, one that urges assimilation on some fronts, but not, as previously mentioned, assimilation in Christian circles. Some Reform congregations, not necessarily in Baltimore, permit Christians to be called to the Torah since it is no longer clear what a Jewish family is or even, for that matter, what an interfaith marriage is.

In 1969, the Reconstructionist movement endorsed the principle of patrilineal descent and more than a decade later it was recognized by the Reform movement. The recognition is valid just so long as the child is brought up as a Jew, and it reflects a reluctance to base Jewish identity solely on the passive fact of inheritance. This recognition has eased defining who is a Jew for these two movements. Despite opposition from the Conservative and Orthodox rabbis, a significant %age of their laity are willing to consider patrilineal Jews as Jews just so long as they identify with Jewish people. Reconstructionists and Reform have also embraced as a matter of principle the inclusion of gay and lesbian Jews.

In mixed marriages a stressful question frequently arises, the "December Dilemma"; of how or if families should celebrate Christmas or Hanukkah or should they celebrate both within the home. There are surface similarities but very deep religious differences between the reasons for the Christian Christmas and the Jewish Hanukkah. Hopefully, parents born into either faith have learned as adults to recognize this -- it is questionable that young children do in their formative years. Pressure from newspaper and television advertisers to buy gifts for both seem to merge the two celebrations and create a confusion for young children and a somewhat dim view of Jewish values. What should mixed couples do about circumcision and Bar Mitzvah and Bat Mitzvah? The question must be asked, "If I'm Jewish and you're Christian, what are the kids?" Workshops for questions and answers are held jointly by the Jewish Family Services and the Baltimore Board of Rabbis. When a rabbi, minister, or priest cannot satisfactorily answer the question, some couples have turned to counseling by mail order parenting guides for interfaith marriages.

The ever increasing willingness of Christians to marry Jews, as is the case since World War II, indicates a growing degree of acceptance of Jews into Baltimore's Christian community. If there is anything positive to be said about interfaith marriages, it must be that they are minor barriers to anti-Semitism as families get to know each other. At least two popular national television shows introduced America to interfaith marriages, and they met with varied feelings. *Bridget Loves Bernie* in the 1970s brought protests from some American Jewish organizations. As evidence of change and possibly because interfaith marriage was more prevalent by this time, *Thirty Something* of the early 1990s produced little reaction. The growing number of interfaith marriages without conversion of the Christian partner, as previously mentioned, poses serious threats to Jewish life. Not to be overlooked are the threats to Judaism of those who have simply abandoned the Jewish communities.

Orthodox leaders put the blame for the dilemma of interfaith marriage and assimilation on the doorsteps of the Reform, Conservative and Reconstructionists. They are of the opinion that religious changes in liberal Judaism that ordains women as rabbis, believes in patrilineal descent, outreachs to Christians, and supports gays and lesbians within the synagogue has abrogated Jewish authenticity.

For all of the social pluses, the country clubs, the vacations, the fancy Mitzvahs, Bar and Bat, the inter-marriages, Jewish post World War II home life began to pay a price and at times it has been difficult to keep Humpty Dumty from crashing. Because alcohol use is limited in Jewish tradition, alcoholism, heretofore almost unknown in the American Jewish culture, has become a minor but growing problem; however, there is a paradox here. In 1995, surveys in Los Angeles and New Haven showed that 13 % of Jewish men have major depression, compared with 5.4 % for non-Jewish men. Researchers can only speculate about what causes the high rate in Jewish men, but it may have to do with their low rate of alcoholism. For a culture that historically does not use alcohol as a release of tension, sadness and distress, problems show up as depression. Now, this gives the modern American Jewish male a real choice; he can have poor mental health or become an alcoholic.

In 1985, two meetings were held at Beth Tfiloh to arouse the concerns of those in attendance about reports of increasing domestic violence in the Baltimore Jewish community. Almost every abused Jewish woman has kept the offense secret because she cannot face the shame of letting her family and the community know. This binds a woman to an untenable situation throughout her married life. Historically, in turn, the close Jewish community is reluctant to acknowledge or respond to the existence of family violence because of the sacrosanct position of the Jewish family and the stigma attached. While the Jewish Family Services of The Associated deals with most cases, incidents of violence in the families of Torah Observant Jews are routinely heard in the Va'ad HaRabonim, the Rabbinical Council. Reform and Conservative Jews put little faith in that jurisdiction. The purpose of the meetings at Beth Tfiloh were to break down that which has been called a conspiracy of silence. The idea is to no longer accept the theory of discussing domestic problems with the congregation's rabbi one-on-one whose advice would most likely be "try harder to make the marriage work." Help for all parties concerned, particularly for child abuse or molestation, is seriously needed. Curiously, findings indicate that among couples 70 years or older, women physically abused their husbands more than the other way around. At last, the Jewish community, long concerned about its image to non-Jews, is becoming more introspective.

A national Jewish women's task force aimed at combating domestic violence has been formed; it began with a national conference on domestic violence in October 1994, by NA'AMAT USA, The Women's Labor Zionist Organization of America. Almost every national women's organization was present at the conference. The NA'AMAT USA is an old hand in involvement with domestic violence matters; as early as 1983 they established domestic violence treatment centers in Israel. Baltimore representatives at the conference said they are going to help sensitize the Jewish community to the realization that domestic violence exists in Baltimore Jewish families. Not all Baltimore homes are as nice and comfortable as they appear. Some that light Shabbat candles and observe holiday celebrations hide dark secrets in the shadows of those flickering candles.

UNCOMMON THREADS

1   *Much that happened in Baltimore happened in other cities with large Jewish populations. New York City has by far the nation's largest Jewish population, and membership in its German Jewish Harmonie Club was exclusive beyond all reason. This club, the bastion of German Jewish society, similar but not exactly a counterpart of Baltimore's Phoenix Club, is located off Fifth Avenue in midtown New York City. The Harmonie's dining rooms and cuisine were and are the finest in New York, so the club was popular as "the" place for lunch and dinner for its German Jewish members. Out-of-town members, including many Baltimoreans who frequented New York on business, rather than to experience the hassle of New York restaurants, preferred to have their dinner at the Harmonie Club. In the evening they dined with friends and competitors and then joined card games or engaged in business conversations.*

Founded in 1852, the Harmonie Club was so German that until World War I, a portrait of German Kaiser Wilhelm hung in the club's entrance hall. What happened to the Harmonie was nearly the same as that which happened to the Phoenix Club when an infusion of new money and new blood was needed to continue its existence. Christians were certainly not interested in joining so the salvation of the club could only be achieved by opening their membership. The club elected a new member to their board, a Russian born Jew, and at his first meeting, he arose to make a suggestion. With a heavy Russian accent he said, "I am well aware that the Harmonie Club has in the past been a German Jewish Club but it is now partly a Russian Jewish Club. I note that the menus are printed in French and I suggest that henceforth they be printed in Yiddish, so everyone can understand them."

By the 1970s, the Harmonie Club's menus included blintzes, chopped chicken liver, and a Jewish version of french toast; challah dipped in egg batter and served with maple syrup. Ten years ago, these foods were removed from the menu but they reappear for Jewish holidays. The menu now reads Caesar salad, roast beef and Welsh rarebit -- more appealing to Americanized Jews.

2   *Until the end of 1993, a club member could play a round of golf with a client and write off part of his club's dues as a business expense. Beginning in 1994, social club dues could no longer be deducted and all deductions for meals and entertainment were considerably lower. Clubs have card rooms in which the girls play cards or mah-jongg, a game played in China since about 500 B.C. A pastime in the United States since 1920, mah-jongg is especially popular among older Chinese-Americans and Jewish women. The Chinese game is slightly different than the one played by the country club girls (termed by some Christians who also play as Jewish ma-jongg), who can play their bams and cracks as well as the best of the Chinese.*

3   *Not all clubs revolved around adult suburban social life. In 1946, Robert I. H. Hammerman, now Baltimore's Chief Judge agreed to be the mentor of the Lancers Club (until 1956 named Corsairs) founded for high school age boys of all races, religions and backgrounds. The club, still in existence and as strong as ever, teaches leadership and responsibility.. Members Alvin "Buzzy" Krongard, Jerry Sachs and Kenny Parker had the original idea for the club and many others of its present 200 members include Mayor Kurt L. Schmoke, Delegate Samuel "Sandy" Rosenberg and other prominent Baltimoreans.*

UNCOMMON THREADS

4   Groucho Marx said it best when he said; "I wouldn't join a country club that would have me." If Groucho Marx were alive in 1996, perhaps he would have been sought after by one of Baltimore's Jewish country club's membership committees. The Baltimore Jewish Times again wrote about the city's Jewish country clubs in its August 9, 1996 issue, an article titled Short of Green. It seems from financial aspects all is not going well financially for the clubs. Fewer than usual younger persons are joining the clubs, partly because of changing life styles that have created a new leisure dollar competition. Today, many outstanding public golf courses, casual and fine restaurants, racquet and fitness clubs and nearby beach resorts offer recreation for a lot less dollars. Then too, Baltimore's Jewish population is beginning a serious dispersal to places such as Columbia, Frederick and Carroll County. It's a big challenge to keep younger people interested, so all of the clubs have used a few obvious weapons available to them; making special offers of reduced initiation fees, lifting the barriers of activities for the young children of members, and, as previously written, seldom denying membership if a person can pay.

5   A father of a bride speaking to the rabbi who would officiate at his daughter's wedding said, "I don't want the ceremony to be too Orthodox. I don't want it to be too Reform. I just want it to be mediocre."

6   One story tells of a man who married a non-Jew, whereupon his brother sat seven days of shiva (mourning for the dead) On one of the days, his intermarried brother paid him a condolence visit.

7   At one synagogue, a girl came to her Bat Mitzvah wearing a cross.

8   The State University of New York at Stoney Brook, after a 70 year study, published some startling facts in September 1995, in the JOURNAL OF PUBLIC HEALTH. They speculated that parental divorce causes increased stress in children which can lead to unhealthy behavior such as substance abuse and poor diet. They say this can result in the shortening of their lives by 5 years.

PART III-12

Associated Agencies move uptown * Park Heights * Pikesville-Stevenson * Jewish voting

For several years after World War II, sections of northwest Baltimore City were thriving centers of Jewish life. Reisterstown Road, north from Mondawmin, and Park Heights Avenue, north from Park Circle, an almost one hundred percent Jewish residential area was known as lower Park Heights. In 1947, the Park Lane Shopping Center at Park Heights Avenue and Cold Spring Lane and the Hilltop Shopping Center at Reisterstown Road and Rogers Avenue were built. To serve the population south of these retail areas, the gigantic Mondawmin Mall was completed in 1950 on the property of the old Brown estate at the corner of Reisterstown Road and Liberty Heights Avenue. A lesser business center at Garrison Boulevard and Liberty Heights Avenue was enlarged and demographics indicated a go ahead sign for the erection of the Reisterstown Plaza on Reisterstown Road north of Northern Parkway; to be anchored by two major Baltimore department stores.

In the early 1950s the agencies of the Associated Jewish Charities prepared to relocate. Plans were made to build major facilities on Park Heights Avenue north of Northern Parkway, easily accessible by public transportation for the majority of the Jewish community. The once large number of Jews requiring financial aid had lessened as had the number of immigrants who needed support and guidance. Therefore the Associated's institutional responsibility to the Baltimore Jewish community was slowly changing, requiring different though not a lessening of services. Modern programs focused on community health, culture, education and recreation. To accomplish the Associated's goals for future decades, the 1950s and part of the 1960s were financially costly for Baltimore Jews yet building goals were achieved through fund raising campaigns, reserve funds, and Federal grants. In the 1950's, The Associated built two major buildings on the west side of Park Heights Avenue, slightly north of Northern Parkway. The first housed the Jewish Community Center (J.C.C.) which combines functions of the Y.W.H.A. with some Jewish Educational Alliance programs, though not designated as such. The second building houses the Baltimore Hebrew University.[1] In 1965, the Associated dedicated a third, the Harry Greenstein Building which is devoted to Social Services.

Not too long after the first two buildings were in place, the demographics of Baltimore's Jewish community in the 1960s began a rapid change. Many fewer Jews lived in the area than the original studies indicated, and most of those remaining were in the process of moving. By the end of the 1970s, few Jews continued to live south and southwest of Druid Hill Park, in the lower Park Height and Forest Park areas or along the west North Avenue sector. Again the Northwest Passage attracted hundreds of Jewish families who abandoned their neighborhoods to move into the Liberty Road corridor up to and past Randallstown, areas that before World War II had been Baltimore County corn fields. Families pushed deeper into the northwest territories of upper Reisterstown

247

UNCOMMON THREADS

Road, upper Park Heights Avenue and on into Pikesville, Stevenson, Owings Mills and beyond. The new northwest neighborhoods are quite diverse. A Randallstown residential address is not looked upon as desirable as one in Pikesville. Housing in the Liberty Road corridor is akin to other middle income suburbia, while Jewish affluence is very visible in Stevenson and the Owings Mills sections of Caveswood and Velvet Valley. Old Court Road, an Indian trail long before the Europeans settled in North America, became the twentieth century Baltimore Jewish trail connecting Randallstown with Pikesville.

In 1959, a new medical center consisting of the Sinai Hospital, Mount Pleasant Home for Consumptives and the Levindale Home for the Aged, built several years before, was dedicated on eighty acres at the corner of Belvedere and Greenspring Avenues. The new Sinai and its research and teaching facilities, no longer considered a charity institution, was built to furnish the best patient care for the entire Jewish and non-Jewish community. Recent additions of a major rehabilitation center, physicians' offices and an Employee and Physicians Resource Center are important additions to the complex. The construction of large additions to the fifth and sixth floors are well under way; projects of the first phase of a long range expansion program expected to cost $125,000,000. Hospital officials anticipate that the total expansion will be completed in 1997-1998, and the up-date is expected to bring the Sinai Medical Center well into the coming century.

Later, the Associated Jewish Charities caught up with some of their constituency when they built a second Jewish Community Center in Owings Mills. For administrative headquarters, the Associated erected a building at 101 W. Mt. Royal Avenue in Baltimore's mid-town cultural center.[2] On July 1, 1991, the Associated Jewish Charities became the ASSOCIATED: Jewish Community Federation of Baltimore, a name that more accurately reflects their mission to preserve and enhance Jewish life in Baltimore and foreign lands.

In the 1960s after Baltimore's Jewish population shifted northwest, the giant Mondawmin Mall, Hilltop, Park Lane and Pimlico, lost their Jewish trade; it has been replaced by Afro-Americans who moved into former Jewish residences. The Jewish move also affected retailing in the giant Reisterstown Plaza; where in time the two large department store anchors closed.

For many years, Belvedere Avenue delineated the upper and lower Park Heights area; Reisterstown Road below Pikesville to Belvedere Avenue was never concise enough to delineate anything. The Pimlico race track, since 1870 on the northeast quadrant of Park Heights and Belvedere Avenues is today a negative in recent attempts to stabilize the old lower Park Heights, now one of Baltimore City's largest drug infestations. About half a mile north of Pimlico is Northern Parkway, a fragile Maginot Line that has established a neighborhood perimeter that in recent years has been penetrated along the Reisterstown corridor. The Beth Jacob Synagogue, the Mount Washington residential area and the buildings of the Associated's agencies, except for the Sinai Hospital and Medical Center, immediately north of Northern Parkway partly remain Jewish neighborhoods.

Heading north, Park Heights Avenue residences are increasingly affluent as the street nears Slade Avenue, a city-county boundary and the location of elegant high rise condominiums. The three huge Reform Jewish temples, smaller Orthodox shuls, a combination of houses, and modest and luxury high and low rise apartment buildings line the street. The Suburban Club and the Dumbarton residences are in the two quadrants north of the intersection of Slade and Park Heights Avenues and the Baltimore Hebrew Congregations synagogues and school are in the southwest quadrant.

Jews, remembering tales of oppression of their progenitors who fled Europe have formed defenses in America and northwest Baltimore is an excellent example. Living as many Jews do in the ethnic cluster of Pikesville, Stevenson and adjacent areas, provides a degree of security and comfort. Consequently, Jewish influence in Pikesville is overwhelming. Over 90% of Pikesville residents are Jewish; a concentration almost like none other in the United States outside of New York City. Many of the German Jewish families, once quite evident in Mount Washington, Dumbarton and upper Park Heights Avenue have disappeared as a group. Some of those remaining are scattered through Pikesville in homes and condominiums on Park Heights Avenue and on Slade Avenue overlooking the once German dominated Suburban Club.

As do most Americans, particularly ethnic groups, Baltimore area Jews take American democracy seriously and voter turnout in Jewish neighborhoods is always a much higher percentage of those registered than in non-Jewish Baltimore City and Baltimore County. The stories of precinct voting in the Baltimore City Glen Avenue firehouse are legendary although the intensity of Jewish political life at that location has become defused in recent years due largely to a lower level of Jewish activity in American public affairs and politics and an infusion of Afro-American families in the neighborhood. Because close knit row house neighborhoods no longer exist in Jewish communities, the old time ward healers have become a phenomenon of the past. Jews involved in education and social work, not big earners and just people, tend to be politically the most liberal, a philosophy that, not too many years ago, was the same for many well to-do Jews. Baltimore is part of the national stage, which in recent years no longer presents a solid national Democratic vote. In recent decades, large numbers of monied Jews have philosophically and financially withdrawn from the Democratic Party; shifting their affection to the more self-serving and conservative Republican platform.[3]

Interestingly, in opposition to the 78% Jewish majority that voted for Democrats in the 1994 elections, large numbers of Baltimore's extremely Orthodox Jews have aligned themselves with the conservatives. By endorsing this agenda, they have, in effect, traded their old ties to fellow Jews and have entered into a political alliance with Republicans and Christian fundamentalists.

Education[4] is a first priority for Jewish parents, and at the Pikesville High School, about 90% of the graduates continue their formal education. More Pikesville Senior High School students meet higher standards than students in the other twenty-one Baltimore County high schools tested. The school also has the lowest dropout percentage.

UNCOMMON THREADS

1 *In August 1996, the Baltimore Hebrew University announced that they were exploring a merger with another institution to expand its facilities by creating a state-of-the-art library, community research center, and a Jewish museum.*

2 *The present Associated's office building is a neighbor of the Meyerhoff Symphony Hall, The Lyric Opera House, the University of Baltimore, the Maryland Institute of Art, the Medical and Chiurgical Faculty of Maryland, the Greek Orthodox Cathedral of the Annunciation. Nearby are Maryland State office buildings, the Fifth Regiment's Armory and Baltimore's Amtrak Station. The Meyerhoff Symphony Hall, home of the Baltimore Symphony Orchestra was made possible by a $15,000,000 gift from Baltimore Realtor Joseph Meyerhoff.*

3 *After World War II, numbers of Jews of Eastern European heritage were appointed to all manner of political offices; in the Fourth District many who ran for public office won consistently.*

4 *As in the mid 1900s at Baltimore City public elementary school #61, with a predominant enrollment of Jewish children, an inordinately large number of its students were sent to the accelerated school #49, Pikesville Senior High School with a predominantly Jewish enrollment, also excels in Maryland State Performance Programs. Due to the large numbers of Jews who have moved into the Owings Mills sector of Reisterstown Road, the enrollment of Jewish children in the Franklin High School has raised that schools performance.*

In the computer age, Jewish religious education need never waiver. Available on compact discs are English authoritative translations of both the Jerusalem and Babylonian Talmuds, the Torah, Jewish Encyclopedias, biographies, graphics, classics, THE JERUSALEM POST and hours of fun for the children with "Dreidels and Dinosaurs." They are reasonably priced, have easy search programs and are accompanied by original Hebrew texts.

PART III-13

The Jewish Historical Society of Maryland * The Jewish Heritage Center * Lombard Street revisited * Jewish population * The Holocaust remembered in bronze, concrete, and stone

*E*xcept for the Jewish Historical Society and Jewish Heritage Center, Lombard Street corned beef, and flashes of nostalgia, there has been little reason in recent years for Northwest Baltimore Jews to visit East Baltimore. As explained in Chapter 5, the founding of the historical society in 1960 was for the purpose of restoring the 1845 Lloyd Street Shul[1]. The completed restoration became the catalyst for the establishment of the Jewish Heritage Center; more than a valid reason for Baltimore Jews to examine and learn about their heritage. The Historical Society library preserves documents and memorabilia which are available to researchers, and the Heritage Center is a fulfillment of the vision of Baltimore attorney Robert L. Weinberg. The reality of its physical being was largely due to his dedication and almost single handed effort to fund it.

The Jewish Heritage Center, America's first Jewish museum, library, and research center combined with a mid-nineteenth century synagogue was dedicated in 1987 on Lloyd Street in the heart of what was once Jewish East Baltimore. In exchange for an arrangement for property upkeep, Baltimore City allowed the center to be built on a strip of city owned land. The property lies between the south wall of the nation's third oldest extant synagogue facing Watson Street and the north wall of Baltimore's oldest shul in continuous use. The restored Lloyd Street Synagogue, now considered to be a museum, and the B'Nai Israel shul, formerly the Chizuk Amuno synagogue, completely restored in 1986 for use by its small active congregation, are integral components of the Jewish Historical Society of Maryland's Heritage Center. Programs of the Center, the core of the Jewish Historical Society of Maryland, embody Jewish related exhibits, tours, publishing and educational programs. Since the construction of the Heritage Center, family heirlooms and other precious objects of Jewish heritage have been generously donated to it. It is now a repository for nearly a half million artifacts, documents, and photographs related to regional Jewish history. The genealogy files of the Maryland Jewish Family History Program grow steadily as do the recordings of Jewish oral histories. The inaugural exhibit, *AND SO THEY CAME,* spanned the Jewish experience of settlement in Maryland 1656-1929, and subsequent exhibits have been equally fascinating and educational.

The growth of the Jewish Historical Society has been rapid and on May 5, 1996, ground was broken for a much needed major addition to the Jewish Historical Society of Maryland. The inspiration for the design of the new structure was drawn from the existing 1845 Baltimore Hebrew Congregation Synagogue, the B'Nai Israel Synagogue and the present Jewish Heritage Center building. The addition makes the Jewish Historical Society the nation's largest and most advanced facility for the study, understanding and appreciation of regional American Jewish History. The Harry & Jeanette Weinberg foundation contributed a large sum of money towards the erection of the new addition and it will carry their name. Weinberg was a former Baltimore billionaire who in 1959 created a charitable trust considered to be the world's largest by a Jewish person. Harry Weinberg had no intention of having his money go to cultural art museums and symphony orchestras; and he specifically stated such; he wanted his money to help people. After his death in November 1990, the interest spent from this reputed to be a $1,000,000,000 foundation has become increasingly noticed in the Baltimore community, particularly in the Jewish sector. The Weinberg name is in place over senior living facilities, soup kitchens as well as the Sinai and Johns Hopkins hospitals. A matching grant to Jewish day schools is establishing a new entity, the Jewish Day School Foundation of Greater Baltimore to be administered by the ASSOCIATED: Jewish Community Federation of Baltimore. The announcement of the grant in 1994 came in time to help solve the tough financial problems of Baltimore's Jewish day schools, particularly the Talmudical Academy, when only two years before their crumbling fiscal condition threatened to destroy this important Baltimore Jewish institution.[2]

    Yale and Peggy Gordon had different ideas where the interest from their largess would be spent. Their large foundation has given generously to musical interests, especially to Baltimore's internationally known Peabody Conservative of Music. In May 1995, The Yale and Peggy Gordon Center for the Performing Arts opened in Owings Mills at the Jewish Community Center

    The present downtrodden Jewish business section of Lombard Street is an urban casualty. A recipient of a nearly fatal blow during the 1968 Baltimore City riots, the 1000 and 1100 blocks have more empty buildings and vacant lots than viable businesses. Hope was that the establishment of the Jewish Heritage Center would anchor an area renaissance, but to date this has not happened, and the possibilities are not good. In a futile effort to restore the ambiance of Lombard Street, former Mayor William Donald Schaefer changed the name of the two block, half demolished stretch to Corned Beef Row. The area has declined too far to imagine that the simplification of giving it a new name could make a difference. Today, three Jewish delicatessens remain on Lombard Street, and only one retains a vestige of Yiddishkeit, where Jewish countermen capable of the traditional wisecracking do so with selectivity and restraint for fear of offending their customers, most of whom are not attuned to Jewish humor. In the largest of the three delicatessens, counter persons are non-Jewish, white and black, male and female, who lack the energy level and personalities of those of past decades. Then too, these out-of-place counter folk are not really sure that pastrami and salami are different and that hot roast brisket of beef can ever taste as it should if it is re-heated by being nuked in a microwave. Sweitzer cheese (swiss) is a lost word so a request for it evokes, "Huh." Fortunately Jews no longer need to exalt Lombard Street corned beef; they can buy as good in Pikesville, and Pikesville's is leaner even if the customer doesn't request it. There is excellent Jewish delicatessen in other parts of Baltimore as well and out-of-town delis advertise in nationally distributed magazines that they can ship kosher salami or pickles anywhere in the country; credit cards accepted.

As the importance of Lombard Street waned, the northwest Baltimore Jewish community fortified by its strength taken from East Baltimore, continued to grow and prosper. The 1973 American Jewish Yearbook estimated that the Baltimore Jewish community numbered 100,000 which made it the eighth largest in the United States and seventeenth in the world. The 1974-1975 Yearbook re-assessed and lowered the figures to 94,000, ranking Baltimore tenth in the nation. Figure compilers are frequently misled by the number of mixed marriages and the question of who is Jewish, who is not and how to classify and count the children?[3]

Moves south and west that have lowered the density of Jewish communities have almost dissolved some of the smaller ones. In larger American Jewish communities, population moves have tended to reduce synagogue membership and community services such as family assistance for senior citizens and other needs; nevertheless, American Jewry has done well in building it's own structure that hopefully insures its survival, establishes a norm for modern Jewish life, and collectively fights anti-Semitism. Unfortunately living greater distances from the synagogue centers, and with many Jewish women in the work force, thousands of Jewish parents have lost their incentive to give their children a Jewish education. An extra hour or two driving time on the days of religious school, for many, has become an unwelcome chore which threatens the Jewish religious structure.

It took fifteen to twenty years after World War II for much of the world to begin to acknowledge the word Holocaust. Perhaps these years were years of shame for non-Jews brought on by universal disgust and rejection of man's inhumanity to man. It was not popular to declare open anti-Semitism, leaving this type of hatred confined to the warped minds of cranks and ranting fundamentalists. Perhaps future generations of all people will come to realize that though the Holocaust was without doubt a Jewish tragedy, it was also a tragedy for all the world. The initial Jewish response to the Holocaust was a natural outpouring of rhetoric, followed by literature that through the years has somewhat subsided. Thoughts of the Holocaust deeply affected the consciousness of Jews, and as the years have passed, there has been a need for representational monuments to visit, to pray at or to learn and to remember.

In 1976, The Baltimore Jewish Council, supported by Baltimore Jews, conceived the idea of a major monument for remembrance of Jewish lives lost in the greatest horror in recorded history. Completed in 1986 in a non-conspicuous one acre site bounded by Water, Gay and Lombard Streets in downtown Baltimore, the Holocaust monument can be seen from Lombard Street when traveling west; that is, if you twist your neck as you drive by. The $300,000 double concrete monoliths face a grassy slope planted with six rows of six trees each. Though not conceived by the designer as such, many view the monoliths as representations of box cars of the type that transported six million Jews to death camps. Few people visit the site because it has been seriously abused by the homeless and druggies. In 1994, the Baltimore Jewish Council considered razing, re-constructing or re-locating the memorial; in 1995 they announced that the imposing concrete structure, more of a shooting gallery for drug addicts and less of a shrine to the Holocaust, will be redesigned.

Dedicated on the 50th anniversary of Kristallnacht and considerably closer to Lombard Street in the same block as the monoliths is a startling sculpture. The monument is a "Gift of Remembrance" from two Baltimore Jewish families, Mr. & Mrs. Melvin Berger and Mr. & Mrs. Jack Luskin. This remembrance was designed by Joseph Sheppard a well-known non-Jewish Baltimore artist who divides his time between Italy and Baltimore. Mounted on a black marble base, the bronze sculpture depicts twisted bodies of emaciated flesh and bones being consumed by a mass of flames.

Inside the entrance to Baltimore Hebrew Congregation's Berryman's Lane cemetery stands an impressive monument, the money for which was donated by Jacob Gottshalk, a congregant. The design was created by Gladys Sauber, a noted Baltimore Jewish sculptor, who also directed the installation. An everlasting memorial flame is in the center of a six pointed Star of David. Each of the six points of the star point to a column representing one of the six million Jewish lives lost in the Holocaust. The composition of the memorial and the interaction of Vermont marble, earth, metal, and concrete evokes a desire for relatives and friends of Holocaust victims and others to stop and to pray in the Jewish tradition for those annihilated in Nazi death camps. In 1995, in the 107 year old United Hebrew Cemetery, a memorial stone designed much like a conventional tombstone has been erected. The Brainchild of Samuel Stone, the memorial features inscriptions of the names of Nazi concentration camps engraved in Hebrew and English. To remember the Holocaust in concrete, stone and metal is one way and another is to remember it spiritually. Concrete, stone and metal tend to outlast the vacillations of human spirituality that changes with the passing of generations.

---

1   *The founding members of the Jewish Historical Society were:*
Dr. Harry Bard--Principal, Baltimore Junior College
Hugo Dalsheimer--business and community leader--philanthropist
Dr. Isaac M. Fein--Professor of History, Baltimore Hebrew College
Louis J. Fox--business man--President of Associated Jewish Charities
Rabbi Samuel Glasner--Chairman, Board of Jewish Education
Rabbi Israel Goldman--Chizuk Amuno Congregation
Harry Greenstein--Director, Associated Jewish Charities
Isaac Hamburger II--business and community leader
Mrs. Elsie Kairys--community leader
Dr. Louis Kaplan--President, Baltimore Hebrew College
Mrs. Amalie S. Katz--community leader
Lester Levy--businessman--former President Associated Jewish Charities
Rabbi Morris Lieberman--Baltimore Hebrew Congregation
Joseph Meyerhoff--Realtor, community leader, philanthropist
Rabbi Samuel Rosenblatt--Beth Tfiloh Congregation
Moses W. Rosenfeld--attorney
Mrs. Marie Rothschild--community leader
Leon Sachs--Director, Baltimore Jewish Council
Dr. Alvin Thalheimer--community leader, philanthropist

2   *In the Spring of 1996, the Harry & Jeanette Weinberg Foundation quietly terminated all contributions to nearly every Orthodox institution and charity in Baltimore; affected were those that considered themselves bound by a Beit din (rabbinical court). The Talmudical Academy of Baltimore bending to the pressure of a New York Beit din, threatened to overturn an agreement made with the Weinberg Foundation that objects to a Jewish community that is part of a secular society, being also bound by religious laws.*

3   *The American Jewish population has shifted; the identity of many Jews has fallen through the cracks and can no longer be counted. In the late 1940s, with a relatively stabilized population, over two thirds of American Jews lived in New England and the mid-Atlantic states. There were signs of a great change in 1970 and a 1990 national Jewish population study reconfirmed that these numbers have been reduced to about half of the 1940 numbers. Baltimore's figures and those of other communities are hard to read because they must take into account the recent movement to the city of the fervently Orthodox and Russian Jews. Offsetting figures are the numbers of Baltimore Jews who have joined those from the Midwest, other Eastern seaboard cities, particularly New England, who now reside full or part time in the sun belt states of Florida, Arizona, and California. By 1990, more Jews lived in San Francisco than in Baltimore, and this is quite a change from earlier statistics.*

PART III-14

2nd Russian migration * The Charedi * N.W.C.P. * The 16 mile Eruv * The 1.5 million dollar Mikvah * Kosher vs. Government * Jews in the news * Avalon * Genetics * Today's et cetera * Har Sinai

*I*n recent years, diverse Jewish groups have moved into Baltimore. Over a century has passed since the first migration of Russian Jews left Mother Russia, and thousands have done it again. The recent migration is in no way a replay of that of the nineteenth century with its trauma. Today's Russians, not quite so bedraggled as the immigrants of one hundred years ago, have lived for decades in an atheistic homeland isolated from their Jewish religion and its traditions. Only a few have any feeling for or a knowledge of Judaism and few have ever entered the Moscow synagogue or other synagogues located throughout the old Soviet Union. To do so could have been risky as special agents of the K.G.B. observed and took photos of those who took such a chance. Though less a product of Jewish culture than of the Soviet system, in present day Russia, the same as in the days of the tsars, Jews are considered a separate nationality by other Russians. It is evident that the cultural gap that exists between Americans and the recently arrived Russian Jews differs from the 1880s when Yiddish speaking Russian Jewish immigrants were confronted by German/English speaking American Jews. Earlier, Russian Jews escaped the terror of the tsars; the new immigrants escaped from the anti-Semitic injustices of the former Communist Soviet Union[1]; however, for each group the dominant reason for departure from Russia was the promise of freedom and a chance for a better economic life.

The migration of Soviet Jews to America began as an organized grass-roots movement by American Jews to Free Soviet Jewry. Through their efforts, congressional and diplomatic pressures were put on the Soviets to convince them to honor the human rights of their Jewish citizens. The resettling of Soviet Jews in Baltimore and other cities was not a smooth transition at the beginning, and though improved, it still is not. Living in the Soviet Union, Jews formed an exaggerated picture of the United States, the same old vision Russian Jews had one hundred years ago, that of the Golden Medina. The majority of newcomers have settled in good but far from golden houses and apartments mostly along the Park Heights Avenue corridor, north of Northern Parkway, south of Seven Mile Lane and in Owings Mills. Because they are disappointed in America, some recent arrivals are bitter and have been demanding and ungrateful to their Baltimore Jewish benefactors.

HIAS (Hebrew Immigrant Aid Society) has assisted the recent arrived Russian Jews with the technicalities of immigration, limited by the United States to 40,000 per year. Social and employment help for the Soviet Jews have come primarily through The ASSOCIATED; Jewish Community Federation of Baltimore's language and job training programs. For those who have shown an interest in Orthodoxy, the ASSOCIATED has made it possible for their children to attend full time religious schools. Orthodox,

257

Conservative and Reform congregations have held out their hands to the Russians, offering free seats for holiday services to those who choose to attend. Arrangements for free circumcision are available for young boys and for adults if they desire.

About half of the 7,000 Soviet Jewish emigrees who have settled in Baltimore are skilled workers. Due to language differences and various licensing requirements for professions and trades, many are forced to accept entry level jobs that require them to start at the bottom of the ladder. America has been a difficult transition for those Jews who have suffered damage to their self esteem by loosing a status they once enjoyed in the Soviet Union. Since May 1991, a Sunday morning Baltimore radio broadcast Zvezda Davida (Star of David) reached Russian Jewish emigrees, helping them acclimate to living in Baltimore. Listeners learned about American Jewish culture. Though the 90 minute program included political commentary, a Torah lesson, and music in Russian, English and Hebrew, it went off the air in July 1996. There are plans for it to return.

Other than the one in Brooklyn, New York, the 20,000 Baltimore Orthodox Jewish community is said to be the strongest in the United States. Contributing to this reputation, are the large number charedi, the Torah observant Orthodox Jews who have recently moved to Baltimore. This city offers a high standard of living for less cost than other large East Coast cities, plus it has the amenity of top rated Jewish religious schools, important to fervently religious Orthodox[2] who would not consider sending their children to public schools. Kosher food markets and community services are in their neighborhoods as well. In the Baltimore area, jobs, particularly good ones, are available for those who are physicians, attorneys, and accountants. Torah observant Jews in Baltimore have let it be known to friends and relatives living in New York, Boston, Washington and as far away as Los Angeles about the favorable aspects of living in Baltimore, long considered one of the premier communities for Jews outside of Israel. Traditionally, Jews here get along well with each other, so those who are Orthodox feel comfortable in their smaller vibrant community with little interference from outsiders. Compared to residential areas in larger cities, upper Park Heights Avenue, Cross Country Boulevard, Cheswolde and Ranchleigh, where new groups have settled, are less prone to serious crime and present residents intend to keep it that way. In 1993, the Maryland State Legislature established the Neighborhood Crime Prevention Grant Program. Funds have been made available to the Mt. Washington Improvement Association, the Millbrook-Colonial Village Citizen's Patrol, the Pickwick Citizen's Patrol as well as the Northwest Citizen's Patrol.

After dark, the fervently Orthodox Jewish community's Northwest Citizen's Patrol, funded mostly by residents and businesses, patrol their residential areas. The 500-600 participating volunteers are members of 22 Orthodox synagogues. Prowl cars are manned each night except on Friday, the Sabbath, by 8 or 10 bearded Orthodox Jews; until recently, two Baltimore City police officers were assigned to the NWCP patrol cars. A sign on the roof of the cars, NWCP RADIO, lets intruders know of the patrol's presence. An attempt in August 1994, by Baltimore's police commissioner to assign a Jewish police major to command the area, a replacement for the present black commander, met with opposition from the black community. A month later the two communities met to iron out their differences, keeping in focus that their common interest is to combat crime. Because Orthodox Jewish customs keep men and women separated outside the home, women can be part of the program only if they accompany their husbands. Contrary to most areas of the city from which residents have moved to the county, the recent influx of Jews has created a concentration of their own that has helped to sustain the stability of their neighborhoods.

Except to go to work, fervently Orthodox Jews rarely go far from their homes, and when they do, they usually go by automobile. Baltimore's upper Park Heights Avenue public transportation system would need modification if extremely Orthodox Jews chose to use it on a regular basis. Possibly they would demand separate busses for each sex or buses with curtains[3] to separate the men from the women. The Talmud forbids men from thinking about women, and with female passengers seated beside them, the temptation would be too great; out of sight, out of mind; the men would have only clean thoughts.

As in New York City and Brooklyn, Baltimore's extremely Orthodox Jewish families practice social insularity and show little interest in the total community. Puritanical Jews attend an assortment of shuls and are partially a political enigma. Probably due to national economic conditions, the number of extremely Orthodox families coming to Baltimore has lessened in the last two or three years so the future growth of the community, except for their internal multiplying, is in limbo. When CHAI (Comprehensive Housing Assistance Incorporated), an agency of the ASSOCIATED Jewish Community Federation of Baltimore, was begun in 1983, it was for the purpose of stabilizing Northwest Baltimore neighborhoods which it has done.[4] By the turn of the century, or shortly thereafter, it is likely that the Jewish population along the Reisterstown Road, Park Heights and Greenspring Avenue areas within the city limits, will be predominantly Orthodox.

Exclusively for the Orthodox shommer shabbat (Sabbath observant Jews), in January 1981, after five years and thousands of man hours, an eruv (an enclosure) was completed and operational by Eruv of Baltimore Incorporated. This symbolic wall encloses extremely Orthodox Jews within a sixteen mile perimeter in northwest Baltimore and Baltimore County. There is little danger of confusing it with either the Great Wall of China or as a tourist attraction. The complete eruv consists of an unbroken chain of fences and telephone wires linked wherever there is a break by stretches of fishing line and wire that connect at the top of telephone and electric power poles. The wall is real where the inside sound barriers of the Baltimore beltway have been incorporated. When installing the eruv, sophisticated surveying equipment made sure that the vertical heights of poles and horizontal planes did not violate traditional codes; a committee of rabbis make frequent inspections of the installation. Baltimore's eruv is one of the largest, perhaps the largest, of about twenty American communities that have installed them. The boundaries include a part of Sinai Hospital, Levindale and Concord House[5]. With the continuous growth of the Baltimore Orthodox community and the popularity of the Baltimore Jewish Northwest Passage, it is likely that in the future, Chizuk Amuno and Beth El synagogues may be absorbed within the walls of a re-drawn eruv. Extremely Orthodox Jews are alerted by radio if breaks in the wall occur and cannot be repaired before the Sabbath; those who miss the radio contact can phone the Eruv Hotline.

This ritual, almost hypothetical wall eases Sabbath restrictions by allowing Baltimore's extremely Orthodox Jews freedoms that would otherwise be forbidden by rabbinical, not biblical law though an Eruvim is mentioned in the Talmud. Within the Eruv on the Sabbath, new social aspects have opened for ultra Orthodox Jews who can arguably now transgress or circumvent ancient religious laws. These laws forbid them from carrying money, wallets, keys, identification cards and such in the public domain outside the home. Theoretically, the eruv is an extension of the home creating a private domain, so within it extremely Orthodox Jews push baby carriages on the Sabbath, an important need for them. The Talmud allows no birth control and families have lots of prams to prove it. Some very religious Orthodox Jews look upon the whole machination with skepticism because they say it stretches the traditional laws too far, and they think it tends to create a self imposed ghetto. For those in favor, it is hoped that the eruv will bring neighbors living within its boundaries closer together in a harmonious society. Tradition has expanded the zone to include Jewish neighborhoods encircled by the unbroken wall, providing structures meet certain qualifications. Those who favor the eruv believe that their interpretation of religious laws and beliefs permit such a wall so why not take advantage of it. For the reader, take note that the concept of an eruv is an excellent example of Jewish law that, through the ages, is subjected to endless rabbinical interpretations[6]

The vitality of the extremely Orthodox Jewish community is strong, and it reaches out to Orthodox needs. In the autumn of 1992, an old and small mikvah was replaced with a modern one and a half million dollar facility for women on Clarks Lane with twenty private changing areas. Married Orthodox Jewish women wearing a tichel (head scarf), frequently yellow but not always, visit the mikvah for spiritual cleansing after their menstrual period and on the eve of a religious holiday. The rite is performed after dark in the kosher waters of the mikvah. Exact details remain an enigma to most non-Orthodox Jewish women, unless perhaps in their earlier days they worshipped as Orthodox. In an older mikvah at another location, extremely pious men immerse their bodies every Friday and on the day preceding religious festivals.

In February 1993, the United States Supreme Court upheld a decision of the Supreme Court of New Jersey, nullifying state kosher regulations[7] similar to those on the books and now enforced under Baltimore and Maryland laws. The Supreme Court said these local laws violate the Constitution's demand for separation of church and state if states use their official authority to enforce Orthodox Jewish kosher standards. Baltimore's kosher meat laws came before a federal judge in Maryland in October 1993 and in an appeal two years later. Judges ruled each time that the Baltimore law is unconstitutional.

The Baltimore based national kosher certification organization Vaad HaKashrus provides kosher supervision of stores, restaurants, and slaughter houses locally and nationally.[8] In August 1994, the organization was called upon to quell major confusion surrounding the use of milk products. Rumors spread through the Orthodox community that a surgical procedure used for years to correct a stomach disorder in cows was leaving punctures in the cow's fourth stomach. Jewish law mandates that cows with such cuts and punctures, and the milk coming from such a cow, is not kosher. After an investigation, the beit din (religious court) of the Vaad determined and announced publicly that the national supply of milk is kosher.

With eruv and the kosher issues put aside, the Baltimore press has brought to the attention of the community, dimensions of Judaism that have awakened some traditions of Orthodox Jewish East Baltimore, traditions and laws that Reform Jews had never been aware of. Relating exclusively to Orthodox Jews, June 1993, was a month of Jews in the News.

In this month and year, the financial problems of the Talmudical Academy written about in Part II-4 were well updated in the *Baltimore Sun*. In June 1993, a custody battle aroused the passions of Baltimore's extremely Orthodox Jewish community when a self-proclaimed religious scholar charged with molesting his children rejected a plea bargain that would have allowed him to avoid going to jail. The charges stemmed from a husband-wife battle being played out in Maryland courts that involved child snatching and molesting. The husband explained to the court that he never held a paying job as his Katubbah, signed at marriage, provided for him and his family to be supported by his in-laws and other members of the community while he was a full-time Talmudic scholar.[9] The Appeals Court agreed the husband had voluntarily impoverished himself despite his obligation to financially support his children. In the opinion quoted from the musical *Fiddler on the Roof,* the fictional lead character Teveya recognizes that a life of study is a luxury when he sings, "If I were a rich man ... Wouldn't have to work hard ... I'd discuss the holy books with the learned men seven hours every day."

In Annapolis in the same month, a small congregation wanted to adhere to Talmudical law and the ancient Jewish tradition of burying old and damaged prayer books in a wooden box in a cemetery. The burial was to be part of the dedication ceremony of a section in a non-sectarian cemetery recently purchased for Jewish burials. The cemetery managers denied permission unless the congregation planned to spend $1,000 to line the burial site with concrete. The congregation hopes to raise the required money.[10]

Possibly because of the unique differences between Jewish religious traditions and laws, happenings foreign to the Christian community make good press, even for fringe groups. Also in June 1993, the stories of an odd group made the public press. A Baltimore area radio station, which thrives on controversial talk shows, told a Messianic Jewish-Christian congregation (Jews who believe Christ is the Messiah), in Owings Mills that its Sunday morning discussion and call-in-hour would be canceled. The station denied the accusations of giving in to pressures from advertisers. The station said they simply made a decision to move away from religious broadcasting.

In the introduction to *Uncommon Threads* the author made a statement, "We don't know for sure but are close to defining our role and where we fit in the jig-saw puzzle of this country." This is probably still true, but an article appearing in the *New York Times* on October 24, 1993, negates this statement somewhat so maybe we are not as close as we think. The article states that departing from a long standing Jewish reluctance to proselytize, the leader of Reform Judaism in North America, President of the Union of American Hebrew Congregations,[11] yesterday encouraged Jews to seek converts among those who do not have their own faith. He announced a $5,000,000 program, "to reach out to those of our neighbors who belong to no church or practice no religion." The rabbi's statement challenged a cherished taboo of modern Judaism and added a new dimension to theological differences between Reform, Conservative and Orthodox Jews.

The justification by the rabbi that the notion that Judaism is not a propagating faith is far from the truth. While this has been only a practical truth for the past four centuries, it was an actual truth for the forty preceding centuries. Abraham was a convert and Isaiah insisted that God's House was a house of prayer for all people. Many of those who oppose conversion argue that those joining Judaism at this time in history have not suffered so they are getting a free ride. They question how it is possible to become a certified Jew without having lived the ages of Jewish oppression. Furthermore, they argue, the proposal undermines the identity, the validity, and the continuity of the Jewish people.

A few years ago, Baltimore Jews waited impatiently for the release of the motion picture *Avalon*. Much of it was filmed locally and the supposition was that viewers would see themselves as part of a rich heritage of Eastern European Jewry in Baltimore; maybe the movie would help them define themselves in this community. The title *Avalon* was meaningful as it was the name of a movie house, long a part of the life of every Jewish person who lived in lower Park Heights. For sure, the Hollywood cum Baltimore producer and director understood the subject because it was part of him when he lived in this city. For shame, *Avalon* omitted religion and this muddled any portrayal of Jewish life. Pseudo ethnic accents of the cast muted *Avalon's* characters and left viewers unsure; was this an Italian, a Jewish, or a generic immigrant family?

Jews, who are about 3% of the population of the United States are certainly not generic families because they as a group are frequenters in the news. According to an article in the *New York Times* of October 5, 1993, researchers claim they have found the gene behind a rare fatal brain disorder that strikes mostly Jews, and they are testing affected families in the hope of finding all the mutations that cause the ailment. If they succeed in their search, a simple blood test could warn prospective parents whether they are likely to bear a child with the disorder called Canavan disease. Like Tay-Sachs, a neurological disease said to be endemic only to Northeastern European Jews, Canavan disease is hereditary, and the article states "it probably had a founding father, a person in whom a genetic mutation first occurred among Ashkenazi Jews of Eastern Europe."

Another, Gaucher disease has been identified as one of the most common Jewish genetic disorders, and two-thirds of those affected are of Eastern European Ashkenazi descent; the remaining one third are scattered through the general world population. Reported in September 1995, in the *Los Angeles Times*, researchers at the National Institutes of Health said a rare genetic defect linked to breast and ovarian cancer is eight times more common among Jewish women of European Ashkenazi ancestry.

Some medical reports in the press would lead us to believe that there are genetic differences between German and Eastern European Jews, and this, probably not true, needs to be clarified. In the Introduction to *Uncommon Threads*, this author told about the Jews who fled to Eastern Europe from Western Europe, and about how those that remained and those that fled developed distinctly differently. This statement applied to social development and not genetic differences.[12]

Reform and Conservative branches of Judaism appear to have less stable parameters than the Orthodox and continue to seek a level that is acceptable to synagogue congregants. In a sermon from the pulpit of one of Baltimore's Reform temples, an associate rabbi suggested that Reform Jews might consider a trial period of observing the dietary laws. Many who heard this sermon reacted negatively to the rabbi's remarks, as disenchantment with dietary laws is a major reason why Reform Jews are Reform Jews. In the May 1994 house organ, the rabbi attempted to clarify his statement by saying that many Reform Jews feel they are exempt from traditional practices and never bother to learn about tradition. The rabbi further stated that this is not Reform Judaism, this is cop-out Judaism.

The Conservative branch of Judaism does its share of shaking the restraints commanded by the Torah and at the same time astounding Orthodox Jews. The Commission on Human Sexuality of the Conservative Rabbinical Assembly,[13] very much aware of the deterioration of Jewish traditional standards, finds that even without marriage, committed and loving relationships can embody a measure of holiness. The Orthodox Jewish Rabbinical Council wasted no time in denouncing the Commission's unpublished document.

Change is not limited to the Reform and Conservative branches of Judaism. Orthodox Jews, too, seek to define their role in today's America. Eight young male students at the P'Tach School for Learning Disabilities at the Baltimore Talmudical Academy entered a Daughters of the American Revolution patriotism contest. Few organizations in the United States could be further afield from American Orthodox Jewry than the DAR. The students submitted *Respect our Flag,* a book of drawings that illustrated flag etiquette; in May 1994, they won the national contest. This was the first time the Baltimore chapter of the DAR had a national winner.

In July 1994 through The ASSOCIATED Jewish Community Federation of Baltimore, not by it, a few individuals gave $36,500 towards an estimated $350,000 needed to erect a 46 foot high sculpture near the foot of President Street The monument honors the 15,400 Polish army officers and intellectuals murdered by the Soviets and buried in mass graves in the Katyn Forest. The proposed soaring abstract bronze will be

Baltimore's loftiest work of art. The Federation made the contribution on behalf of a group of 10 or 12 donors. Words were spoken about the historic friendship between the Polish and Jewish peoples and how Polish and Jewish destinies have been closely entwined for more than 1,000 years. Not completely aware of the circumstances surrounding this gift, news of it came as a surprise to many Baltimore Jews, particularly those who had survived while living in Poland.

In September 1944, a Baltimore mohel (certified Orthodox circumciser) stated in print, "I've had a bris in practically every synagogue in town, in a bowling alley out in Bel Air. I had a bris in a jail, any place imaginable I've had a bris. I'm going to these things constantly. The only problem with that is that sometimes it can hurt your diet. With all that food around, you can get a little heavy, but I'm not complaining." Recently a synagogue was thought not to be the place where a Baltimore family wanted to have a brit milah (circumcision), a very important Jewish life ritual and a cause for celebration. Planning this forthcoming event, the family inquired about the possibility of having the ceremony at a Baltimore County country club where they were members. It became a slight dilemma for the board; club facilities had no precedence for such an event though there was nothing in club rules to prevent it. The club's president, a bit unsure of his footing, contacted another country club and the Baltimore County Health Department for their opinions. They second club had never had a circumcision so they could be of no help. The Health Department gave positive approval with a condition that the circumcision not be held in the club's kitchen. They didn't know at the time how on target their decision was, as shortly thereafter a member of the same club requested that they consider the installation of a kosher kitchen.[14] On the first and second evenings of Pesach (Passover), the gathering of the family for the seders is thought of by most Jews to be a celebration that lends itself to the comfort of the Jewish home. Some, however, shy away from dealing with the burdensome cooking, cleaning and changing of dishes for the holiday so they leave Baltimore and let someone else do it. They go to the Catskills, to the Poconos, to Florida and some to Hawaii and the Caribbean islands where many resort hotels offer rabbi-conducted communal Pesach services to groups and to individuals. Nine day packages that include sports activities and educational programs are popular. At several of the more upscale resorts where families prefer it, intimate services are conducted at individual tables within the questionable seclusion of open ballrooms.

Much of this chapter deals with change; some of it with the demographics of upper Park Heights Avenue. A question must now be asked: Though the three large Reform congregations are located there, does Reform Judaism have a future on Park Heights?

In October 1994, trustees of the Pimlico Road day school Yeshivat Rambam (Maimonides Academy) approached the Har Sinai Congregation's board with an offer of $4,000,000 to purchase their property at 6300 Park Heights Avenue. The Academy is primarily interested in Har Sinai's school buildings, and the offer included an agreement that will allow Har Sinai to occupy its domed sanctuary for twenty years. In January

1995, members of the nation's oldest Reform congregation voted overwhelmingly to accept the offer. Har Sinai, located a distance south of Baltimore Hebrew and Oheb Shalom, is in the heart of what is now an Orthodox neighborhood. Occupancy of the school buildings by Yeshivat Rambam is scheduled for the end of 1996.[15] Meanwhile, Har Sinai has selected property on Walnut and Greenspring Avenues in Baltimore County where they hope to break ground by 1997 for their new home. Neither Oheb Shalom nor Baltimore Hebrew plan to move at this time, but it may not be too many years before there is a knock on their doors, a knock they may have to answer. Because it has recently made a huge investment in their Park Heights Avenue complex, The Baltimore Hebrew Congregation probably can't even think of moving. In September 1995, they dedicated a very expensive library and education center and not long ago erected a building for their day school program. Not germane to Baltimore because it happens everywhere for every move Jewish communities make, be it residences, institutions or synagogues, neighborhoods have changed in a relatively few years and Jews must wander on, and their synagogues must follow.

The Baltimore Jewish scene is fluid. In July 1995, a battle over Beth Tfiloh Synagogue's proposed senior housing and assisted living project broke into open warfare. On its 35 acre site, Beth Tfiloh wants to build three luxury condominiums for senior adults, an assisted living facility and two additions to their school. The neighborhood is up in arms. NIMBY (not in my back yard) sentiment has spread throughout this high rent district zoned for low density residency. Objections have come from neighborhoods nearby and not so nearby and from their associations. The synagogue is being of accused of loving money more than people and hearings before the Baltimore County Planning Board and other agencies are just the beginning. This is a sensitive issue, and it is possible that the intensity that surrounds the issue is in some way related to Jews who live with the guilt of having placed their parents in a senior care facility when they didn't have to. A strong tradition of Judaism is to have elderly parents live at home with their children. An ad appearing in the September 15, 1995, of the *Baltimore Jewish Times* offers a senior care group plan "How Your Parents can Live at Home, and you can live without guilt."

Many changing social issues and fads run headlong into Jewish law and tradition. The latest issue is the rapid growth of tattoos injected by needle into the body skin, an interesting way of projecting one's self as being only slightly eccentric. Leviticus 19:28 states that "Ye shall not make any cuttings in your flesh for the dead, nor imprint of any marks upon you." It's rather difficult at times to follow the law strictly, because for years Jewish women have had nose jobs, face lifts, and tummy tucks without any thought that these procedures were against Jewish law.

UNCOMMON THREADS

1   *After 1965, when the Soviet Union severed relations with Israel, Russian emigration to that country became negligible. The cost for a visa to Israel rose from forty rubles to four hundred rubles, and in order to leave the country, an affidavit was required from a relative living in Israel. Even so, in 1972, 31,500 Soviet Jews left for Israel; by 1973 the number increased to 35,300, and by 1976, nearly one half of those Jews allowed to leave the Soviet Union chose to emigrate to Israel.*

2   *Orthodox rabbis and lay persons do not use the word ultra to describe themselves, although this adjective is in general usage by non-orthodox. Since the noun orthodox means strict observance, technically there can be no degree of orthodoxy, therefore there is no need for an adjective such as ultra; a Jew is either orthodox or he or she is not. In actual practice however, there is a difference between the Orthodox Jews who observe Jewish law to the letter and those Orthodox who do not. Orthodox rabbis prefer the more prudent fervently Orthodox or extremely Orthodox or the simple straightforward Charedi.*

3   *In Monsey, N. Y., in March 1995, a commuter bus company catering to religious Jews had been outfitted with a curtain hung in the aisle so that men would not be in the sight of women during prayers. In March 1995, the bus company agreed to remove the curtain separating passengers by gender after a woman refused to give up her seat so men could pray. There will no longer be segregated seating in Monsey.*

4   *In recent years through the Harry & Jeanette Weinberg Foundation, interest free and low interest home ownership loans can be obtained.*

5   *The Conservative synagogues Chizuk Amuno and Beth El located a short distance north of the beltway are not included but Eruv of Baltimore has made it clear that if they want to be at a later date, they can be.*

6   *Charges of alleged mishandling of advertising revenues and membership dues were made in July 1994, against the president and principal founder of the Eruv that is registered as a public charity. An annual 430 page eruv membership directory lists 1,000 families and 500 ads to raise funds for maintenance. An emergency meeting of the Vaad HaRabonim was held and the rabbis determined that Eruv of Baltimore should no longer be conducted by an autocratic dictatorship. In August, the president of Eruv of Baltimore resigned his office though he remains as the executive director. In December 1994, he announced he would publish a new list for profit; possibly his own, that is. Working with the Vaad HaRabonim, a board of directors has been formed, and they have determined that the Eruv list belongs to Eruv of Baltimore, Inc.*

7   *Under the 1946 law a Bureau of Kosher Meat and Food Control was established with a six person staff of inspectors. They not only check to make sure the kosher ritual of killing is observed, but also that the prescribed tools of the trade are used properly. For beef slaughter, the knife must be 17 inches long and have no imperfections that could cause the animal undue pain. The Bureau also checks bakeries to make sure that a small pinch of dough from each batch is burned, a symbol of sacrifice. The Baltimore case was brought to court when an inspector determined that a retail food store sold as kosher, hot dogs that had been cooked on a rotisserie next to non-kosher meat.*

8 *Vaad Hakashrus of Baltimore Cholov Yisroel deals with dairy products. The Vaad Hakashrus of Baltimore with a national jurisdiction uses the mark of a letter "k" within a five pointed star, and kosher buyers look for this symbol. A Rabbinical Council of Greater Washington supervises some local caterers as does the Metropolitan Rabbinical Kashrus Association, neither of which are as strict as the Va'ad Hakashrus.*

9 *In Part I-16, a reference is made to a marriage gift of years of family support by parents for newlyweds, to allow the husband to spend his days in study for several years. In January 1994, in a Baltimore City Circuit Court, the prosecutors dropped the charges when the defendant pleaded guilty of assault by entering an Alford Plea. Using this plea, a defendant declines to plead guilty but concedes that the evidence is against him. The judge granted probation before judgment. Allegations of child molestation are not unheard of in custody fights though almost unheard of in the Orthodox Jewish society.*

10 *As previously written, because of the Jewish tradition of settling their own problems and because of their dislike for them to be aired in the public press, a few years ago, religious issues would have been settled by Rabbinical tribunals and Jewish Courts of Arbitration.*

11 *The Union of American Hebrew Congregations represents 850 Reform congregations in North America with a combined membership of 1,300,000 persons.*

12 *The author consulted the Johns Hopkins world famous eugenicist, Dr. Victor McKusick who said there are 12 or 15 diseases attributed to Eastern European Jews. Tests have been made by extremely sophisticated researchers, completely familiar with the facts of the 15th century movement of Jews who fled the Rhineland to areas near Vilna, Minsk and other parts of Poland and Russia. Researchers have drawn maps of Europe showing conclusively that these diseases have occurred heavily in Eastern European Ashkenazis and rarely in German Ashkenazis. The conclusion is that when hundreds of Jews left Germany for Eastern Europe, there was a founding father, a person in whom a genetic mutation first occurred and the gene was carried to Eastern Europe. As the Eastern European Jewish families multiplied, so did those carrying the gene from the original mutation. In their upcoming study on genetic inheritance patterns that contribute to the development of Schizophrenia, researchers at the Johns Hopkins Hospital are specifically recruiting Ashkenazic Jews who have had the mental illness. This is because Jews are a more homogenized inbred population; an advantage for the identification of the causes for diseases.*

13 *The Conservative Rabbinical Assembly represents 1,500 Conservative rabbis in the United States and Canada, and its Commission on Jewish Law and Standards is expected to deliberate on this recommendation in the Fall of 1994.*

14 *After writing about the brit milah at a country club, the author and his wife attended such a ceremony at a local country club. The mohel spent much time orchestrating and explaining the ritual after which, more than 100 guests enjoyed a beautiful luncheon.*

15 *Dr. Rita Shloush, principal of Yeshivat Rambam, is a Sephardic Jew. She estimates there are between 200 and 300 Sephardic families living in Baltimore. They worship in the three year old Sephardic Orthodox Synagogue Netzach Yisrael on Park Heights Avenue. Dr. Shloush also estimates that sixty Iranian Jewish families worship at the Ohr Mizrach Synagogue.*

In 1921, the downtown UNITED HEBREW CHARITIES merged with the uptown FEDERATED JEWISH CHARITIES to form the ASSOCIATED JEWISH CHARITIES. This merger began to join the German and Russian communities as "ONE".

Have You Done YOUR Duty?

Hundreds of Baltimore's Hebrews have taken part in the campaign, increased their annual subscriptions to meet and with which THE UNITED HEBREW CHARITIES is doing such wonderful work among the poor and unfortunate persons of the Jewish faith—men, women and children who vitally need assistance.

HAVE YOU SEIZED THE OPPORTUNITY TO DO YOUR DUTY?

Have YOU signed up a new pledge card? Have you done YOUR part toward insuring the maintenance of those associations which are caring for the orphans, the aged persons and the aged incurables?

Have YOU considered the vast amount of suffering that is annually relieved by THE UNITED HEBREW CHARITIES?

Have YOU realized that the carrying on of this great work is of vital importance to the community?

Have YOU grasped the fact that by each subscriber to THE UNITED HEBREW CHARITIES increasing his subscription, the $50,000 annual addition can be raised by next Friday and without burdening anyone?

Share Your Prosperity With Others

If YOU have been one of the thousands of business men who have prospered in the last few years, do not delay in renewing and increasing your present subscriptions. Sign the minute a campaign worker calls on you.

If YOU are not a subscriber, join as soon as the campaign workers call on you.

THE UNITED HEBREW CHARITIES.

MAINTAINING THESE INSTITUTIONS:

Baltimore Talmud Torah Society
Hebrew Free Loan Association
Jewish Court of Arbitration
Hebrew Children's Sheltering and
 Protective Association

Hebrew Friendly Inn & Aged Home
Home for Aged Incurables
Immigrants' Protective Association
Putzel Memorial Library
Young Ladies' Benevolent Societies

A UNITED HEBREW CHARITIES circular - 1917

A scene from the second-act cast of THE PASSING YEARS, a play dramatizing the philanthropic history of the Baltimore Jewish Community. Performed at Ford's Theater - 1922

Brooks Lane - 1917

Abe Sherman's news stand
Battle Monument Square
(1921 - 1971)

On the boards in
Atlantic City - 1925

upper Eutaw Place
circa 1923

SINAI HOSPITAL - Monument & Rutland Streets (1926 - 1959)

Unrelated "THIS and THATS"

Original club house Woodholme Country Club
Pikesville, Md. - 1927

In the 1920s, and today, few Baltimore banks had Jewsh board members. The First National had two; the Savings Bank of Baltimore none.

The International Ladies Garment Workers Union, (I.L.G.W.U.) played "Pins and Needles" at the Ford's Theater - 1938.

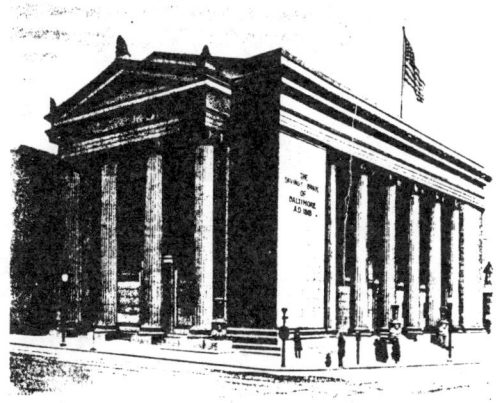

Streetcars disappeared from Northwest Baltimore in the 1950s. This mode of transportation was an important factor in the development of the northwest Jewish community.

At the intersection of Reisterstown Road and Liberty Heights Avenue, the No. 32 line continued west on Liberty Heights.

The No. 32 line crossed the busy intersection of Garrison Blvd. and continued to Gwynn Oak Juntion; terminating at Gwynn Oak Park.

At Park Circle, the Nos. 5 and 33 cars ran north on Park Heights Ave. At Pimlico, the No. 33 line branched off to West Arlington and terminated at Gwynn Oak Junction. The No. 5 cars ran north past Reisterstown and as far as Emory Grove.

Fat & thin headed Nazi Storm Troopers

These rare photographs were taken by Philip Kahn, Sr. in Nurnberg - 1929

In the early 1930s, Baltimore Jews continued to sail on North German Lloyd ships.

Starting in 1937, Germany issued passports to Jews stamped with the letter "J".

Jews in Germany owned many large commercial establishments such as:

The Herman Tietz Department Store, Alexanderplatz, Berlin

Bais Yaakov, classroom and
1st schoolhouse 1947
4637 Park Heights Avenue

Study Hall,
Ner Israel
Rabbinical College

Baltimore Jewish community leaders plan Jewish Medical Center mid-1950s:

Lester S. Levy
Abraham Krieger
Elkan R. Myers
Dr. Alvan Thalheimer
J. Benjamin Katzner
Joseph Meyerhoff
Robert H. Levi
Isaac Hamburger
Joseph Sherbow

Baltimore Zionists played a major role in the establishment of the State of Israel

Haganah ship "EXODUS 1947" formerly the Old Bay Liner PRESIDENT WARFIELD

Youths dance the "HORAH" the popular folk dance of Israeli settlers

East Baltimore

Sign of the 1930s

First block of S. High St. 1934

Lombard St. re-visited-closing the door on the chickens-1979

Baltimore Holocaust Memorials
of metal - of stone - of concrete and earth

United Hebrew Cemetery
Washington Blvd. &
Sulphur Spring Road
Artist: Kevin Conley

Chevra Ahavas Chesed
Cemetery Gateway

Dedicated on 50th Anniversary
of Kristalnacht -
Lombard near Gay Street
Artist Joseph Sheppard

Baltimore Hebrew Congregation
Berryman's Lane Cemetery
Artist: Gladys Sauber

Mid 20th century Russian Jews wait for an opportunity to emigrate to the United States or to Israel.

Map of the Baltimore Eruv

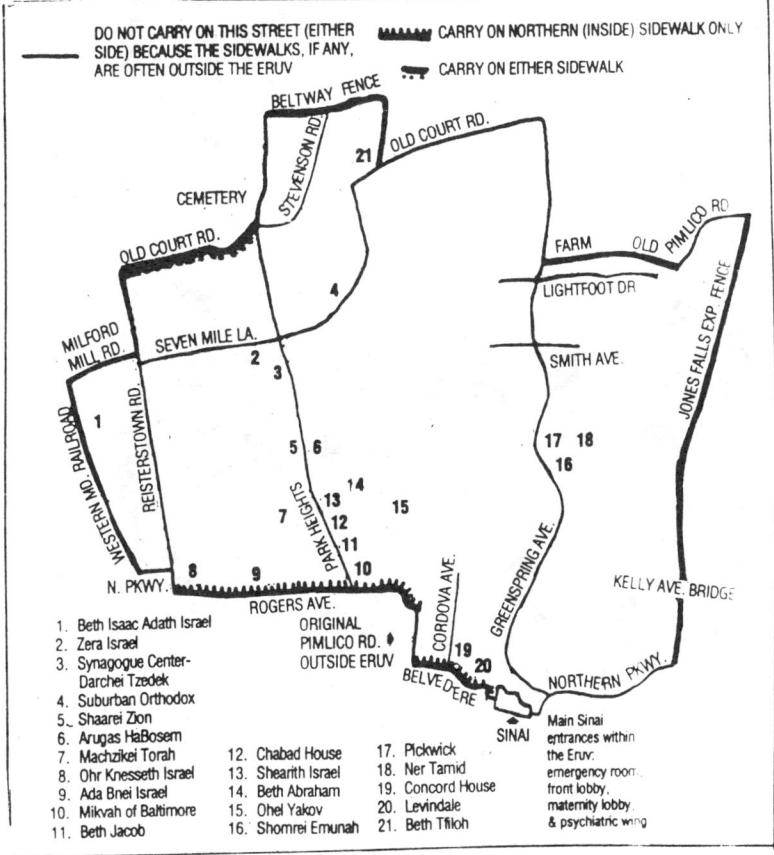

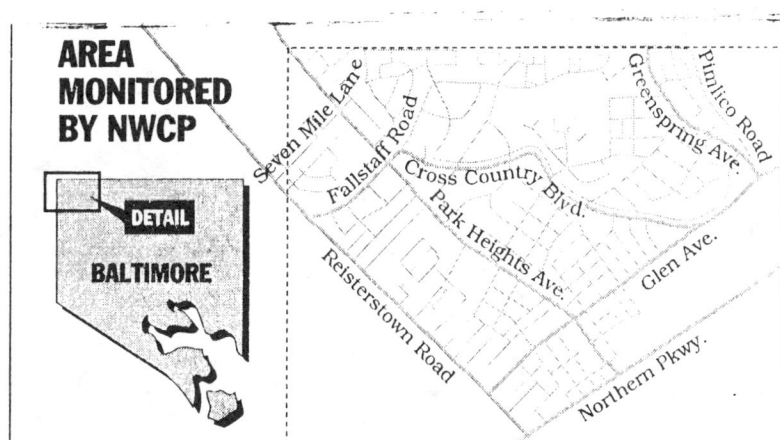

Map of the Northwestern Citizen's Patrol N. W. C. P.

BALTIMORE'S TORAH OBSERVANT JEWS - THE CHEREDI

A "SOFAR" (scribe) at the Ner Israel Rabbinical College scribing a Torah

The 1.5 million dollar Clark's Lane Mikvah

The Baltimore Shmurah Matzo Company - South Baltimore

CONCLUSION

*T*he conclusion is that for the present there is no conclusion for the Baltimore Jewish community; as well as elsewhere, Jews live in a world of flux and change. During the years of weaving the "Uncommon Threads into the Fabric of Baltimore Jewish life," Reform and Conservative, Germans and Russians are actively engaged in running soup kitchens and social action committees for the secular community; moderate Orthodox, and the fervently religious, give much of themselves to their religion and to its institutions.

Though not encompassing everyone, there is a communal embracing of Baltimore's Reform, Conservative, moderate Orthodox, the less structured groups, and non-affiliated Jews. Arguably, they have put dissimilarities aside, which has enabled them to weave a strong though still somewhat diversified fabric of a progressive Jewish community. Differences between Baltimore Jews are no longer so much whether one is German or of Eastern European heritage, moderate Orthodox, Conservative or Reform because all are part of mainstream Judaism. According to Ed Wynn, the hat switching comedian who, in 1922, came from Broadway to be part of the Associated Jewish Charities production *The Passing Years,* there is a real distinction in the demeanor of persons who wear different hats. For the Jews, there are differences in the hats Jews do or do not wear: the frum (very religious) black hatters, sometimes hatters, and the no hatters. Praying with or without a covered head,[1] or praying in English, German, Hebrew or Yiddish does not in and of itself divide the Baltimore Jewish community, but hat identification is a barrier that makes it difficult for each group to learn to know one another. Baltimore's present Jewish community is complex, and on a larger and more diverse scale than in the days when Germans and Russians drew lines. Torah observant Jews have, and may always have, theological differences that make it difficult for them to recognize those worshipping on a less than the orthodox level as actually being Jewish. To the fervently Orthodox, Reform and Conservative simply do not meet the definition of Judaism. This is a one sided area of friction, wherein all denominations of worshipping Jews consider themselves to be Jewish. Clearly though, the religious fervor of the Torah observant Jews positions them as the defenders of the faith and the hope for the future of traditional Judaism.

In 1947 in New York, a merger established the Hebrew Union College-Jewish Institute of Religion, an institution that has strongly influenced changes in the manner of worship in Reform Jewish synagogues. After World War II, large numbers of Eastern European Orthodox Jews joined the cloistered German Reform congregations, most of whose members opposed Zionism and men wearing head coverings and prayer shawls in their synagogues. The establishment of the New York institution and congregational changes in the temples insured for the future that the practice of Reform as dictated by the isolationist mid-west cocoon of Cincinnati's Hebrew Union College would end, thus, the staid and stilted decorum of Reform Jewish services has gradually changed to meet the preferences of today's congregants. The Central Conference of American Rabbis combined the old with the new when they introduced for Reform worship, three new Union prayer books: in 1975, Gates of Prayer and Gates of Repentance for the Days of Awe, and in 1977, Gates of the House. Reform services now include congregational participation and are less decorous and impersonal. Though early Reform regarded women as equals in Judaism, equality was not practiced until recent years when women rabbis and cantors began to officiate. Presently, over half of the rabbinical students at the Hebrew Union College in Cincinnati are women.

With the vanishing of the German Jew in Baltimore, their identities and customs within the Reform synagogues has nearly ended. Today, in almost every Reform synagogue, religious school teachers with little knowledge, teach Eastern European customs and traditions as Jewish customs and traditions. As it was difficult during the days of Brooks Lane for Eastern European Jews to explain to their children the reasons that some German Jews had Christmas trees in their homes, it is now difficult, but not as, for German Jews who want to keep their German Jewish heritage alive to explain to their children that fifty years ago German Jews never heard of a latke, and although they knew of bagels, they had never eaten one. Recently, the National Museum of American History, The Smithsonian Institution recently hoisted its revisionist colors by considering references to German Jews as Western European Jews. In their anxiety to produce with as little study as possible, it is unfortunate that many present day historians reach historical conclusions based upon shallow research and little knowledge. For their purpose, whatever that may be, The Smithsonian could erase in shame from their institution, the significant contribution of German Jews to world Judaism.

In years past in Baltimore, German Jews who never had a real love for the Fatherland enjoyed their singing societies and turnvereins. The few who could afford memberships delighted in their Concordia, Phoenix and Suburban Clubs and sought fashionable residential addresses. Those with highly developed social finesse danced and dined at the Harmony Circle's balls. Today, very few drink beer with their frikadellen, sauerbratten, gansebratten and kartoffel kloese; in fact they seldom eat these foods, and it is not possible to find Goodman's round matzos in the marketplace.

With the passing of today's elders, Eastern European Jews will have completely buried their foreign past and disdain for the tsars. Only a few now perspire in Russian steam baths, drink slivovitz and dance the kazotzky. They are far past the need to sew garments in a relative's sweatshop and no one would think of starting one of their own. Yet they continue to eat a little taste of cholesterol laden chopped liver and lots of corned beef and brisket, gefilte fish, latkes fried in oil at Chanukah, and Manischewitz square matzos.

To objectively measure the evolution of the Baltimore Jewish community, the accounts of the ASSOCIATED:[2] Jewish Community Federation of Baltimore graphically indicate a reversal of dominance of Baltimore's German and Russian Jews. Indicating the prominence of each in its own time; the members and officers of the ASSOCIATED'S boards reflect a significant transfer of Jewish influence.

German Jews are rapidly disappearing as an identifiable Baltimore sub-Jewish culture, abetted by marriages between German and Russian Jews and interfaith marriages with Christians. It is the hope of many Jews that strengthening the identities of the young through Jewish worship and education will diminish the temptation to intermarry; this seems to be an unlikely scenario in an America where, nearing the end of the 20th century, over half the Jews that marry are wed to Christians.

The problems Jews in Baltimore face are no different than for Jews all over America. A common denominator is study and learning, but this just may be the Achilles heel of the Jewish people. Thousands of young impressionable Jews attend colleges and universities where more and more they are socially accepted by Christians. These associations frequently lead to interfaith marriage, so from this unsuspected arena, the campuses of America, a major battle is taking place for the survival of Judaism.[3] When interfaith marriages occur, most often it is a male Jew who marries a blonde, blue eyed shikse (non-Jewish female). Marriages between shaygetz (non-Jewish male) and dark eyed Jewish women are fewer in number. Does the appeal to Jewish men have anything to do with beauty parlor peroxide blonde Jewish mothers and grandmothers? Has a Jewish male the yearning to experience the real thing? In many instances, the conversion to Judaism by a partner born a Christian results in a very good Jewish marriage, but no one knows how many Jews who, because of interfaith marriage, have chosen to join the Christian community or have entered a world of no religion. The problems of interfaith marriage are many: where to marry, who will marry them, where to live, what to eat? If I'm Jewish and you're Christian, what are the kids?[4] Do we baptize them or circumcise them? Some parents seek the advice of rabbis or clergy or counsel themselves by reading mail-order parenting guides published for inter-faith couples. Most important, assuming a couple has spiritual needs, who is God in their lives and where is God? Frequently, interfaith marriage is a manifestation of the on-going insecurity and anxieties of the Jewish people.

A new dimension to Baltimore Judaism as we have known it has been the founding in 1983 of the newest East Baltimore synagogue, Beth HaShem. Members of the congregation are brown eyed African-Americans and though the congregation's rabbi has an Irish surname, he favors the strict observance of Hasidic Judaism.

In the past, most Baltimore Jews constituted a dependable Democratic vote in national, state and city elections. By the 1970s-1980s, many well to-do Russian Jews joined a political minority of conservative German Jews who have for years voted Republican in national elections. Politicians can still depend on a Democratic Jewish Vote in state and city elections, but this may change.

For the Reform, Conservative and Orthodox, and others in lesser denominations with different instincts and view points, there is no single way to worship as a Jew. Because Jews are children of one people and one basic heritage, there is a single Judaism of purpose. The mention in these chapters of the variances of religionists and the binding together regardless of these differences has everything to do with the strong philosophical and spiritual forces of being a Jew. The very fact that there was a separateness of factions adds to the animation and charisma of world Jewry, and in a lesser way this is true for Baltimore Jewry. The Jew persists and has survived the rise and fall of centuries of governments and cultures, the Diaspora and forces of evil that have worked to eliminate them from the earth. Not now and not ever has this been without a toll. Other than those who perished, it is understandable that all Jews who escaped the Holocaust and their American born children have not to date, and probably never will, fully reconcile themselves to the loss of their relatives in the German and Eastern European death camps. In this present age, Jews are endangered by outside and inside perils including that of their own prosperity, something Jews have striven for throughout the ages. Money has always helped them buy peace, security, and freedom so Jews are fearful of being without it.

While synagogue affiliation is good, at the same time factors on the horizon indicate an irreversible weakening of communal ties, so there are questions to be asked. Are we Jews standing on another threshold? For all practical purposes, the founding of Israel in 1948 eliminated anti-Zionism because its founding was a fait accompli. Does the present peace process in the Middle East portend the end of Zionism because it appears now that the goals set by the founders over one hundred years ago are within reach? Will there be a sincere and lasting peace in the Middle East? Can Jews who isolate themselves in neighborhoods and barricade themselves behind the teachings of fervently Orthodox Jews and their past history, theoretically and intellectually progress beyond their irrelative mentality? Will Christian acceptance in America, that has ignited assimilation and interfaith marriage, contribute additionally to Jewish discontent for Judaism? The continuous weakening of some Jewish communal ties appears to be irreversible and seems to answer the question: Can Judaism, through respect and communication within itself, ever reach a common ground?

If the past is prologue, Jewish strength has come from an unbreakable faith in unchangeable moral laws, the Five Books of Moses containing the Ten Commandments and six hundred thirteen laws. Teachings begin with the creation and conclude with the death of Moses. To date, the religion lives through an endless chain of Jewish scholars who study the written doctrines and Jewish history and interpret their learnings for today's Jewish life. Though Judaism has many ideological differences, theological assumptions, different types of observances and commitments, Jews have lived a few thousand years through a shared history and destiny.

Though it is quite clear that there is no single practice of Judaism, the segments of the Baltimore Jewish community in these years are chained together albeit some links are weaker than others. THE ASSOCIATED: Jewish Community Federation of Baltimore, articulated *"WE ARE ONE"* in their slogan for their 1995 campaign. For all Jews -- Baltimoreans, Americans of German, Eastern European, Sephardic, or Middle Eastern extraction, the Torah is the central force of Judaism -- confirmed in the ritual of some synagogues when it is held high and a rabbi proclaims: "Behold, a good doctrine has been given unto you. Forsake it not. It is a tree of life."

1   *The covering of one's head at all times is a sign of piety derived from Sephardic and Babylonian Jews and a custom that followed into Persia. During the Middle Ages, Ashkenazi European Jews adopted the custom.*

2   *When founded in 1921, the ASSOCIATED was dominated by German Jews. After fifty years, in 1970, using the author's quasi-accurate method of identification by presumed origin of last names, none of the eight officers and only sixteen of the seventy-eight board members were of German Jewish extraction.*

Twenty-five years later in 1995, the year of the Associated's 75th Anniversary, the one hundred and eleven person board of the ASSOCIATED has a markedly less ratio of German Jews to Russian Jews; it appears less than fifteen are of German heritage. An Associated is People insert in the Jewish Times of September 16, 1994, lists the names of seventy 1995 campaign leaders of which perhaps two or three appear to have German Jewish names.

Data for giving to the Associated Jewish Charities is explicit. In 1936, sixty-eight separate gifts of over $1,000 each were pledged to the Associated. The three largest gifts were substantially higher than the other sixty-five and two of the three were given by Eastern European Jews. Of the total pledges over $1,000 that year, eleven came from Eastern European Jews and fifty-seven from German Jews.

The 1996 Associated: Jewish Community Federation of Baltimore Campaign Honor Role indicates a stunning reversal of those that gave over a period of seventy-five years. The annual report lists twenty-nine gifts of over $100,000 from Baltimore Jewish families and foundations; only four of these pledges are from persons recognized by their names as being German Jews. Present Baltimore's Eastern European Jewish giving compared to that of the German Jews could mean they as a group are more charitable, but this is a poor supposition as it is likely their level of giving indicates a measure of wealth. Of the twenty-nine $100,000 pledges, only four came from families engaged in traditional Jewish businesses such as retailing, garment manufacturing, and dry goods wholesaling.

3   *A recent publication predicts that in the next fifty years, "The Tribe of American Jews will be reduced as much as seventy-five percent." It says "The remaining will spend more time in their synagogues, vote for more conservative politicians, and worry less about anti-Semitism and Israel." Already, a quarter of all Jews in America are so detached from the group that their identification is primarily a matter of nostalgia. Another quarter identify mainly as a defense reaction to anti-Semitism that will tend to disappear from the core group as anti-Jewish sentiment subsides.*

4   *It is not unusual to see blonde haired, blue eyed Jewish children whose dark-eyed grandfather or great-grandfather migrated to America wearing payes that matched his heavy black beard. The author recently observed a Park School kindergarten class on a field trip. Park School was founded primarily by and for Jews and has retained a large Jewish enrollment. All of the class of perhaps 20 to 25 children had either blonde or light brown hair; several had blue eyes.*

APPENDIX

UNCOMMON THREADS

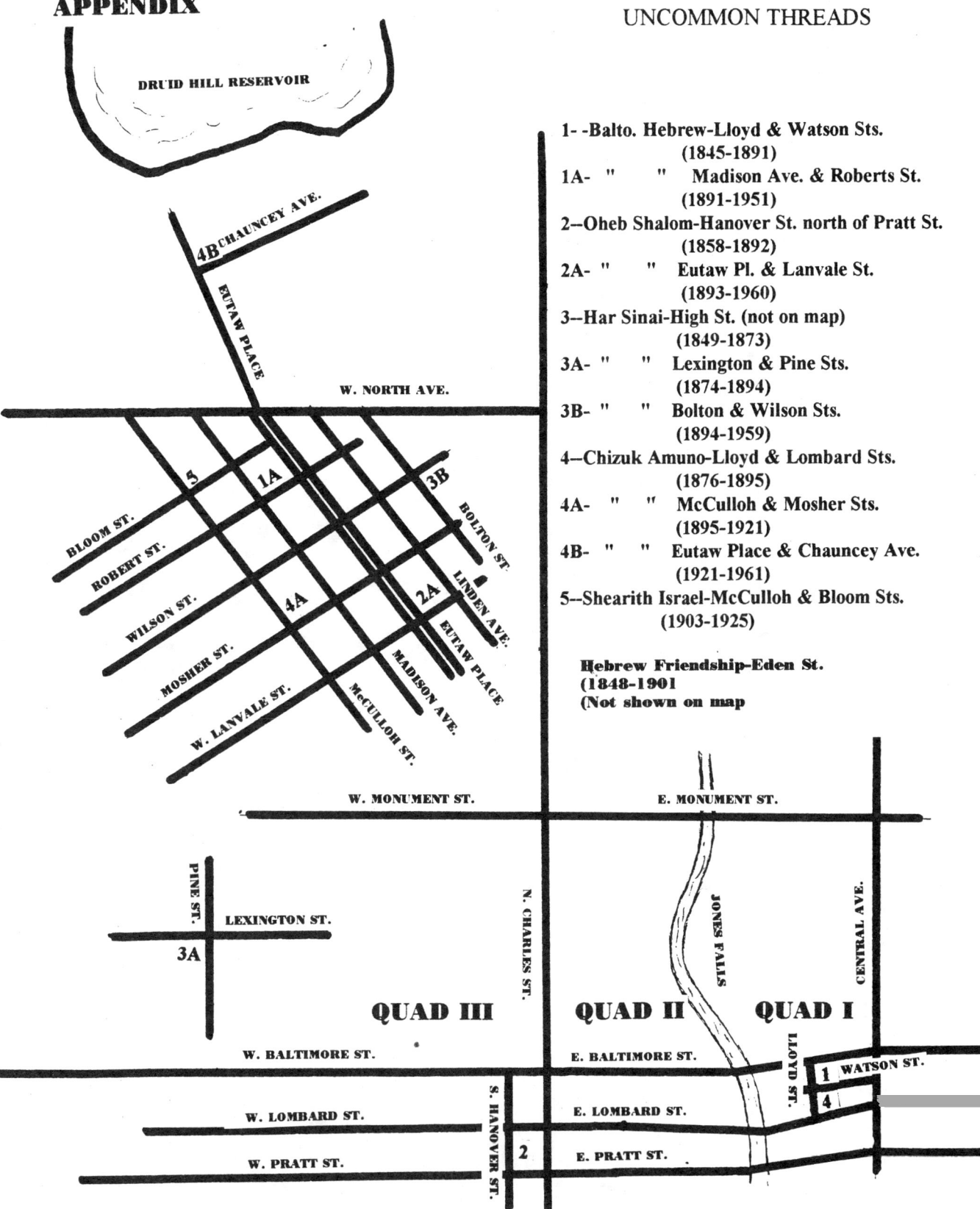

1--Balto. Hebrew-Lloyd & Watson Sts.
(1845-1891)
1A- " " Madison Ave. & Roberts St.
(1891-1951)
2--Oheb Shalom-Hanover St. north of Pratt St.
(1858-1892)
2A- " " Eutaw Pl. & Lanvale St.
(1893-1960)
3--Har Sinai-High St. (not on map)
(1849-1873)
3A- " " Lexington & Pine Sts.
(1874-1894)
3B- " " Bolton & Wilson Sts.
(1894-1959)
4--Chizuk Amuno-Lloyd & Lombard Sts.
(1876-1895)
4A- " " McCulloh & Mosher Sts.
(1895-1921)
4B- " " Eutaw Place & Chauncey Ave.
(1921-1961)
5--Shearith Israel-McCulloh & Bloom Sts.
(1903-1925)

Hebrew Friendship-Eden St.
(1848-1901
(Not shown on map

GLOSSARY

GERMAN GLOSSARY

Ashkenazi/Ashkenazim: Jews of medieval tradition and descent
Ausgespeilt: Played out; exhausted
Ausgelassen: Care free; high spirited
Besturzt: Mentally unbalanced
Brummel: Grumble
Der Wecker: The Awaker
Der Weiser: The Wise
Deutsche: German
Frau: Woman; wife
Fraulein: Young unmarried lady
Frikadellen: Cone-shaped ground meat ball
Gansebraten: Roast goose
Genug: Enough
Gemutlich: Comfortable; cozy
Grieben: Goose skin rendered crispy
Kartoffel Kloese: Potato dumpling with croutons in the center
Kristallnacht: Night of broken glass
Neulich: Recent
Nuremberg Laws: Nazi racist legislation, Sept.,1935"
Sauerbraten: Sour meat
Schnorrer: Door to door beggar
Shicker: Inebriated
Turnvereins: Tourner associations
Umbaschrien: Thankful for being lucky
Verien: Club; association

HEBREW GLOSSARY

Anshe: People of
Arba Canfot: Small friged 4 corner shawl worn by Orthodox Jews under their garments
Bar Mitzvah: At age 13, ceremony initiating a boy's entry into the Jewish community"
Bat Mitzvah: At age 13, ceremony initiating a girl's entry into the Jewish community"
Bet/Beth/Beit din: Jewish civil court of law
Bet ha-midrash/Bet midrash: Synagogue area for prayer and study
Bimah: Elevated platform in synagogue for the reading desk
B'Nai B'rith: Jewish fraternal organization
Bris/Brith/Berit milah: Circumcision ritual
Chabad: Wisdom; understanding; knowledge
Challafim: Ritual knife
Chanukah: Festival commemorating the re-dedication of the First Temple
Chazzin/Hazzan: Cantor or reader
Chassidic/Hasidic: A religious philosophy and movement
Cheder/Heder: Traditional Hebrew elementary school
Chevra/Hevra: Jewish burial society
Chevra/Hevra Kadisha: Holy brotherhood
Cholla: Braided ceremonial egg bread
Chuppah/Huppah: Marriage canopy
Dreidel: 4 sided spinning top with 4 Hebrew letters
Erev: Day before the Sabbath or holiday
Eruv: Area confine for Sabbath worshippers
Gemara: Discussions and comments on the Mishnah
Hadassah: Woman's Zionist Organization of America
Haganah: Israel defense agency
Halakhah: The ancient canon of Jewish law; rules of conduct
Hamidrash: (See bet ha-midrash)
Hanukah: (See Chanukah)
Hasidic: (See Chasidic)
Haskalah: Cultivation of the mind See maskilim)
Hazzan: (See Chazzin)
Heder: (See Cheder)
Hevra: (See Chevra)
Hora: Dance of the Zionist pioneer spirit
Hovevei Zion: Lovers of Zion
Huppah: (See Chuppah)
Israelites: Children of Israel; ancient Hebrews
Judaism: Living faith and spiritual way of the Jewish people
Kabbalah: Jewish mystical traditions and precepts
Kashrut: (See Kosher)
Ketubbah: Marriage contract
Kibbutz: A commune based on agriculture
Kiddush: Sanctification traditional benediction ushering in the Sabbath and festivals
Kitel: Burial shroud; white rove worn by rabbis and cantors at Rosh Hashanah
Kosher: Food in accordance with rabbinic law
Loshen Kodesh: Holy tongue
Maskilim: The scholarly and enlightened (See Haskalah)
Matzoh/Matzoth/Matzot: Unleavened bread
Melamed: Teacher
Menorah: Seven branched ritual candelabrum
Midrash: Legendary explanation and understanding of Torah
Mikvah: Ritual bath for purification and cleanliness
Minhag: Well-established local prayer rites
Minyan: Required number present for Jewish worship service
Mishnah: First part of the written Talmud
Mitzvah: Commandment; good deed
Mogen David: Star of David
Mohel: Certified Orthodox ritual circumciser
Palestine: Country of Israel before 1948
Pesach: Passover
Phylactories: See Tiffilah)
Poalei Zion: Workers of Zion; The Labor Zionist party
Rabbi: Teacher; spiritual leader; interpreter of Jewish Law
Rosh Hashonnah/Hashanah: Jewish New Year
Schmurrah: Guarded

UNCOMMON THREADS

Schnorrer: Beggar, generally door-to-door"
Schochet/Schochetim/Schohet: Ritual slaughterer of animals
Schulchan/Shulchan Aruch: Code of Jewish Law
Seder: Feast of Passover
Sefer Torah: Torah scribed by a pious and learned soferim
Shabbas/Shabbot: Jewish day of rest; the Sabbath
Shema: ""Hear"", the first word of the Jewish Shemah prayer"
Shiva: Seven day period of mourning
Shmous: Things heard
Shoah: Holocaust
Sinai: Sacred mountain on which most Jews believe God gave the Ten Commandments to Moses
Soferim: Pious and learned scribe; authority on biblical texts
Sphard: Spain
Sukkah: Booth
Sukkot: The Feast of Tabernacles, the fall harvest festival"
Synagogue: House of Jewish worship, study and assembly"
Tallit/tallis: Prayer shawl worn for Orthodox Jews
Talmud: Written body of Jewish law interpreted from the Torah
Talmud Torah: Religious school
Tefillah/Tefflim: Black leather cubes worn by Orthodox Jews for morning prayers
Temple: Synagogue for all Reform and some Conservatives
Terefah/Traif: Non-kosher
Tikkum olam: Healing of the world
Torah/Sefer Torah: Scroll of the Law
Tzedakah: Charity expressed through righteousness
Tzorchei Tzibur: Responding to communal needs
Yarmulke: Head covering worn by Orthodox Jews
Yehudim: Jews
Yerusholaem: Jerusalem
Yeshiva: Highest institute of Jewish learning
Yom Kippur: Day of Atonement
Yom tov: Good day; good holiday
Zion: Ancient name for the land of Israel

RUSSIAN GLOSSARY

Borscht: Soup made primarily of beets
Pogrom: Organized massacre of Russian people, usually Jews"
Slivovitz: Plum brandy
Tsar/Tzar/Czar: Russian ruler
Uajido: Kewosj
Zverda David: Star of David

SPANISH GLOSSARY

Ladino: Jewish dialect; Judeo Spanish
Sephardim/Sephardic: Spanish-Portuguese Jews

YIDDISH GLOSSARY

Babushka: Triangular kerchief worn on the head
Bund: Eastern European Jewish social democratic workers' organization
Charedi/Haredi: Torah observant Jews
Fabrenta: Red hot
Frum: Extremely religious
Galitzianer: Galician
Glatt: Kosher meat from animals showing no sign of ill health
Goy: Non-Jew
Hasid: Devout
Hazir: Pig
Kapote: Long black caftan
Katerinka: Sewing machine head
Klezmorim: Musician
Kreplach: Dumpling
Landsmanshaften: Compatriot Jews from same European area
Latke: Potato pancake cooked in oil
Litvac: Lithuanian
Lokshen: Noodles
Lubavitcher: Hasidic sect
Mama Loshen: Mother tongue
Mavin: Expert
Mashgeach/Mashgichim: Kosher overseer
Medina: Land; domain
Mushullach: Agent to collect funds for accredited Jewish institutions
Mithnagdin: Opponents to Hasidism
Nusach: Version
Oysesn: To dine out
Pushke: Charity box, usually made of tin"
Rebbe: Hasidic rabbi
Rebitsen: Wife of an Orthodox rabbi
Schmooze: (See Hebrew Shmous/Yiddish Shmues)
Shaygetz: Non-Jewish male; literally, male abomination"
Sheitel: Woman's wig
Shiksa: Non-Jewish female; literally, female abomination"
Shlemiel: Awkward; inept
Shmues: Conversation
Shommer Shabbat: Sabbath observer
Shtadlanuth: Pleading with an acquaintance
Shtetl: Small Eastern European town or settlement
Shtreimel: Round fur hat
Shul/schul: Synagogue; school
Tichel: Woman's head scarf
Tzaddick: Righteous man
Vaad Hakashrus: Koshser certification organization
Vaad HaRabonim: Rabbincal Council
Yahudim: Jewish
Yiddishkeit: Eastern European Jewish verve
Yikkes: High family pedigree or status

BIBLIOGRAPHY

PUBLISHED SOURCES, Books-Periodicals-Pamphlets

Dr. Moses Aberbach, SOLOMON BAROWAY, Farmer, Writer, Zionist and Early Baltimore Social Worker.
    Baltimore, The Jewish Historical Society of Md.-The Jewish Heritage Center 1990.

Michael J. Anuta, SHIPS OF OUR ANCESTORS.
    Menominee, Michigan: Ships of Our Ancestors, Inc., 1983.

Eli Barnavi, (Editor) A HISTORICAL ATLAS OF THE JEWISH PEOPLE, From the Time of the Patriarchs to the Present.

Dr. Charles S. Bernheimer, THE RUSSIAN JEWS IN THE UNITED STATES
    Philadelphia: The John C. Winston Co., 1905.

Stephen Birmingham, THE REST OF US, The Rise of America's Eastern European Jews.
    Boston-Toronto: Little, Brown & Co., 1984.

Isadore Blum, THE JEWS OF BALTIMORE, An Historical Summary of their Progress and Status as Citizens of Baltimore from Early Days to the Year 1910.
    Baltimore-Washington: Historical Review Publishing Company, 1910.

Dr. Frank W. Brecher, RELUCTANT ALLY, United States Foreign Policy toward the Jews from Wilson to Roosevelt.
    New York-Westport-London: Greenwood Press, 1993.

Alexander C. Brown, STEAM PACKETS ON THE CHESAPEAKE, History of the Old Bay Line.
    Cambridge, Md. Cornell Maritime Press Inc., 1961.

Robert H. Burgess & H. Graham Wood, STEAMBOATS OUT OF BALTIMORE
    Md. Tidewater Publishers, 1968.

Abraham Cahan, THE RISE OF DAVID LEVINSKY.
    New York: Harper & Brothers, 1917.

Louis F. Cahn, THE HISTORY OF OHEB SHALOM (1853-1953).
    Baltimore. Oheb Shalom Congregation. 1953

Abraham Cohen, EVERY MAN'S TALMUD.
    New York,: Schocken Books, 1975.

Louis F. Cahn, MAN'S CONCERN FOR MAN, The First Fifty Years of the Associated Jewish Charities and Welfare Fund of Baltimore.
    Baltimore: Associated Jewish Charities and Welfare Fund, 1970.

Louis F. Cahn, RESTORATION OF THE LLOYD ST. SYNAGOGUE.
    Baltimore: The Jewish Historical Society of Maryland, October, 1973.

Louis F. Cahn, BALTIMORE JEWS AND BALTIMORE HORSES.
    Baltimore: The Jewish Historical Society of Maryland, not dated.

Rod Chernow, THE WARBURGS, The Twentieth Century Odyssey of a Remarkable Jewish Family.
    New York: Random House, 1993.

Dr. John B. Colletta, THEY CAME IN SHIPS.
    Salt Lake City; Ancestry, 1989.

Drs. Neil M. Cowan & Ruth Schwartz Cowan, OUR PARENTS LIVES, The Americanization of Eastern European Jews.
    New York: Basic Books Division of Harper Collins, 1989.

Dieter Cunz, THE MARYLAND GERMANS.
    Princeton N.J.: Princeton University Press, 1948.

Malka Drucker, THE FAMILY TREASURY OF JEWISH HOLIDAYS.
    Boston-New York-London-Toronto: Little, Brown & Co., 1994.

Ben M Edidin, JEWISH COMMUNITY LIFE IN AMERICA.
    New York: Hebrew Publishing Co., 1947.

Robert Ernst, IMMIGRANTS LIFE IN NEW YORK, 1825-1863.
    Port Washington, N.Y.: Ira J. Friedman Inc., 1965.

Eli N. Evans, THE PROVINCIALS, A Personal History of Jews in the South.
    New York: Athenaeum, 1976.

Dr. Isaac M. Fein, THE MAKING OF AN AMERICAN JEWISH COMMUNITY, The History of Baltimore Jewry from 1773 to 1920.
    Philadelphia: The Jewish Publication Society of America, 1971.

UNCOMMON THREADS

Dr. Henry L. Feingold, (General Editor) THE JEWISH PEOPLE IN AMERICA.
  Baltimore & London, The Johns Hopkins University Press & The American Jewish Historical Society, Waltham, Mass.
    Volume I, A TIME FOR PLANNING, Volume IV, A TIME FOR SEARCHING.
      Dr. Eli Faber, The First Migration (1654-1820). Dr. Henry L. Feingold, Entering the Mainstream (1920-1945).
    Volume II, A TIME FOR GATHERING, Volume V, A TIME FOR HEALING.
      Dr. Hasia R. Diner, The Second Migration ((1820-1880). Dr. Edward S. Shapiro, American Jewry since World War II.
    Volume III, A TIME FOR BUILDING.

Dr. Harry Friedenwald, LIFES, LETTERS & ADDRESSES, of AARON FRIEDENWALD, M.D.
  Baltimore: The Lord Baltimore Press 1906.

Abraham D. Glushakow, TERCENTENARY JEWISH BOOK (1634-1934).
  Baltimore: 1934.

Abraham D. Glushakow, PICTORIAL HISTORY OF MARYLAND JEWRY.
  Baltimore: Jewish Voice Pub. Co., 1955.

Abraham D. Glushakow, MARYLAND BICENTENNIAL JEWISH BOOK.
  Baltimore: Jewish Voice Pub. Co., 1975.

Harry Golden, ONLY IN AMERICA.
  Cleveland-New York: The World Publishing Co., 1944.

Eric L. Goldstein, THE JEWS OF COLONIAL MARYLAND, 1656-1776 (Oxford Center for Postgraduate Hebrew Studies, 1991).
  Baltimore: Jewish Heritage Center, Jewish Historical Society of Maryland, 1993.

Dr. Suzanne Ellory Greene, AN ILLUSTRATED HISTORY OF Baltimore.
  Woodland Hills, California: Windsor Publications Inc., 1980.

Rose Greenberg, THE CHRONICLES OF BALTIMORE HEBREW CONGREGATION, (1830-1975).
  Baltimore: Baltimore Hebrew Congregation, 1976.

Benjamin H. Hartogensis, Esq., THE SEPHARDIC CONGREGATION OF Baltimore.
  American Jewish Historical Society, # 2, 1915.

Leon Harris, MERCHANT PRINCES, An Intimate History of Jewish Families who Built Great Department Stores.
  New York-Hagerstown-San Francisco-London: Harper & Row, 1979.

Dr. Uri P. Herscher, THE EAST EUROPEAN JEW IN AMERICA (Editor) (1881-1891).
  Cincinnati: American Jewish Archives, Hebrew Union College, Jewish Institute of Religion, April, 1981.
    WORKER ON THE LAND   THE GREATFUL THREAT
      Harris Rubin   Jeanette W, Bernstein
    CHAPTERS FROM MY LIFE   MY OWN STORY
      Alexander Harkavy   Bessie Schwartz
    LETTERS OF AN IMMIGRANT.
      Isaac Don Levine

Dr. John Higham, SEND THESE TO ME, Immigrants in Urban America.
  Baltimore-London: The Johns Hopkins University Press, 1984.

Dr. John Higham, STRANGERS IN THE LAND, Patterns of American Nativism, 1860-1925.
  New Brunswick-London: Rutgers University Press, 1988.

Gertrud Hirschler, "TO LOVE MERCY."
  Jewish Historical Society, Unpublished, not dated.

George W. Howard, THE MONUMENTAL CITY, Its Past History and Present Resources.
  Baltimore: J.D. Ehlers & Co., 1873.

Irving Howe, WORLD OF OUR FATHERS, The Journey of the East European Jews to America and the Life they found and Made.
  New York: Simon & Schuster, 1976.

Franz Hubman, THE JEWISH FAMILY ALBUM, The Life of a People in Photographs.
  Boston-Toronto: Little, Brown & Co. 1974.

Philip Kahn, Jr., A STITCH IN TIME, The Four Seasons of Baltimore's Needle Trades.
  Baltimore: Maryland Historical Society, 1989.

Abraham J. Karp, THE JEWS IN AMERICA, A Treasury of Art and Literature. 1994, Hugh Lauter Levin Associates Ltd.

Deborah Karp, HEROES OF AMERICAN JEWISH HISTORY.
  New York: KTAV Publishing House Inc. Anti-Defamation League of B'Nai Brith, 1972.

Jacques Kelly, BYGONE BALTIMORE.
  Norfolk: Donning Co., 1982.

Roland Klemig, JEWS IN GERMANY, Under Prussian Rule.
> Berlin: Bildarchiv Preussischer Kulturbesitz, 1984.

Robert Kotlowitz, HIS MASTER'S VOICE.
> New York: Alfred A Knopf, 1992.

Alexandra Lee Levin, VISION.
> Philadelphia: The Jewish Publication Society of America, 1964.

Alexandra Lee Levin, THE SZOLDS OF LOMBARD STREET.
> Philadelphia: The Jewish Publication Society of America, 1960.

Lester Levy, JACOB EPSTEIN.
> Baltimore: Maran Press, 1978.

Jennifer M. Lowe, (Editor) JEWISH JUSTICES OF THE SUPREME COURT REVISITED.
> Washington, D.C.: The Supreme Court Historical Society, 1994.

Rabbi Lee J. & Elma Ehrlich Levinger, THE STORY OF THE JEW.
> New York: Behrman House Inc., 1928.

Kay MacIntosh, (Editor) The Baltimore JEWISH TIMES, 75th Anniversary Special Edition (1919-1995).
> Baltimore: 1995.

Harold R. Manakee, MARYLAND IN THE CIVIL WAR.
> Baltimore: Maryland Historical Society, 1961.

Dr. Sherry H. Olson, Baltimore, The Building of an American City.
> Baltimore: The Johns Hopkins University Press, 1980.

Rabbi Albert Plotkin, RABBI ALBERT PLOTKIN D.H.L.,D.D.,L.L.B.
> Tempe: Arizona State U. Libraries, 1992.

Earl Pruce, SYNAGOGUES, TEMPLES, and CONGREGATIONS, Past and Present.
> Baltimore: Jewish Historical Society of Maryland, 1993.

Lizette Woodworth Reese, A VICTORIAN VILLAGE, Reminiscences of Other Days.
> New York: Farrar & Rinehart, 1929.

Mary Helen & Rosenbaum Stanley Ned Rosenbaum, CELEBRATING OUR DIFFERENCES, Living two faiths in one Marriage.
> Boston, Kentucky: Ragged Edge Press and Black Bear Productions, 1994.

Rabbi William Rosenau, A BRIEF HISTORY OF CONGREGATION OHEB SHALOM.
> Baltimore: Baltimore Jewish Times Publishing Co., 1903.

Rabbi William Rosenau, HISTORY OF CONGREGATION OHEB SHALOM.
> Baltimore: Baltimore Jewish Times Publication Co., 1928.

Rabbi William Rosenau, JEWISH CEREMONIAL INSTITUTIONS AND CUSTOMS.
> New York: Bloch Pub. Co. Inc., 1929.

Leo Rosten, THE JOYS OF YIDDISH.
> New York, Toronto, London, Sydney: McGraw Hill Book Co., 1968.

Norman Rucker, THE PORT, Pride of Baltimore.
> Baltimore: 1982.

Ronald Sanders, SHORES OF REFUGE, A Hundred Years of Jewish Emigration.
> New York: Henry Holt & Co., 1988.

J. Thomas Scharf, THE CHRONICLES OF BALTIMORE, Complete History of Baltimore Town and Baltimore City.
> Baltimore: Turnbull Brothers, 1874.

J. Thomas Scharf, HISTORY OF BALTIMORE CITY & COUNTY.
> Baltimore: Regional Publishing Co., 1971.

John C. Schmidt, WIN-PLACE-SHOW.
> Baltimore: G.W.C. Whiting School of Engineering, The Johns Hopkins University, 1988.

Jean Thompson Sharpless, THE PARK SCHOOL OF BALTIMORE, The first Seventy-five Years.
> Baltimore: June, 1988.

Yuri Suhl, AN ALBUM OF THE JEWS IN AMERICA.
> New York: Franklin Watts, Inc., 1972.

Rabbi Abraham Shusterman, THE LEGACY OF A LIBERAL.
> Baltimore: Har Sinai Congregation, 1967.

Rabbi Joseph Telushkin, JEWISH HUMOR, What the Best Jewish Jokes say About the Jews.
> New York, William Morrow and Co., Inc. 1992.

UNCOMMON THREADS

Robert L. Weinberg, THE MURDER OF A GRAVEYARD.
    Baltimore: The Jewish Historical Society of Maryland, 1990.

Robert L. Weinberg THE SUBURBAN CLUB OF BALTIMORE COUNTY, A History from 1900 to the present.
    Baltimore: The Suburban Club of Baltimore County, 1995.

Maralyn A. Wellauer, GERMAN IMMIGRATION TO AMERICA IN THE NINETEENTH CENTURY.
    Milwaukee: Roots International, 1985.

Harold A. Williams, Baltimore AFIRE.
    Baltimore, Md. Schneidereith & Sons, 1954.

Jane Bromley Wilson, THE VERY QUIET BALTIMOREANS, A Guide to the Historic Cemeteries and Burial Sites of Baltimore,
    Shippensburg, Pa. White Mane Publishing Co., 1991.

Rabbi Herbert S. Rutman, RABBI DAVID EINHORN.
    Baltimore, Md. The Jewish Historical Society of Maryland, 1979

70 Years NORTH GERMAN LLOYD, BREMEN 1857-1927.
    Berlin: Atlantic Verlag G.M.B.H., circa 1928.

ENCYCLOPEDIAS

AMERICAN JEWISH YEARBOOK
    Philadelphia: The Jewish Publication Society of America 1902-1903.

ENCYCLOPEDIA BRITANNICA
    Chicago-London-Toronto-Geneva-Sydney-Tokyo-Manila-Paris-Auckland-Madrid-Rome-Seoul, 1966-1993.

THE NEW JEWISH ENCYCLOPEDIA
    New York: Behrman House Inc., 1962.

THE ENCYCLOPEDIA OF JUDAISM
    Jerusalem: The Jerusalem Publishing House Ltd., 1989.

THE READERS COMPANION TO AMERICAN HISTORY
    Boston: Houghton Mifflin Co., 1991.

ORAL HISTORIES

THE ASSOCIATED: Jewish Community Federation of Baltimore

Louis Fox	1986
Richard Lansburgh	1990
Eleanor Kohn Levy	1991
Jerold C. Hoffberger	1991
Marie L. Rothschild	1991
Leon Sachs	1991
Mendel (Mickey) Silverman	1984
Beatrice K. Stern	1985

The Jewish Historical Society of Maryland

Seymour Attman	1982
Louis F. Cahn	1977
Gerson Eisenberg	1978
Arthur J. Gutman	1992
Emanuel Hettleman	1980
Joseph R. Hirschmann	1979

INTERVIEWS

Marie Lowenstein Rothschild (Mrs. Stanford Z. Rothschild), November, 1992.

Eleanor Kohn Levy (Mrs. Lester Levy), November, 1992.

Naomi Kellman, Historian, The Associated: Jewish Community Federation of Baltimore, November, 1994.

LECTURES & PAPERS

Dr. Moses Aberbach. (Lecture) THE EARLY GERMAN JEWS OF Baltimore.
    The Society for the History of the German Jews in Maryland, Feb. 10, 1970.

Louis F. Cahn. (Lecture) A TREE GREW IN LLOYD STREET,
    Dedication ceremonies of the Lloyd Street Synagogue.
    The Jewish Historical Society of Maryland, November 8, 1964.

Louis F. Cahn. (Paper) Baltimore JEWISH HISTORY FOR SCHOOL GROUPS VISITING THE LLOYD STREET SYNAGOGUE,
    1965.

Dr. Ruth Schwartz Cowan. (Lecture) OUR PARENTS' LIVES, The Americanization of Eastern European Jews.
  The Jewish Historical Society of Maryland, November 15, 1992.
Dr. Hasia R. Diner. (Lecture) A LEGACY OF TOLERANCE, Milestone in Maryland History.
  Har Sinai Congregation, Baltimore: 150th Anniversary Program, Nov. 14, 1991.
Dr. Hasia R. Diner. (Lecture) A TIME FOR EVERY PURPOSE, The Jewish People in America, 1830-1900.
  The Jewish Historical Society of Maryland, Baltimore, October 11, 1992.
Leonard Fein. (Lecture) LOOKING BACKWARD, LOOKING FORWARD.
  150 Anniversary of the Lloyd Street Synagogue.
  The Jewish Historical Society of Maryland, Baltimore, October 29, 1995
Bernard Fishman (Lecture) THE SYNAGOGUES OF OLD BALTIMORE, What They Were and What They Are.
  Baltimore Hebrew Congregation, March 14, 1955.
Dr. Neil Gilman. (Lecture) CONSERVATIVE JUDAISM, The Problem of Tradition and Change
  The Baltimore Hebrew University, October 23, 1994.
Dr. Samuel Heilman. (Lecture) DEFENDERS OF THE FAITH, Inside Ultra Orthodox Jewry,
  Adult Institute of Jewish Studies, November 2, 1993.
Wilbur Harvey Hunter, Jr. (Lecture) Annual Meeting of the Jewish Historical Society of
  Maryland, May 26, 1963.
Dr. Leon Jick .(Lecture) REFORMING REFORM JUDAISM, The Problem of Tradition and Change.
  Baltimore Hebrew University, October 23, 1994.
Dr. Jenna Weissman Joselit. (Lecture) AMERICA'S JEWISH JEWS, THEN AND NOW, Orthodoxy in Historical Prospective.
  Baltimore Hebrew University, October 23, 1994.
Philip Kahn, Jr. Baltimore'S JEWISH HERITAGE.
  Resident Associate Program tour.
  Smithsonian Institution, Washington, D.C., August 17, 1986.
Barry A. Kessler. (Lecture) CORNED BEEF WITH BEDLAM ON THE SIDE, The Jewish Delicatessen in Baltimore.
  Baltimore Hebrew Congregation, April 4, 1995.
  Lester S. Levy.(Lecture) Jewish Historical Society, May, 1965.
Rabbi Mark Loeb. (Lecture) GERMANY AND THE JEWS, A Tortured Relationship.
  Adult Institute of Jewish Studies. October 19-26: November 2-9-16, 1993.
Rabbi Mark Lobe. (Lecture) A LIFE IN GHETTOES.
  Adult Institute of Jewish Studies. October 18-25, November 1-8-15, 1994.
Rabbi Mark Lobe. (Lectures) THE JACK PEARLSTONE INSTITUTE FOR LIVING JUDAISM.
  October 31, December 5, 1994; January 9, February 6, 1995.
Rabbi Joel Mishkin. (Lectures) THE WORLD OF OUR FATHERS AND OUR MOTHERS.
  Adult Institute of Jewish Studies, October 19-26; November 2-9-26, 1993.
Avrum K. Rifman, Esq.(Lecture) Baltimore AS A GATEWAY CITY, Centennial of Eastern Jewish Immigration 1882-1982.
  Jewish Community Center, Washington, D.C., May 16, 1982.
Dr. Marsha Rosenblit. (Lecture) THE STRUGGLE TO MODERNIZE JUDAISM, Was Baltimore Unique?
  Baltimore Hebrew Congregation, March 10, 1995.
Dr. Marsha Rosenblit. (Lecture) GERMAN JEWS AND RUSSIAN JEWS, The creation of The Baltimore Jewish Community.
  Baltimore Hebrew Congregation, March 11, 1955.
Dr. Marsha Rosenblit. (Lecture) ARE JEWS IN BALTIMORE MORE JEWISH THAN OTHER AMERICAN JEWS TODAY?
  Baltimore Hebrew Congregation, March 12, 1995.
Gilbert Sandler (lecture). THE HISTORY OF BALTIMORE JEWISH NEIGHBORHOODS, A Northwest Passage Through the Years.
  Baltimore Hebrew Congregation, March 28, 1995
Rabbi Ira Schiffer. (Lecture) A TASTE OF TALMUD, An Introduction to the Time and Texts of Rabbinic Judaism.
  Adult Institute of Jewish Studies. October 18-25, November 1-8-15, 1994.
Rabbi Alexander M. Schindler. (Lecture) THE REFORM JEW, Values, Practices, Vision.
  61st General Assembly of the Union of American Jewish Congregations, Baltimore: November 2, 1991.
Albert Schumacher. (Speech) MAIDEN VOYAGE, S.S. BALTIMORE, NORTH GERMAN LLOYD STEAMSHIP CO.
  Baltimore-Bremen Line, March 26, 1868.
Alfred Strauss. (lecture) ROOTS OF REFORM AND BALTIMORE HEBREW CONGREGATION.
  Baltimore Hebrew Congregation, March 7, 1995

UNCOMMON THREADS

Henrietta Szold. (Lecture) "THE NIGHT SCHOOL OF THE HEBREW LITERARY SOCIETY.
   November 1889.

LETTERS
Marie Lowenstein Rothschild (Mrs. Stanford Z.) to Dr. Isaac M. Fein, February 21, 1969.
Bernhard Kahn in Baltimore to his mother in Germany, July 25, 1865.
Bernhard Kahn in Baltimore to his sister and brother-in-law in Germany, October 1, 1889.
Sherva Sandelman in Odessa to her sister in America, October 27, 1905.

UNPUBLISHED ARTICLES
Richard H. Kress. The Amity Club-The Woodholme Club

PUBLISHED SPECIALIZED ARTICLES
Arthur C. Abramson. URBAN ILLS RAVAGE BALTIMORE'S HOLOCAUST MEMORIAL.
   The Baltimore Sun, November 26, 1994.
Rafael Alvarez. ROVING RABBIS.
   The Baltimore Sun, March 12, 1987.
Rafael Alvarez. HAR SINAI CONGREGATION MAY MOVE TO OWINGS MILLS.
   The Baltimore Sun., January 12, 1995.
Rafael Alvarez IN THE SHELTER OF A JEWISH COVENANT.
   The Baltimore Sun, March 5, 1995.
Rafael Alvarez AT 75, SYNAGOGUE STILL CALLS BALTIMORE HOME.
   The Baltimore Sun, May 21, 1995.
Rafael Alvarez. HONORING HIS FATHER AND MOTHER.
   The Baltimore Sun, September 9, 1995.
Rafael Alvarez THE HAT OF MANHOOD.
   The Baltimore Sun, January 18, 1996.
Jay Apperson. WIFE MOLESTATION.
   The Baltimore Sun, June 8, 1993 & January 11, 1994.
Jay Apperson HAR SINAI SIGNS DEAL TO SELL LAND.
   The Baltimore Sun, January 22, 1996.
Benjamin S. Appleton. EARLY JEWISH SETTLERS IN BALTIMORE.
Liz Atwood. JEWS IN MARYLAND.
   Maryland Magazine, Summer 1993.
Paul Benson. END OF THE TUNNEL.
   Baltimore Jewish Times, December 30, 1994.
Paul Benson. DOWN TO THE WIRE.
   Baltimore Jewish Times, January 20, 1995
Paul Benson. ON GAUCHER DISEASE.
   Baltimore Jewish Times, February 10, 1995.
Paul Benson. COMING OF AGE.
   Baltimore Jewish Times, March 18, 1994.
Paul Benson. DEAL OF THE DOME.
   Baltimore Jewish Times, October 7, 1994.
Paul Benson. UDDER PANIC.
   Baltimore Jewish Times, August 26, 1994.
Paul Benson. END OF THE TUNNEL.
   Baltimore Jewish Times, December 30, 1994.
Paul Benson. TAKING CENTER COURT.
   Baltimore Jewish Times, February 10, 1995.
Paul Benson. IT INSURES THE SCHOOL CAN CONTINUE.
   Baltimore Jewish Times, May 19, 1995.

Irwin M. Beret. THE EAST EUROPEAN JEWISH IMMIGRANT IN AMERICA; An Index to the 1900 Baltimore Census.
    Maryland Historical Magazine, Fall, 1985.
Elizabeth Kessin Berman. THREADS OF LIFE CATALOGUE, Overcoming the Conflicts between Jews Employers and Jewish Workers in Baltimore's Garment Workers.
    April 30, 1991-January 26, 1992.
James Beser. A HISTORY LESSON.
    Baltimore Jewish Times, December 29, 1995.
Rabbi Marcel Blitz. KASHRUT POLICY IS RIDICULOUS.
    Baltimore Jewish Times, February 3, 1995
James Bock. CHEAPER LIVING: STRONG COMMUNITY LURE ORTHODOX JEWS.
    The Baltimore Sun, September 8, 1991.
Judith Bolton-Fasman. IMMIGRATION AND ASYLUM IN AMERICA.
    Congress Monthly, February/March, 1994.
Lee Boolean. OLD COURT ROAD.
    The Baltimore Sun, December 18-19, 1972.
Susan Brafman. CHEVRA AHAVAS CHESED, Inc.
    From book by Gertrude Hirschler, Jewish Historical Society Vertical file, not dated.
William Braiterman. THE JEWISH LEGION OF WORLD WAR I.
    The Baltimore Sun Magazine, April 23, 1967.
James H. Bready. MARYLAND RYE: A Whiskey the Nations Long Fancied-But Now Has Let Vanish.
    Maryland Historical Magazine, Winter, 1990.
David Briggs. INTERFAITH FAMILIES MUST CHOOSE ONE RELIGION FOR KIDS.
    The Baltimore Sun November 27, 1995.
Martha Bristow FAMILY TO.SEEK HOME IN ANCIENT CULTURE OF ISRAEL.
    Baltimore Messenger, August 7, 1996.
Lynn Buhlmahn. EARLY WARNING OF BIRTH DEFECTS.
    The Baltimore Sun, November 23, 1983.
Henry G. Burke. MY MEMORIES OF THE YIDDISH THEATER.
    Generations: the Jewish Historical Society of Md., December, 1979.
Lawrence Bush. THE GOOD NEWS AND BAD NEWS ABOUT JEWS AND MONEY.
    Reform Judaism Spring 1994.
Larry Carson AN INSPECTOR CALLS.
    The Baltimore Sun, November 28, 1995.
Larry Carson. TALMUDICAL ACADEMY OF BALTIMORE.
    The Baltimore Sun, May 12-June 12-July 16, 1993.
Avraham Cohen. STRINGS ATTACHED.
    Baltimore Jewish Times, December 23, 1994.
David Conn. YAKETY YAK.
    Baltimore Jewish Times, June 9, 1995.
David Conn SOUL SEARCHING.
    Baltimore Jewish Times, March 15, 1996.
David Conn 75 AND COUNTING.
    Baltimore Jewish Times, June 22, 1996
David Conn SHORT OF GREEN.
    Baltimore Jewish times, August 9, 1886.
Helen Bond Crane. EUTAW PLACE IN ITS FINEST DAYS.
    The Baltimore Sun, August 12, 1956.
Mary Irene Cupinger. Baltimore HAS A COLORFUL OLD WORLD MARKET.
    The Baltimore Sun, April 13, 1924.
JoAnna Daemmrich. PROFANED HOLOCAUST MEMORIAL TO BE RAZED.
    The Baltimore Sun, November 28, 1995.
Douglas Danoff. A SIGN UPON THY ARM.
    Forward, October 20, 1995.
Lloyd R. Dennis. LOMBARD STREET STORES OFFER OLD WORLD VARIETY.

UNCOMMON THREADS

    The Baltimore Sun, August 2, 1964.
Lyle Denniston. KOSHER.
    The Baltimore Sun, February 23, 1993.
Lyle Denniston. BOY SCOUTS-SUPREME COURT.
    The Baltimore Sun, December 7, 1993.
James D. Diltz. THE BLOCK; NOT WHAT IT USED TO BE.
    The Baltimore Sun, February 1, 1994.
Connie P. Dufner. HOLIDAY PARTYING FIT FOR A QUEEN.
    The Baltimore Sun, February 28, 1996.
Alan Doelp. THE NEIGHBORHOOD SPANS, POVERTY TO RICHES AREAS.
    The Baltimore Sun, February 14, 1972.
Patrick Dunne & Charles L. Mackie. BREAD UPON THE WATER.
    Historic Preservation Magazine, September/October, 1993.
Jorg Echternkamp. EMERGING ETHNICITY, The German Experience in Ante-bellum Baltimore.
    Maryland Historical Magazine, Spring, 1991.
Mat Edelson. THE BIG BIOTECH GAMBLE.
    Baltimore Magazine, December, 1994.
Daniel J. Elazar. REORGANIZING AMERICAN JEWRY.
    Congress Monthly, February/March, 1994.
Daniel J. Elazar. THE PEACE PROCESS & THE JEWISHNESS OF THE JEWISH STATE.
    Congress Monthly, November/December, 1994.
Patrick Ercolano. AVALON.
    The Evening Sun, October 3, 1991.
Robert A. Erlandson. YAAZOR.
    The Baltimore Sun, December 1, 1991.
Alan H. Feiler. WANDERING ISRAELITES.
    Baltimore Jewish Times, March 11, 1994.
Alan H. Feiler. "IT'S A FREE COUNTRY".
    Baltimore Jewish Times, December 2, 1994.
Dr. Isaac M. Fein. Baltimore JEWS DURING THE CIVIL WAR.
    American Jewish Historical Quarterly, December, 1961.
Dr. Isaac M. Fein. MARYLAND JEWISH HISTORY, Dreams and Realities, Baltimore Jewry at the end of the NINETEENTH century.
    Jewish Historical Society, of Md., May, 1963.
Bernard Fishman. THREADS OF LIFE, Exhibit Catalogue Introduction.
    Jewish Historical Society of Md., April 30, 1991-January 26, 1992.
David Folkenflick. JEWISH SCHOOL WITH A MISSION.
    The Baltimore Sun, December 3, 1995.
Gail Forman. CHARTING MELTING-POT EFFECTS ON JEWISH FOOD IN AMERICA.
    The Baltimore Sun, February, 23, 1994.
Elyssa Gabray. PINS AND NEEDLES.
    Baltimore Jewish Times, April 26, 1991.
Estelle Gilson. ON SCHINDLER'S LIST.
    Congress, Monthly, American Jewish Congress, February/March, 1994
Abraham. D. Glushakow. JEWS AMONG THE EARLIEST SETTLERS IN MARYLAND. Maryland Bicentennial Jewish Book, Baltimore: Jewish Voice Publishing Co., 1975.
Lisa S. Goldberg. CLASSY DONATION.
    Baltimore Jewish Times, April 7, 1994.
Lisa S. Goldberg. A MATTER OF URGENCY.
    Baltimore Jewish Times, September 9, 1994.
Lisa S. Goldberg. MONUMENTAL TASK.
    Baltimore Jewish Times, September 30, 1994.
Lisa S. Goldberg. A SCHOOL GROWS IN PIKESVILLE.
    Baltimore Jewish Times, December 30, 1994.

Lisa S. Goldberg. SEARCHING FOR THE BOTTOM LINE.
>   Baltimore Jewish Times, December 30, 1994.

Lisa S. Goldberg & Paul Benson. DOES REFORM HAVE A FUTURE ON PARK HEIGHTS?
>   Baltimore Jewish Times, January 6, 1995.

Ira L. Goldman. THRUWAY REST STOP PROVIDES PLACE FOR JEWS TO PRAY.
>   The New York Times, July 25, 1993.

David Green. SMOOTH SAILING.
>   Baltimore Jewish Times, June 28, 1996.

Harry Greenstein. THE PASSING YEARS, 1922.
>   The Baltimore Sun, 1956.

Edward Gunts. SINAI HOSPITAL.
>   The Baltimore Sun, May 12, 1993.

Edward Gunts. MIKVAH, Its waters offer spiritual Cleansing.
>   The Baltimore Sun, January 21, 1993.

Edward Gunts. RENAISSANCE PLAZA.
>   The Baltimore Sun, December 9, 1993.

Edward Gunts. HISTORIC HAR SINAI VOTES TO SELL PROPERTY.
>   The Baltimore Sun, January 23, 1995.

Edward Gunts. CITY JEWISH CONGREGATION DEDICATES LIBRARY.
>   The Baltimore Sun, September 18, 1995.

Clyde Haberman. JERUSALEM'S STONES YIELD TO CHANGE.
>   The New York Times, January 8, 1995.

Constance L. Hays. STARTING OVER IN A NEW WORLD.
>   The New York Times, December 5, 1993.

Theodore W. Hendricks. RUSSIAN JEWS.
>   Generations, The Jewish Historical Society of Md., January, 1982.

Peter Hermann. DISPUTED POLICE TRANSFER.
>   The Baltimore Sun, August 10-12, 1994.

Ross Hetrick JEWISH NEWS GROUP SEEKS TO EXPAND.
>   The Baltimore Sun. March 6, 1995.

Robert Hilson Jr. TRASHED HOLOCAUST MEMORIAL.
>   The Baltimore Sun, October 25, 1995.

Arthur Hirsch. NICE WORD FALLS ON HARD TIMES.
>   The Baltimore Sun, January 10, 1996.

Rona S. Hirsch. CUSTOM-MADE SEDERS.
>   The Baltimore Jewish Times, March 29, 1996.

Simon L. Isaacson. HEBREW PAROCHIAL SCHOOLS. A Pictorial History of Maryland Jewry.
>   A. D. Glushakow, Baltimore: Jewish Voice Publishing Co., 1955.

Joan Jacobson. IMMIGRATION MUSEUM.
>   The Baltimore Sun, December 9, 1993.

Joan Jacobson. BAKERY MAKES MATZO ACCORDING TO JEWISH LAW.
>   The Baltimore Sun, March 14, 1994.

Joan Jacobson. BROTHERS KEEPERS; Jewish Volunteers Monitor Streets.
>   The Baltimore Sun, December 13, 1993.

Carleton Jones. A VOICE OF 20th CENTURY FAITH.
>   The Baltimore Sun, April 15, 1992.

Edgar L. Jones. JEWISH COLONY'S ROLE IN BALTIMORE.
>   The Jewish Historical Society of Md. vertical files, not dated.

Philip Kahn, Jr. AND SO THEY CAME AND SEW THEY DID.
>   Threads of Life Exhibit Catalogue.
>   The Jewish Historical Society of Md. April 30, 1991-January 26, 1992.

Chris Kaltenbach. A PAPER'S TRAIL.
>   The Baltimore Sun, July 31, 1994.

Donald Kann & Arthur Volk INTERPRETING THE HOLOCAUST MEMORIAL.

UNCOMMON THREADS

November, 1980.

Stanley Karnow. YEAR IN, YEAR OUT.
Smithsonian Magazine, Washington D.C., January, 1994.

Jacques Kelly. THREADS OF LIFE.
The Evening Sun, Balto., May 2, 1991.

Robert Kotlowitz. Baltimore BOY.
Harpers Magazine, December, 1965.

Terese Loeb Kreuzer. GETTING AT THE ESSENCE.
Baltimore Jewish Times, May 12, 1995.

Diane LaMorte. MAKING ITS MARK.
The Messenger, February 1, 1995.

Kathy Lally. RUSSIAN EXTREMIST LEADER.
The Baltimore Sun, December 15, 1993.

Kenneth Lasson. THE HEIGHTS OF POPULARITY.
The Baltimore Jewish Times, September 15, 1995.

Will Lester. TOSSING IN THE LONG WHITE GLOVE.
The Baltimore Sun, December 30, 1994.

Alexandra Lee Levin. A MEMORIAL FOR TWO WORTHY BALTIMOREANS.
Generations, Jewish Historical Society of Maryland, Summer, 1991.

Harry O. Levin, Esq. MARYLAND JEWS IN POLITICS. A Pictorial History of Maryland Jewry.
A. D. Glushakow, Baltimore: Jewish Voice Publishing Co., 1955.

Simon J. Levin.   Baltimore, The Cradle of Zionism. The Tercentenary Jewish Book (1634-1934)
Baltimore: A. D. Glushakow, 1934.

Henry W, Levy. THE ASSOCIATED JEWISH CHARITIES, Brief Historical Resume A Pictorial History of Maryland Jewry.
A. D. Glushakow, Baltimore: Jewish Voice Publishing Co., 1955.

Rabbi Mordechai Liebling. RECONSTRUCTIONIST.
Reform Judaism, Summer 1995.

G. Lipsitz, J. Kristall & B. L. Hecht. THE BOOK IS NEVER CLOSED.
Baltimore Jewish Times, Nov. 25, 1994.

Solomon Liss, Esq. PUBLIC BATHS.
The Baltimore Sun, not dated.

Yvonne Koelle Lyons (Editor) OVERTURE.
The Baltimore Symphony Orchestra, January 19-March 2, 1996.

Deidre Nerreau McCabe. HUSTLE, BUSTLE.
The Baltimore Sun, March 26, 1995.

Arthur J. Magida. BEYOND THE TRIPLE WHAMMY.
Baltimore Jewish Times, February 24, 1995.

Aron-Hirt Manheimer. WHY JEWS SHOULD SEEK CONVERTS.
Reform Judaism, Spring 1994.

Jeffry Marsh: IN GOD'S HANDS.
The Baltimore Jewish Times, May 10, 1996.

Simeon J. Maslin. "WHO ARE THE AUTHENTIC JEWS?"
Reform Judaism, SUMMER, 1996.

Maryln Maushard. DAR HONORS STUDENTS, Book on Flag.
The Baltimore Sun, May 6, 1994.

Lori Moody. MAH-JONGG'S ADHERENTS.
The Baltimore Sun, 1993.

Marcia Myers. JUDGE UPSETS KOSHER RULES.
The Baltimore Sun, October 2, & 9, 1993.

Marcia Myers. Baltimore KOSHER-FOOD LAW IS STRUCK DOWN ON APPEAL.
The Baltimore Sun, October 6, 1995.

Eric Nelson. FROM TRADITIONAL TO FUTURISTIC, JEWISH EXPO TOUTS IT ALL.
The Baltimore Sun, December 20, 1993.

Jacob Neusner. A JUDAISM OF MEMORY ALONE.

The Baltimore Sun, April 21, 1993.

Tom Nugent & Edward Olshaker, THINGS YOU ALWAYS WANTED TO KNOW ABOUT COUNTRY CLUBS AND MORE.

    The Baltimore Jewish Times, October 7, 1977.

Angela Winter Ney. BURYING PRAYER BOOKS.

    The Baltimore Sun, June 12, 1993.

Gene Oishi. SOVIET JEWS.

    The Baltimore Sun, June 4 & 5, 1993.

Michael Ollove. CORNED BEEF ROW.

    The Baltimore Sun, April 18,1986.

Michael Ollove. ORTHODOX JEWS FIND CONFLICT IN ENCLOSURE.

    The Baltimore Sun, August 5, 1994.

Judy Oppenheimer. WE OURSELVES,

    December 30, 1994.

Phyllis Orick NORTHWEST EXODUS.

    City Paper, June 5-11, 1987.

Barbara Pash. THE JOKES ON US.

    The Baltimore Jewish Times, April, 14, 1995.

Barbara Pash. SIGNS IF RESISTANCE.

    The Baltimore Jewish Times, July 14, 1995.

Rabbi David W. Pearlman. THE Y.M. & Y.W.H.A. The Tercentenary Jewish Book (1634-1934).

    Baltimore: A.D. Glushakow, 1975.

Antero Pietila. THE NECESSITIES OF A JEWISH HOME.

    The Baltimore Sun, January 28, 1995.

Scott Ponemone. A SEARCH FOR JEWISH CULTURE.

    The Baltimore Sun, July 9, 1995.

Chaim Potok. THE SUBTLE EFFORT TO RECONSTRUCT THE SHTETL.

    The New York Times, October 23, 1994.

Rabbi James Prosnit. RECONFIRM CONFIRMATION.

    Reform Judaism, Spring, 1994.

Richard & Elizabeth Pearson and David & Nancy Fierstein. RANDALLSTOWN JEWRY IS ALIVE AND WELL.

    Baltimore Jewish Times, February 7, 1986.

Isaac Rehert. Baltimore HEBREW CONGREGATION HOLOCAUST MEMORIAL.

    The Baltimore Sun, August 29, 1981.

Isaac Rehert. PIONEER CLUB.

    The Baltimore Sun, July 1, 1980.

Rabbi Schlomo Riskin. UNDERSTANDING THE SH'MA.

    Baltimore Jewish Times, July, 1994.

Rabbi Schlomo Riskin. USING ONE'S HEAD.

    Baltimore Jewish Times, October 14, 1994.

Rabbi Schlomo Riskin. WHAT IS AN INHERITANCE?

    Baltimore Jewish Times, December 30, 1994

Israel Rosen, M.D. BICENTENNIAL EXHIBIT, 1975.

    A Pictorial History of Baltimore Jewry.

    A. D. Glushakow, Baltimore: Voice Publishing Co., 1975.

Rabbi William Rosenau. JEWS IN EDUCATION.

    The Tercentenary Jewish Book (1634-1934).

    Baltimore: A.D. Glushakow, 1934.

Rabbi Samuel Rosenblatt. JEWS AT THE JOHNS HOPKINS UNIVERSITY.

    The Tercentenary Jewish Book (1634-1934).

    Baltimore: A. D. Glushakow, 1934.

Dr. Marsha L. Rosenblit. ORTHODOX AND REFORM IN THE NINETEENTH CENTURY BALTIMORE JEWISH COMMUNITY.

    Arts & Humanities Magazine, Fall, 1985.

UNCOMMON THREADS

Dr. Marsha L. Rosenblit. CHOOSING A SYNAGOGUE: THE SOCIAL COMPOSITION OF TWO GERMAN CONGREGATIONS IN NINETEENTH CENTURY BALTO.
   The American Synagogue, Fall, 1985.
Ira Rosenwaike. THE JEWS OF BALTIMORE, 1810.
   American Jewish Historical Quarterly, Volume LXIV, January, 1975.
Ira Rosenwaike. THE JEWS OF BALTIMORE, 1810-1820.
   American Jewish Historical Quarterly, Volume LXVII, December, 1977.
Ira Rosenwaike, Baltimore'S FIRST JEWISH CONGREGATION, FACT vs FICTION.
   American Jewish Historical Quarterly, Volume LXVI, November, 1976.
Ira Rosenwaike. Baltimore JEWRY, 1868.
   Baltimore Jewish Times, January 20, 1995.
Ira Rosenwaike. THE JEWS OF BALTIMORE, 1820-1830.
   American Jewish Historical Quarterly, Volume LXVI I, March, 1978.
Ira Rosenwaike. CHARACTERISTICS OF BALTIMORE'S JEWISH POPULATION IN A NINETEENTH CENTURY CENSUS.
   American Jewish Historical Quarterly, Volume 82, 1994.
Maryland Rowland. ITS TOUGH TO KEEP UP THE FAMILY.
   The New York Times, December 26, 1993.
Gilbert Sandler. SALUBRIOUS TURKISH BATHS.
   The Baltimore Sun, Date?
Gilbert Sandler. ISSAC DAVIDSON: A MAN, A SCHOOL, A LEGACY.
   Baltimore Jewish Times, July 26, 1996.
Henry Scarupa & Wm. L. Kendler. CHABAD.
   The Baltimore Sun Magazine, December 13, 1981.
Rabbi Ira A. Schiffer. REWARD AND PUNISHMENT.
   Baltimore Jewish Times, August 18, 1995.
Lisa Schiffren. JUDAISM'S CRISIS: "ASSIMILATION AND ITS DISCONTENTS"
   The Baltimore Sun, March 5, 1995.
Daniel Schifrin. PIKESVILLE MAKES THE GRADE.
   Baltimore Jewish Times, November 2, 1992.
Carl Schoettler. IN BULGARIA.
   The Baltimore Sun, July 30, 1994.
Carl Schoettler. FAITH IS PROOF ENOUGH.
   The Baltimore Sun, August 12, 1995.
Carl Schoettler. KLEZMER KICKS UP ITS HEELS AGAIN.
   The Baltimore Sun, December 21, 1995..
Laura Scism. JEWISH BALTIMORE.
   Baltimore News American Supplement.
   Jewish Historical Society of Maryland vertical file, not dated.
Elaine Seagal. I WANT TO STAY IN BUSINESS, I LIKE TO BE IN BUSINESS.
   The Smithsonian Magazine, April, 1994.
Herman Seidel M.D. CORNERSTONE OF LABOR ZIONISM, A Pictorial History of Maryland Jewry.
   A. D. Glushakow, Baltimore: Voice Publishing Co., 1955.
Rabbi Avi Shafran TAKING UMBRIDGE AT "ULTRA".
   The Baltimore Jewish Times, February 9, 1996.
Deborah Shapiro. CHERISHED AND REMEMBERED.
   The Baltimore Jewish Times, October 27, 1995.
Deborah Shapiro. MONUMENTAL ACHIEVEMENT.
   The Baltimore Jewish Times, November 24, 1995.
Edward S. Shapiro. JEWS BY CHOICE: ONLY IN AMERICA.
   Congress Monthly, May/June 1995.
Stephanie Shapiro. RUSSIAN LANGUAGE BROADCAST.
   The Baltimore Sun, December 9, 1993.
Kevin Smokler. DOME DIASPORA.

Dr. Leivy Smolar. BALTIMORE HEBREW UNIVERSITY.
>   The Scribe, Baltimore Hebrew University, February, 1988.

Lois K. Solomon. AWAY FOR THE HOLIDAY.
>   The Baltimore Jewish Times, November 17, 1995.

Frank P. L. Somerville HIDDEN VIOLENCE IN JEWISH MARRIAGES.
>   The Baltimore Sun, November 10, 1985.

Frank P. L. Somerville DEPARTING EDITOR SEEKS JEWISH UNITY.
>   The Baltimore Sun, May 4, 1993.

Frank P. L. Somerville. COMPLETION OF THE TORAH.
>   The Baltimore Sun, March 17, 1991.

Frank P. L. Somerville. MESSIANIC JEWISH CHRISTIAN RADIO SHOW.
>   The Baltimore Sun, June 8, 1993.

Frank P. L. Somerville. HOLIDAYS POSE DILEMMA FOR INTER-FAITH COUPLES.
>   The Baltimore Sun, December 9, 1993.

Frank P. L. Somerville. JOY AND SORROW.
>   The Baltimore Sun, August 2, 1993.

Frank P. L. Somerville. NER ISRAEL COLLEGE AT 60.
>   The Baltimore Sun, November 30, 1993.

Frank P. L Somerville. JEWS, CHRISTIANS RAISING MONEY SIDE BY SIDE.
>   The Baltimore Sun, December 17, 1993

Frank P. L. Somerville. PROSPERITY DOES NOT CONFLICT WITH ORTHODOXY.
>   The Baltimore Sun, November 10, 1985.

Joseph W. Spector. JEWS IN ECONOMIC LIFE OF BALTIMORE.
>   A Pictorial History of Maryland Jewry.
>   A.D. Glushakow, Baltimore: Voice Publishing Co., 1955.

Peter Steinfels. REFORM JUDAISM SEEKS CONVERTS.
>   The New York Times, October 14, 1993.

Ira Stoll. LIVING AS A TRIBE IN THE UNITED STATES.
>   Review 0f 1995 book JEWS AND THE NEW AMERICAN SCENE.
>   Martin Lipset and Earl Raa Forward, October 27, 1995.

Amy Stone. NOW SHOWING: SHTETL LIFE.
>   Baltimore Jewish times, October 28, 1994.

Christine Stutz. A PERFECT MARRIAGE.
>   Baltimore Jewish Times, January 19, 1996

Christine Stutz A SUMMER PLACE.
>   Baltimore Jewish Times, November 17, 1995,

Christine Stutz. BOYS TO MEN.
>   Baltimore Jewish Times, June 14, 1996.

Christine Stuts DR. ANN PULVER ON SCHIZOPHRENIA.
>   Baltimore Jewish Times, June 28, 1996

Christine Stutz CLASS ACT.
>   Baltimore Jewish Times, August 16, 1996

Rabbi Israel Tabak. WE ARE AN INSEPARABLE PART OF MARYLAND.
>   A Pictorial History of Maryland Jewry.
>   A. D. Glushakow, Baltimore: Voice Publishing Co., 1955.

B. J. Tenenbaum, Jr. WHO IS A GOOD JEW?
>   Reform Judaism, Summer 1994.

Max Vanger. MEMOIRS OF A RUSSIAN IMMIGRANT.
>   American Jewish Historical Quarterly.
>   Volume LXIII, September, 1973.

Lawrence Van Gelder. SPIRITUALITY AS A BUSINESS., Rabbis Are Standing By.
>   New York Times, December 31 1995

Albert Vorspan. IS AMERICAN JEWRY UNRAVELING?
>   Reform Judaism, Summer 1995

UNCOMMON THREADS

Rabbi Daniel Weiner. A CLARIFICATION.
    Baltimore Hebrew Congregation Bulletin, May 13, 1994.
Stephen J. Whitfield. OBSERVING AMERICAN JUDAISM.
    Congress Monthly, Sept./Oct. 1994.
Andrew Wohlberg. TEAMING UP.
    Baltimore Jewish Times, October 28, 1994.
Tom Weisser. TORAH.
    City Paper, December 25, 1987.
Amy Worden. JEWISH LIFE IN BALTIMORE
    The Washington Post, June 21, 1991.
David B. Wroblewski. THE DAY THE MUSIC DIED.
    Baltimore Jewish Times, July 12, 1996
Leonard Zeskind. AND NOW, THE HATE SHOW.
    The New York Times, November 16, 1993

EXHIBITIONS

AND SO THE CAME: Bicentennial Exhibit, The Jewish Community Center, 1975 The Jewish Experience of Settlement in Maryland, 1656-1929, The Inaugural Exhibit of the Jewish Heritage Center of the Jewish Historical Society of Maryland, October 25, 1987-June 19, 1988.
    Curator: Elizabeth Kessin Berman.
SOLOMON NUNES CARVALHO, The Jewish Heritage Center of the Jewish Historical Society of Maryland, April 9, 1989-September 29, 1989.Curator: Elizabeth Kessin Berman.
THREADS OF LIFE Jewish Involvement in Baltimore's Garment Industry. The Jewish Heritage Center of The Jewish Historical Society of Maryland, April 30, 1991-January 26, 1992. Curator: Elizabeth Kessin Berman.
FERTILE GROUND, Two Hundred Years of Jewish Life in Baltimore. The Jewish Heritage Center of The Jewish Historical Society of Maryland, May 17, 1982-February 28, 1993. Curator: Barry Kessler.
FREEDOM'S DOORS. Immigrant Ports of Entry to the United States. An exhibition in the museum of the Balch Institute for Ethnic Studies. Edited by Gail Stern. March 11,1986-September 30, 1992.

CHRONOLOGIES

FERTILE GROUND, Two Hundred Years of Jewish Life in Baltimore. The Jewish Heritage Center of the Jewish Historical Society of Maryland, May 17, 1982-February 28, 1993. Curator: Barry Kessler.
MARYLAND'S PIONEER JEWISH CHRONOLOGY, The Tercentenary Jewish Book, (1634-1934), Baltimore;A.D. Glushakow, 1934.

NEWSPAPER, PERIODICALS & PAMPHLETS

BALTIMORE SUN		BALTIMORE JEWISH TIMES	
Har Sinai Synagogue	July 12, 1849	Conservatism	January 27, ?
Har Sinai Synogogue	September 8, 1849	Mercantile Club	October 3, 1975
Enjoy Wit and Viands	November 8, 1882	Mercantile Club	October 10, 1976
Kosher	September 15, 1891	Mercantile Club	December 16, 1977
Phoenix Club	November 23, 1893	Country Clubs	October 7, 1977
Mercantile Club	January 29, 1895	Eruv	January 30, 1981
Hebrew Hospital	March 14, 1923	Reconstructionism	December 11, 1981
Woodholme Club	June 27, 1927	Tour Through Baltimore	November 26, 1981
Old Court Road	December 18, 1972	Bessarabian Society	November 26, 1982
Mercantile Club	September 16, 1975	Mercantile Club	October 23, 1987
Jews Building Invisible Wall	June 8, 1978	Sephardum	January 27, 1992
Soviet Jews	June 4 & 5, 1987	An Orthodox Celebration	February 19, 1992
Eruv	June 8, 1987	Ultra Orthodox	September 11, 1992
Baltimore Hebrew University	November 29, 1987	Sephardum	February 5, 1993
Falafel Flap	April 15, 1992	Erov Lists Finances	July 29, 1994

Talmudical Academy	February 19, 1992	Charles St. Eatery	August 5, 1994
Judaica for Judaism	April 21, 1993	Eruv President Resigns	August 5, 1994
Numbers Killed in Holocaust	April 21, 1993	A School Grown in Pikesville	December 30, 1994
Old Court Rd.	December 18, 1972	Strings Attached	Order in the Court
Park Heights Avenue	January 13, 1992	Mama Mia	February 24, 1995
A Lesson on Shofars	September 15, 1993	Baltimore, Not a Lubavitch Stronghold	March 15, 1916
High Court to take look at Religion	November 30, 1993	Lord Arthur James Balfour	March 29, 1996

Temple Emanuel
   Congregation moving — December 9, 1993
Reservoir Hill Grande Dames — December 22, 1993
Rabbi disagrees over "Holiness"
   of unmarried sex — May 5, 1994

BALTIMORE NEWS AMERICAN
Baltimore Jewish Population — January 20, 1975

Judaism and Human Sexuality — May 14, 1994
Obituaries — August 9, 1994

BALTIMORE MAGAZINE
Orthodox Judaism — September, 1987

Jewish Center to Celebrate — January 13, 1995
Prayer Curtain Removed from Bus — March 16, 1995

MARYLAND MAGAZINE
Jews in Maryland — Summer, 1993

High Incidence of Depression in
   Jewish Males — May 23, 1995
Rare Breast Cancer Link — September 29, 1995

ILLUSTRATION AMERICAN
Mercantile Club — June 7, 1892

Congregation now will
   pray to Matriarchs — November 17, 1995

TIME MAGAZINE
Reform Jews Approach Limit on level
   of Religious Toleration — December 1, 1995
Forward — December 28, 1962

THE SUN MAGAZINE
This Week — June 25, 1995

BALTIMORE JEWISH CHRONICLE
January 6, 1926

THE EVENING SUN
Baltimore Jewish Population — January 22, 1974.

THE SOURCE, The Associated Jewish Federation of Baltimore
Fall, 1972 — Winter 1993/1994

THE NEW YORK TIMES
Key Found to Fatal Brain Disorder — October 5, 1993.
Need More Help to Help the Neediest — December 5, 1993.
God and Country — December 5, 1993.
Harmonie Club — May 31, 1995
Syrian Jews, Refuge on Jersey Shore — May 26, 1996
2nd Gene defect linked to breast cancer — October 2, 1996

Spring 1993 — Spring, 1994

THE TORCH
Talmudical Academy of
   Baltimore — June, 1946

THE AMERICAN HEBREW — October, 1885

REFORM JUDAISM — Winter, 1993

BALTIMORE HEBREW CONG. BULLETIN — December 27, 1991

PURPOSE
Ner Israel Rabbinical College — 1933
Ner Israel Press Release — 1952

THE WASHINGTON POST
Jewish Life in Baltimore — June 21, 1991.

MARYLAND HISTORICAL MAGAZINE
Maryland Jewish History, — May, 1963
The East European Jewish
Index to 1900 Baltimore
Census

THE PALESTINE POST, JERUSALEM
Nazi Activity — March 15, 1933.
Nuremburg Laws — October 28, 1935.
Nazi Savagery — November 13, 1938.
Refugees — August 13, 1944.
EXODUS 1947 — July 26, 1947.

SUBURBAN NEWS, The NORTHWEST
August, 1946 — Decemberr, 1947

UNCOMMON THREADS

GENERATIONS
The Jewish Historical Society of Maryland
   June, 1982   December, 1988
   Spring, 1988   Summer, 1991

BURIAL & CEMETERY
Sol Levenson & Brother, Baltimore Cemetery Directory
Tripartite Committee on Jewish Funeral Standards,
   Brooklyn, N. Y.

BALTIMORE BEACON
May, 1948   December, 1960

NATIONAL PUBLIC TELEVISION
THE AMERICAN EXPERIENCE, America and
the Holocaust: Deceit and Indifference April, 1994.

INDEX

A

Abell, Arunah S. 185
Abraham xvii
Abramawitz, Irving 220f
Abramson, Leon 162
Academy of Visitation 53
Adath B'Nei Israel Cong./Syn. 172f
Adath Chaim 225
Adath Yeshurin Cong./Syn.(Shadover Shul) 113, 117f, 226
Adler, Blanche 79f
Adler, Irvin 162
Agudas Achim Anshe Sphard Cong./Syn. 227
Agudas Achim Anshe Chernigov Nusach Ari Cong./Syn. Chernigov Shul) See Lubavitz Nasach Ari 113, 117f, 235
Agudath ha-Rabbanim. 114
Ahavas Achim Cong./Syn. 117f, 167
Ahavas Sholom-Agudas Achim Anshe Sphard (See Randallstown Syn. Center)
Aitz Chaim Cong./Syn. (Prushnitz Shul) 20, 57, 113, 117f, 226
Albanians 86
Aleichem, Sholem (Solomon Rabinowitz) 156
Alexander II, Tzar 83, 84
Alexander III, Tzar 84, 85, 86
Allen, Joseph 216f
Allenby, General Edmund Henry Hynman 151
Alliance Israelite Universelle 84, 87, 91, 92
Alpha Omega 195
Altfeld, E. Milton 161
Amalgamated Clothing Workers of America (ACW) 133, 238
Ambach Family 55
American Association of Rabbinical Theological Seminaries 234
American Council for Judaism 212, 218
American Hebrew, The 37, 45f
American Jewish Archives 77
American Jewish Committee 151, 219
American Jewish Congress 151
American Jewish Historical Society 88f
American Relief Committee 160
Amity Club 183, 184
Amsterdam 92
Anglo- American Committee of Inquiry 213
Anglo-American Conference of 1924 211, 212
Anti-Defamation League 154
Anshe Bobruisk Nusach Ari Cong./Syn. 235
Anshe Chesed Bialystok Cong./Syn. (See Ohel Yakov)
Anshe Emunah Tavriger Cong./Syn. (Tavriger Shul) (See Liberty Jewish Center)
Anshe Neisen Nusach Ari Cong./Syn. (Nesina Shul) 113, 117f, 235
Anshe Shalom Cong./Syn. 173f
Anshe Sphard Cong./Syn. 117f, 172f
Anshe Wolyn Cong./Syn. (People of Wolyn) 113, 117f
Anti-Defamation League 154
Antwerp 92, 93
Arabs 211, 217, 218
Arbeiter Ring (See Baltimore Workmen's Circle)
Arion 43
Anti-Defamation League 155
Ashkenasi/Ashkenazum xiii, xv, 23, 87, 113, 114, 263, 267f, 273f

Associated Jewish Charities 29, 76, 104, 176-178, 183, 209f, 213, 238, 247, 248, 269, 273f
ASSOCIATED: Jewish Community Associated: Federation of Baltimore 226, 233, 248, 252, 257, 259, 263, 270, 272, 273f
Association of Rabbis (See Agudath ha-Rabbanim)
Atlantic City & Hotels 71, 196-199, 200f
Austria 9, 81, 83, 205, 213
Austrian, Dr. Charles 200f
Austro-Hungarian Constitution xvi, 83
A Victorian Village 97, 98
Avalon 262
Avodot Israel 22

B

Baal Shem xix
Bacharach, Carl 162
Baernstein, Charles & Lina Kraus 53f, 111f
Bais Yaakov School 233
Balfour Declaration 151
Balfour, Lord Arthur James 151, 152f
Baltic Sea 81
Baltimore x, xi, xii, xvii, 5f, 7, 9, 10, 17
Baltimore Asylum for Israelites 42
Baltimore Beacon 147
Baltimore Board of Rabbis 243
Baltimore-Bremen Line 102
Baltimore and Ohio Railroad 10, 102, 105f
Baltimore Civic Opera Co. (see Meyerbeer Singing Society)
Baltimore City College 194
Baltimore Fire 1904 78, 157
Baltimore German Jewish Social Register 68, 69, 185
Baltimore Hebrew College/University 145, 183, 234, 247, 250f
Baltimore Hebrew Congregation Cemetery 26, 35, 241, 254
Baltimore Hebrew Cong./Syn. 17-21, 24-26f, 35, 44, 45f, 52, 57, 60, 61, 61f, 73, 222-224, 233, 241, 249, 251, 265
Baltimore Jewish American 146
Baltimore Jewish Council 155, 253, 254
Baltimore Jewish Family Services 242
Baltimore Jewish Population 1
Baltimore Jewish Times 146, 147, 183, 236f, 239, 240, 265
Baltimore Jewish Voice 147
Baltimore Museum of Art 79f
Baltimore Public Baths 122
Baltimore Purim Association 42
Baltimore Rabbinical Council (See Beit Din)
Baltimore Schmurrah Matzo Co. (See Schmurrah Matzo)
Baltimore Sheltering Home 137
Baltimore, S.S. 10, 11
Baltimore Talmud Torah Society (See Talmud Torah Society)
Baltimore Workmen's Circle (Arbeiter Ring) 132
Baltimore Young Men's Relief Assoc. 137
Bamberger, Dr. Florence 200f
Bamburg 207
Bar & Bat Mitzvah 58, 142, 168, 174f, 224, 229, 230f, 231f, 243, 244, 246f
Bard, Dr. Harry 254f
Baron de Hirsch (See Hirsch, Baron de)
Basel 85, 218

UNCOMMON THREADS

Bavaria 3, 4, 7, 36, 78
Begin, Menachim 217
Beit Din (Baltimore Rabbinical Council) 115, 255f, 261
Beit Tikvah Cong. 236
Belair Market 48
Belair Road Cemetery (See Baltimore Hebrew Cong. Cemetery)
Belgium 92, 206
Belvedere Hotel 74
Ben Gurion, P.M. David 214, 217, 219
Bendann Family 55
Benesch Memorial Collection 79f
Bereditchev 81
Berger, Mr. & Mrs. Melvin 254
Berlin 78, 82, 207
Berman, Paul 162
Bernheimer 49f
Bessarabia/Bessarabians xvi, xvii, 86
Bessarabia Society 88f
Beth Am Cong./Syn. 235
Beth El Cong./Syn. 224, 225, m260, 266f
Beth Elohim Cong./Syn. 18
Beth Hamedrosh Hagodol Cong./Syn. 24, 117f
Beth HaShem 271
Beth Israel (Sephardic Cong,) Cong./Syn. 23
Beth Israel Eden St. Cong./Syn. (Little Eden St. Shul) 117f
Beth Israel (Liberty Road Conservative) Cong./Syn. 225, 277, 228
Beth Jacob Cong./Syn. 172f, 173f, 249
Beth Jacob Anshe Kurland Cong./Syn. People of Kurland 113, 117f, 227
Beth Jacob Anshe Riga Cong./Syn. (People of Riga) 113
Beth Jacob Anshe Veshear Cong./Syn. (People of Visheyer) 113
Beth Tfiloh Cong./Syn. 173f, 224, 233, 244, 265
Beth Yehuda Cong./Syn. 227
Beth HaMidrash 82, 115
Bialystok 59
Bible xviii
Bikur Cholim Cong./Syn. (Prushnitz Shul) 59, 117f
Biltmore Hotel Turkish Baths 122
Bismarck, Prince Otto Von 4
Black Death xv
Blaustein, Jacob 211, 219
Block, Dr. James A. 196
Bloom, Mike 153
Blue Ridge Mountains 71
Bloomberg, Michael 196
Blum, Irving 183
Blumenberg, Gen. Leopold 37
B'Nai Brith 154
B'Nai Israel Cong./Syn.(Russiche Shul) 19, 59, 117f, 251
B'Nai Jacob Cong./Syn. 117f, 226, 227
Board of the Jewish Congregations in Baltimore 61
Boas, Dr. George 200f
Bohemians 84
Bolsheviks 159, 160
Bolton Street Cong./Syn. (see Har Sinai)
Bolton Street Cong./Syn. (Non Affiliated) 235
Bond, Dr. Thomas 55
Bonnie View Club 238, 239
Borscht Belt 199
Boston 11, 196
Bowley's Lane Cemetery 114
Braddock Heights 70

Brager Family 49f
Brandeis, Louis Dembitz 160
Bremen 7, 9-11, 11f, 92, 93
Bremen, S.S. 10
Bremen & Baltimore Steamship Line 10
Brit Milah 264, 267f
Britains/British (See England/English)
Britain Hotel 197
Britain/British (see England/English)
Brith Shalom 154
British Foreign Office 215
British Mandate for Palestine 212, 217
British White Paper 211, 217
Broadway Market 48
Brody 83, 84
Brooklyn 214
Brooks, Chauncey 55, 56, 183, 185
Brooks Lane (900 block) 185, 186, 187f, 270
Bruchey, Elinore 72f
Bureau of Kosher Meat and Food Control 266f, 267f
Bulgaria 113, 117f
Burlesque 157, 158
Bund (Der Algemeiner Juddisher Arbeiter Bund) 85, 86
Byelorussia xvi, 85

C

Cahan, Abraham 148f
Camden Street Market 48
Camp Airy 138
Camp Louise 138
Canavan Disease 262
Cardin, Meyer 162
Cardin, Morris 162
Carpathian Mountains 83
Carroll, Charles of C. 24
Carvalho, Simon Nunes & Sara 23, 24
Cass Co., N.D. 111f
Catherine the Great 81
Catskills 70, 72f, 157, 199, 264
Central Committee 91, 92
Central Conference of American Rabbis 161, 269, 270
Central Scholarship Bureau 178
Centre Market 47
Chabad 235
CHAI (See Comprehensive Housing Assistance Incorporated)
Charedi xi, xix, 234, 235, 258, 266f
Charleston 5f
Charlevoix 71
Chattolanee Hotel 70
Cheder 142
Chernigov Shul (See Agudas Achim)
Chesed Schel Eme (See Hebrew Orthodox Free Burial Society)
Chestnut Ridge Club 238
Chevra Ahavas Chesed , 208
Chevra Kadisha 25, 208
Chevrei Tzedek Cong./Syn. 225
Children's Sheltering and Protective Assoc. 110
Chizuk Amuno Cong./Syn. 24, 31, 44, 45f, 53f, 59-60, 62f, 167, 168, 173f, 218, 224, 225, 233, 235, 260, 266f
Chofetz Chaim Cong. & Syn. 172f
Cholor Yisroel (See Va'ad Hakashrus)
Church of St. John the Babtist (See Lloyd Street Synagogue) 57

Cincinnati 10, 77, 159
Circumcision (See Brit Milah)
City College of New York 201f
Civil War xi, xvii, 11, 22, 35, 36, 41-43
Cliosophic Association 32
Clover Club 73
Clover Theater 157
Coblenz 207
Cohen Family 23-25, 35
Cohen, Dr. Abraham 200f
Cohen, Jacob I., Jr. 24
College of Dental Surgery 195
Columbia University 200f
Commission on Jewish Law & Standards 267f
Community Benevolent Society 108
Comprehensive Housing Assistance Inc. (CHAI) 259
Concord House 259
Concordia Club, Hall and Opera House 43, 44, 73, 270
Cone, Dr. Clarabel & Etta 79f
Confirmation 168
Congress of Vienna, 1815 3, 4
Conservative xix, xx, 223-228, 230f, 241, 242, 244, 263, 269, 272
Conservative Rabbinical Assembly 263, 267f
Cordish, Paul 162
Corned Beef Row 252
Corsairs Club (See Lancers Club)
Cossacks 84, 86, 87
Cotillion 237, 238
Coughlin, Father Charles C. E. 182, 182f
Council of Orthodox Jewish Congregations of Baltimore 167, 242
Council of Jewish Federations 242
Cross Street Market 48
Crescent Club 73
Crimean War 87
Crusades xv
Czechoslovakia 205

D

Dalsheimer, George H. 79f
Dalsheimer, Hugo & Helen 223, 254f
Daughters In Israel 109, 138, 153
Davidson, Isaac (See Isaac Davidson Hebrew School)
Deal 70
Dearborn Independent 181
Debutante Balls (See Harmony Circle)
Denmark 211
Der Algemeiner Juddisher Arbeiter Bund (See Jewish Socialist Bund)
Der Baltimore Israelite 146
Der Deutsche Correspondent Der 32, 35
Der Wecker 32, 35
Der Weiser 146
Deutsche Amerikanische Bank 45f
Deutsche Auswanderer-Zeitung 11f
Deutsche Bank von Baltimore 45f
Deutsche Central Bank 45f
Deutsche Haus 186
Deutsche Sparbank von Baltimore 45f
Diaspora xv
Dickens, Charles 43
Die Irische Hebra Cemetery 20
Displaced Persons Act 218, 219
Dnepropetuvsk 81

Donetsk 81
Dropsie College 77
Druid Hill Park 55, 70, 71, 165, 185, 247
Dunn, Msgr. William Kailer 226
Dutch xvii

E

Easterwood Park & Boy's Club 166
Eden Street Shul 20
Edict of Emancipation 1861 83
Egypt 218
Egyptian Expeditionary Forces 151
Einhorn, Rabbi David 22, 23, 26f, 32, 35
Eisenberg Family 49f
Eisenberg, Abraham 79f
Elbe River 7
Elberon 71
Elizabethgrad 88
Elks Club 43, 154
Ellis Island 88f, 104f
Emancipation Edict, 1812 3
Emersonian Apartments 56, 61f, 168
England/English xii, 8, 9, 92, 93, 205, 206, 211, 213, 215, 217
Ensor Town 24
Epstein, Jacob 79f, 175-176, 178f
•rlanger Family 56
Eruv of Baltimore Inc. 259-261, 266f
Esplanade Apartments. 56, 61f
Ethnic Germans 9
Etting Family 23, 24
Etting, Solomon 24
Eutaw Place 55-56, 58, 61f, 73, 183, 185, 237
Eutaw Place Temple (See Oheb Shalom)
Exodus 1947 214-215, 216f
Ezras Hovevei Zion Kadina 150

F

Fagin, Dr. N. Bryllion 200f
Family Circles 168, 169
Federated Jewish Charities (Uptown Charities) 76, 110, 138, 160, 175, 176, 209f
Federation of American Zionists 150
Federation of Orthodox Jewish Congregations 114, 115
Fein, Dr. Isaac M. 254f
Fells Point xvii, 9, 10, 29, 48
Fells Point Market (See Broadway Market)
Fells Point Hebrew Friendship Cong./Syn. (See Hebrew Friendship)
Fifth Regiment Infantry 37
Fine, Melvin P. 161
Finney, Dr. James M. T. 65f
First Crusade xv
First Jewish Labor Congress 150
First Zionist Congress 85
Fisher, Judge Morton P. 161
Five Books of Moses xviii, 272
Flexner, Dr. Simon 200f
Ford, Henry 181
Ford's Theater 177
Forest Park 165
Fort Armistead 10
Fox Family 71
Fox, Louis J. 254f
France/French 9, 205, 206, 211, 212, 215, 216

UNCOMMON THREADS

Frank, Eli 65f
Frank Family 56
Frank, Simon & Co. 38f
Frankfurt 193, 207
Frankfurter Zeitung 190
Frantsoisishe Shul (See Ohel Yakov)
Frederick II, The Great 82
Free Soviet Jewry 257
Friedenwald Family 9, 56, 173f, 204
Friedenwald. Chayim and Merle 8, 11f
Friedenwald, Dr. Harry 101, 150, 151, 200f, 209f
Friedenwald, Jonas 8, 9, 29
Friedenwald, Dr. Jonas 200f
Friedenwald Shul (see Chizuk Amuno)
Friendly Inn 109, 110
Friends School 64
Froelicher, Hans Sr. 65f
Front St. Theater 155, 156

G

Galicia/Galicians/Galitzianers ix, xvi, 83, 84, 87, 103, 133, 143
Galician Synagogue (See Mogen Abraham)
Gamara xviii, xix
Garment Industry xii
Garrison Blvd. 165
Gates of the House, Prayer & Repentance 270
Gaucher Disease 263
Gay Street 48, 49
Gayety Theater 157
German/English schools 51
German Mannerchor 43
German Sozialdemocratisch Turnverein 43
German Zion Church 43
German and English Institute 51
Germany/Germans xvii, 4, 7, 9, 13, 27, 91, 104, 203-207, 213, 214
Glassner, Rabbi Samuel 254f
Glyndon 70
Goldman, Rabbi Israel 254f
Goldschmidt, Jonas 52
Good Fellowship Club 183
Goodman, Philip 162
Gordon, Jacob 156
Gordon, Yale and Peggy 252
Gottschalk, Jacob 254
Grand German Opera Co. 43
Great Britain (See England/English)
Greek Orthodox Cathedral 250f
Great Synagogue of Sofia 117f
Greece/Greeks/Greecuian xvii, 86
Greenebaum, Stewert J. & Marlene 196
Greenhorn 124
Greenspring Valley Synagogue and Center (See Ner Tamid)
Green Valley Club 239
Greenstein, Harry 213, 247, 254f
Greif Family 56, 61f
Greif, Leonard 65f
Gropius, Walter 223
Gutman Family and Store 56
Gutman, Joel 49f
Gutman, Julius 49f

H

Hadassah 141
Haganah 214, 215, 217
Haifa 215
Halachah xix, 115, 174f, 236f
Hamburg 7, 9, 27, 92, 93, 101, 193, 207
Hamburger Family 56
Hamburger, Adolph 214
Hamburger, Dr. Ferdinand 200f
Hamburger, Isaac II 254f
Hamburger, Jonas 65f
Hamburger, Dr. Louis 65f
Hammerman, Judge Robert I. H. 245f
Hanover 207
Hanover Street Market 48
Hanukkah 243
Hapisga 146
Harmonie Club 245f
Harmony Circle 41, 42, 74-76, 185, 237, 238, 270
Harrison Street 48
Harvard University 200f
Har Sinai (Verein) Cong./Syn. 19, 21, 22, 25, 37, 57, 61, 63, 174f, 219, 223, 226, 230f, 264, 265
Har Zion Cong./Syn. 172f
Hasidic/Hasidim xix, 25, 114, 143, 167, 214, 234-235, 271
Hasidic Lubavitchers 167, 234-235
Haskalah 82-83, 141
Hazir Market 150
Hebrew American 33f
Hebrew Benevolent Society 29, 41, 42, 76, 110, 177
Hebrew Burial and Social Services 25
Hebrew Children's Sheltering & Protective Assoc. 110, 137
Hebrew Colonial Society 108
Hebrew Directory 68
Hebrew Education Society 110
Hebrew and English Benevolent Academical Assoc. 31
Hebrew Emigrant Aid Society 107
Hebrew Free Burial Society 25
Hebrew Free Loan Assoc. 110
Hebrew Free School (See Baltimore Talmud Torah)
Hebrew Friendship Cemetery 26f, 59
Hebrew Friendship Cong./Syn. (P'int Shul) 19-21, 25, 31, 52, 57, 222
Hebrew Home for Incurables 109, 137
Hebrew Hospital and Asylum (see Sinai Hospital) 42, 101, 108, 110, 114, 115, 175, 177, 178
Hebrew Immigrant Aid Society (HIAS) 33f, 100, 107, 137, 206, 219, 257
Hebrew Immigrant Protective Society 107, 108
Hebrew Independent Association 32
Hebrew Kindergarten and Day Nursery 153
Hebrew Literary Society 141
Hebrew Noble Ladies 137
Hebrew Orphan Asylum 42
Hebrew Orthodox Free Burial Society (Chesed Schel Emes) 114, 135f
Hebrew Sheltering Home 137
Hebrew Society for the for the Education of the Poor and Orphan Children 143
Hebrew Talmudical Seminary & Parochial School (See Talmudical Academy of Baltimore)
Hebrew Union College, Jewish Institute of Religion 77, 223, 269, 270
Hebrew Young Men's Literary Assoc. 23
Hebrew Young Men's Sick Relief Assoc. 109
Hecht Family 56
Hecht, Judge Lee I. 161

Hecht, Robert H. & Ryda 79f
Heidelberg 207
Helfer, Rev. Dr. Frederick 226
Hendler, L. Emanuel 198
Herman, Rabbi Floyd L. 174f
Hess Family 56
Hesse 4, 7, 78
HIAS (See Hebrew Immigrant Society)
HICEM 206
High Street Bath 122
Higham, Dr. John ix
Hill Street Synagogue (See Oheb Hasholom)
Hilltop Shopping Center 247, 248
Hinter Berliners xvii, 104
Hirsch, Baron Maurice de 84, 91, 92, 108, 142
Hirsch, Moritz Von 91
Hitler, Adolph 182, 190, 204, 205, 212
Hochschild Family & store 49f, 56
Hoffberger, Jerold Charles 213
Holland 92
Hollander, Dr. Jacob 151, 175, 200f
Hollander, Sidney 178f
Hollins Market 48
Hollofield (See Yaazor Community)
Holocaust ix, 212, 213, 253, 254
Holocaust Memorials 253, 254
Hoover, President Herbert 190, 204
Hopkins, Johns 25
Hovevei Zion 150
Howard, John Eager School No.61 186, 250
Hull, England 9
Hungary/Hungarians ix, 9, 87, 219
Hunner, Dr. Guy S. 65f
Hunter College 200f
Hunter, Dr. Wilbur 19
Hutzler Family and Store 49f, 56
Hutzler, Moses 21

I
Illoway, Rabbi Bernard 35
Immigration Service and Laws 10, 103, 177, 204-206, 214, 219
Independent Ladies Farein of Baltimore 137
Institute of Notre Dame 53, 53f
Interfaith marriages 271
International Ladies Garment Worker's Union (ILGWU) 132, 133
Iraq 218
Irgun Tzevai Leumi 217
Irische Chevra 19, 20
Isaac Davidson Hebrew School 145
Israel x, 214, 216f, 216-219, 266, 266f, 272
Israel, Rabbi Edward 21, 216f
Israel Bond Dinner 219
Israelite 33f
Israelitisch Allianz 84
Italy/Italians xvii, 103, 206, 212, 213

J
JEA (See Jewish Educational Alliance)
JEA Fellowship Association 154
Japan 206
Jerusalem 217
Jerusalem Post 250f
Jeshurun Lodge 154

Jew Alley 24
Jew Bill 1
Jewish Agency 213, 217
Jewish Big Brother League 155
Jewish Board of Education 144
Jewish Children's Bureau 137, 178f, 195f
Jewish Chronicle 33f
Jewish Colonization Association (JCA) 206
Jewish Comment 146
Jewish Community Center 154, 247, 248, 252
Jewish Convalescent Society and Home 138
Jewish Court of Arbitration 123, 176, 267f
Jewish Daily Forward 148f
Jewish Day School Foundation 252
Jewish Educational Alliance (JEA) 123, 142, 153, 154, 247
Jewish Exponent 146
Jewish Family Services 242, 244
Jewish Heritage Center 19, 59, 60, 251, 251
Jewish Historical Society of Md. 18, 19, 60, 216f, 251
Jewish Institute of Religion 223
Jewish Legion 151
Jewish Messenger 33f, 146
Jewish National Fund Council of Baltimore 129, 184
Jewish National Workers Alliance 150
Jewish Reconstructionist Federation 236
Jewish Record 33f
Jewish Social Register 68
Jewish Socialist Bund 85, 86, 149
Jewish Theological Seminary xx, 58, 225
Jewish Welfare Agency 205
Jewish Welfare Fund 209f
Jewish Workers Federation 85
Johns Hopkins Hospital 194-196, 252
Johns Hopkins University 77, 194-196, 200f, 234
Johnson Act, 1924 (See Immigration Service & Laws)
Joint Distribution Committee (JDC) 206, 219
Jones, Miss (School) 186
Jordan 218
Journal of Public Health 246f
Junior Cotillion 75, 76, 237, 238

K
Kahn, Bernhard 38f, 39f, 134f
Kahn, Elizabeth (Betsey) 11f
Kahn, Philip Sr. 187f
Kairys, Mrs. Elsie 254f
Kaiser, Cantor Alois 31
Kaiser, Samuel J. 216f
Kann, Sigmund 65f
Kaplan. Dr. Louis 196, 254f
Katerinka 99, 132, 150
Katyn Forest memorial 263
Katz, A. Ray 176
Katz, M. Shakman & Amalie Sonneborn 216f, 254f
Katzenberg, Meyer 38f
Katzenberg, Alexander Stephens 38f
Katzner, J. Benjamin 216f
Kaufman, Judge Frank A. 161
Ketubah 127, 240, 261
Key, Francis Scott Monument 56
Khal Ahavas Yisroel Cong./Syn. 235
Kharkov 81
Kibitzing Market 150
Kielce 213, 220
Kiev xv, 81

UNCOMMON THREADS

King David Hotel 220f
Kishinev xvii, 81, 86, 87, 88f
Knapp, Frederick 51, 53f
Know Nothing's 36, 181
Kolker, J. Benjamin 214
Kol Tikvah Cong./Syn. 225
Kosher Dining Club 228
Krakow 83
Kraus, Lina (See Baernstein)
Kraus, Myra 30f
Krieger, Zanvyl 196
Kristallnacht 205, 206, 254
Krongard, Alvin (Buzzy) 245f
Kuntz, Henry 216f

L
Labor Zionists 110, 150
Ladino xv, 87
Lafayette Market 48
Lake Drive Apartment 56176
Lancers Club 245f
Lansburgh, Richard M. 176
Lansburgh, Sidney
Laucheimer, Brig. Gen. Charles H. U.S.M.C. 78
Lazaron, Rabbi Morris 21, 212, 216f
Lazarus, Emma xi, 104
Lazarus, Morton 187f
League of Nations 211, 212
Lebanon 218
Lee, Robert E. School No.49 186, 187, 250f
Lever, Dr. Barry 216f
Lehmyer, Martin 63
Lenin, Ulyanov Vladimir Ilyich 85
Lester, Rabbi Jacob 23
Levi, Robert H. and Ryda 79f
Levi Yitzchok-Bais Lubavitch Cong./Syn. 235
Levin, Harry O. 161
Levin, Louis H. 65f, 146, 151, 160, 176
Levindale Home for the Aged. 109, 178, 248, 259
Levinson, Ruben 216f
Levinson, Sol & Bro. 59
Levy, Jacob 52
Levy, Julius 79f, 153, 176, 193
Levy, Lester 254f
Levy, William 153, 176
Lewis, Jack 59
Lexington Market 47
Liberty Heights Ave & Liberty Road 225-228, 247
Liberty Jewish Center (See Ansche Emunah) 113, 226-227
Liberty Road Conservative Cong./Syn. (See Beth Israel)
Lieberman, Rabbi Morris 254f
Liebhold, Amelia Marie 11f
Liederkranz 43
Lisbon 206
Lithuania/Lithuanians/Litvaks ix, 1, 59, 81, 84, 85, 87, 109, 143, 234
Little Russia xv
Liverpool 9, 92
Lloyd Street Shul. (See Baltimore Hebrew and Shomrei Mishmeres Hakodesh Congs.).
Locust Point 10, 97, 101, 102, 105f
Lombard Street 122, 123, 170-172, 174f, 252, 253
London 92
Long Branch 71, 72f

Long, Robert Carey, Jr. 18
Louise, brig 9
Lowell, A. Lawrence 200f
Lowenstein, Malcolm 179f
Lubavitch (See Hasidic Lubavitchers)
Lubavitch Center for Jewish Education 235
Lubavitz Nasach Ari Cong./Syn. 167, 235
Luebeck 10
Luskin, Mr. & Mrs. Jack 254
Lutzker Social Relief Society 137
Luxembourg 206
Lyric Opera House/Theater 74, 76, 160, 176, 214, 250f

M
Maccabeans 153
Machine Strike 132, 133
Madison Avenue Temple (See Baltimore Hebrew)
Maggid's Turkish Bath 122
Maimonides Academy (See Yeshivat Rambam)
Maine Camps 71
Mandel, Gov. Marvin 161
Marburg, Charles L. 56
Marsh (Mash) Market (See Centre Market)
Marseilles 215
Marx, Karl Heinrich and Marxist Party 85
Maryland Country Club 230f
Maryland General Assembly 1, 17, 161
Maryland Institute of Art 69, 250f
Maryland Public Health Association 122
Maryland School for Boys 153
Maryland State Constitution of 1776 1
Maryland Theater 158f
Mashgiach 93, 94, 96
Maskilm 83, 141, 143
Masons 21, 26f, 43, 154
Matzo 29, 228, 229, 230f, 270
May Laws xvi, 85
May, Sadie 79f
McKim School 31
McKusick, Dr. Victor 267f
Mechina High School 234
Medical & Chirurgical Faculty of Md. 186, 250f
Mein Kampf 190
Mencken, H. L. 51
Mendelssohn Literary 32
Mendelssohn, Moses xvi, 82
Menorah Lodge 154
Mercantile Club #1 73
Mercantile Club # 2 73, 183, 184, 227, 237
Messiah xix
Messianic Jewish-Christian Congregation 261
Meyerbeer Singing Society 153, 154
Meyerhof, Joseph 250f, 254f
Meyerhof Symphony Hall 250f
Middle Ages 3
Mikro Kodesh Cong./Syn. (Pokroyer Shul) 59, 113, 117f, 225
Mikvah 128, 225, 260
Mikvah Israel Cong./Syn. 17
Milk and Ice Fund (See National Council of Women)
Millbrook-Colonial Village Citizen's Patrol 258
Milwaukee 159
Minhag Amerika 22
Minsk 81, 194
Mishna xviii, xix

Mithnagdim 143
Mogen Abraham Cong./Syn. (Galician Shul) 117f, 226
Moldavians 86
Mondawmin Mall 247, 248
Monsey, N.Y. 266f
Mordecai, Moses 1
Morrison, George C. 65f
Mosaic Code xviii
Moscow 81, 194
Moser, Judge Herman 161
Moses xviii
Moses, Jacob 63, 272
Moses Montefiore Emunath Israel Cong./Syn. 117f, 226
Moss, Leon 88f
Mount Pleasant Home for Consumptives 175, 248
Mount Sinai xviii
Mount Washington 70, 165, 248, 249
Mount Washington Improvement Assoc. 258
Mueller, Dr. Steven 196
Murder Inc. 162f
Myers, Elkan 216f

N
NA'AMAT USA 244
Napoleonic Wars 3, 4
Nathans, Dr. Daniel 196
National Council of Women 110
National Labor Zionists 150
Nat'l Museum of American History, The Smithsonian Institution 270
National Register of Historic Places 19, 59
National Union of Social Justice 182f
Native American Party (See Know Nothings)
Nazi Germany 203-208, 218
Neighborhood Crime Prevention Program 258
Ner Israel Rabbinical College 88f, 233, 234, 236f
Ner Tamid Cong./Syn. 235
Netherlands 206, 213
Netzach Yisrael Cong../Syn. 267f
New Assembly Rooms 74
New Orleans 11
New York Beit Din 233
New York City xvii, 5f, 17, 102
New York Stock Exchange 189, 190
New York University 200f
New York Workmen's Circle 132
Nicholis, I , Tzar 82
Nicholas II, Tzar 86, 87, 159
Nidche Israel Cong. (See Baltimore Hebrew).
Niles, Hezekiah 152f
Northeast Market 48
Northwest Citizen's Patrol 258, 259
Northwest Suburban News 147
North German Federation 10
North German Lloyd Steamship Co. 7, 10, 11, 69, 102
Notre Dame, Institute of 53
Nuremberg Laws-1935 204
Nuremberg Trials 208

O
Oasis Night Club 157
Occident 33f
Odd Fellows 43, 154
Odessa 81, 87, 88f
Offit, Morris W. 196

Oheb Hasholom Cong./Syn. (First Hill Street Synagogue) 117f
Oheb Israel Cong./Syn. (See Hebrew Friendship)
Oheb Shalom Cong./Syn. 22, 36, 42, 52, 56-60, 61f, 62f, 141, 265
Ohel Yakov Bialystoker Cong/Syn.(Bialystoker Shul) 59, 113, 117f, 223, 227
Ohr Knesseth Israel Cong./Syn. 117f, 172f
Ohr Mizrach Cong./Syn. 267f
Olath Tamid Prayer book 22
Old Bay Line 214
Old Court-Liberty Rd., /Cong./Syn. (See Talmud Torah V'Emunah)
Old Testament xviii
Old Town 48, 49
Olmstead, Frederick Law, Sr 70
Oppenheim, Eli 65f
Oppenheim, Isaac 65f
Orthodox xix, xx, 28, 168, 223, 224, 226, 228, 243, 249, 255f, 258, 259, 260, 263, 265, 266f, 267f, 269, 271
Orthodox Jewish Rabbinical Council 263
Oriental Railway 9
Ottoman Empire xv, xvi, 87
Owings Mills 227, 228, 233, 248, 250f, 252, 257, 261

P
Pale of Settlement xvii, 81-83, 85, 91, 143, 149, 159, 160
Palestine 151, 211, 212, 214, 217, 218
Paris Peace Conference of 1919 211
Park Circle 165
Park Heights Ave. 165, 222-223, 233, 234, 247, 248, 249, 257, 258, 259, 264, 265
Park Lane Shopping Center 247, 248
Park School 65, 65f, 186, 273f
Parker, Kenny 245f
Patz, Dr. Arnall 200f
Peabody Conservatory of Music 69, 252
Pearl Harbor 206
Pegram, Francis E. 65f
Peddlers 13- 15, 131
Pen Mar 70
Pentateuch, The (See The Five Books of Moses)
Perlman, Philip B. 162
Petach Tikva Cong./Syn. 173f
Phi Epsilon Pi 195
Philadelphia 5f, 11, 17, 69, 77
Phoenix Club 73-77, 183, 184, 237, 238, 245f, 270
Pickwick Jewish Center 173f
Pickwick Citizen's Patrol 258
Pikesville xi, 165, 200f, 222, 227, 229f, 233, 239, 248, 249, 252
Pikesville Senior High School 201f, 249, 250f
Pimlico 165, 248
P'int Shul (See Hebrew Friendship Cong./Syn).
Pioneer Club 154, 158f
Pioneer Women's Organization 137, 150
Pins and Needles 133
Pinsk 81
Pisga Community (see Yaazor)
Playground Athletic League 166
Poalei Zionists 150
Pocono Mountains 240, 264
Pogroms 83-87, 88f
Pokroyer Cong./Syn. (See Mikro Kodesh) 59

UNCOMMON THREADS

Poland/Polish/Poles ix, 9, 27, 59, 81-84, 85, 86, 88, 93, 103, 203, 205, 213, 214, 218, 220f, 228, 234, 235, 264
Pollack, James H. (Jack) 162
Portuguese Sephardic 23, 97
Posners 49f
President Warfield (See Exodus 1947)
President's Advisory Committee on Political Refugees 206
Pressman, Hyman 162
Progressive Labor Lyceum Assoc. 132
Protestant Reformation xix
Protocols of the Learned Elders of Zion 181, 182, 182f, 190
Prussia 81
Prushnitz Shul (See Aitz Chaim)
Public Athletic League 123
Public Primary School # 2 52
Public Secondary School # 3 52
Public School # 61 (John Eager Howard School) 250f
Public School # 49 (Robert E. Lee School) 250f
Purim Ball 75
Pushke 129
Putzel, Louis 63

R

Rabbinical Council of Baltimore (See Va'ad HaRabonim)
Rabbinical Tribunal (See Beit Din)
Rabinowitz, Solomon (See Sholem Aleichman)
Radomer Russian-Polish Verein 110
Randallstown xi, 247, 248
Randallstown Synagogue Center Cong./Syn. (See Ahavas Sholom-Agudas Achim Anshe Sphard & See Talmud Torah V'Emunah)
Rangley Lakes 71
Rayner, Sen. Isador 63, 73
Rayner, Wm. S. 42, 56
Reconstructionist Rabbinical Assoc. 236
Reconstructionists xx, 226, 236, 243
Red Eye 99
Red Men's Hall 23
Reese, Lizette Woodworth (See A Victorian Village)
Reform xix, xx, 22, 24, 27, 28, 58, 62f, 77, 113, 168, 219, 222, 223, 224, 226, 227, 230f, 241-244, 249, 262, 263, 265, 269, 270, 272, 264
Reisterstown xi, 225
Reisterstown Jewish Center 224, 225
Reisterstown Plaza 247, 248
Renaissance Plaza 61f
Residential Restrictive Covenants 221
Rhine River xv, 3
Rice, Rabbi Abraham 18, 21, 20, 23
Richmond 5f
Richmond Market 48
Riggs, Gen. Lawrason 65f
Riviera Apartments 56
Robinson, Jerome 161
Rodef Tzedek Cong./Syn. 117f
Rodeph Shalom Cong./Syn/ 17
Rogers, Lloyd Nicholas 55
Roland Park 193
Romania/Romanians ix, xvi, 9, 81, 84, 87, 88, 103, 113, 143, 213
Rome 212
Roper Poll 209f
Roosevelt, President Franklin Delano 190, 204-206, 212, 217
Rosenau, Rabbi William 30f, 143, 200f

Rosenberg, Del. Samuel (Sandy) 245f
Rosenblatt, Rabbi Samuel 254f
Rosenblit, Dr. Marsha 62f
Rosenfeld Family 56
Rosenfeld, Goody 45f
Rosenfeld, Moses W. 255f
Rosenfeld, Rosa (see Rosa Wiesenfeld)
Rosenthal, Gertrude 79f
Rothschild, Lord (Baron Edmond De Rothschild) 151, 152f
Rochschild, Mrs. Marie 255f
Rotterdam 93
Rowland, Dr. J.M.H 65f
Russia/Russians ix, 9, 27, 81, 83-88, 91, 92, 102, 103, 108, 121, 149, 203, 228, 257
Russian Jewish Hebrew Literary Society (See Jewish Hebrew Literary Society)
Russian Jewish Night School 141, 142
Russian Jewish Opera Company 158f
Russian Relief Assoc. 109
Russian Revolution 86
Russian Social Democratic Party 86
Russische Shul (See B'Nai Israel)
Ruthenians 83

S

Sachs, Jerry 245f
Sachs, Joseph 52
Sachs, Leon 254f
St. John the Babtist Church (See Lloyd Street Synagogue) 57
St. Louis 10, 159
St. Petersburg 81
Sandelman, Sherva 88f, 89f
Sauber, Gladys 254
Savannah 5f
Schadehen 127
Schaffer, Rabbi Schepsel 24, 220f
Scheib, Heinrich 51, 53f
Schloss Family 56, 61f
Schmoke, Mayor Kurt L. 245f
Schneeberger, Rabbi Henry W. 60
Schoeneman Family 61f
Schmurrah matzo (See Baltimore Schmurrah Matzo Company) 228, 229, 231f
Schnorers 129
Schohet 171
School No.49 (See Lee, Robert E.)
School No. 61 (See Howard, John Eager)
School No.79 186
Schulcan Aruch xvi, xvii, xix, 25
Schwartz, Rabbi Avrum Nachman 19, 116, 173f
Sea Bright 71
Second Presbyterian Church 18, 19
Second Temple (70 CE) xv, xvii
Seesen, Westphalia xx, 27
Seidel, Dr. Herman 150
Seligman, Prof. M. 52
Sephardic/Sephardim xv, 23, 24, 84, 87, 97, 101, 107, 113-115, 267f, 273f
Serbia/Serbs 86
Shaarei Tfiloh Cong./Syn. 173f, 226
Shaarei Zion Cong./Syn. 172f
Shabus Goy 130
Shadova Shul Cong/Syn 113
Shapiro, Samuel 216f
Shaw, Rabbi Abraham 187f

Shearith Israel Cong./Syn. 23, 24, 218, 220f
Sheppard, Joseph 254
Shevet Achim Cong./Syn. 23, 24
Shield of David window 18
Shloush, Dr. Rita 267f
Shmooze /Shmuos 130f
Shomrei Hadath Cong./Syn. 117f, 235
Shomrei Mishmeres Hakodesh Cong./Syn. (Volhynia Shul)(See Lloyd St. Syn.) 19, 57, 113, 117f, 167, 172, 173f
Shtetl xvi, 81, 82, 85, 101, 105, 143, 156
Shulcan Aruch (See Schulcan Aruch)
Shusterman, Rabbi Abraham 226, 230f
Siberia 81
Silberman, Tanchum 143
Silesians 84
Silver Birch Club 239
Sinai 22, 32, 35
Sinai Hospital 42, 196, 248, 249, 252, 259
Singer, Isaac Basjevis 148f
Singewald, Karl 65f
Sixth Massachusetts Regiment 37, 38
Sklar, Judge Albert L. 161
Slaves 38f
Slovakia/Slovakians 22, 84
Sobeloff, Judge Simon E. 151, 162
Social Justice 182
Society for the Education of the Poor and Orphan Hebrews 31
Society of Friends 31
Society of Truth Seekers 77
Society Visiting List (1899) 55, 56
Solomon, Levi 24
Sondheim, David & Sons 58, 193
Sonneborn Family 56, 61f
Sonneborn, Henry & Co. 72f
Sonneborn, Rudolph 150, 214
Sonneborn, Siegmund B. 65f, 150
Sozialdemocratische Turnverein 43
Soviet Union Jews 213, 217, 219, 257, 258, 266f
Soypher, Maurice 161
Speert, Herman 216f
Speert, Moses 214
Sperry, Joseph Evans 58, 167, 168
Stadt Shul (See Baltimore Hebrew Cong.Syn.)
Stalin, Joseph 85, 212
Stein Family 56
Stevenson 222, 248
Stone, Samuel 254
Straus, Henry (Harry) L. 71, 72
Strauss, Isaac Lobe 63
Strauss Family 56, 77, 204
Strauss, Aaron & Lillie 73, 138
Strauss, Myer & Julia 209f
Strauss Shul (See Shearith Israel)
Strouse Family 56, 61f
Strouse Bros. 61f
Strouse, Eli 65f
Suburban Club 76, 77, 184-185, 222, 237-239, 249, 270
Suburban Orthodox Cong./Syn. (See Toras Chaim)
Sudbrook Park 70, 72f
Sultan of Turkey 87
Summit Club 239
Sweat shops 121
Sweden 211

Switzerland 9, 206
Symphony Hall (see Myerhoff Symphony Hall)
Syria 218
Szold, Rabbi Benjamin 22, 36, 53f, 60, 141
Szold Henrietta 53f, 111f, 141, 142

T
Talmud-Talmudical Law xvii, xix, 101, 115, 123, 127-130, 130f, 141, 142, 166, 171, 229, 234, 236, 250f, 260, 261
Talmudical Academy of Baltimore 116, 145, 227, 233, 252, 255f, 261, 263
Talmudical Seminary of Baltimore 145
Talmud Torah 124, 142, 143
Talmud Torah Society 143, 145
Talmud Torah V'Emunah Cong./Syn. (See Randallstown Synagogue Center)
Tannersville 70
Task 121
Tau Epsilon Phi 195
Tay-Sachs Disease 262
Tefillin 127
Teheran 212
Tel Aviv 215
Telz 1
Temple Emanuel 224, 227
Temple Gardens Apartments 56, 61f
Ten Commandments xviii, 272
Thalheimer, Dr. Alvin 254f
The Passing Years 177, 269
Thomashefsky. Boris & Bessie Kaufman 155, 158f
Three Power Conference (1943) 212
Tiferith Israel Anshe Sphard Cong./Syn. 173f, 226
Tikkum Olam xviii
Titus xv
Tobacco 7
Torah xviii, xix, 58, 142, 218, 224, 230f, 236, 250f, 272
Toras Chaim Cong./Syn. 226
Towson State University 234
Treaty of 1832 82, 83, 88f
Trenton Democratic Club 162
Triennial 224
Trotsky, Leon 85
Truman, Pres. Harry S. 211, 217, 218
Turkey 87
Turnverein Vorwarts 43
Tuttle, Prof. & Mrs. 69
Two O'Clock Club 157
Tzedakah 129
Tzemach Tzedek Cong./Syn. 235

U
Ukraine/Ukrainians 81, 83, 84, 87, 92, 93, 108, 143, 213
Ulman, Jacob 63
Ulman, Judge Joseph N. 161
Union of American Hebrew Congregations 58, 241, 262, 267f
Union Prayer Book 22, 223
United Garment Workers of America 132
United Hebrew Assistance Society (See Hebrew Benevolent Society)
United Hebrew Benevolent Society 20
United Hebrew Cemetery 114, 254
United Hebrew Charities (Downtown Charities) 110, 137, 138, 175, 176, 209f
United Jewish Appeal 206, 209f

United Nations 211, 217
United Nations Special Committee on Palestine (UNSCOP) 217
United Palestine Appeal 206
United Railways & Electric Co. 70
United States Immigration Service (see Immigration Services & Laws)
University of Baltimore 234
University of Maryland 194-196, 234
UNSCOP 217

V

Va'ad HaRabonim (Rabbinical Council of Baltimore) 115, 244, 267f
Va'ad HaKashrus 261, 267f
Van Sickle, James H. 65f
Vichy Government 206
Vilna 81, 85
Vineland 109, 110f
Visheyer Shul (See Beth Jacob Anshe Vesheyer)
Visiting List 68
Volga River 9
Volhynia/Volhynians xvi, 81
Volstead Act 160

W

Wagner-Rogers Bill 205
Walters, Henry 122
War Refugee Board 212
Wars of Liberation 3
Warsaw 81
Weddings 240, 241
Weinberg, Robert L. 251
Weinberg, Harry & Jeanette Foundation 196, 251, 252, 255f, 266f
Weisgal, Fred 220f
Weitzman, Pres. Chaim 214, 218
Wesser River 7
West Arlington 70
Western Female High School 53, 53ff
Western Maryland Railroad 70
Weston Trading Co. 214, 215
Westphalia (see Seesen)
Whitechapel 92
White Russia (see Byelorussia)
Wiesenfeld Family 56, 105f
Wiesenfeld, Moses & Betsey Friedenwald 38f, 45f, 97, 98
Wiesenfeld, Rosa 53f
Willehad, S.S. 78
Wilhelm. German Kaiser 245f
Wilmars 207
Wilson, Pres. Woodrow 211
Winans Rd. Synagogue Center (See Beth Yehuda & Beth Jacob Anshe Kurland)
Winans, Thomas 88f
Windsor Hills 70, 165
Wise, Rabbi Isaac M. 22
Wise Men of Chelm 156, 158f
Wolman, Dr. Abel 200f
Women's Labor Zionist Organization of America (See Na'Amat)
Women's Turkish Bath Club 122
Woodholme Country Club 184, 237, 238
Woodmore Hebrew Cong./Syn. 226
Workmen's Circle Branch No. 9 132

World Zionist Organization 214, 216f, 217
W.W. I 11, 78, 103, 107, 114, 147, 159, 161, 165, 175, 176, 194, 206
W, W, II x, xii, xiii, xx, 165, 183, 186, 204, 205- 208, 212, 217, 221, 222, 225, 230f, 237, 240, 242, 243, 250f
Wurtzburg 207
Wurtzburger, Allan and Janet 79f
Wynn, Ed 179f, 269

Y

Yaazor 108, 109, 158f
Yale and Peggy Gordon Center for the Performing Arts 252
Yalta Conference (1945) 212
Yeshiva 142, 143, 233, 234
Yeshiva High School 145
Yeshivat Rambam 264, 265 , 267f
Yeshivath Chofez Chaim and Parochial School 145
Yeshivath Torah'Emunah Hebrew Parochial School of Baltimore City 145
Yiddish xv, xvi, 8, 82-84, 87, 95, 101, 108, 124, 131, 132, 141-143, 146, 148f, 149, 153, 156, 167, 168, 221, , 235, 269
Yiddish Press 116, 146, 169
Yiddish Theater 44, 155-157, 158f
Yiddishkeit 169, 170, 252
Yikhes 128
Yom Kippur 171
Young Men's Hebrew Association (YMHA) 31, 154
Young Men's Hebrew (Literary) Assoc. 31
Young Men's Progressive Club 132, 150
Young Women's Hebrew Association (YWHA) 154, 247
Yugoslavia/Yugoslavs 213

Z

Zeta Beta Tau 195
Zichron Yaakov Cong./Syn. 117f
Zion Lutheran Church 51
Zion xvii
Zionism x, xi, 77, 82, 85, 146, 149, 151, 152f, 154, 184, 189, 211-212, 214, 217-219, 224, 241, 269, 272
Zionist Congress 85, 218, 220f
Zvezda Davida 258